CONTENTS

Electronic Design Automation for Windows: A User's Guide

David Pellerin

Prentice Hall PTR
Englewood Cliffs, New Jersey 07632

Library of Congress Cataloging-in-Publication Data

Pellerin, David
Electronic design automation for Windows: a user's guide / David Pellerin.
p. cm.
Includes bibliographical references and index.
ISBN 0-13-348988-4
1. Electronic apparatus and appliances--Design and construction--Data processing. 2. Electronic circuit design--Data processing. 3. Computer-aided design. I. Title.
TK7870.P382 1995
621.381'0285'5365--dc20—dc20 95-5779
CIP

Editorial/production supervision: *Kerry Reardon*
Cover design: *Anthony Gemmellaro*
Manufacturing buyer: *Alexis R. Heydt*
Acquisitions editor: *Karen Gettman*
Cover photo: *Patrick Doherty/The Image Bank*

Prentice-Hall, Inc.
A Simon & Schuster Company
Englewood Cliffs, New Jersey 07632

The publisher offers discounts on this book when ordered in bulk quantities. For more information, contact:

Corporate Sales Department
PTR Prentice Hall
113 Sylvan Avenue
Englewood Cliffs, NJ 07632

Phone: 201-592-2863/800-382-3419
Fax: 201-592-2249
E-mail: dan_rush@prenhall.com

Printed in the United States of America

10 9 8 7 6 5 4 3 2 1

ISBN 0-13-348988-4

Prentice-Hall International (UK) Limited, *London*
Prentice-Hall of Australia Pty. Limited, *Sydney*
Prentice-Hall Canada Inc., *Toronto*
Prentice-Hall Hispanoamericana, S.A., *Mexico*
Prentice-Hall of India Private Limited, *New Delhi*
Prentice-Hall of Japan, Inc., *Tokyo*
Simon & Schuster Asia Pte. Ltd., *Singapore*
Editora Prentice-Hall do Brasil, Ltda., *Rio de Janeiro*

also represented on the CD-ROM. It's worth your time to try out packages from a number of vendors before making any purchasing decision.

Why and How This Book Was Written

Why a book on low-cost EDA tools? For some people (particularly the high priests of the workstation EDA business) this question is unanswerable. Let me explain how I came to believe that this book is needed.

At the 1993 Design Automation Conference in Dallas I noticed a few things that, when put together, made me change my thinking about EDA tools and the engineers who use them.

The first thing I noticed at DAC was that the booths and products being set up in the vendor show by the large EDA companies (the ones who get all the headlines) were getting larger, louder, and more colorful. These booths were also getting more full of people but, when I looked closer, I noticed that all the badges being worn by the people going in and out of those booths were labeled with the names of the same companies who had put up those booths in the first place. There weren't any real users! It seems that conferences like DAC attract either academics (who go to the technical sessions) or EDA vendors and the industry press. Very few working engineers actually attend these events.

The second thing I noticed at DAC was that, along the walls and in odd corners of the building, there were a number of small companies demonstrating software—often highly focused EDA point tools—that ran on personal computers, and most often under the Windows user interface. There were simulators, PCB layout tools, VHDL and Verilog tools, and even tools that did things only workstation tools were supposed to do, like signal integrity analysis and ESDA (whatever *that* is). In many cases, the tools that I saw running under Windows had better integration, and were clearly easier to use, than their workstation counterparts. Somehow this had, for the most part, escaped the notice of industry presses, who continued to churn out articles about the "big names" in EDA. And what was the big news being printed about these large companies? Mergers, acquisitions, strategic partnerships, and high-priced new products based on emerging technologies that had little to do with the actual day-to-day work of an average engineer.

It appeared to me then (and even more now) that there is a great lack of information available to mainstream electronic system designers—engineers who cannot afford the time to go chasing off to a major conference to look at design tools, or to research the dozens (perhaps hundreds) of sources for affordable tools. This book is an attempt to capture as much data about the state of low-cost EDA tools—and the ways that they are used—as is possible using a combination of traditional and nontraditional information gathering methods. The design tools are out there, and they are usable on personal computers today. The problem is information, and that is what this book is all about.

A Note on Style

The text of the book has been written in an informal style, reflecting the exciting and nontraditional ways in which the new generation of low-cost EDA tools can be combined and used. The intent of the book is to show that computer-based design methods can be fun and easy. To this end, formal descriptions of design languages, circuit analysis methods and obscure data formats have been de-emphasized in favor of technology overviews, product tutorials and examples, and tips obtained from designers in the field. This approach reflects the major goal of *Electronic Design Automation for Windows: A User's Guide*: to remove EDA tools and technologies from their high pedestals and place them in the hands of the average working engineer.

So welcome to the revolution. Pop in the CD-ROM, turn the page, and let's begin our march forward.

David Pellerin
Duvall, Washington

ACKNOWLEDGMENTS

A book attempting to cover as much ground as this one is obviously not something that any one person can create. I would therefore like to extend my appreciation to the many people who lent their support, helped to fill in technical details, and corrected my sometimes outrageous assumptions about EDA tools, and about computer-based electronic design techniques in general.

Special thanks go to the following individuals and their respective companies for their help and support:

- ☐ Renee Anderson, InterHDL
- ☐ Stan Baker, TechWin
- ☐ John Birkner, Quicklogic
- ☐ Larry Blessman and Warren Miller, Actel Corporation
- ☐ Andy Bloom and Riky Escoto, Visual Software Solutions
- ☐ Brian Carlson, Hyperception, Inc.
- ☐ David Carron and Peter Robinson, Innovative Synthesis Technologies
- ☐ Chris Dewhurst and Neil MacKenzie, Capilano Computing
- ☐ Antony Dennis, Esperan Limited
- ☐ Jeff Deutsch, Deutch Technology
- ☐ Suresh Dholakia and Sanjiv Kaul, Frontline Design Automation

- Nancy Eastman, ACCEL Technologies
- Jeff Edson and Kuhoo Goyal, Intergraph
- Bruce Edwards, Protel
- Jon Englebert, Beige Bag Software
- Aggie Frizzell, Frizzell Communications
- Bob Hanz and Don Faria, Altera Corporation
- Bob Hunter, Model Technology
- Charles Hymowitz, Intusoft
- Steve Kaufer and Kellee Krisafullee, Hyperlynx
- Sanjeev Kaul, Frontline Design Automation
- David Kohlmeier, Data I/O Corporation
- Larry Lewis and Mike Merideth, Chronology Corporation
- Michiel Ligthart and Rob Dekker, Exemplar Logic
- James Lindauer, Tanner Research
- Maribeth Matre, Wellspring Solutions
- Clive Maxfield, Intergraph Electronics
- Scott McGrath, Viewlogic
- Nancy McHugh, MicroSim Corporation
- Donna Mitchell, SynaptiCAD
- Ray Schnorr, ACCEL Technologies
- Alisa Yaffa, Synplicity
- Gregor Ziwinski, ALDEC

And thanks once again to Karen Gettman at Prentice Hall for supporting and promoting this project.

Trademark Acknowledgments

This book contains many product names, terms, and acronyms that are registered or claimed as trademarks or service marks by their respective holders. The author has made every attempt to use appropriate capitalization, spelling, and punctuation of these terms. The author and publisher attest that these trademarked designations have been used solely for editorial purposes, with the intent of benefiting the trademark holder. There is no intent on the part of the author or publisher to infringe on any trademark, and the use of terms in this book should not be regarded as affecting the validity of any trademark or service mark.

Microsoft is a registered trademark, and Windows is a trademark of Microsoft Corporation.

FOREWORD

Since its inception in the early 1980s, commercial electronic design automation (EDA) software has helped drive the electronics revolution. Leading-edge IC and systems designers throughout the world have adopted EDA software, and today's complex electronic systems, ranging from desktop computers to avionics guidance systems, wouldn't be possible without it. Still, for many would-be users, EDA remains an elusive mystery. EDA tools usually run on Unix workstations, and are expensive and difficult to use.

Today, however, there's a second wave of EDA software. These new EDA tools are showing up on PCs running either Windows 3.1 or Windows NT. The proliferation of inexpensive, powerful software is now bringing EDA to tens of thousands of people, from hobbyists to engineers working for large electronics manufacturers. Yesterday's complicated tools are giving way to "shrink-wrapped" software that's high in quality, low in cost, and very easy to install and use.

What you hold in your hands is a comprehensive guidebook to this new world of affordable, accessible EDA. Whether you're a long-time EDA user or a novice, this book and its accompanying CD-ROM will bring you up to date on every major area of Windows-based EDA software.

Following a primer that defines the scope of EDA, you'll find "Focus on Technology" chapters that provide overviews for such topics as schematic entry, analog and digital simulation, and logic synthesis. In a straightfoward, informal style, this book will give you a description of each topic and relate both history and current issues. But this book provides more than just background reading. It also includes "Hands-on EDA" chapters that walk you through several examples using commercially available tools.

Don't just read the book. Use the CD-ROM as you go through the Hands-on chapters, and try Windows-based EDA software yourself. Many of the tutorials correspond to evaluation software that's included on the CD-ROM.

You'll also find references at the end of each chapter, as well as an appendix that includes an EDA vendor directory and a list of on-line resources. You can use this book as a basis for future exploration. In Internet terminology, this book is a "home page" for users and prospective users of Windows-based EDA tools.

As a consultant, trainer, product developer and writer, David Pellerin is uniquely qualified to guide you through this journey. And since this book wasn't written by an EDA vendor, there's no hidden sales pitch. Just good, solid information you can start applying right away to any electronic design task, no matter how large or small.

Richard Goering
Technology Editor
Electronic Engineering Times

CHAPTER 1

INTRODUCTION

The engineering workstation is dead.

Did that statement get your attention? If not, then little of what I say in this book will seem like big news. You already know that electronic design automation tools available on personal computers—particularly those equipped with Microsoft Windows or Windows NT—can be just as powerful as their higher-priced cousins, the Unix workstation EDA products. If, on the other hand, my proclamation causes you to raise your eyebrows, or to deny that personal computers can ever rival the powerhouses from Sun, HP, DEC, and IBM, then you are in for some surprises, because low-cost, personal computer-based design tools will soon dominate the electronic design tool industry.

Of course, these lower-cost tools may not dominate the EDA industry in terms of the money they earn for their developers and vendors—not yet, anyway. But in the sheer number of users who buy them and put them to productive use, they will eclipse the currently fashionable high-priced tools.

Product marketers often describe the expanding EDA market in terms of a potential number of "seats." The more seats a vendor can capture, goes the theory, the more users can be hooked into that vendor's exclusive tool set. One strategy that is sometimes used is to create a lower-cost, entry-level version of a more expensive product. The goal of this is to get a large number of customers using the entry-level product, then migrate those customers up to ever-increasing levels of product. The problem with this strategy, of course, is that the entry-level product must not directly compete with its more expensive siblings, and is therefore doomed from the start to second-class status as an EDA tool.

This is one reason why there is a sudden explosion in the number of independent, focused technology suppliers appearing in the EDA industry. These small companies, many of whom have fewer than a dozen employees, are exploiting two factors that have emerged in the software world in recent years: a standard user interface and standard data formats. With a standard user interface—Microsoft Windows—and standard EDA data formats like EDIF, VHDL, and Verilog HDL, it is becoming easier for small technology suppliers to compete, and there is becoming less need for a design tool user to become dependent on any one design tool vendor. If you are an EDA customer, you can shop around for EDA tools in the same way you might shop around for electronic components, creating a design system that best suits the requirements of your unique product or application, and your unique engineering style.

This new freedom gives you, the design engineer, great flexibility and power. To work effectively in this new, decentralized environment, you need to be aware of the kinds of tools that are available and understand how product "features" such as integration, application support, and customer service are going to be affected—and possibly even eliminated—in the new lower-cost EDA tools. You need to learn how to create your own design environment by selecting and combining the EDA tools that are available, and you need to understand how the loss of proprietary (or EDA-specific) user interfaces and integration methods is more than offset by new standards such as Windows, OLE (Object Linking and Embedding), and other personal computer de facto standards.

What This Book Is About

This book is about low-cost tools for electronic design automation. The products, design methods and user interviews presented in this book will provide you with a wealth of information about the exciting and fast-changing world of Windows-based EDA. With the addition of the companion CD-ROM, you will have the ability to actually try out the concepts and tools that are discussed in the book, and you will learn first-hand about the many products that are available to help address your electronic design needs. This book covers design tools and methods including

- ☐ Design capture
- ☐ Digital and analog simulation
- ☐ Circuit synthesis
- ☐ PLDs and FPGAs
- ☐ ASIC design
- ☐ Printed circuit board (PCB) layout
- ☐ Signal integrity analysis

and many other important areas of the electronic design process.

What This Book Is Not

This book is not intended to be a vehicle for product benchmarks or comprehensive product reviews. EDA tools are constantly being updated, and new tools are certainly being developed by as-yet unknown companies. (It is also quite possible that some of the EDA tool vendors mentioned in this book could go out of business, or be acquired by other companies, by the time you read this.) To provide complete product reviews or comparisons would be unfair, since it is only possible to capture the state of the industry at one point in time.

Although I have selected a number of Windows-based EDA tools to use as examples in this book, I want to stress that my choosing a particular design tool does not necessary constitute an endorsement of that product over any other. (In many cases, I used whatever design tools were easiest to obtain at the time, even if I might have preferred to use others.)

If you want more current evaluation versions of products mentioned in this book, you should contact the vendors (all of whom are listed in Appendix A) directly and request their most recent demonstration software or product literature. Another option is to join the TechWin user group, which acts as an educational organization and clearing house for product information, as well as being a useful forum for communication with other EDA users. Detailed information about TechWin can be found in Appendix D.

How to Use This Book

This book is not meant to be read cover to cover. It is not an academic treatise on digital or analog design nor is it a replacement for the detailed documentation and application notes available from design tool and hardware vendors. Instead, this book should be used as a product reference, a technology guide, and a reality check against the often-exaggerated claims of EDA vendors. Use this book where and when you need it. Use it when you are considering new tools, or when you are evaluating new implementation technologies and device alternatives. Use it, and the companion CD-ROM, as a tool for experimentation as you explore new design techniques.

About the Tutorials

To help illustrate how EDA tools work and how they are used, I have included a number of product tutorials in this book. These tutorials usually involve rather small circuits and walk through the various steps necessary to use a design tool or related set of tools. Some of these tutorials have been adapted from examples or tutorials provided by design tool vendors, while others were developed by the author to illustrate various points about the tools being described. When reading through these tutorials (or, better yet, duplicating them with the actual software) keep in mind that they are intended as primers, rather than as case histories or detailed product investigations. The electronic engineering process is often complex, and the design tools you choose may or may not make your job any easier. (If the tools work as they should, they will increase your productivity so you can get on to more challenging, more interesting, and just as difficult work.) I certainly don't want you, the reader, to think that these brief tutorial descriptions, in which no mistakes are ever made, and the software never crashes, are representative of the real world; they're not.

The tutorials should also be viewed as representative, rather than as being sales pitches or endorsements for a particular product or vendor. The product features that I mention or make use of during a tutorial are almost always available in some other competitive product. (If, however, I feel that a particular product has done a particularly good—or bad—job of providing a feature or capability, then I don't hesitate to say so.) When possible, I have used products from more than one vendor to illustrate areas of technology. While this does at times interrupt the continuity of the tutorials, I feel that it is beneficial to provide as much variety as possible in the tools being spotlighted.

In short, the tutorials in this book are not intended to show you how to go about the task of designing a piece of hardware or to convince you to buy a particular vendor's product. Instead, they are intended only to show you how representative EDA tools operate in the much larger world of electronic design.

The Companion CD-ROM

The companion CD-ROM includes dozens of demonstration products and EDA vendor-supplied tutorials and examples. To use the CD-ROM, you will need a CD-ROM drive compatible with Microsoft Windows. If you want to take full advantage of the multimedia features of the presentations and tutorials on the disk, you should have a computer that meets the requirements of the MPC2 (Multimedia Personal Computer) specifications: a double-speed CD-ROM drive and the appropriate Windows multimedia drivers. To learn how to install each software demonstration package from the CD-ROM drive to your system, just follow the instructions printed on the disk.

Let's Go!

So let's begin! The next chapter will be taking you on a quick tour of EDA technology, so you can have a good head start in your understanding of where specific EDA tools fit. After that introduction, we'll go on to explore the EDA world in detail, focusing in close when necessary to understand important technology areas.

CHAPTER 2

GETTING STARTED: AN EDA PRIMER

Electronic design automation (EDA) is the application of computer-based tools—and automated methods—to speed the process of creating complex electronic circuits, systems, and products. EDA covers a broad area of technology, including design capture, simulation, synthesis, test and verification, board layout, signal integrity analysis, IC design and packaging, and many other segments of the electronic product development process.

Because the development of an electronic system or product involves more than just creating circuitry on a board, the borders of EDA are not well defined—nor should they be. The best electronic system designers take a holistic view of the process, and take the time to explore issues such as the mechanical constraints of the product (such as what kind of housing it will be contained in, or how heat will be dissipated) and its testability and manufacturability. There are also other engineering disciplines, such as embedded software, digital signal processing algorithm development, and data acquisition, that are closely related to traditional electronic engineering tasks.

In this book, I have chosen to focus on the following EDA tools and disciplines:

- ☐ Design capture
- ☐ Digital simulation
- ☐ Digital circuit analysis
- ☐ Analog simulation

- Hardware description languages
- Circuit Synthesis
- Programmable logic
- ASIC design
- Board layout

I have selected these topics because they represent the areas of greatest concern to mainstream electronic system designers and are also the areas in which EDA tools—particularly those tools available at a reasonable cost—can provide the most help.

Design Capture

Design capture is the process of entering a design concept into an electronic design automation system. Designs entered into such a system may be represented using a wide range of possible formats, and may represent the system being developed at a very high level of abstraction (as a block diagram, for example), or at a very low level of abstraction (transistors on a custom chip).

Advanced EDA tools allow circuits to be specified using a mixture of design entry formats, so that each part of the design can be represented in the form that is most natural, and easiest to comprehend. For example, a product that includes a large state machine controller, some RAM blocks and a digital signal processing (DSP) chip may be best represented using a combination of state diagrams, block diagrams, and C language source code. While some parts of a design such as this (the C language statements and their resulting object code) fall outside of the domain of most EDA environments, trends in EDA tools suggest that such a design may soon be relatively easy to develop using one integrated design environment.

Whatever the capabilities of the tools today, and in the future, it will always be true that different parts of a complex product require different fundamental representations, and different methods of design capture. In chapters 3 through 5 we'll be examing some of these capture methods and products. We'll also be examining design capture using hardware description languages (HDLs) in more detail later in the book.

Digital and Analog Simulation

One of the most compelling reasons to use EDA tools is their ability to reduce development costs. Creating a complex electronic system is an expensive proposition. Design errors can be a major factor in the overall cost of a product, both in terms of money and in terms of the development schedule. Simulation was developed as a way to minimize the chance of failure in a complex system. Simulation reduces the cost risks associated with complex systems and makes it possible to develop systems of far greater complexity than would otherwise be possible.

Digital and analog simulation tools allow you to model the behavior of a system under normal and abnormal operating conditions, and to quickly detect problems in its implementation. Simulation also allows you to defer the implementation of portions of your design, so you can create and model the system using a top-down approach.

There are many points in the product development process where simulation can be used, and each point requires different simulation strategies and tools. As your design moves from its high-level conceptual phase to its prototype and final implementations, you may find yourself needing simulation tools that can help you test your design assumptions (model the interface between two devices, for example, or check out the signal response of a specialized analog filter), debug specific components (such as a programmable logic device or an ASIC), or test the entire system's ability to deal with environmental factors such as RF interference or power fluctuations. Simulation tools can help in all of these areas.

We'll spend quite a lot of time on the various aspects of simulation in this book. Chapters 7 through 10 focus almost exclusively on simulation, and later chapters make extensive references to simulation issues and products.

Digital Circuit Analysis

The need for systems to operate at ever-increasing speeds, and to be implemented using smaller and smaller physical areas, has given rise to a new set of problems that must be dealt with during design. Signal integrity—the relationship between signals in a system and the physical environment—is one such problem. Because the problems of crosstalk, ground bounce, inductance, and capacitance are so prevalent in electronic systems, there are now a number of design tool vendors who are offering products in this area.

We'll be examing the problem of signal integrity in Chapter 9, and will see how specialized analysis tools can help to solve complex problems in printed circuit board and ASIC design.

Hardware Description Languages

Hardware description languages—HDLs—are a relatively new concept in electronic design. HDLs provide an alternative to traditional design representations (most notably schematics) and are being used increasingly in the areas of simulation and circuit synthesis.

For simulation purposes, HDLs provide both a means of describing (modeling) the behavior of components in the system and of describing the actual test environment, the input stimulus and expected response. HDLs are becoming the standard way for providers of simulation models (models for fixed-function devices or other standard components) to describe detailed circuit behavior, and are also finding use as netlist formats to describe the interconnection of components in a system.

For design capture and circuit synthesis, HDLs allow designs to be entered at a higher level of abstraction than is possible using traditional gate- or component-level schematics. Used in this way, HDLs begin to approach traditional software programming languages (such as C or Pascal) in their ability to speed the design process. Like software programming environments, HDL synthesis and simulation tools provide features like source-level debugging, higher-level code generation, and an ability to create designs using a structured or object-oriented approach.

Chapters 13 through 15 provide a solid introduction to HDLs (specifically VHDL and Verilog HDL), and later chapters on synthesis and programmable logic also feature HDLs extensively.

Synthesis

Synthesis technology is gaining importance as designs become more complex and as implementation technologies become more highly integrated. Synthesis is what allows a design to be entered using a representation that more closely matches the design concept, rather than a form that matches the implementation technology. Synthesis is also what allows designs to be written at a high level, by describing the desired behavior of the circuit, instead of at a low level, using gates or transistors.

Synthesis tools can operate on virtually any input format, from gate-level schematics to HDL descriptions. Whatever input format is used, the job of synthesis is to convert the design into an alternate form that is appropriate for the target technology, be it a simple programmable logic device or a complex ASIC.

Advanced synthesis tools accept not only a design description as input, but synthesis constraints as well. Constraints accepted by sythesis tools may include timing and area constraints, as well as physical constraints imposed by the target technology.

Synthesis is covered in great detail in Chapter 16 and is also featured in later chapters relating to programmable logic.

Programmable Logic

Programmable logic devices (PLDs) have been in widespread use in digital designs for nearly two decades and are now familiar to most engineers who have created small- to medium-scale digital designs. Programmable logic is the ideal technology for sytems that must be developed in a hurry, and has also become a popular technology to use for prototyping large ASIC-based systems.

Design tools are critical to the success of programmable logic designs, and the tools offered for PLD users include many of the same features and technologies found in larger EDA systems. PLD design tools can be used as a model for larger EDA systems and are an excellent starting point for designers who have little or no experience with EDA tools.

When using programmable logic, it is important to understand that there are fundamental differences between the two major types of programmable logic devices being offered by chip vendors. Traditional PLDs (such as the ubiquitous PAL devices offered by Advanced Micro Devices and others) require much simpler design tools and techniques than do the more complex field programmable gate arrays (FPGAs) offered by companies such as Xilinx, Actel, Quicklogic, and others. These higher-density devices more closely resemble gate arrays in both their internal structures and in the design methods required to use them. Tools for FPGAs, then, tend to be more complex than tools intended only for PLD design.

Because programmable logic is such an important part of today's designs, I'll be devoting three chapters to describing basic device types and design tools for these devices. Chapter 18 provides an introduction to PLD and FPGA architectures and tools, while Chapters 19 and 20 demonstrate how representative PLD design tools can be used.

ASIC Design

Application-specific integrated circuits (ASICs) are seen by many engineers as a technology that is only accessible to design teams with specialized expertise and large budgets. While it is true that a large custom chip can be quite expensive and time consuming to develop, there are alternative ASIC technologies that require only a fraction of the time and cost of previous technologies. FPGA conversion services, laser programming techniques, and an acknowledgment from ASIC vendors that lower-cost, lower-risk solutions are required have all contributed to a new set of low-cost ASIC options.

In addition to advances in ASIC architectures, ASIC design tools are now appearing that rival FPGA tools in cost and simplicity. These tools can be used on personal computers and support technologies ranging from mask-programmed gate array devices to full custom chips.

Chapter 21 surveys the types of ASICs in common use today and presents information on relative costs for these different chip technologies. In Chapter 22, we'll see how low-cost ASIC development tools can be used to create actual ASIC devices.

Board Layout

Although the process of laying out a circuit board has often been thought of as a purely mechanical or preproduction process, it is actually an integral part of the product engineering process. This has become even more true as design speeds have increased and as device packaging technologies have advanced. It is no longer possible to consider the process of laying out a board to be distinct from the process of designing a circuit. Issues such as crosstalk, heat dissipation, power consumption, and manufacturability must all be considered during the design process.

Modern printed circuit board layout tools provide not only the ability to place and route components on a board, but also include features to help analyze and correct problems of signal integrity, heat, power, and manufacturability.

Chapter 23 provides a general overview of printed circuit board layout tools and describes some of the issues surrounding board design.

Many Applications, Many Design Environments

Because electronic applications—the end products being designed and built—are so diverse, it is difficult to characterize the design environment or to present a "typical" design flow. We can, however, try to map the EDA design process onto various models of an engineering project and see where each kind of design tool fits in those models.

Formal Engineering Projects

In the environment of a large engineering project, there are usually many engineers of various disciplines working together to produce a product or prototype. In these project team environments, the problem being solved (or product being created) must be approached in a methodical way, and a major part of the engineering time will be consumed in project management, design partitioning, and integration issues. In this environment, there is a sequence of critical milestones (such as the design and fabrication of a custom chip) that indicate when the disparate elements of the design must come together to form the end product or one component of the end product. Because of the coordination of schedules and interfaces required, the formal engineering project has evolved into a complex system of specifications, reviews, milestones, and test cycles (and, it may seem, endless project status meetings).

This is the design environment for which traditional, workstation-based EDA systems have been designed. The companies that use the most formal project engineering methods are most often associated with military contractors, telecommunications, aerospace and transportation, and large-scale industrial control. These large companies often have centralized CAD departments that handle the aquisition of EDA software and computers and usually have design entry standards that limit an individual engineer's choice of design tools and methods.

Design teams that are working in one of these structured design environments must be able to partition their tasks, describe and test the interfaces to each design module, and have constant visibility over design changes. In this design environment, design management and design tool integration are most important, and complete, broad-line CAD/CAE systems (such as those produced by IBM, Intergraph, Cadence, Mentor, and others) are prevalent. These large-scale environments may include everything from mechanical engineering tools to software configuration management, and are beyond the reach of the mainstream electronic designer.

But the fact that the largest electronics companies invest in large-scale CAD/CAE systems for their engineering needs does not prove that these expensive systems are actually needed to do formal project engineering. All of the functions that are associated with formal engineering environments can now be obtained on Windows-based personal computers. Many of these tools work well in a networked enviroment, so a team of engineers can work just as effectively on their personal computers as their pals at the defense contractor down the road do on their networked engineering workstations.

The tools that are used in this environment? They range from full-featured schematic editors and hardware description language tools to expensive digital and analog simulation products with extensive model libraries. High-level electronic system design automation (ESDA) tools may also be used to help design a system (or custom IC) as a whole. Increasingly, however, large design groups that use broad-line EDA tools are seeing the value of decentralization and are buying personal computer-based EDA tools that can integrate loosely (perhaps at the level of a standard netlist) with workstation-based tools.

The Fast Prototype Project

An alternative to the traditional, formal engineering environment can be found in the *fast prototype* method of design. In this design environment, the formal product specification is replaced by an actual working model of the product, often produced in a crash effort by a small group of engineers. The prototype may lack important features of the final product, but it allows management, salespeople, potential customers, and other less technical types to see just what it is the engineers intend to offer the world.

In a fast prototype design environment, elegance and efficiency take a back seat to design speed. There is a single, overriding goal in the minds of the engineers: getting the prototype ready in time for the first dog and pony show—be it a meeting with the vice president of sales and marketing or booth duty at the consumer electronics show. To meet deadlines, *off-the-shelf* components are used whenever possible, and old designs are canabalized for their hardware, software and firmware contents. This bottom-up approach often results in a prototype that must be thrown away and reimplemented from scratch to make it economically viable or functionally competitive.

What kind of design tools are used in this environment? Programmable devices are often employed in prototype hardware, with the intent being to eventually replace the programmable chips with a gate array or semi-custom ASIC. Programmable logic development tools of many flavors are therefore usually found in these environments. It is also more likely that you will find a wide variety of design tools existing on the same desktop machine, and being used by a single multidisciplinary team or individual, since the effort of creating the prototype may involve not only the core electronic design effort, but the mechanical and other aspects as well. In this environment, it is not unusual for the same small group of engineers to be switching from design entry, to test vector generation, to PCB layout, all in the space of a few days. Using many tools in this way makes it all the more important that the learning curve is short, and the interfaces between the tools are straightforward.

Although the intent of the prototype project is to simply hasten the formal engineering process, as often as not the prototype is cleaned up, given a shiny plastic cover, and becomes instead...

The Instant Product

Instant products—those that are released before there is even a complete product specification—represent the "bleeding edge" of technology. Speed is everything; in both time-to-market and performance. The mottos of this class of designer? Be creative; shoot from the hip; and don't be too concerned when the occasional product misses its target. (Just make sure you've got a half-dozen follow-on products ready to release in its place.)

These are the products that are released seemingly overnight, often by small entrepeneurial companies, in response to ever-shrinking market windows and highly competitive vertical markets. It is here that low-cost, high performance design tools excel, and where new tools are tested to their limits and either quickly accepted or just as quickly thrown in the trash.

The project teams that crank out these leading-edge products are often willing to take great risks to get ahead of the competition. It is in this environment that you will find Beta release EDA software, new (and single-sourced) programmable devices, and the most creative solutions to design problems.

Standards, Standards, Standards

As an industry pundit once pointed out, the great thing about EDA standards is there are so many to choose from. Unless you buy every EDA (and mechanical CAD) tool from the same EDA vendor, you will have to think about standards. It's not enough to buy the fastest simulator, or the most efficient circuit board auto-router. If you can't transfer your design data into and out of these tools, then you might as well have purchased a box full of air.

Standards also come into play when you plan to migrate your designs to different design environments (perhaps so you can use an entirely different implementation technology). If you have invested months of work into creating a set of source files for, say, a family of programmable logic devices, and then later decide to combine some of those designs into a single gate array device, you will be better off if you had entered the designs originally in a standard design entry language, or using a schematic editor that supports standard netlist formats.

Standard EDA data formats fall into a number of categories. Some data formats are languages that you actually learn and write yourself (for data entry) while others are used strictly for data transfer between tools and are generated by the tools. Some standard formats are accepted and promoted by standards organizations such as the IEEE or by industry consortiums, while others are de facto standards accepted and supported by a large number of EDA tool vendors. Let's examine some of these standards and see where they are used. In later chapters, we'll see how the standards fit into specific areas of the design process.

Schematic Standards

There are an amazing number of schematic entry products available today. Some of these products include simulation, PCB layout, or other features, while others are simply drawing packages with netlist output. Every schematic entry tool out there has a unique set of features, and a particular focus (be it simulator integration, multiple drawing views or some other specialized feature). If there is one thing that almost all of these tools have in common, it is that they all use a unique, proprietary data format for their drawings, interconnections and symbols. Although a standard schematic format has been proposed and specified (EDIF schematic), few, if any, schematic entry tools actually use this representation as their primary data format. The only schematic format in existence that even smells like a de facto standard is the OrCAD schematic. Because OrCAD was able to gain so many users on the PC, any new would-be competitor provides an OrCAD schematic reader with their product.

Another format that is in widespread use is the Viewlogic schematic. Viewlogic Systems has put a tremendous amount of effort into creating OEM relationships with major vendors of ASICs and FPGAs, which has helped the company to create a large base of users and designs. For various technical reasons (mostly involving the encription of symbol libraries), the Viewlogic schematic format has not appeared in competitors tools as an input option, so this format cannot be considered a de facto standard among EDA tools. (Viewlogic schematics are a good choice if you will be interfacing to many different FPGA and gate array design tools and services, since the Viewlogic tools are widely supported in these environments.)

Netlist Standards

Rather than focusing on creating a standard schematic format (a difficult task, since the data format of an electronic schematic depends a great deal on the kind of data included, and schematic entry tools are continuously evolving), EDA vendors and standards organizations have instead concentrated on the intermediate data formats that allow schematics (or other design entry data) to be transferred into other tools (such as simulators and printed circuit board layout tools) that are needed to complete a design.

The most common official standard for netlist data is EDIF (Electronic Design Interchange Format). Most schematic capture packages include an EDIF netlist writer (either as a standard feature or as an extra-cost option), and many post-processing software tools (such as board layout packages, ASIC tools, or simulators) will accept EDIF netlist as input. EDIF netlist, however, does not in itself provide enough information to describe an entire design. Because an electronic design consists of components (or primitives) as well as interconnection information, the use of a standard netlist format such as EDIF does actually help very much; the components referenced within the standard netlist are very often proprietary and nonstandard.

Practically speaking, there is no standard netlist in use today; instead, vendors of postprocessing tools must support a wide variety of commonly used netlist formats to have a marketable product.

Hardware Description Languages

Although it seems that a standard schematic format (such as EDIF schematic) is unlikely to gain widespread acceptance, and standard netlist formats have failed to catch on because of nonstandard component primitives, there have been two notable standards (or de facto standards) for language-based design for some time. Both VHDL and Verilog HDL (which are described in detail in Chapters 13, 14 and 15) allow designs to be entered, simulated, and otherwise processed using a wide variety of design tools sold by a large number of EDA vendors.

Standardization (or the perception of standardization) has been one of the primary reasons for the success of these languages; when you have confidence that a design can be quickly transferred between design systems, or retargeted to different implementation technologies, then you have more opportunity to try alternatives, both in the tools that you use and in the final implementations of your design.

CFI: The CAD Framework Initiative

The CAD framework initiative was formed in May 1988 as an industry consortium (in the form of a nonprofit corporation) with the goal of defining industry-wide standards for interoperability of EDA tools and the integration of EDA tools into larger CAD environments and existing frameworks.

In the *standard framework* view of the world, a well-defined, vendor-independent CAD framework allows users to launch tools, manage the operation of those tools and organize data in a common user interface and interprocess communication environment. Standard interapplication communication methods and protocalls make it possible for CFI compliant tools to share data, send messages to one another, and otherwise operate with a high level of integration.

CFI released its first version of a framework specification in January 1993. Eleven EDA tool vendors, including Cadence, Mentor and Viewlogic have announced that they will be shipping products compatible with CFI. CFI, in turn, announced a certification program give a CFI stamp of approval to CFI-compliant products.

As of this writing, all of the activity surrounding CFI has been occuring in Unix workstation-based products. How does CFI relate to low-cost, Windows-based tools? It's not clear at this point; much of the interprocess communication that is defined by CFI is duplicated by off-the shelf Windows technology, and that technology is evolving at such a rapid pace (from Windows message-based communication, to DDE, to OLE versions 1 and 2) that it may not be practical or desirable to attempt a version of CFI for the Windows environment at this point in time. Perhaps when Windows and Windows NT have matured to the point where we don't have new interprocess (or interobject, as the case may be) communication features being announced each year, a Windows implementation of CFI will be feasible and desirable.

Where Is EDA Going?

Much of what I will be covering in this book is technology that has existed for some time in workstation-class design environments. This is an exciting time for EDA, however, because of some important trends in hardware design and in the changing approaches to the design process.

In the final chapter of this book, I'll be describing some of the fundamental changes in the electronics and EDA industries, and in the tools that are being produced as a result. In the meantime, let's focus in on some of the more important areas of EDA and see what today's tools can offer.

CHAPTER 3

FOCUS ON TECHNOLOGY: DESIGN CAPTURE

In this first *focus on technology* chapter, we'll be examining how designs are initially entered using electronic design automation tools. We'll look at a variety of tools and design representations, and see that there are many possible ways to represent an electronic circuit. Some of these design representations will be immediately familiar, while others may be new to you and may seem quite removed from the actual circuitry being designed.

Concept to Hardware: Taking the First Step

The first step in an automated design process is to get your product concept entered into a computer-based design system. This phase of the development process is called *design entry*, or *design capture*. Both of these terms are actually a little antiquated; if the point of automated design tools is to aid in the overall process, then you will not be using the tools to simply enter or capture an existing design. Instead, you will be using the tools in an iterative way, as you refine your concept into a form that is closer to reality—closer to an actual working piece of hardware.

Design Metaphors

A well-designed software product, be it an ASIC development system or a tax preparation program, is built around some kind of visual or processing *metaphor* familiar to that product's users. Most electronic design capture systems in use today rely on the electronic schematic as the overriding concept—the metaphor—for

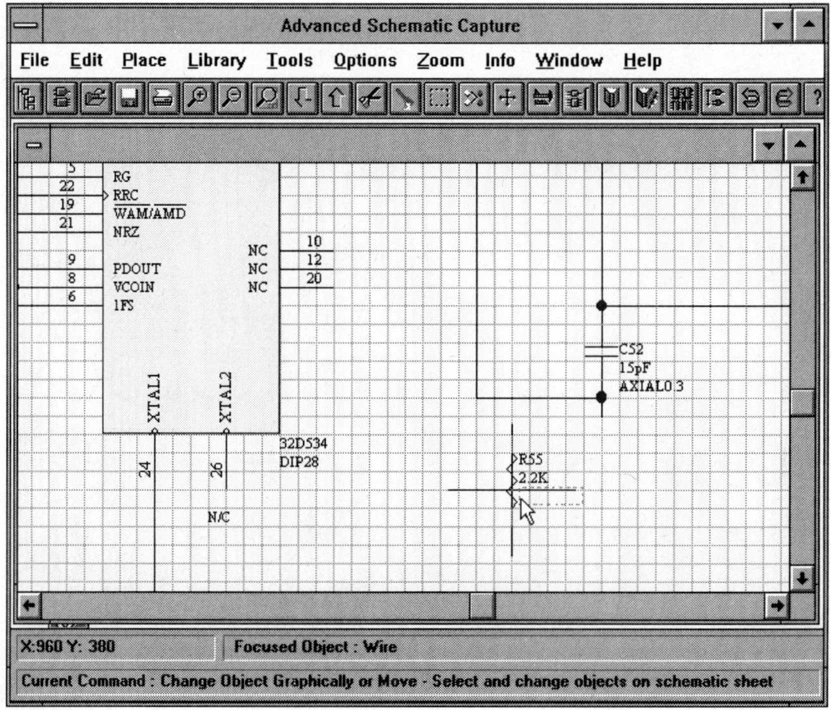

Figure 3-1
A schematic editor is a drawing program optimized for electronic applications. (Protel Advanced Schematic.)

design capture. When using a software product oriented around a schematic view of the design process, you enter your design by selecting schematic symbols from a library, placing those symbols in some arrangement on the screen, and connecting the symbols with lines representing wires or traces (Figure 3-1). The result is a graphic representation that consists of familar elements such as logic gates, flip-flops, or higher-level functional blocks that perform well-understood functions.

If you have used EDA tools of any kind, then chances are you have used a schematic capture package at some point. There are dozens of such packages available today, ranging from free design entry tools available on computer bulletin boards to advanced, hierarchical schematic tools with built-in simulation and design management capabilities.

The schematic is a valuable tool for design entry and documentation, and is unlikely to be replaced as the most common design entry method any time soon. But, as we will see later, there are ways other than a schematic to represent a design. For many circuits, these alternate representations—*alternate metaphors*—can be more understandable, faster to enter, and easier to maintain.

Since schematic capture is ubiquitous in the electrical engineering world, I won't spend a great deal of time describing it here. (The first *Hands-On EDA* chapter provides a detailed tutorial on schematic capture.) I will, however, present an overview of what general features schematic capture packages have, and will spend most of the chapter describing alternate forms of design capture, such as higher-level graphical tools, hardware description languages and other nontraditional design representations. I will also be focusing in on how other components of an EDA environment—such as simulation and synthesis—interface to design entry tools. Before doing so, however, let's take a moment to examine just what design capture is, in the context of electronic design automation.

What Is Design Capture?

Design capture is a way of creating a computer-based representation of a design concept. This design concept may be a simple schematic showing how the components on a board are laid out and interconnected, or may be a more abstract concept that initially describes only the interfaces of a system, and perhaps the bare minimum of functionality for each component in the system. These two extremes—a representation that directly corresponds to hardware and a higher-level representation that may not even result in a completely hardware-based implementation—demonstrate an important concept for design capture: the differing levels of abstraction that are available.

Levels of Abstraction

If you scribble a high-level concept onto a napkin and tuck that napkin into your pocket for later reference (Figure 3-2), you are performing a high-level form of design capture. In all likelihood, the concept that you scribble on the napkin will be missing most of the important details, will ignore important interface issues, and will be obscured by beer or lipstick stains. No matter; you know you will be changing the entire concept later anyway, but the act of capturing the design concept in some form for later reference is the start of a continuing process of design refinement. A design such as this normally starts out at a fuzzy, conceptual level and is described using high level of abstraction. As the design is refined, that level of abstraction is lowered, bringing the concept closer and closer to its possible implementations until a point in time arrives where the design, or portions of the design, can be entered into a design system or implemented directly using off-the-shelf hardware and/or software.

At what point in this process can electronic design capture begin? That depends on the tools you use. While there are EDA tools now appearing that attempt to address issues such as hardware/software co-design, and are intended to help with the entire design process, these tools are not yet accessible to mainstream designers using low-cost design tools. There are, however, many niche tools now appearing

Figure 3-2
A napkin is sometimes used as an initial method of design entry. (The design? A notebook computer fish finder.)

on the Windows platform that can help you with some of the higher-level aspects of the design process; state machine design tools are good, although somewhat specialized, examples of this.

Since design capture is the first step in any automated design system, just about every EDA vendor has design capture tools to offer. Even design tools that are focused on highly technical, back-end processes (such as board routing) must have a method of capturing the design, and these back-end tools will often come bundled with a schematic capture package in addition to supporting standard netlists or other data formats.

Integration Issues

Although many of the design entry tools sold today are integral parts of larger design systems, and may include tightly integrated simulation, synthesis, or other functions, there are other tools that are more focused, and operate in a stand-alone environment. Examples of this approach include graphic front-ends for HDL generation (such as the tools offered by Summit Design, Visual Software Solutions, R-Active Concepts, and others) and low-cost, standalone schematic capture programs that generate standard netlists. When you are using these tools, you must generally provide your own integration, but this integration may require no more effort than keeping track of a few data files and managing your own flow of data through the design process.

Whatever the state of today's low-cost tools may be for high-level design, you can be sure that they will be improving rapidly in the future, as workstation EDA vendors begin moving their tool suites to the new environments and begin lowering their prices in response to competitive pressures.

Schematic Capture

In the early days of schematic editors, the schematics generated as a result of the design process were good for two things: documentation of a board design and postprocessing of that design into a netlist that could be processed with a batch-oriented simulator to verify the design, by a parts lister to generate reports, by a printed circuit board layout tool for manufacturing, or for other tasks that were considered distinct from the actual design entry process. As more tools appeared

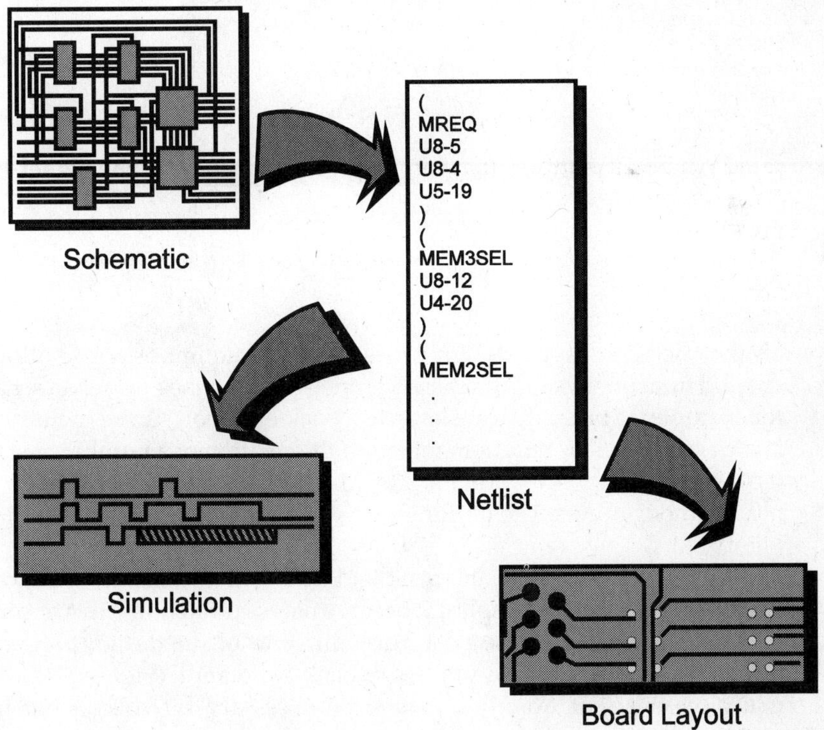

Figure 3-3
The simplest design flow using a netlist-based system is one-way: from design entry to netlist.

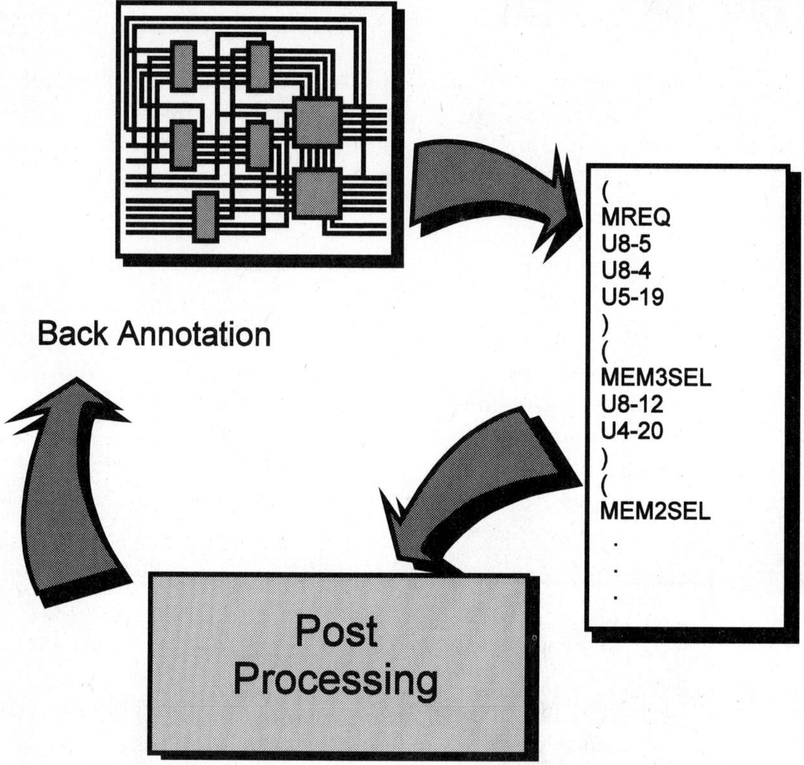

Figure 3-4
Adding back-annotation makes it possible to update the design to reflect back-end changes or added design contraints.

on the back-end of the design process, it became important to allow schematics entered from one system (a schematic entered using the FutureNet schematic editor, for example) to be easily translated to a back-end tool (such as a Racal-Redac board layout system). This requirement led to the creation of a number of standard (or de facto standard) netlist formats, including EDIF, FutureNet pinlist, and OrCAD netlist among others. The design flow using systems such as this is diagrammed in Figure 3-3.

As the capabilities of the back-end software became more powerful and the designs became more complex, it became necessary to find ways of communicating information created at the postprocessing end of the design process back to the design capture phase. This process of back-annotation (Figure 3-4) is necessary for many reasons. For example, it may be necessary for component locations, pin numbers or post-route signal delays to be back-annotated to the original schematic from the board layout process. For simulation, it may be desirable to view the simulation results directly on the schematic.

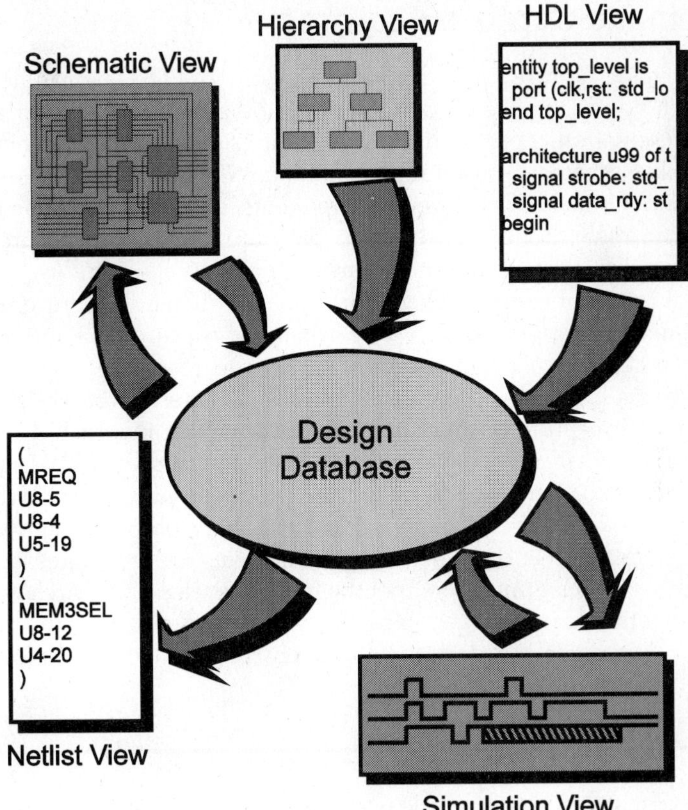

Figure 3-5
An integrated design environment makes it easier to quickly move between design entry, simulation and other functions.

More recently, schematic capture packages have appeared that blur the distinction between design entry and other tasks, such as simulation, that have been traditionally been considered "back-end" processes. Products like Capilano Computing's DesignWorks seem more like interactive software breadboards than schematic capture systems, allowing designs to be entered and simulated using "live" components, including voltage supplies, waveform generators, and various types of meters.

In these highly integrated tools, there may be a central design database (Figure 3-5) through which the applications communicate. Rather than relying on the user invoking the correct sequence of processing tasks and generating output files, a system such as this may provide a variety of "views" of the design, ranging from the familiar schematic view to more abstract views like hierarchy trees, or more simulation-oriented views such as waveforms.

Schematic Capture Features

Schematic capture is an important part of any EDA environment. No matter how much you make use of synthesis technology, HDLs, or other advanced forms of representation, there are many applications that just naturally lend themselves to a graphic, schematic-based representation. When you are developing a board with a certain number of predefined components, and are going to be feeding that design to a printed circuit board layout program, schematic capture is really the only practical method of design capture.

Just about every EDA vendor offers a schematic capture package; it is worth noting, however, that very few schematic capture packages can read and write schematic files or symbol libraries in the format of other schematic capture packages. Because of this, you should think carefully before choosing a particular schematic capture product or larger EDA system that includes an integrated (and proprietary) schematic capture system. If design portability is an issue, you might want to consider a schematic capture product that can import and export files in a standard format (such as an EDIF schematic) or can read and write schematics in the format of widely used schematic capture packages such as OrCAD or Viewlogic. Remember, too, that the money you save by purchasing a very-low-cost schematic entry package can be offset many times over by the time you may spend later to reenter the design into an environment that supports more advanced capabilities such as simulation.

Component Libraries

A schematic editor is of little use without a library of component symbols that you can select and place on your schematic to represent your circuit (Figure 3-6). A schematic editor specialized for certain application areas (such as analog circuits, IC design, or printed circuit board layout) will usually come packaged with a library of components appropriate for that application area. In most cases, the schematic editor will provide ways to add new components as needed.

Depending on the capabilities of the schematic entry package and other tools (such as a simulator) that are integrated with it, a component library may consist of not only the graphic representation of each component, but information about the function or physical characteristics of that component as well. Components used in a schematic may represent actual devices (such as a 74138 TTL device) or may be purely functional representations (such as NAND gates and flip-flops).

One of the most critical aspect of a schematic capture package is the library of components that it supports. If you are designing for an ASIC or FPGA, or intend to use the schematic tool to enter board-level designs containing hundreds (or even thousands) of different discrete components, then you will need to have a access to comprehensive libraries of component symbols specific to your application, in addition to having access to the right netlist formats. All other features are secondary; no matter how intuitive or pretty the drawing tools are, or how large a

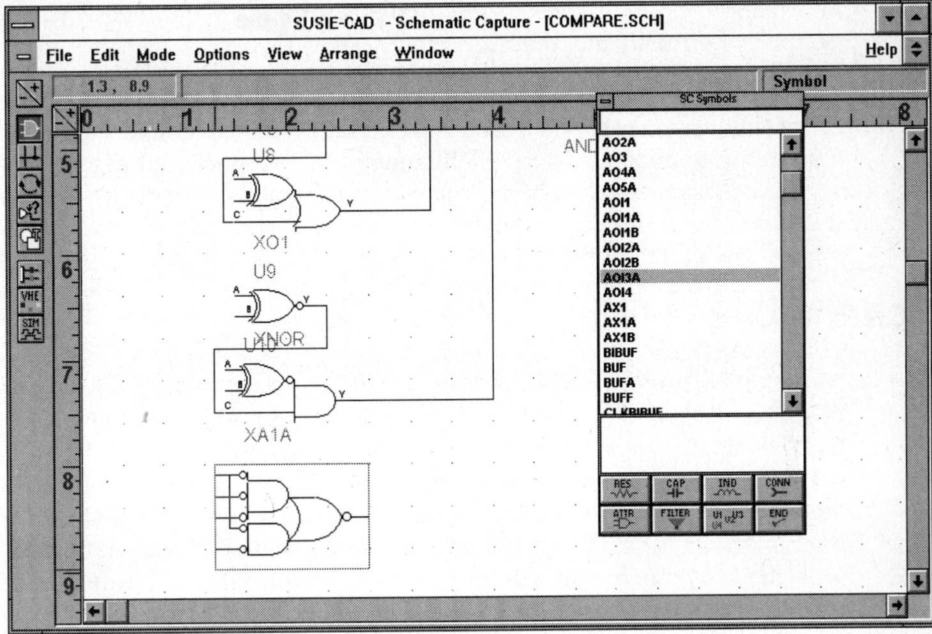

Figure 3-6
Libraries are critical to a schematic entry package. (ALDEC's SUSIE-CAD.)

schematic the program will handle, if you can't enter your design due to a lack of libraries or can't translate the design to the right netlist format, then you are not going to get very far with your design.

Before investing time and money in a new schematic capture product (and after all, the time you spend creating your first few schematics is worth far more than you will pay for most schematic packages), be sure the product comes with adequate libraries and that the libraries you will need in the future will be readily available. In some cases, such as ASICs, libraries are provided by someone other than the producer of the schematic capture product. If this is the case, be sure that the schematic library supplier supports the schematic entry package you have chosen.

Symbol Editors

Because component libraries are so important to a schematic, all modern schematic editing tools include facilities for creating and maintaining your own library of component symbols. Symbol editors can be simple extensions of the schematic editor itself, allowing you to create block symbols with pin stubs and other information, or may be complex drawing programs that allow you to create symbols of virtually any shape or size.

Whatever the features of a symbol editor, you must keep in mind that your library of schematic symbols will become increasingly valuable, and increasingly time consuming to maintain, over the lifetime of the product. You can help to protect your investment in schematic symbols by using a schematic entry system that is well-known and likely to be still in use and supported in the future.

Schematics for Higher-Level Design

Although schematics are most often used to create circuits consisting of gate-level primitives or board-level components, there is no reason why schematic capture has to be thought of as a low-level way of entering a circuit. Schematic capture tools that support hierarchy are quite useful for designing with a top-down design methodology. Using schematic capture in this way, the schematic that you enter into a schematic editor may actually have little or no relationship, other than functional, with the final implementation of your design as a piece of hardware. Schematic capture can be used to draw the actual layout of chips on a board, but, increasingly, schematic representations are used to represent an electrical/logical function, or a higher-level, system-oriented view of a design, rather than an actual circuit.

Hierarchy

Most schematic capture packages now support hierarchy as a means of creating designs using a top-down approach. Hierarchy allows multiple lower-level circuit diagrams to be collected together under one or more higher-level diagrams, forming a treelike structure (Figure 3-7). When hierarchy is used, it is possible for a team of designers to work on a large design with parts of the design being clearly distinguished—and their interfaces defined—by the hierarchy boundaries. Hierarchy also promotes design reuse, since lower-level circuits may be easily incorporated into new top-level designs.

Hierarchy can also be used (if the design tool allows it) for *mixed-mode* design entry. In a later chapter, we'll see how a design that is initially described at a high level using a schematic block diagram is represented at the lower levels as a set of hardware description language statements. The reverse is also possible; it is quite possible that a hardware description language will be the most natural representation for a top-level design description, even if some of the lowest-level circuit descriptions are entered in the form of schematic drawings.

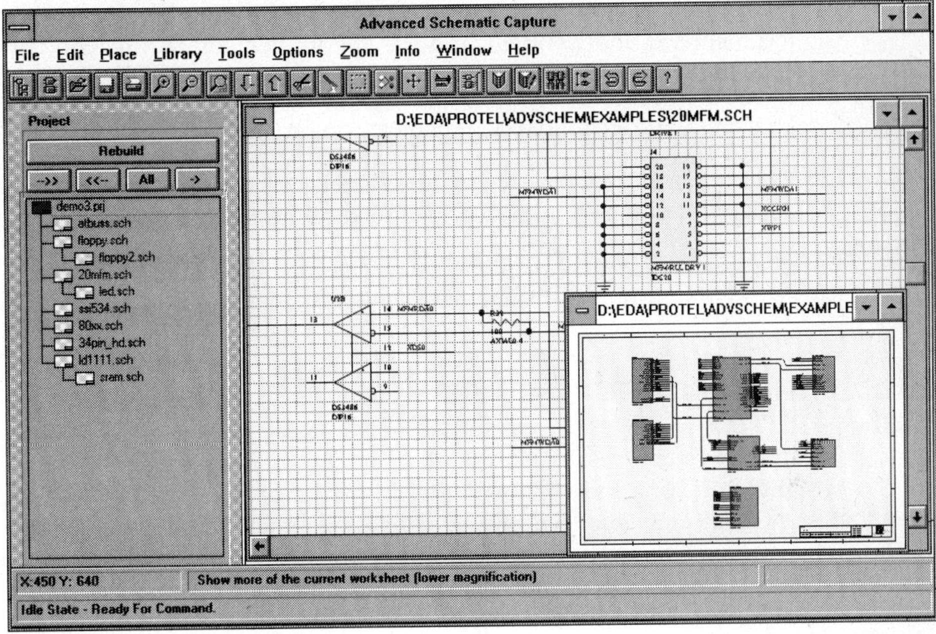

Figure 3-7
Many schematic editors provide a hierarchy view of the design. (Protel's Advanced Schematic.)

Hardware Description Languages

Hardware description languages are becoming increasing popular as a way to capture a complex design in a form that is conscise, understandable, and portable. An HDL is a programming language that is intended for the specification of hardware or, more precisely, for the specification of the *observable behavior* of hardware. Like high-level software programming languages (such as C, C++, or Pascal,) HDLs have features that allow designs to be entered in a modular fashion, and are ideal for designs that will be developed in team environments. HDLs differ from software programming languages in that they are primarily intended to describe systems that have a high level of *concurrency*—systems that are parallel rather than sequential.

Designs that are captured using HDLs can be easily simulated, are more likely to be adaptable to multiple implementation technologies (through a process called *synthesis*) and can be archived for later modification and reuse. HDLs have significant advantages over other design entry methods:

- ☐ HDLs raise the level of abstaction during the design process, allowing designs to be entered independent of a specific implementation technology (FPGA, standard cell, etc.).
- ☐ HDLs provide a common language for design entry and testing.
- ☐ HDLs are widely supported in design tools from many vendors, allowing your design to be quickly migrated to different types of tools.

We'll be spending a great deal of time discussing HDLs in later chapters, and you can expect to see more of this powerful new way of designing circuits in the future.

Electronic System Design Automation

Electronic System Design Automation, or ESDA, is a relatively new concept in design automation tools. The long-term goal of ESDA is to allow systems to be designed at a high level, without concern for whether the eventual implementation is hardware, software, or some mix of the two. A secondary goal is to provide design representations that more closely match the application being designed, rather than matching the implementation technology. In reality, it is still not possible to completely insulate yourself from the underlying implementation technology. Today's ESDA tools provide a glimpse of what may come in the future, but are really only applicable to a fairly narrow range of applications.

What ESDA tools do provide today is a higher level of design abstraction during the design entry and top-level simulation phase of a project. ESDA tools generally approach the design process using a graphical, block diagram oriented approach, and usually include simulation capabilities that operate at this higher level of abstraction.

While most tools that fit into the catagory of ESDA are available only on engineering workstations, there is likely to be a shift of these tools to Windows in the near future. Even if complete ESDA solutions (with integrated simulation and advanced synthesis capabilities) are not available to mainstream designers using personal computers, there are a variety of point tools that fill some of the need for higher-level design tools.

Combining Multiple Forms of Entry

Design entry tools that take a more holistic view of the design process often include more than one form of design entry. These tools are useful when you are creating a large, system-level design that has many widely divergent components (perhaps mixing hardware and software components in the same design) and may include design entry formats ranging from hardware description languages to high-level block diagrams. All these design entry methods may be accessible from the same primary interface (Figure 3-8).

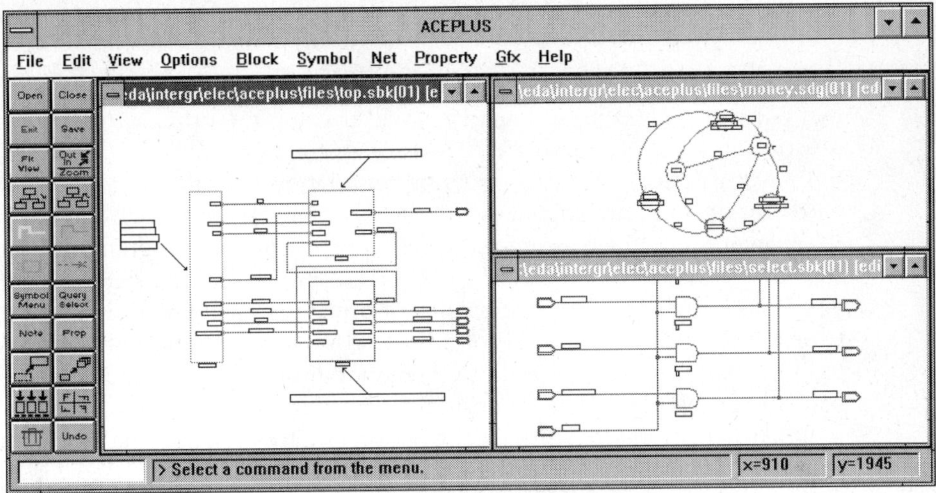

Figure 3-8
Higher-level design tools combine alternate forms of entry in a single project. (Intergraph's ACEPlus.)

State Diagram Tools

One example of where nontraditional forms of design entry are beginning to appear is in the area of state machine design. State diagrams are used to represent sequential state machines, and typically use circles or boxes to represent the possible states of a machine (as stored in its internal state registers) and all of the possible transitions between the various states. State diagram entry tools are about as close as you can get to the napkin metaphor I presented earlier. They allow complex state machines to be quickly entered, using the bubble diagram representation familiar to most engineers, and allow the state and transition information to be entered in much the same way gates and wires are edited with a schematic editor. As in a schematic, additional data in the design (such as the actual transition and output logic) is captured in the form of text.

A state machine design entered into such a tool can be quickly analyzed for conflicting transitions and for other potential bugs. From the diagram, the design entry system generates an output that is appropriate for the type of hardware being used for implementation. For example, in an ASIC implementation, the system might generate VHDL, C, Verilog or a netlist format, while for an embedded controller implementation, the system might generate C source code.

Future Directions in Design Capture

Where are design capture tools going in the future? Some observers have predicted that hardware description languages will become the primary method of design description, since HDLs provide a level of abstraction that is, for hardware, similar to that provided in software programming languages. But is it really likely that hardware description languages will usurp schematics and block diagrams? I think the answer is no. The reason for this opinion? Traditional programming languages as actually falling out of favor for software programming. Rather than writing applications by entering line after line of procedural statements in a language like C or Pascal, many developers of advanced software applications are now using tools that look, in some sense, like schematic editors. The new catch-phrases among software developers are *object-oriented design* and *component-based* software.

Component-based software development tools speed the development of complex applications by providing libraries of commonly used (and already debugged) component objects. These objects (which may or may not be objects in a strict object-oriented sense) are often designed for specific application areas such as communications, networking, data bases, or user interface. In some programming environments (such as Visual Basic) the components may be graphical, while in other environments the components are accessed using a text-oriented source code browser.

Component-Based EDA Tools

So what do component-based software tools have to do with electronic design automation? If trends in software tools can help to forecast future trends in EDA, then component-based methods are likely to become common for hardware design. Graphical programming environments are well suited for hardware applications, and there are tools now available for embedded software design (most notably digital signal processing) that give us a hint of how the hardware design process could look in the future.

One such system intended for DSP application development is the Hypersignal for Windows product sold by Hyperception of Dallas, Texas. The Hypersignal product (Figure 3-9) is based on a block diagram design representation, and includes component libraries for DSP applications. The block diagram symbols each represent either a common function used in DSP applications or are pointers to lower-level block diagrams. The block diagram editor allows the design to be immediately simulated as shown, and can also generate source code allowing designs to be implemented in a variety of specialized DSP processors. The component libraries that are included with Hypersignal include math, display, signal generation, and DSP algorithms. Other libraries are available for specialized areas of DSP, and the product allows its users to create their own, custom libraries of components.

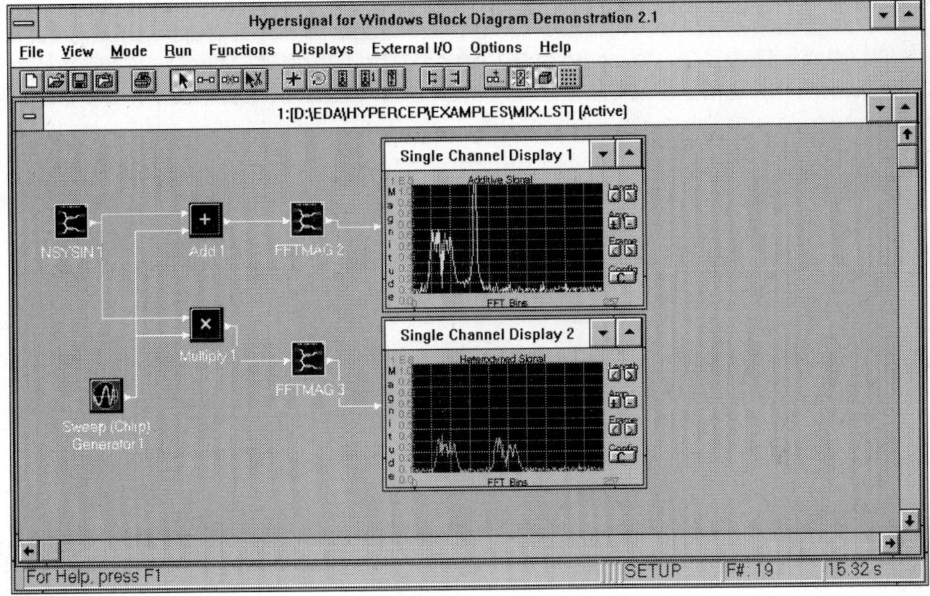

Figure 3-9
A block diagram editor provides a high-level view of a design and encapsulates the actual implementation within each block. (Hyperception's Hypersignal.)

The ability to place graphic representations of circuit components on a diagram and simulate them is nothing new, of course; schematic capture packages have had those capabilities for years. Instead, the value of component-based design tools may be in their emphasis on application-specific component libraries—libraries that allow extremely complex systems to be assembled quickly and efficiently, without the need to create the entire design from scratch. It is not difficult at all to imagine a design tool that is oriented around the idea of high-level components—components that represent high-level functions and encapsulate multiple implementations (software, hardware, HDL, etc.) within themselves. Such a tool could be what is needed to turn the promise of ESDA into reality.

Moving On

Now that we have seen some of the existing technologies and trends in design capture, we are ready to begin looking at specific design entry methods in more detail. In the next two chapters, you will have an opportunity to try out two very different methods of design entry: schematics and state diagrams. In later chapters, you will be introduced to more abstract forms of design entry using HDLs.

If you are already proficient with schematic editing tools, you may want to skip the next chapter and move on to more advanced EDA topics. In any event, be sure to check out the contents of the companion CD-ROM. There are many more design entry systems and evaluation software products contained on the CD-ROM than could possibly be described here.

CHAPTER 4

HANDS-ON EDA: SCHEMATIC CAPTURE

In this chapter, we're going to take a detailed look at a representative schematic entry package, Intergraph's ACEPlus. This tutorial will introduce you to schematic capture concepts such as symbols and drawings and will show you how hierarchy and multisheet designs are entered in a typical schematic entry environment.

During the tutorial, we're going to focus in on the process of creating and maintaining schematics, see how the most important features of schematic editors are used, and learn how concepts such as hierarchy can be used to simplify large schematic-based designs.

Note: *The information in this chapter has been adapted from a tutorial provided by Intergraph Electronics with their ACEPlus system. Additional tutorials that build upon this sample circuit can be found on the companion CD-ROM, in the ACEPlus on-line help files. An evaluation version of the ACEPlus software has been provided on the CD-ROM, as have sample versions of many other schematic entry products.*

Intergraph's ACEPlus Design Entry System

The ACEPlus Design Entry System is versatile design entry package that allows designs to be represented not only as schematics, but as mixtures of hierarchical blocks, state diagrams, and hardware description languages such as VHDL, Verilog HDL, and ABEL. ACEPlus supports analog, digital, and mixed-signal designs and can be used in conjunction with other tools such as simulators and board layout tools to form a complete electronic design environment.

Invoking the Schematic Editor

When ACEPlus has been correctly installed on your system, you can invoke the schematic editor by double-clicking on the ACEPlus icon (Figure 4-1).

Note: *When the instructions in this or other tutorials refer to clicking or double-clicking, you should use the left mouse button unless another button is specified.*

Command Styles

ACEPlus supports many methods of command entry, ranging from keyboard commands (such as **PP** for place property) to the familar point-and-click methods of other Windows applications: pull-down and pop-up menus, single- and double-click mouse actions on objects (using either verb-object or object verb command styles), and menu accelerators (such as ALT-F for the File menu).

Most ACEPlus features can be accessed using multiple methods of command entry. The command styles used in this tutorial are not necessarily the quickest, and you should experiment with the commands and mouse actions to become

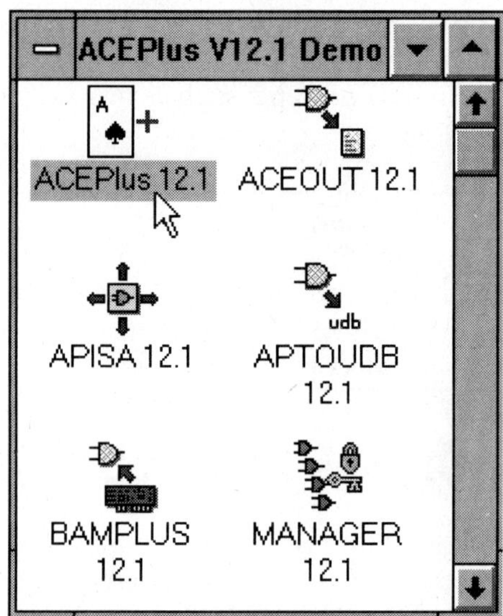

Figure 4-1
Double-click on the AcePLUS icon to start entering a schematic.

acquainted with alternate methods of entry. As in most Windows applications, the most commonly used commands have icon buttons arranged in a tool pallette (the button bar located on the left side of the schematic editing window) as an alternative to the pull-down and command line styles.

Creating a New Schematic

To begin working with the schematic editor, you are going to create a simple schematic representing a 4-bit binary to gray code converter. The completed schematic that you will be entering is illustrated in Figure 4-2.

Note: *This tutorial makes occasional reference to the middle mouse button. If you are using a two-button mouse, you will need to make a change to the ACEPlus initialization file* **aceuser.asc** *before continuing. Refer to the help files that are installed with the ACEPlus demonstration software for more information about this file and about using a two-button mouse.*

1. To create a new schematic, invoke the schematic editor (as described previously) and click on the Open icon on the button bar. When you click on the Open icon, the schematic editor responds with a window in which you need to enter the schematic name.
2. Type **BCD2GRAY** into the schematic name field. This will be the name of your new schematic.
3. After entering the name **BCD2GRAY**, ensure that the **Editor** field reads **SCHEMATIC**. If not, click on the down arrow next to the **Editor** field and select **SCHEMATIC** from the resulting pull-down menu.
4. Press the Enter key or click the **OK** button to open the new schematic. The blank schematic diagram for this design is shown in Figure 4-3.

Working with Borders

The new schematic sheet that has been created is not exactly blank. By default, the schematic is opened with a border (Figure 4-3), and with other configurations (such as size) set up for you. This initial configuration of ACEPlus is specified with a set of files known as configuration or side files. A newly installed copy of ACEPlus is typically configured so as to automatically place a C-size border in new schematics, and to include a border.

You can change or delete the default border and size if you need to. (Refer to the on-line help provided with ACEPlus for information on how to work with borders.)

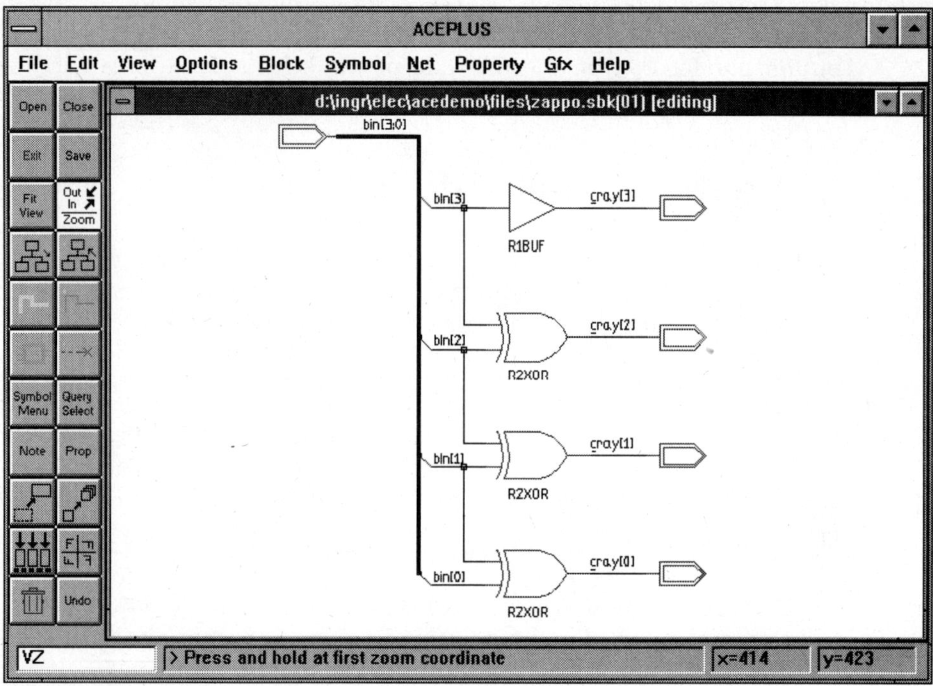

Figure 4-2
The sample schematic is a 4-bit binary to gray code converter.

Placing Symbols on the Schematic

Follow the steps below to place the four gate component symbols (three exclusive-OR gates and one buffer) and the five hierarchy connector symbols on the schematic:

1. Click on the Symbol Menu icon in the button bar.
2. If the Library Name field contains an entry other than **basic**, click on the down arrow next to the field and then click on the **basic** entry in the pull-down list.
3. Click in the form's **Browse Window** check box to open the Browse window in the lower left-hand corner of the schematic window. Note that the highlighted entry in the Symbol Name list is displayed in the Browse window.
4. Click on one of the symbol names. The Browse window immediately changes to reflect the symbol you selected.

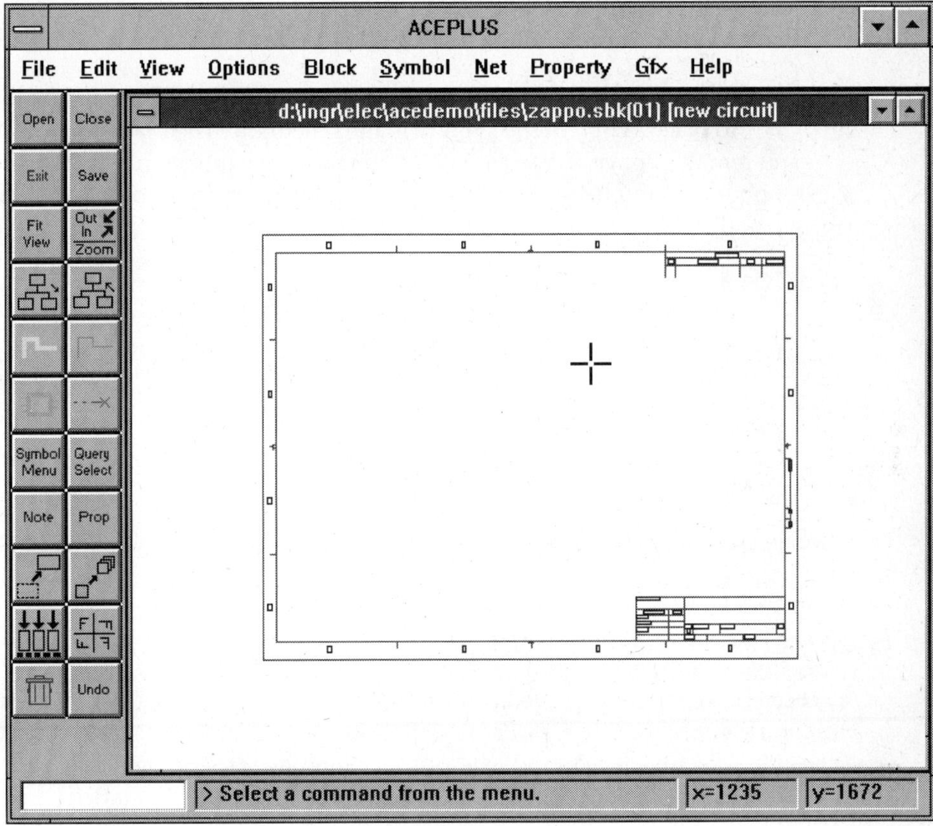

Figure 4-3
A newly created schematic diagram includes a standard border.

5. Press the down arrow key on the keyboard two or three times. Every time you press the key, the Browse window changes to reflect the currently selected symbol.

6. Now click in the Symbol Name field to make this field active.

7. Enter the name **R2XOR**. Note that every time you type a new character, the scroll list and Browse window immediately jumps to the first entry that satisfies the criteria.

8. Double-click on the **R2XOR** entry in the scroll list.

9. Move the mouse cursor into the schematic window. As soon as the mouse cursor enters the schematic window, a white copy of the selected symbol follows the cursor around.

10. Click to place a copy of the symbol in the schematic. The Place action is "sticky" and remains active. Thus, as soon as you move the mouse cursor away from the symbol that you have just placed, a new copy of the symbol follows the cursor around.

11. Place two more copies of the **R2XOR** symbol on the schematic by clicking the left mouse button and moving the mouse cursor between each copy.

12. To reset out of the Place command, click the right mouse button while the mouse cursor is somewhere in the schematic window.

13. Move the mouse cursor back into the scroll list of symbols and select the **R1BUF** symbol.

14. Place the **R1BUF** symbol on the schematic above the exclusive-OR gates in the position shown earlier.

Hierarchical Connectors

Hierarchical connectors have implications in terms of both hierarchical design and for simulation. For the purposes of this part of tutorial, you can consider hierarchical connectors to indicate primary interfaces to the outside world. (There are other kinds of connectors that are used for multisheet schematics.)

1. Activate the Symbol Place command by typing **SP**. Type **con_hier_i** to select a hierarchical input connector and press the Enter key (Figure 4-4).

2. Move the mouse cursor until the highlighted symbol is in the upper left of the schematic. (Check Figure 4-2 for the approximate position.) Click the left mouse button to place a copy of this symbol, then click the right mouse button to reset out of this command.

3. Type **SP** again to open the Symbol Place form. Type **con_hier_o** to select a hierarchical output connector and press the Enter key.

4. Move the mouse cursor until the highlighted symbol is to the right of the buffer gate. Click the left mouse button to place a copy of this symbol.

5. Now move the mouse cursor until the new highlighted symbol is to the right of the first exclusive-OR gate and click to place another copy. Once again, do not spend a lot of time trying to align the connectors precisely under each other

Figure 4-4
Select a hierarchical connector using the **Symbol Place** *command.*

because you are going to use the Align command to do this. Repeat this step two more times so that each exclusive-OR gate has an associated connector.

6. Click the right mouse button to reset out of the command.

7. Use the Zoom command from the button bar to magnify the schematic so that the connectors and gates fill the window. This will make the following tasks easier to see.

Aligning the Symbols and Connectors

ACEPlus has a special Align command to make it easier to align symbols precisely:

1. First click the right mouse button to ensure that you have de-activated the bounded Zoom command from the previous exercise.

2. Select the buffer gate and exclusive-OR gate symbols by pressing and holding the shift key, clicking the left mouse on the symbols, and releasing the shift key. Note that the symbols turn white when selected.

3. Type **EA** to open the Align Symbols window. This is equivalent to selecting the **Edit** menu followed by the **Align** option (Figure 4-5). Based on where you placed the symbols, ACEPlus makes the assumption that you wish to align these symbols vertically (as a column), so the **Column** button is already selected for you.

4. Press the Enter key to align the symbols.

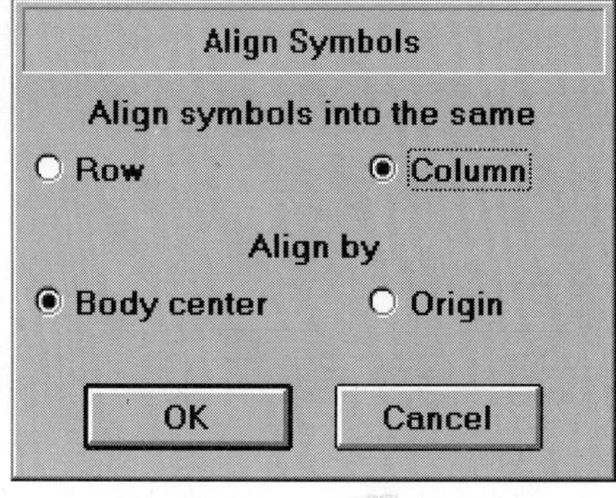

Figure 4-5
Automatic symbol alignment features simplify the drawing process.

5. Now move the mouse cursor a little above and to the left of the upper output connector symbol on the right side of the schematic.

6. Area-select the four output connector symbols by pressing and holding the left mouse button, dragging the mouse down and to the right so that the bounding box touches all four connectors, and releasing the mouse button. Note that this automatically deselects the previously selected symbols.

7. Once again, type **EA** to access the Align Symbols window, then press the Enter key to align the connector symbols. (If necessary, you can also use the **Align** command to align symbols horizontally.)

Creating Wires and Buses

Placing the Bus

In this example, the inputs to the circuit are in the form of a 4-bit bus:

1. Click on the Bus icon in the button bar. Note that the bus and wire icons are similar, but the bus icon is yellow while the wire icon is green.

2. Click the left mouse button on the right-hand tip of the hierarchical input connector.

3. Move the mouse cursor to the right until the highlighted bus is approximately halfway between the connector and the gates. Next, move the cursor down

until the highlighted bus is a little below the bottom exclusive-OR symbol (about 2 cm lower than that shown in Figure 4-2).

4. Double-click the left mouse button to terminate the bus. Note that the red star at the free end of the bus is automatically placed to alert you that it is not connected to anything. You will return to correct this later.

5. Click the right mouse button to reset out of the Bus command.

Naming the Bus

It is not necessary to name buses immediately after placing them. However, for the purposes of this example, you are going to name the bus that you just placed:

1. Click on the horizontal portion of the bus halfway between the hierarchical input connector and the vertex (corner).

2. Activate the Property Place command by typing **PP**. This is equivalent to using the Property pull-down in the menu bar followed by the Place option.

(You can use the Type field to select which type of property you wish to attach to the bus. However, each schematic object has its own default type; in the case of a bus, the default type is the Net Name, which is what you want.)

3. Click in the Value field to make it active, then type **bin[3:0]** (Figure 4-6). This informs the system that the bus contains 4-bits: **bin[3]**, **bin[2]**, **bin[1]**, and **bin[0]**.

4. Press the Enter key to attach the name to the bus.

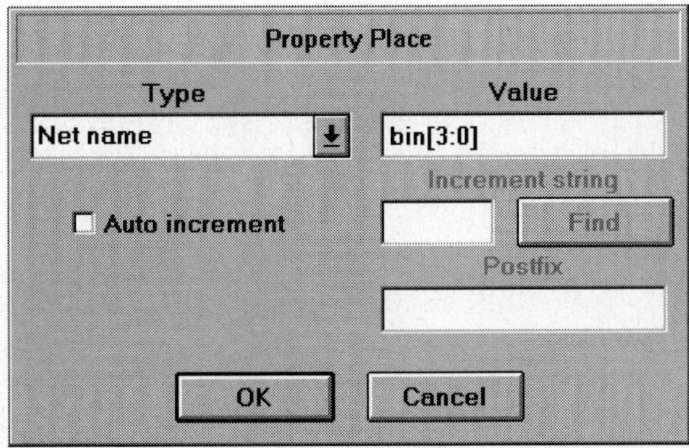

Figure 4-6
The Property Place command is used to give names to signals.

5. Click the right mouse button to deselect the bus.

Placing the Wires

In this example, the outputs from the circuit are in the form of four scalar (1-bit) wires. However, before you connect these outputs, you are going to wire the gate inputs to the bus.

1. Click on the Wire icon in the button bar. Remember that the Wire icon is green while the Bus icon is yellow.

2. Click on the left-hand tip of the input to the buffer gate, move the mouse cursor to the left until the highlighted wire touches the bus, and double-click to terminate the wire. By default, terminating a wire on a named bus automatically invokes the Select Net Name form (you can change this default if desired.)

3. By chance, the net name that you want, **bin[3]**, has been selected as the default. Press the Enter key to attach this name to the wire.

4. Repeat the previous steps to connect the other three exclusive-OR gate inputs to the bus. When you are connecting the other wires to the bus, you will need to select the names **bin[2]**, **bin[1]**, and **bin[0]**. You can do this by double-clicking on the name in the list.

5. The Wire command is still active, so click on the left-hand tip of the top input to the exclusive-OR gate below the buffer gate. Move the mouse cursor to the middle of the wire that you placed above and double-click to terminate the wire (refer to Figure 4-2). Repeat this step to finish wiring the exclusive-OR inputs.

6. Now connect the outputs: click the left mouse button on the right-hand tip of the output from the buffer gate. Move the mouse cursor to the right until the highlighted wire is on the left-hand tip of the hierarchical connector associated with the buffer gate and double-click to terminate the wire.

7. Repeat the above operations until you have connected all the wires as shown in Figure 4-2.

8. Click the right mouse button to reset out of the Wire command.

Naming the Wires

You can attach names to the output wires in a similar manner to the way you named the bus. That is, individually naming each wire by first selecting the wire then executing the Property Place command. However, ACEPlus offers a variety of more sophisticated alternatives. For example

1. Activate the Property Place command by clicking on the Prop icon in the button bar or by typing **PP**.

2. The Property Place window appears with the Net Name property selected by default. Click in the **Value** field to make it active, delete the entry (if one exists), and type **gray[0]**. Do not press the Enter key at this time.

3. Click on the **Auto Increment** check box.

Note: *ACEPlus uses the name you enter in the Value field to automatically fill in the Increment String and Postfix fields.*

---

4. Now press the Enter key to close the window. The command line at the bottom of the ACEPlus window prompts you to select a pin or a net.

5. Move the mouse cursor over the wire connecting the bottom exclusive-OR gate's output to its connector and click the left mouse button to place the name.

6. Move the mouse cursor over the wire above and click the left mouse button to place that name. Repeat for the remaining two wires.

7. Click the right mouse button. Note that this does not reset you completely out of the Property Place command. Instead it resets out of the current properties that you were placing and reinvokes the properties window. This is a useful time-saving feature if you are naming a lot of wires. However, in this instance you have named all the wires you need to, so click on **Cancel** to close the window.

Delete the Dangling Bus

To complete the schematic you will need to delete the dangling part of the bus indicated by the red star. To do this

1. Click on the dangling part of the bus just above the red star.

2. Click on the Delete button in the button bar (it's the button with a trash can icon).

The schematic is now complete. To save your work

3. Click on the Save icon in the button bar. The schematic will be written to the file **BCD2GRAY.SBK**.

Using Hierarchy in Schematics

ACEPlus, like most modern schematic entry systems (and other forms of entry such as VHDL or Verilog HDL) supports any combination of top-down and bottom-up design methodologies. This allows you to start each design, or portion of a design, at the most appropriate level of abstraction.

This section focuses on a top-down approach, meaning that you first specify your design at a high level of abstraction (in this case a block symbol), and then move the design forward to the implementation level. In this context, the implementation level is taken to be the lowest level with which you are concerned: usually gate-level in the case of a digital design and transistor level in the case of an analog design.

With ACEPlus you can represent your design as a hierarchy of functional blocks and the connections between them. The blocks represent design units, thereby allowing you to easily visualize your design at a high level of abstraction. When pushing into a block, you can choose the most appropriate way to represent its contents; for example, schematic, graphical state diagram, or a textual hardware description language such as VHDL or Verilog. These alternative forms of representation are known as *views*. ACEPlus allows each block to have multiple views at different levels of abstraction, and also allows you to quickly and easily select between views.

In this section of the tutorial, you are going to create a schematic containing a single hierarchical block. You are then going to push into the block and create a gate-level schematic representation of its contents. Begin by creating a new schematic called **TOP_DOWN** using the same methods used earlier:

1. Click on the Open button.

2. Type **TOP_DOWN** in the data entry field and click **OK**.

3. Move the mouse cursor into the middle of the schematic area. Hold the shift key and click the middle mouse button to zoom in (magnify). Continue to zoom in until the grid points are clearly visible.

Creating a Block

In this exercise you are going to create a functional block measuring 10 grid points across and 15 grid points down, as shown in Figure 4-7.

1. Click on the Block button (it's the one that looks like a blue box with pins sticking out of it).

2. Move the mouse cursor into the upper left quadrant of the visible schematic area. Press and hold the left mouse button and drag the mouse to the lower left

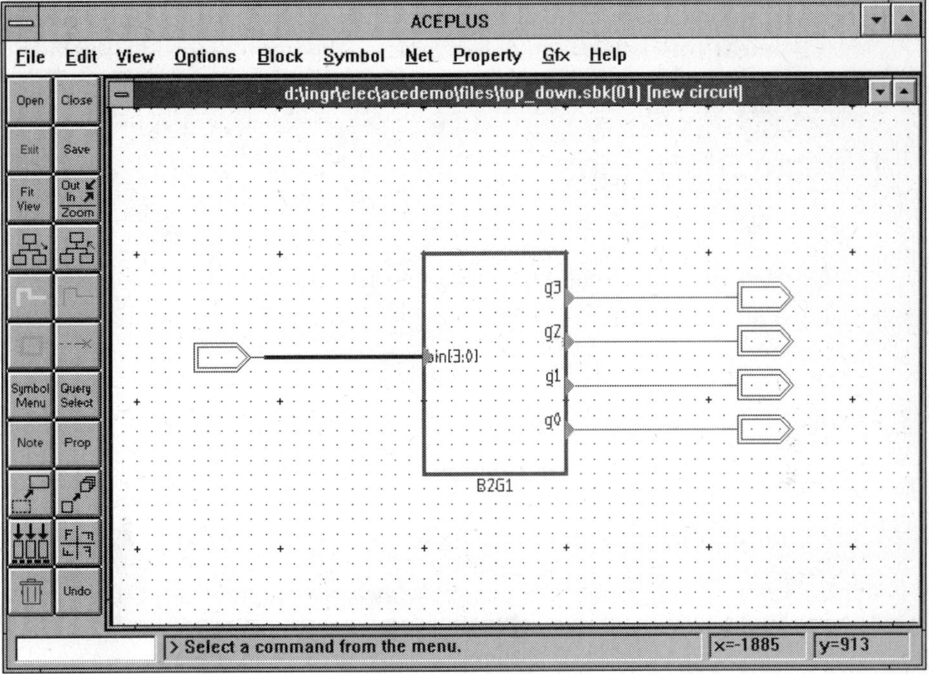

Figure 4-7
A schematic top-level block is used to reference lower-level schematics in a hierarchy.

until the resulting box is 10 grid points across (horizontally) by 15 grid points down (vertically). Then release the left mouse button.

3. The Block Name form automatically comes up. Type **B2G** using uppercase characters and press the Enter key.

4. Click the right mouse button to reset out of the Block command.

Placing Block Pins Manually

Now you will need to place pins on the **B2G** block:

1. Click on the Pin button (located next to the Block button). Refer to the figure when placing pins.

2. Move the mouse cursor to the middle of the left-hand side of the **B2G** block and click to place a pin.

3. Move the cursor to the right-hand side of the **B2G** block, three grid points from the top corner and click the mouse button to place another pin.

4. Move the cursor down three grid points and click again. Repeat two more times so that you have a total of four pins on the right-hand side (see the figure).

5. Click the right mouse button to reset out of the Add Pin command.

Naming Block Pins

Now you are going to name the pins on the **B2G** block:

1. Click on the left-hand (input) pin to select it (it turns white).

2. Type **PP** to open the Property Place window. Note that the **Type** field is defaulted to **Pin Name**.

3. Click in the **Value** field to make it active and type in **bin[3:0]**, then press Enter.

4. Click the right mouse button to deselect the input pin.

5. Type **PP** again to bring up the Property Place window.

6. Click in the **Value** field to make it active (if the **Value** field contains text, double-click) and type **g0**.

7. Click on the **Auto increment** button. Note that this action moves the **0** into the **Increment String** field and that, in this case, there is no entry in the **Postfix** field.

8. Press the Enter key to close the window and activate the command.

9. Click on the bottom pin on the right-hand side of the **B2G** block, then on each of the other pins from the bottom up.

10. Click the right mouse button, then click the **Cancel** button to close the Property Place window.

Placing Buses and Hierarchical Connectors

The next step is to connect the inputs and outputs of the block. In this example, the input is a bus, while the four outputs are wires. While creating the input and outputs, you are going to attach hierarchical connectors.

1. Move the mouse cursor half way between the left-hand side of the window border and the **B2G** block. Press and hold the shift key and click the middle mouse button until you can see the grid points. Then release the shift key.

2. Click on the Bus icon (the yellow one).

3. Click on the input pin of the **B2G** block and move the mouse cursor to the left until it is about 3/4 of the way to the border.
4. Click to place a vertex, then press and hold the middle mouse button to open a pop-up menu.
5. Select **Add Input Hierarchical Connector** from the resulting pop-up menu to place an input hierarchical connector at the end of the bus.
6. Note that the Bus icon is still active. Select the Wire button.
7. Click on pin **g3**.
8. Move the mouse cursor to the right until it is about three-fourths of the way to the border.
9. Press and hold the middle mouse button to open a pop-up menu.
10. Select **Add Output Hierarchical Connector** from the resulting pop-up to place an output hierarchical connector at the end of the wire.
11. Repeat the preceding four steps to create wires and output connectors for **g2**, **g1**, and **g0**.
12. Click the right mouse button to exit the Wire command.
13. Click the Save button to save the work you have done so far. Your block schematic should resemble Figure 4-7.

Pushing into a Block

Now you will traverse the hierarchy of this simple circuit by pushing into the block you just created:

1. Select the block symbol by clicking inside of it.
2. Click on the Push button (the left-most button icon that looks like a hierarchy diagram). This opens a new schematic with the Schematic view (by default).

Note: *ACEPlus automatically places hierarchical connectors in the schematic along with the pin names specified on the block at the top level of the hierarchy.*

3. Double-click on the automatically generated input connector and move it to the left-hand side of the schematic.
4. Click the right mouse button to deselect the connector.

5. Move the mouse cursor to the middle of the four connectors. Hold the shift key and click the middle mouse button to zoom in. Note that ACEPlus has automatically propagated the block's pin names down into the block and attached them to the hierarchical pins on the hierarchical connectors.

6. Click the Fit View icon.

7. Click the Save icon.

Copying from One Window to Another

Now you are going to copy the previously drawn schematic to the new schematic by copying the symbols and wires.

Note: *To save time, you could have named the top-level symbol BCD2GRAY and pushed directly into the BCD2GRAY schematic. The following excercise, however, will help you to understand how ACEPlus allows you to work with multiple schematic files.*

To copy components from the **BCD2GRAY** window to the **B2G** window:

1. Resize the **B2G** schematic window by dragging the top left-hand corner of the **B2G** window to the middle of the ACEPlus window (drag to the lower right) so that the schematic only takes up one-fourth of the ACEPlus window. You can now see the **TOP_DOWN** schematic behind the **B2G** schematic.

Note: *If you choose to, you could make the* **TOP_DOWN** *schematic window active and edit it, then make the* **B2G** *schematic window active again and edit. That is, you can edit or flip between multiple levels of a hierarchical schematic.*

---

2. Click on the Open button to invoke the File Open window.

Note: *You will notice that there is an entry for* **B2G.SBK**. *When you pushed into the block, edited the schematic contents, and saved it, ACEPlus automatically created the file* **B2G.SBK**.

---

3. Select **BCD2GRAY.SBK** with a single click, and then click **OK**. Note that a double-click on **BCD2GRAY.SBK** would have selected page **01** (the only page of this schematic) by default and immediately opened the schematic.

4. Drag the bottom right corner of this window to the middle of the ACEPlus window (that is, to the upper left) until it is approximately one-fourth the size of the ACEPlus window.

Now you will copy the schematic (minus the connectors) from the **BCD2GRAY** schematic to the **B2G** schematic:

5. Area-select the gates, wires, and wire names but not the connectors in the **BCD2GRAY** schematic.

6. Click on the Copy icon then click on the selected area.

7. Move the mouse cursor to the **B2G** schematic. A white copy of the selected area follows the cursor until the cursor moves out of the **BCD2GRAY** schematic. Click in the **B2G** schematic to make it active and the white copy reappears. Move the copy to the middle of the **B2G** schematic and click to place the copied symbols.

8. Another copy appears. Click the right mouse button to exit the Copy command and dismiss the second copy.

9. Click the right mouse button on the banner of the **BCD2GRAY** schematic to push this window to the back.

10. Double-click on the banner of the **B2G** schematic to make this window fill the screen.

11. Press and hold the shift key and click the middle mouse button to zoom in so that you can see the left connector and the bus on the left-hand side.

12. Ensure that nothing is selected and double-click on the left-hand connector for a quick move. Move the connector so that its pin is over the end of the bus and click to place it. Click the right mouse button to deselect the connector. Note that the connector symbol automatically connects to the bus, and the red asterisk on the bus disappears to indicate a good connection. Note also that the pin name is different than the bus name. The pin name is used to connect to the hierarchical level above.

13. Pan via the mouse (or the numeric keys) to the right-hand side of the schematic. Do similar moves on the right-hand connectors to connect them to the appropriate wires.

14. Click on the Fit View icon.

15. Click on the Save icon.

You now have a hierarchical schematic.

Moving On

This tutorial has shown the basics of schematic editing and has illustrated many of the important features of modern schematic editing packages. Many of the products described in this book include schematic editors, and these editors have their own sets of features and benefits.

It is important to understand, however, that schematic entry is not the only method of design entry. Increasingly, experienced electronics system designers are turning to alternative forms of entry such as hardware description languages and graphic state diagrams to express their designs. In future chapters, we'll be learning more about these other forms of design entry.

CHAPTER 5

HANDS-ON EDA: USING STATE DIAGRAM TOOLS

State machines are used in many digital systems, and are most often found in controllers, sequence generaters or detectors, and in interface circuitry. There are many possible ways to implement such machines in both hardware and software. For this reason, state machine designs are good candidates for higher-level forms of representations—forms that allow the design concept to be isolated from the underlying implementation technology.

In this tutorial, we'll be examining a specialized design entry tool that is intended for the description and implementation of state machine circuits. The design tool is called StateCAD, and is produced and sold by Visual Software Solutions of Coral Springs, Florida. With StateCAD, state diagrams are used to represent sequential finite state machines (FSMs). Circles and arrows are used to represent the states (as stored in its internal state registers) and transitions between states, in much the same way you might diagram the machine using pencil and paper.

Note: *Information in this chapter has been adapted from a product tutorial provided by Visual Software Solutions. The companion CD-ROM includes an evaluation version of the StateCAD software, so you can follow along with this tutorial. Additional StateCAD examples and tutorials can also be found on the CD-ROM.*

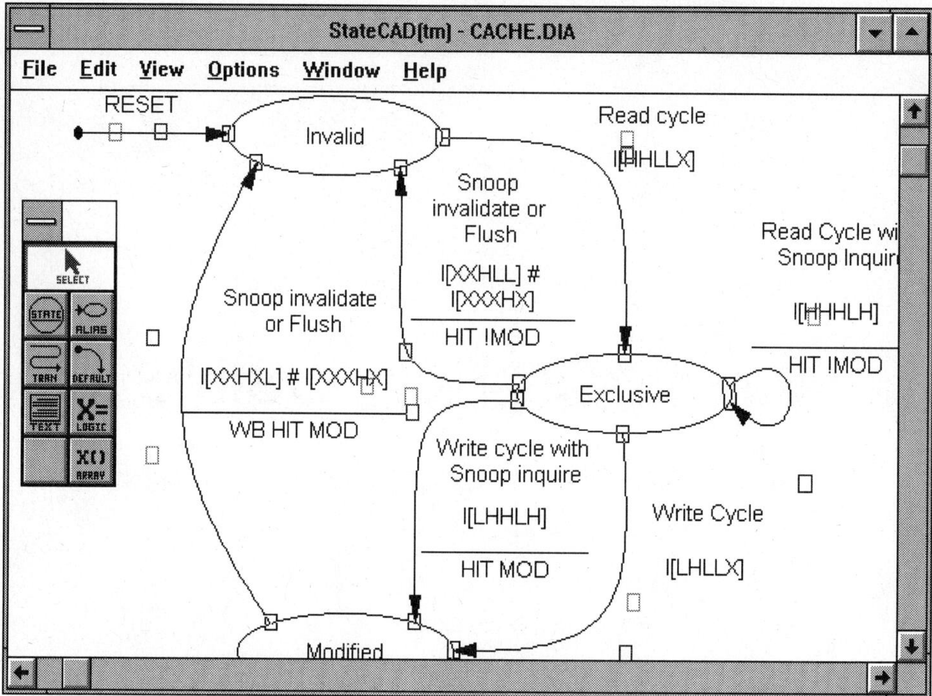

Figure 5-1
A state diagram entry package allows a design to be expressed graphically. (StateCAD, Visual Software Solutions.)

Visual Software Solution's StateCAD™

Figure 5-1 is a screen from the StateCAD state diagram editor. StateCAD allows complex state machines to be quickly entered, using the bubble diagram representation familiar to most engineers, and allows state and transition information to be entered in much the same way gates and wires are edited with a schematic editor. As in a schematic, additional data in the design (such as the actual transition and output logic) is captured in the form of text.

A state machine design entered into StateCAD can be quickly analyzed for conflicting transitions and for other potential bugs. From the diagram, the program generates output in a variety of common forms, including Boolean equations, ABEL language (described in Chapter 18), or VHDL (described in Chapter 14). StateCAD also has an option that allows C source code to be generated for embedded controller applications. This makes StateCAD one of the few low-cost tools on the market that supports both hardware and software implementations from the same design description.

Simulating State Machines

Since the intent of alternative design entry formats is to provide a view of the design that is closer to the way a designer might concieve of the circuit, it is useful if a design entry tool includes simulation features that operate at that same level of abstraction. Since a state diagram provides a flow-chart oriented view of a sequential machine, it makes sense to provide simulation features that allow that machine to be "operated" graphically. StateCAD provides this feature as an option to their product, allowing you to observe a state machine as it transitions from state to state, decoding its inputs and driving its outputs.

Another method of simulation supported by StateCAD is the use of its ANSI-standard C language output feature. A design can be specified using StateCAD's graphic state diagram features, then compiled into a C language form and executed as software for testing purposes. For synthesis, the design can be recompiled into VHDL or ABEL and implemented in a PLD or ASIC.

StateCAD Features

The StateCAD product has the following features useful for graphical state machine design:

- ☐ Graphic editor specialized for state diagram applications
- ☐ Automatic error checking for over 100 common design problems
- ☐ Support for both Mealy and Moore state machines
- ☐ Automatic generation of source code using either VHDL, ABEL, or C language
- ☐ Support for large combinational logic functions for transition and output logic

A Sample Design

To see how graphical state tools can help speed the design process, we'll be entering a sample circuit provided with the StateCAD product. This sample circuit is a controller for a coin-operated washing machine (Figure 5-2). This washing machine will include controls for the water temperature (hot or cold) and for the wash and spin cycles.

Although this sample circuit is quite small, it will demonstrate the important features of StateCAD, and of state machine design entry tools in general. To keep the controller simple, the design makes the following assumptions:

- ☐ An external mechanism exists to determine when the correct amount of money has been deposited in the machine's coin slots. This mechanism activates signal **PAID**.
- ☐ The cycling time of the machine is controlled by an external timer that counts from 0 to 31 minutes. This timer is reset by the signal **RST_TIMER**.
- ☐ A switch exists on the machine to select hot or cold water. This switch activates signal **HOT**.
- ☐ The washing machine has three valves to regulate the flow of water. **FILL_HOT** and **FILL_COLD** allow water to enter the machine, while **DRAIN** allows water to exit.
- ☐ When power is applied to the machine, the signal **POWERUP** is activated, and the washing machine is initialized.
- ☐ The motor that spins the washing machine's basket is activated by the signal **ROTATE**. If the signal **CHURN** is active, the motor agitates the clothing.

The complete design that we will be entering is illustrated in Figure 22-7.

Entering the State Machine

The first step in entering this design is to invoke the StateCAD application and create a new diagram.

1. Invoke StateCAD from the Program Manager by double-clicking the left mouse button on the StateCAD icon. The StateCAD application will display a message indicating that the demo version does not save files. Click **OK**.

After you have invoked the StateCAD application, you will begin creating the diagram by selecting and placing four state bubbles.

2. To create a state bubble, click on the state button on the tool bar (Figure 5-3) to enter State mode. This allows states to be drawn. Drawing modes allow different types of objects to be added to a diagram. Notice that the cursor reflects the current mode so you won't be confused about what kind of object you are creating or modifying.

Mouse operations in StateCAD have been optimized for drawing and editing state diagrams. StateCAD uses the convention that the left mouse button adds or edit objects, while the right button moves or reshapes them. This can be a little confusing at first, but speeds the drawing process when you get used to using the right button.

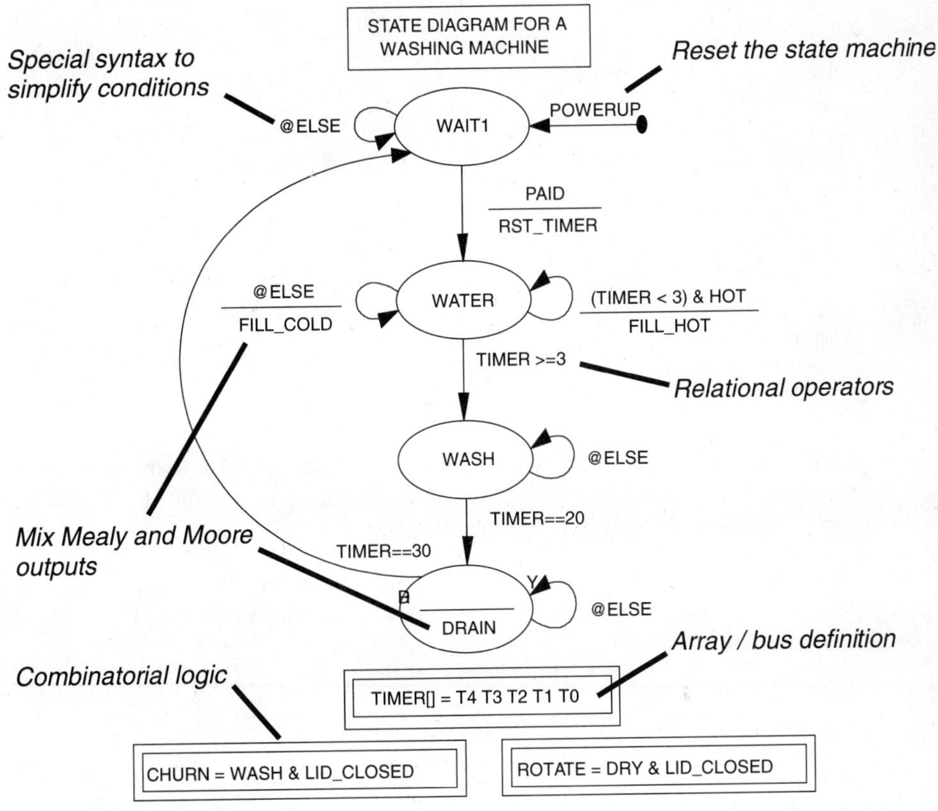

Figure 5-2
The washing machine state diagram.

3. To add a state to the diagram, position the cursor in the upper part of the drawing region and click the left mouse button. A new state will be added, and will appear highlighted as shown in Figure 5-4.

4. Now add three more states and arrange them as shown in Figure 5-5. (Increase the size of the application window if necessary to make more space.) When moving the states into position, remember that the right mouse button is used to move objects and the left button to edit them.

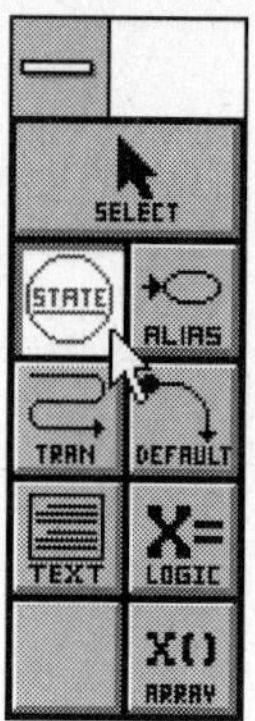

Figure 5-3
Selecting the state drawing mode.

Now you will need to add state names and state output information (if any) to the four states. You do this by clicking once on a state to highlight it and then clicking again on the state to edit its information.

5. Double-click on the topmost state, and enter the state name **WAIT1** as shown in Figure 5-6. Repeat this process for each of the states **WAIT1**, **WATER**, **WASH** and **DRY**.

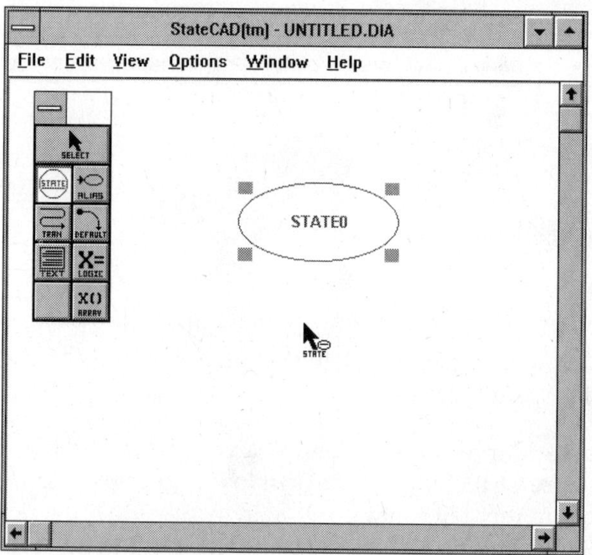

Figure 5-4
Placing states on the diagram.

StateCAD[tm] - UNTITLED.DIA
File
Edit
View
Options
Window
Help
STATE0
STATE1
STATE2
STATE3

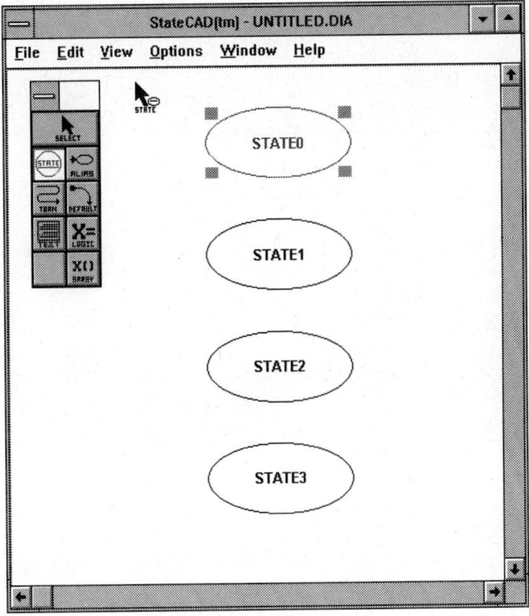

Figure 5-5
The four states of the machine.

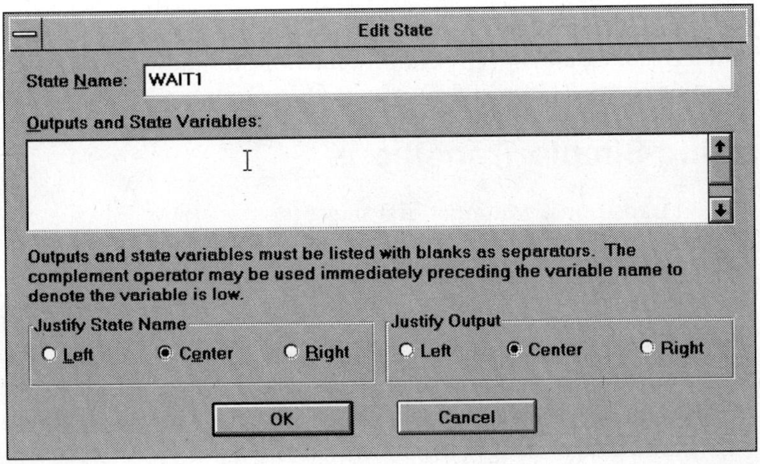

Edit State
State Name:
WAIT1
Outputs and State Variables:
Outputs and state variables must be listed with blanks as separators. The complement operator may be used immediately preceding the variable name to denote the variable is low.
Justify State Name
Left
Center
Right
Justify Output
Left
Center
Right
OK
Cancel

Figure 5-6
Naming a state.

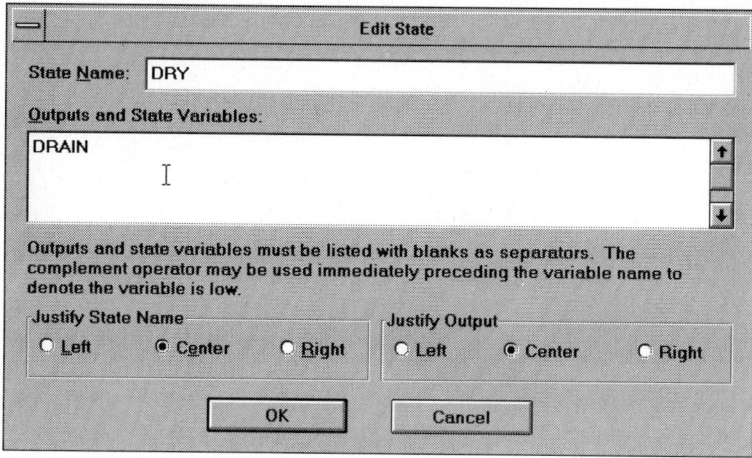

Figure 5-7
Adding a state output to state **DRY**.

The **DRY** state, in addition to requiring a state name, also requires that an output be defined, **DRAIN**.

6. To define the **DRAIN** output, add the name **DRAIN** to the **Outputs** and **State Variables** fields in the Edit State dialogue box as shown in Figure 5-7. When you enter the state name with an output in this fashion, you will see the output name(s) listed below the state name on the diagram.

Now that the diagram has its states defined, you will need to add transitions between states, and specify conditional logic for these transitions. You will start by drawing the transition arrows, using the diagram presented earlier to guide you.

Drawing Simple Transitions

To add transitions, you must first select the transition drawing mode:

1. Click on the transition button on the toolbar (Figure 5-8). The cursor will change, indicating that you are in transition drawing mode.

2. Start by drawing the transition from state **WAIT1** to state **WATER** (Figure 5-9). To draw a simple, straight-line transition arrow, place the cursor inside the first state (in this case **WAIT1**) near the place where you want the arrow to begin (the bottom of the bubble, in this case).

3. Click the left mouse button to begin the arrow. Release the button and move the cursor to the destination state (in this case, state **WATER**).

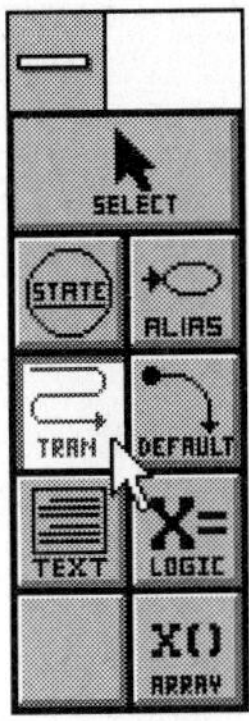

Figure 5-8
Selecting the transition drawing mode.

When you move the cursor inside of the destination state, you will see an arrowhead appear on the end of the transition line, indicating that you can complete the arrow.

4. Move the cursor to adjust the arrow's position, then click once on the left mouse button to complete the transition arrow. (You can use the cursor and right mouse button to adjust the beginning and ending postion of the line at any time.)

Repeat these actions to create the two remaining straight-line transitions that exit from states **WATER** and **WASH**.

Drawing Curved Transition Arrows

To draw curved transition arrows, you will use a similar method of locating the begin and end points of the transition, but you will have to specify two additional points (called control points) to define the curve of the line. Try this to create the transition from state **DRY** back to state **WAIT**:

1. Move the cursor inside the leftmost half of the bubble representing state **DRY**. Then click and release the mouse button.
2. Move the cursor up and to the left, about one-third of the way up the display area toward the bubble representing state **WAIT1**. Pause at this point and click the mouse button once to create a control point.
3. Now move the cursor up (vertically) until it is about two thirds of the way to the **WAIT1** state. Click the mouse button again to create the second control point.

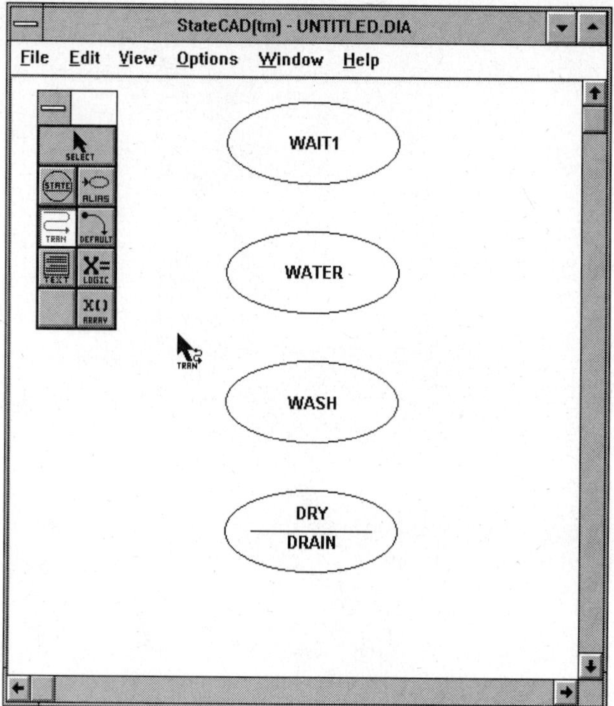

Figure 5-9
Drawing state transitions.

4. Finally, move the cursor to the inside of the **WAIT1** state bubble and click the mouse one more time to complete the transition arrow. (If your transition arrow is not shaped the way you want it, you can use the cursor and right mouse button to move the two control points and reshape the line.)

5. Repeat this process to create transition arrows representing each of the nine state transitions shown earlier. To draw the five small transitions that represent holds, click the mouse when the cursor is inside the state bubble, then add two control points outside of the state bubble, and then complete the arrow by clicking a fourth time within the same state bubble that you began.

Note: *The reset transition (the upper rightmost transition) "powerup" is drawn later. Do not try to draw it at this time.*

Adding Transition Conditions

Each of the nine transitions represented by an arrow must have a transition condition associated with it. Transition conditions are logic expressions that specify when the machine is to transfer control to another state. To add a transition condition to each transition arrow:

1. Use the left button and click on any of the four control points for an arrow. A dialogue box will appear.

2. Enter the condition expression into the **Condition** field of the dialogue box and click on **OK** to exit the dialogue box.

The **WAIT1** to **WATER** transition and the right-hand hold transition for state **WATER** require that some additional information be entered to describe the state of the **RST_TIMER** and **FILL_HOT** outputs. StateCAD allows outputs to be defined from within states (as in state **DRY**) or from within transitions. To activate an output signal from within a state transition, you enter the output signal name in the transition condition dialogue box as shown in Figure 5-10.

3. Use the left button and click on a control point for the transition from **WAIT1** to **WATER**. A dialogue box will appear.

4. Enter the signal name **PAID** into the **Condition** field, and enter the signal name **RST_TIMER** into the **Output** field as shown.

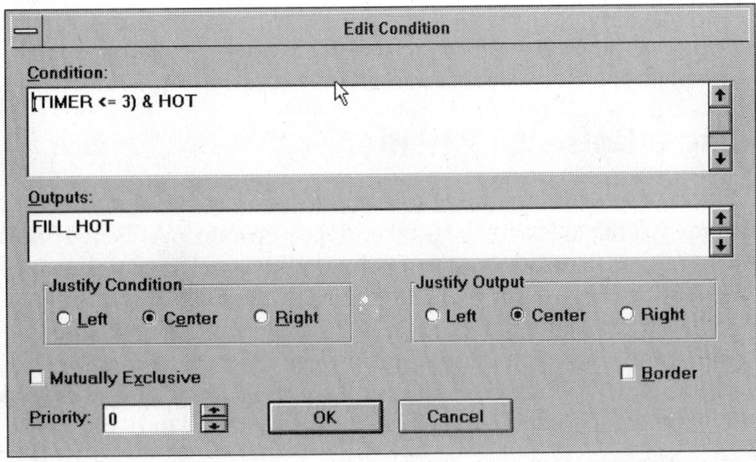

Figure 5-10
Adding a transition condition.

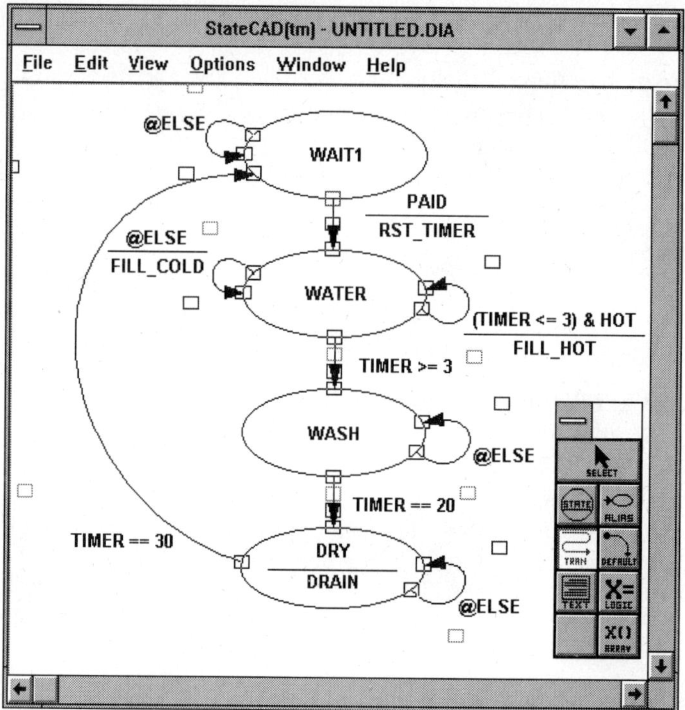

Figure 5-11
Transitions added to the diagram.

5. Repeat these procedures to add condition and output expressions to the remaining transitions as shown in Figure 5-11.

Adding a Default Transition

This state machine requires one additional transition before being complete. To ensure that the machine starts up correctly in state **WAIT1**, a default transition must be specified. This default transition will specify that the machine transition unconditionally to state **WAIT1** whenever the **POWERUP** signal is active.

To add the default transition to the diagram, select the default button from the toolbar, and create a default transition arrow. To create this arrow, do not begin from within a state bubble. Instead, start the arrow from outside a bubble, and complete the arrow inside the bubble representing the initial or default state.

1. Click on the default button in the toolbar. The cursor will change to indicate the new drawing mode.

2. Start the default transition arrow by clicking the mouse button when the cursor is to the right of the **WAIT1** state bubble, and complete the transition arrow inside of state **WAIT1**. (Refer to the earlier diagram of the completed state machine to see where the default transition should be located.)

3. Complete the default transition by adding a transition condition, and assigning a condition expression consisting of the signal name **POWERUP**.

Adding the Time Array

To complete the state machine portion of the design description, you will need to add a definition for the array representing the **TIMER** input. This array is a collection of single-bit signals that form an integer value. To add an array definition, you click on the array button in the toolbar, then click on the area of the diagram where you want the array definition to be located.

1. Click on the array button (the bottom right button) in the toolbar. The cursor will change to indicate the new drawing mode.

2. Click on the area just below state **DRY** to place the array definition at the bottom of the drawing. Double-click on the array object. An array definition dialogue box will appear.

3. Enter the definition for the **TIMER** array in the dialogue box as shown in Figure 5-12, then click on **OK** to exit the dialogue box.

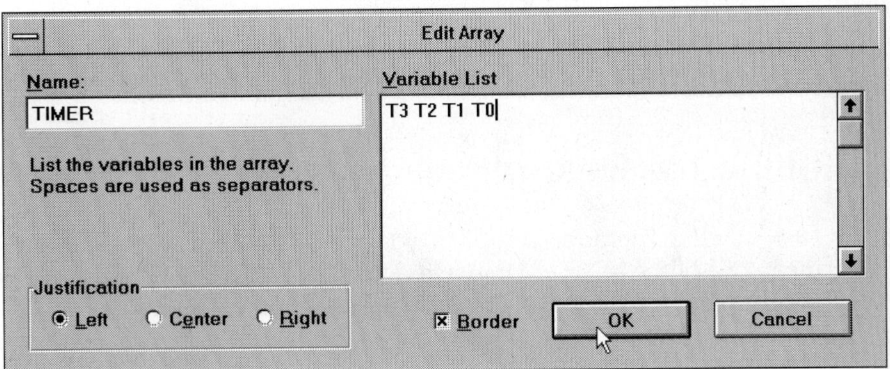

Figure 5-12
Entering an array definition.

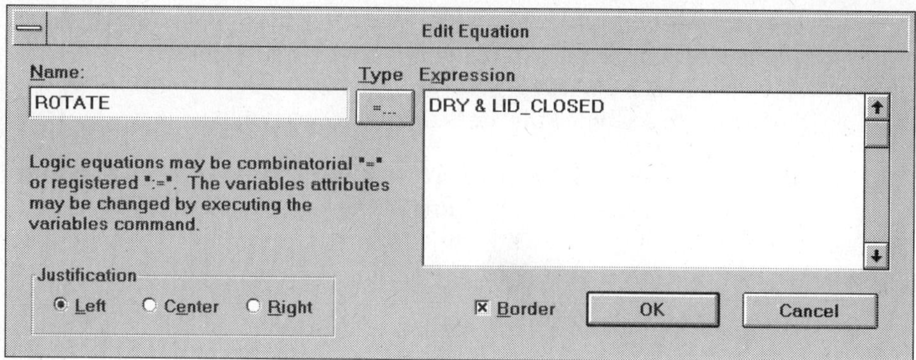

Figure 5-13
Adding a logic equation.

Adding Logic Equations to the Diagram

In addition to the state diagram portion of the design, StateCAD allows logic equations for combinational and registered functions to be entered on the drawing. For the washing machine controller, there are two such equations required: one to turn on the spin cycle (signal **ROTATE**) and one to turn on the agitator (signal **CHURN**).

1. To add a logic equation to the diagram, click on the logic button in the toolbar, then click on an empty space on the diagram.

2. Edit the equation as shown in Figure 5-13. Click on **OK** to exit the dialogue box and update the equation on the drawing.

3. Repeat this process to create an equation for **CHURN**, with the expression **WASH & LID_CLOSED**. The complete diagram is shown in Figure 5-14.

Compiling the Design

Now that the diagram is complete, you can invoke the compiler to create a source file in one of the selected languages (VHDL, ABEL, or C language). During this process, you will see how StateCAD catches errors in the design.

Generating VHDL

VHDL (VHSIC Hardware Description Language) is a standard language used for simulation modeling and logic synthesis. The language (which is described in more detail in later chapters) includes constructs that allow for the design of

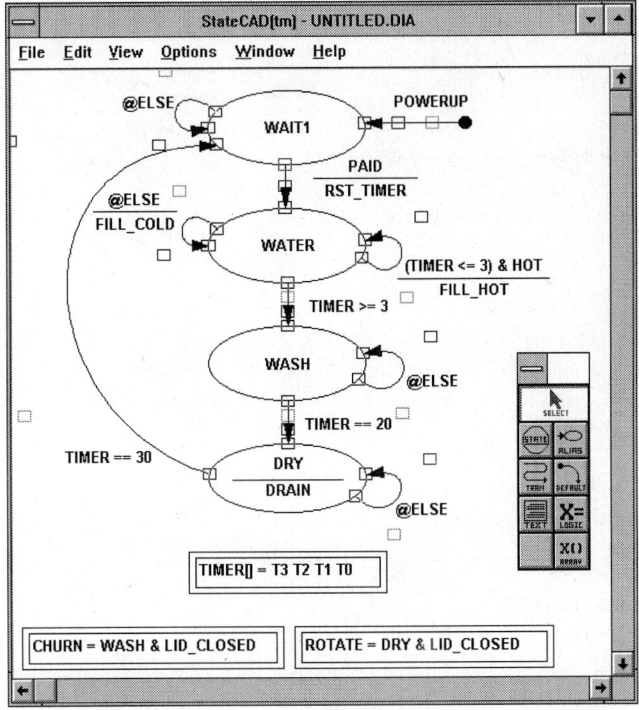

Figure 5-14
The complete diagram, ready for processing.

combinational and sequential circuits and is well suited to state machine designs. To generate VHDL source language

1. Select the **Configuration** menu item from the **Options** menu (Figure 5-15) and select the **VHDL** option in the lower center of the dialogue box.

The Configuration dialogue box includes many options that you can set, depending on the output format selected, to control how the design is processed, and what kinds of error checking are to be performed. For this example, leave the default settings intact and exit the dialogue box by clicking on **OK**.

2. Select **Compile** from the **Options** menu to process the design (or simply press CTRL-S). The design will be processed and, if there are no errors, converted to the chosen output format. (Note, however, that the demonstration version of StateCAD supplied on the CD-ROM does not save the compiled output files.)

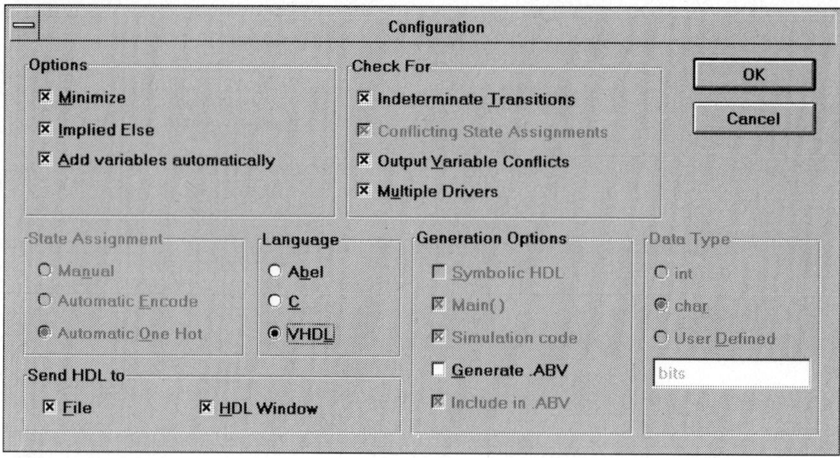

Figure 5-15
Selecting VHDL output.

Correcting Errors

If you have followed this tutorial exactly, then you will be confronted with an error dialogue box at this point (Figure 5-16). The error you will encounter indicates that the constant value specified on a transition condition is too large to be mapped to the 4-bit **TIMER** input array.

1. To correct this error, exit the error viewer and change the definition for **TIMER** to add another bit, **T4**, so the text in the array definition contains the signals **T4**, **T3**, **T2**, **T1**, and **T0**.

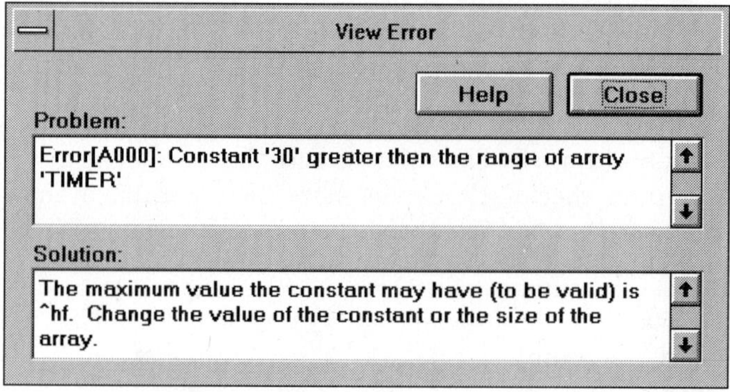

Figure 5-16
StateCAD has detected an error in the diagram.

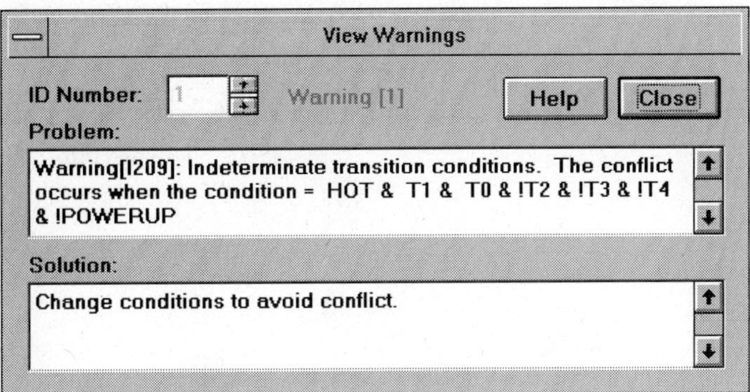

Figure 5-17
The warning display helps you identify common errors.

2. Compile the design again. This time a warning message should appear (Figure 5-17). This warning error is an indication that two transitions are conflicting by having overlapping conditions. The location of the error is highlighted on the drawing and is related to state **WATER**. Correct the error by changing the condition **(TIMER <= 3) & HOT** to **(TIMER < 3) & HOT**. The modified diagram, with the errors corrected, is shown in Figure 5-18.

3. Recompile the design once again; this time the VHDL source code should be successfully generated and displayed in the HDL output window. This VHDL source code (shown in Figure 5-19) is compatible with a variety of VHDL-based simulation and synthesis tools, some of which are described later in this book.

Generating ABEL and C Language Outputs

For programmable logic applications, you may want to generate ABEL (Advanced Boolean Expression Logic) output files. ABEL, described in more detail in Chapter 18, is a widely used design entry language for programmable logic devices, and is well suited to PLD and FPGA implementations of state machines and other types of digital circuits.

To generate ABEL language statements from this diagram:

1. Select the **ABEL Language** option in the Configuration dialogue box, then recompile the diagram. The generated ABEL source code is ready to be compiled using the ABEL software available from Data I/O corporation and other suppliers.

For embedded software applications, and for software simulation, C language statements are the prefered representation for the generated logic. StateCAD can produce C code, and this code can be either compiled and executed directly for

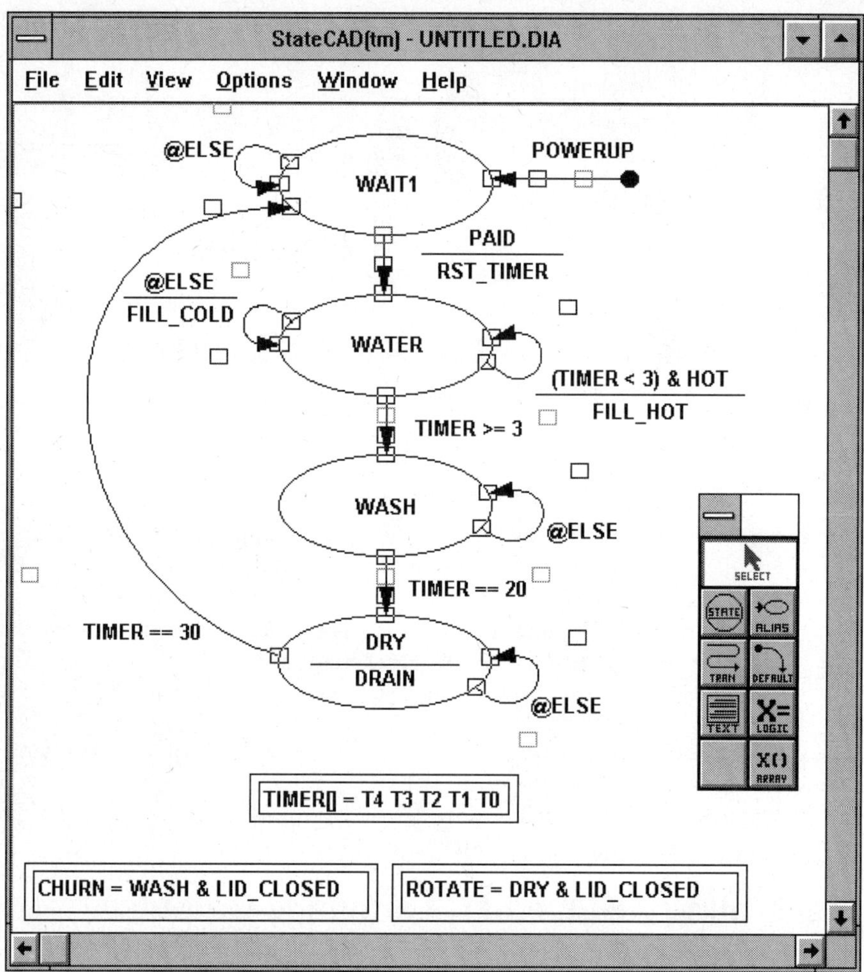

Figure 5-18
Complete diagram, with errors fixed.

simulation purposes or modified for use in a larger microprocessor-based implementation.

2. Change the language option in the Configuration dialogue box to **C**, then recompile the drawing. The C language statements generated by StateCAD can be modified as needed for use in embedded processors or for larger software control systems.

Figure 5-19
Generated VHDL source file.

```
LIBRARY ieee;
USE ieee.std_logic_1164.all;
ENTITY WASH3 IS
    PORT (CLK, T4, T3, T2, T1, T0, POWERUP, LID_CLOSED, HOT,
         PAID: IN std_logic;
    CHURN, DRAIN, FILL_COLD, FILL_HOT, RST_TIMER,  ROTATE : OUT
std_logic);
END;

ARCHITECTURE BEHAVIOR OF WASH3 IS
    TYPE type_sreg IS (DRY, WAIT1, WASH, WATER);
    SIGNAL sreg, next_sreg : type_sreg;
    SIGNAL next_DRAIN,next_FILL_COLD,next_FILL_HOT,
           next_RST_TIMER : std_logic;
BEGIN

PROCESS (CLK)
BEGIN
    IF CLK='1' AND CLK'event THEN
        sreg <= next_sreg;  DRAIN <= next_DRAIN;
        FILL_COLD <= next_FILL_COLD; FILL_HOT <= next_FILL_HOT;
        RST_TIMER <= next_RST_TIMER;
END IF;
END PROCESS;

PROCESS (sreg,T4,T3,T2,T1,T0,POWERUP,HOT,PAID)
BEGIN
    next_DRAIN <= '0'; next_FILL_COLD <= '0';
    next_FILL_HOT <= '0';  next_RST_TIMER <= '0'; next_sreg<=DRY;
    IF (POWERUP='1') THEN
        next_sreg<=WAIT1;
    ELSE
        CASE sreg IS
            WHEN DRY =>
                IF (NOT T4='1' AND NOT POWERUP='1') OR (NOT
                    T3='1' AND NOT POWERUP='1') OR (NOT T2='1'
                    AND NOT POWERUP='1') OR (NOT T1='1' AND NOT
                    POWERUP='1') OR (T0='1' AND NOT POWERUP='1') THEN
                        next_sreg<=DRY;
                        next_DRAIN<='1';
                END IF;
                IF (NOT POWERUP='1' AND NOT T0='1' AND T1='1'
                    AND T2='1' AND T3='1' AND T4='1') THEN
                    next_sreg<=WAIT1;
                END IF;
            WHEN WAIT1 =>
                IF (NOT PAID='1' AND NOT POWERUP='1') THEN
                    next_sreg<=WAIT1;
                END IF;
                IF (NOT POWERUP='1' AND PAID='1') THEN
                    next_sreg<=WATER;
                    next_RST_TIMER<='1';
                END IF;
            WHEN WASH =>
                IF (NOT T4='1' AND NOT POWERUP='1') OR (T3='1' AND NOT
                    POWERUP='1') OR (NOT T2='1' AND NOT POWERUP='1') OR
                    (T1='1' AND NOT POWERUP='1') OR (T0='1' AND NOT
                    POWERUP='1') THEN
                    next_sreg<=WASH;
                END IF;
                IF (NOT POWERUP='1' AND NOT T0='1' AND NOT T1='1' AND
                    T2='1' AND NOT T3='1' AND T4='1') THEN
                    next_sreg<=DRY;
                    next_DRAIN<='1';
                END IF;
```

```
            WHEN WATER =>
                IF (NOT POWERUP='1' AND HOT='1' AND NOT T0='1' AND NOT
                    T2='1' AND NOT T3='1' AND NOT T4='1') OR (NOT
                    POWERUP='1' AND HOT='1' AND NOT T1='1' AND NOT
                    T2='1' AND NOT T3='1' AND NOT T4='1') THEN
                    next_sreg<=WATER;
                    next_FILL_HOT<='1';
                END IF;
                IF (NOT HOT='1' AND NOT T0='1' AND NOT T2='1' AND NOT
                    T3='1' AND NOT T4='1' AND NOT POWERUP='1') OR
                    (NOT HOT='1' AND NOT T1='1' AND NOT T2='1' AND NOT
                    T3='1' AND NOT T4='1' AND NOT POWERUP='1') THEN
                    next_sreg<=WATER; next_FILL_COLD<='1';
                END IF;
                IF (NOT POWERUP='1' AND T4='1') OR (NOT POWERUP='1' AND
                    T3='1') OR (NOT POWERUP='1' AND T2='1') OR (NOT
                    POWERUP='1' AND T0='1' AND T1='1') THEN
                    next_sreg<=WASH;
                END IF;
        END CASE;
    END IF;
END PROCESS;

PROCESS (sreg,LID_CLOSED)
BEGIN
    IF (((sreg=WASH) AND LID_CLOSED='1')) THEN CHURN<='1';
    ELSE CHURN<='0';
    END IF;
END PROCESS;

PROCESS (sreg,LID_CLOSED)
BEGIN
    IF (((sreg=DRY) AND LID_CLOSED='1')) THEN ROTATE<='1';
    ELSE ROTATE<='0';
    END IF;
END PROCESS;
END BEHAVIOR;
```

Moving On

This chapter has provided us with a look at an alternative form of design entry. In later chapters, we will be looking at other, text-based forms of entry when we examine hardware description languages. For the next few chapters, however, we are going to be focusing on simulation.

CHAPTER 6

FOCUS ON TECHNOLOGY: DIGITAL SIMULATION

The ability to simulate a system before building it is one of the most compelling reasons to use computer-based circuit design methods, and the existence of powerful, relatively low-cost simulation tools for the Windows environment makes this technology available to all circuit designers. There are literally dozens of simulation tools that you can choose from, each having its own particular emphasis on designing and debugging circuits.

Computer-based simulation allows design concepts to be tried before a decision is made on the final implementation and allows large systems to be tested before all of the component parts actually exist. Simulation has become increasingly important as designs have become more complex and as new implementation technologies (such as ASICs, or surface mount packaging) make it more difficult to debug a design using traditional breadboard techniques.

Because simulation is such an important part of the overall EDA environment, I'll be devoting many chapters to describing the different aspects of simulation tools now available. In this chapter I'll focus on digital simulation tools, and examine some of the different ways that these tools can fit into a primarily schematic-oriented digital design environment. In later chapters we'll be taking a look at analog simulation tools and simulation from a hardware description language perspective.

What Is Digital Simulation?

Digital simulation allows you to model the behavior of a circuit, in terms of logical values on signals and the timing of events, before actually building it. All digital simulators in widespread use today are *event-driven* simulators, meaning that they calculate and store changes on signals (or *nodes*) in a circuit's network. Modern digital simulators can work efficiently on very large circuits because they assume that each node in the circuit can be represented using a relatively small number of unique values, or states. These states are typically a combination of a logic level (e.g., 0, 1, or unknown) and signal strength (high impedence, drive level, etc.) Unlike analog simulators (the subject of a later chapter), digital simulators do not have to calculate precise voltage or current values for nodes in a circuit; they only have to track changes to the state of each node in the system being simulated.

The accuracy of a digital simulator depends on many factors, including

- The number of logical states defined by the simulator (with each state being a unique combination of logic level and signal strength)
- The type of delay model used (e.g. gate delays only)
- The method used to model delays and rise/fall times on signals
- The method used (if any) to model the effect of fan-in, fan-out, loading, temperature, and power

When using a digital simulator, you apply *stimulus* to a software *model* of a circuit and view the resulting circuit outputs. Stimulus can provided to the simulator in many forms, including waveforms, simulator commands, and test vectors. When the simulation runs, the *response* of the design under test—the output that it generates over time—may be displayed dynamically (as changing values on the schematic, or the values of signals in a debugging window) or may be reported as tabular or waveform data after the simulation has finished processing all the stimulus that you have provided. In some simulation environments, you can interact with the simulation in much the same way you might interact with a hardware breadboard, applying stimulus and observing responses interactively.

Simulation can allow you to check the function of your circuit as though it was operating normally, or it can be used to test abnormal conditions that you would never expect to occur in the final product. The latter is useful for modeling how the circuit would react if other parts of the design were functioning incorrectly. If your design has been developed using modular design methods, then simulation can be used to test individual circuit elements (functional blocks of the overall circuit) or can be used to test the entire system, even before all the component parts have been completely specified (using a top-down approach).

To understand simulation, it is useful to think of analogies to actual hardware. Figure 6-1 show shows how a conceptual design, consisting of a collection of

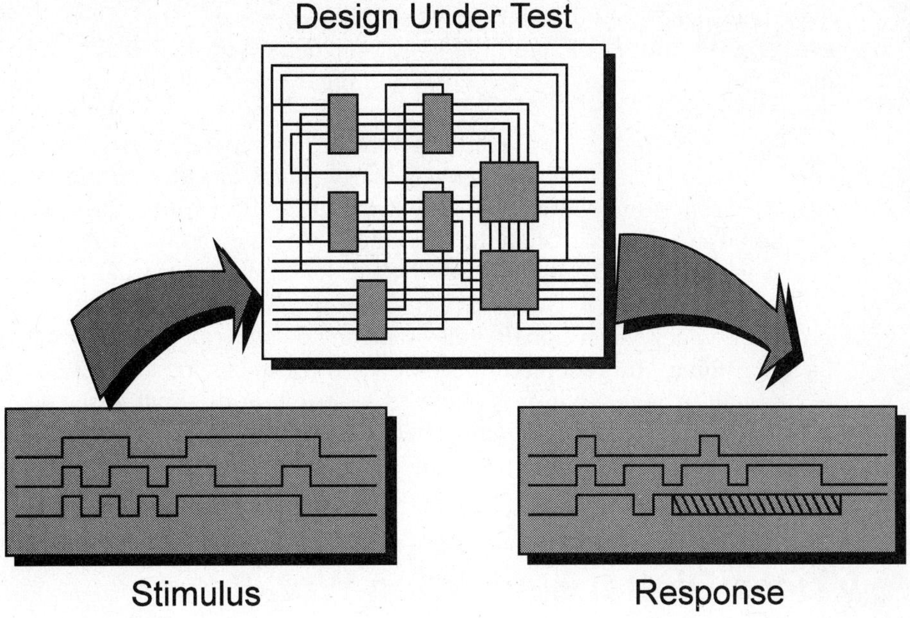

Figure 6-1
Simulating a digital circuit requires a circuit model and input stimulus.

component devices, is processed during simulation. The simulator accepts your test stimulus (either interactively or in a batched sequence) and applies that stimulus to the circuit. The simulator then models your design (using knowledge that the simulator has about your design and its components) and reports how the design reacted to the stimulus over time.

Simulation Time Versus Real Time

The notion of simulation time is an important concept to understand when you begin using simulation tools. In all electronic systems, signals values throughout the system change state, data is passed from circuit element to circuit element, and other events occur, sometimes in parallel and sometimes in sequence, over whatever period of time you allow the system to run. Since actual hardware devices (logic gates, flip-flops, and other circuit elements) can operate at speeds much faster than the equivalent software can execute, a simulator must create not only a software model of the design being simulated, but of time as well. In *functional simulation*, this model of time is restricted to a sequence of events, with zero units (or some fixed unit) of time assumed to go by between each event. (If measured in actual time, the simulator would appear to be stepping forward from event to event, with essentially zero time elapsing between each event.) Using this event-centric model of time, the simulator helps you to determine if the basic operation of the circuit is correct, without regard to its actual operating speed and internal delays.

Functional simulation is valuable because it is generally fast, cheap and easy to comprehend. Since most errors in the early phase of a design are related to the design's function (rather than its implementation and timing constraints), functional simulation is often the first step in verifying a new design.

In the case if a true *timing simulation*, the simulator actually calculates and models the delays between events, based on knowledge that it has about propagation delays on signals, gate switching delays, rise and fall times, and other factors. Timing simulation is important when you are trying to determine how your design will behave when it is operated at speed, in the final implementation. I'll describe more about the differences between functional and timing simulation later in this chapter. First, let's peer inside a simulation environment and try to understand how a typical digital simulator does its job.

How Does Digital Simulation Work?

Most digital simulators in use today operate at the gate level (as opposed to a lower-level, such as at the transistor level). Gate level simulation typically involves the following components: the simulation engine (the core simulator) a set of simulation primitives (such as AND and OR gates, and more complex primitives such as flip-flops) and some kind of user interface that provides control and visibility over the simulation as it runs (or, in the case of a batch mode simulator, after it has finished running). To complete the simulation environment, the simulator must include a well-defined method of capturing the design (such as a standard netlist or schematic interface) and a useful set of output formats (such as waveform displays, reports, and messages.)

To simulate a design, a gate-level simulator models the design being simulated as a collection of interconnected simulation primitives and, as the simulation progresses, keeps track of the input and output values of each primitive in some kind of database. During simulation, the simulator has many events to keep track of, and it must schedule the processing of those in such a way that the inherently parallel operation of the hardware being simulated is accurately reflected in the inherently serial operation of the simulator software. To speed the processing of the simulation and reduce the number of calculations that must be performed, most simulators operated in an *event-driven* manner, meaning that the outputs of the simulated gates in the circuit are recalculated only when qualifying events (such as changes in that gate's inputs) occur.

Let's look at an example of how this works. Figure 6-2 is a schematic of a simple circuit consisting of three logic gates: an inverter (**U1**), a 2-input AND gate (**U2**), and a 2-input OR gate (**U3**). Figure 6-3 shows a possible set of input stimulus

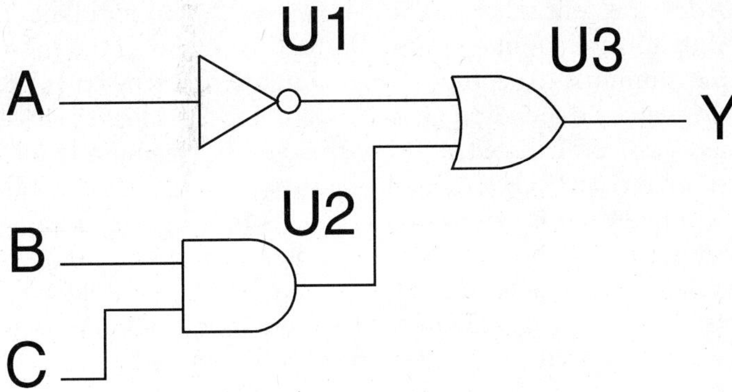

Figure 6-2
A simple circuit.

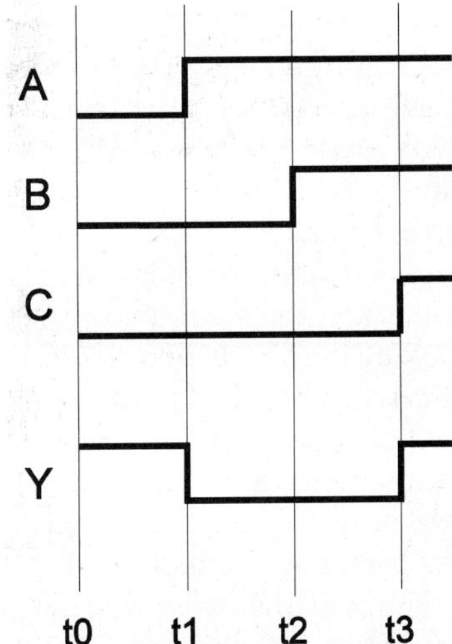

Figure 6-3
Stimulus and response for the simple circuit.

waveforms, one for each input **A**, **B**, and **C**, and the resulting waveform for output **Y** when this simple design is functionally simulated. Let's examine how the output waveform for **Y** is calculated during functional simulation. To simulate this design, the simulator first initializes each input to the specified value at simulation time **t0** (in this case all inputs are low). It then calculates the values for all gates in the system based on the logical function of each primitive and the connections provided between them. In this case, at time zero the output of the inverter gate is high, the output of the AND gate is low, and the resulting value of the output of the OR gate (signal **Y**) is high.

After this initial calculation takes place, the simulator advances (in what amounts to zero simulated time) to the first event in the input waveform. In our sample stimulus, that point in the simulation is labeled **t_1**. At **t_1**, all gates in the system that are dependent on a change in the signal **A** (the inverter gate **U1**, in our example) are recalculated, and any changes that result from these recalculations are placed on an *event queue*, or are in some other way captured. Since, in this example, the output of the inverter gate **U1** feeds into the input of the OR gate **U3**, the changing value of the **U1** output generates an event the affects the OR gate **U3**. This event in term generates another event on the output of the OR gate, and the signal **Y** gets a new value: low. Before the simulator can advance to the next input event, all events that occur in the system must be completed—the event queue must be empty.

After all the events at **t_1** have been processed and the signal **Y** is assigned its new value, the simulator can advance to the next event in the input stimulus, which is marked **t_2**. At **t_2**, the simulator detects that an event has occured that might affect AND gate **U2**, and recalculates the output of that gate. Since the changing of only one of the AND gate's inputs to a high value does not result in a change in the value of the AND gate's output, no additional events are generated and the simulation can advance to **t_3**, where the next change in the stimulus occurs. At this point, the input **C** goes from low to high, causing the output of the AND gate to go high. This, in turn, generates an event that affects the OR gate, so the value of that gate's output (signal **Y**) is recalculated and changes back to a high value. At this point the simulation is complete, and the resulting simulation waveform is displayed.

Take a close look at the waveform for output **Y**. Since this was a functional simulation, all events were assumed to take place in zero time, so the two changes in the value of **Y** line up perfectly with the changes in signal **A** (at **t_1**) and signal **C** (at **t_3**). Is this an acurate reflection of the real world? Of course not; consider what would happen if we built this circuit in such a way that the propagation delay through the inverter gate was significantly longer (perhaps due to a long routing path in an FPGA) than was the delay through the AND gate. In this case, if the actual period of time between **t_1** and **t_3** were sufficiently short, the output **Y** would never go to a low value. To detect situations such as this, you need to run a timing simulation. In a timing simulation, actual delays are attached to each gate in the simulated *network*, and propogation delays may also be attached to each signal (or *net*) in the network. These delays may be fixed units of delay that you assign for all gates and nets prior to simulation or may be back-annotated delay values that are based on the actual type of hardware (PLD, FPGA, gate array, etc.) being used for implementation.

Unit Delay Simulation

It is possible to improve on the level of information that you get from simple functional simulation without having to assign real timing values throughout the simulated circuit. If your goal in simulation is to find race conditions and the

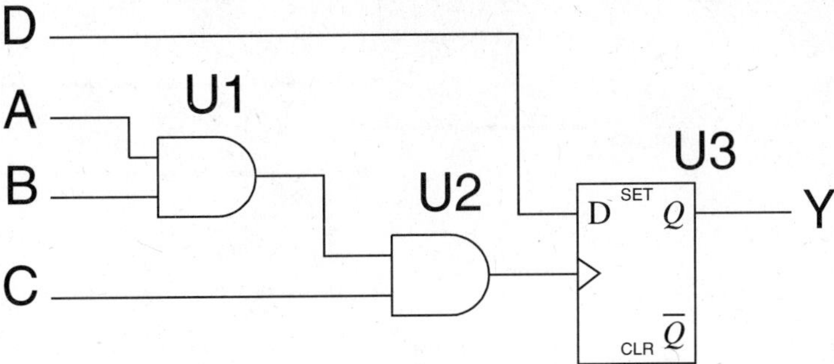

Figure 6-4
A circuit with a clocking hazard.

glitches and other circuit errors that result from such conditions, then a *unit delay* simulation may be all that you need. With a unit delay simulator, a single delay time is assigned to every gate in the design. Since many timing errors are caused by unequal numbers of gates in the paths of different signals, common timing problems can be uncovered by running a unit delay simulation with various delay values and observing the result.

Figure 6-4, for example, shows a simple circuit consisting of two AND gates feeding the clock input to a flip-flop to create a clock enable function. If each gate in this design is assigned a delay value of 5 ns, and we apply a stimulus to the circuit such as that shown in Figure 6-5, then we may find at simulation time that there is a potential for the clock input to the flip-flop to have a brief pulse, or false clock, due to the unequal delays between the **A** and **B** signal propogation (through AND gate **U1**) and signal **C**. Functional simulation, which assumes zero delay for all circuit elements, would not be capable of detecting such a situation.

Timing Simulation

Simulating a design with complete timing will obviously result in a more accurate reflection of the actual design's performance, but there's a catch: Where do all the timing numbers come from? Obviously you can't just plug in arbitrary numbers when performing timing simulation. Instead, you must either wait until you have decided on an implementation technology (PLD, ASIC, TTL, etc.) and let the simulation models define the timing for you (perhaps adding in or ignoring the propagation delays on your board) or define worst case delay values that you have calculated or estimated for large segments of the design.

In any case, it is unlikely that you will be able to model the precise timing values for your completed system, and you will simply have to find a compromise position. If you are implementing your entire design in a single ASIC or FPGA, you

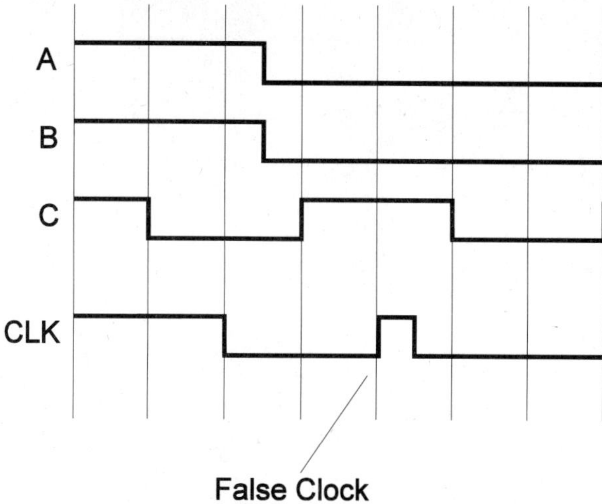

Figure 6-5
A false clock can be created by gate delays.

can expect to achieve a level of accuracy from simulation that is sufficient for virtually any application.

Clearly, a simulator that models actual gate and signal delays has a lot more to keep track of than does one that only operates in a functional (zero delay) manner. Each simulation primitive must be modeled with a number of timing parameters, including most of the parameters you might see in a data book (tpdHL, tpdLH, fMAX, etc.) Because the timing data being applied for each primitive is specific to the type of technology being used, timing simulators include libraries of simulation primitives representing the actual components (such as 7400 series devices) or macros (such as gate array blocks) being used in the final implementation. These libraries are often sold as extra cost options, since the cost (to the simulator vendor) of keeping these libraries up to date may actually exceed the cost of maintaining the simulator itself.

Simulation Models

All timing simulators have one or more libraries of primitives that you will used to simulate your design. These primitives are called *simulation models* and may be represented in a proprietary format (such as the simulation vendor's own data format) or in a standard format such as Verilog HDL or VHDL. Depending on the complexity of the simulator, the models may contain only the minimum information required to decode each component's output for any set of inputs (assuming zero delay, for functional simulation) or may contain extremely detailed information about the exact behavior for every possible set of input events.

Simulation models are generally provided by simulator vendors (usually at an added cost) but may also be provided by third parties who specialize in simulation modeling. Simulation models may also be provided by the vendors of the actual hardware being simulated (as in the case of FPGAs and gate arrays). Simulators that use a standard modeling data format (such as Verilog HDL or VHDL) can read models obtained from a wide variety of sources (including Internet newsgroups and FTP sites, or from simulation model vendors) and these simulation environments also make it possible to write your own simulation models that are are portable to a wide variety of simulators.

The Test Environment

When you have your design in a form that your simulator can understand (such as a netlist of primitives) you are ready to simulate. To begin a simulation, however, you will need to supply the simulator with some information about the data to be applied to the design's inputs. This data can be provided in the form of simulator commands typed into a command window or script file, or it can be entered in advance using a waveform editor, script language, or test vectors.

Using either a script language or test vectors is the most efficient way to define stimulus for simulation. Command languages tend to be tedious to type, and are practical only for the smallest circuits. Waveform editors make it easy to visualize the relationships between input events, but are impractical when it comes time to set up repetitive events, or events that are dependent on previous circuit output conditions.

Script languages are often extensions of the simulator's basic command language and often include looping constructs, subroutines, and other types of statements that are useful for describing lengthy test sequences. Hardware description languages such as VHDL and Verilog HDL can also be used as scripting languages, if the simulator being used supports the respective HDL.

Test vectors are long, tabular lists of values that are applied to the circuit in a regular, timed sequence. Test vectors usually include not only input values to stimulate the circuit, but expected output values as well. Test vectors are quite useful for later use in hardware testing, as many hardware testers can accept and use test vector data.

Simulation Interfaces

The way in which an engineer interacts with a simulator can have a large impact on the speed with which a complex design is debugged and the completeness with which the design is tested. There are two basic methods of integration in use today for simulation: graphical and language based.

Graphical Simulation Environments

In a graphical simulation environment, you interact with the simulator using methods familiar to users of schematic capture systems. In fact, a schematic capture program is often used in combination with a waveform editor/viewer as the primary interface to the simulator (Figure 6-6). This approach to simulation is easy for most engineers to learn and comprehend, as it models traditional methods of design interaction such as schematics and logic analyzers. This method of simulation interaction is well suited to those designs that have been entered using

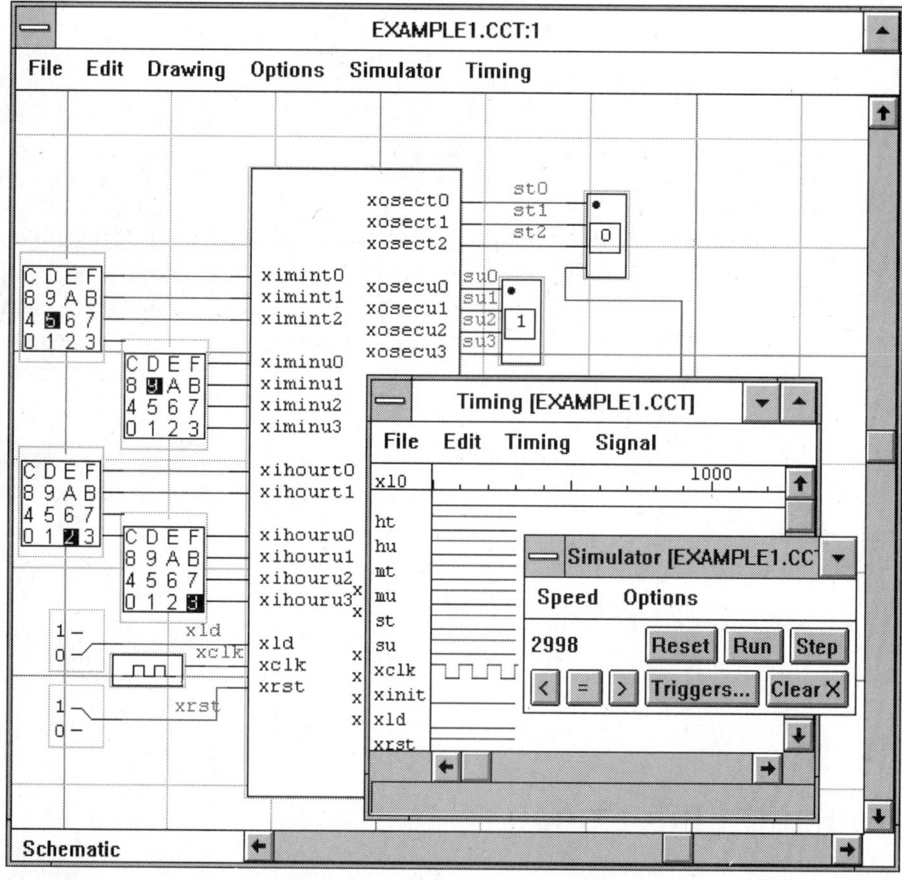

Figure 6-6
An interactive, schematic oriented simulation environment. (DesignWorks, Capilano Computing.)

a schematic approach, since the *simulation view* of the design matches the design entry format.

To perform functional simulation in such an environment, each schematic primitive used in the design is mapped to a corresponding functional model (typically composed of lower-level simulation primitives) and provided to the simulator in the form of a netlist. The simulation results are then back annotated to the schematic during simulation, allowing any signal used in the design to be probed on the screen.

To perform timing simulation using such as simulator, detailed timing data for the device (whether in the form of a database of timing parameters, an annotated netlist or a detailed timing model written in C, Verilog, or VHDL) must be provided to the simulator for each element of the design. If the design has been synthesized (as is the case in PLD and FPGA implementations, or in ASICs), the simulation model of the circuit may bear little structural resemblance to the original design. In this case, the simulator cannot always display the simulation results directly on the schematic, since the actual structure of the design may have changed dramatically during the device mapping process.

Language-Based Simulation Tools

Language-based simulation environments are becoming more prevalent as the use of hardware description languages (HDLs) becomes more widespread. In this approach, the test data for the design (which is often called a *test bench* or *test fixture*) is entered using the same language (typically VHDL or Verilog HDL) as is used to enter the design. During simulation, the user of an HDL simulator will typically interact with the simulation using a combination of design representations and methods, including waveforms, simulator commands, and source-level debugging (Figure 6-7).

When using HDLs for design entry and simulation, the design entered into the system is inherently able to be simulated and requires little or no special processing or conversion. This means that the design entry and simulation process can proceed in parallel; the simulator can actually become the primary tool used during design entry.

To simulate such a design with complete timing information, a timing-annotated version of the circuit must be provided to the simulator. The actual method used for this varies widely depending on the implementation technology (e.g., FPGA, PLD, ASIC).

Do You Need Simulation?

It is not always necessary to simulate; if you are building a circuit using programmable hardware (such as an erasable PLD or low-capacity FPGA), you may find it easier to simply breadboard the circuit and apply some stimulus by

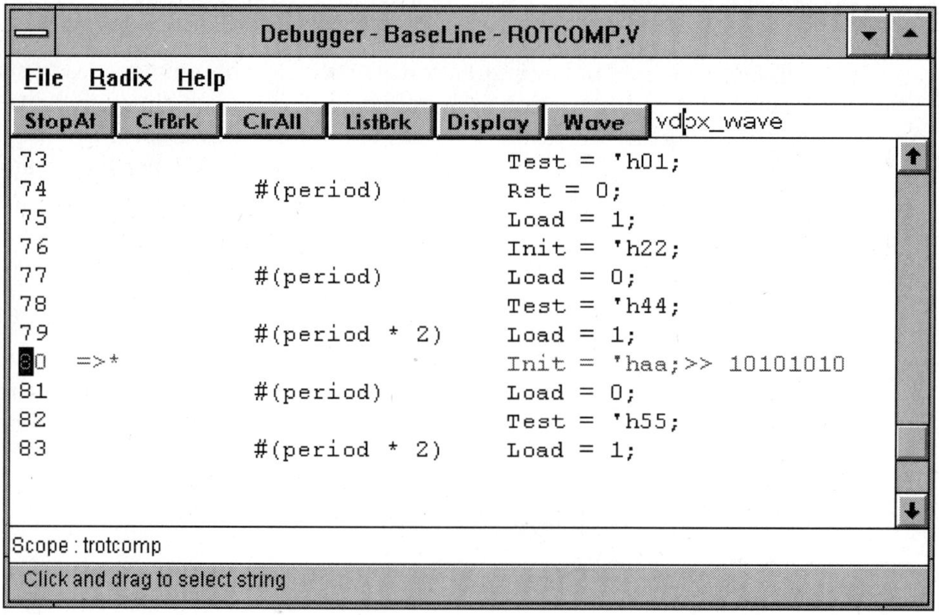

```
Debugger - BaseLine - ROTCOMP.V
File  Radix  Help
StopAt  ClrBrk  ClrAll  ListBrk  Display  Wave  vdpx_wave

                    Test = 'h01;
  #(period)         Rst = 0;
                    Load = 1;
                    Init = 'h22;
  #(period)         Load = 0;
                    Test = 'h44;
  #(period * 2)     Load = 1;
=>*                 Init = 'haa;>> 10101010
  #(period)         Load = 0;
                    Test = 'h55;
  #(period * 2)     Load = 1;

Scope : trotcomp
Click and drag to select string
```

Figure 6-7
Language-based simulation environments provide features such as source-level debugging. (BaseLine Simulator, FrontLine Design Automation.)

hand, using a signal generator and logic analyzer. If your design will be running at high speed, however, or if the design is large enough that applying and checking all the necessary stimulus and response combinations by hand is impractical, then you have only two options: put the design together with all the other circuit components and turn it on (the "smoke test" method) or use simulation.

Even if your design is relatively small and consists primarily of standard components, simulation has significant advantages over hardware breadboarding:

- Using simulation, you will not have to waste time trying to determine whether a problem is in your design or in the breadboarded implementation of that design.

- You can add and remove complicating factors as needed to zero in on a problem. For example, you can choose to simulate your design in a purely functional sense (assuming zero delays) or add simulation parameters to test for timing violations, find critical timing paths, or observe how the design would operate at its specified environmental limits. You can also test your design using varying timing values.

- Simulation allows you to experiment with components that you don't actually have available. For example, simulation allows you to try implementing your circuit in a PLD or FPGA without having to purchase an actual device.

- Simulation saves time. Once you have become familiar with simulation methods, you will find that setting up and running a simulation takes far less time that would be required to create and test a hardware prototype.

- Simulation gives you greater observability. Unlike a breadboard, which allows you only to observe the inputs and outputs of each component, simulation allows you to observe what is happening within each component, and allows you to quickly zero in on problems. Even the simplest simulator software gives you as much observability and data collection power as a high-end logic analyzer. The data display options of most simulators allow you to observe your simulation results in many formats, depending on the type of problem being diagnosed.

- Simulation gives you greater control. In addition to giving you the ability to see inside the components of your design, simulation allows you to modify the design as needed *during simulation* to isolate signals, check unusual input conditions, or set up lengthy tests by artificially loading registers with known, but abnormal, values.

Moving On

This chapter has provided the basics of digital simulation. We have learned about the differences between functional and timing simulation, and have examined how event-driven digital simulators operate. In the next chapter we're going to look at a typical low-cost digital simulation package.

CHAPTER 7

HANDS-ON EDA: USING DIGITAL SIMULATION

In this chapter, we'll be examining a representative low-cost simulation system, the SUSIE-CAD simulator offered by Automated Logic Design Company, Inc. (ALDEC) of Newbury Park, California.

Note: *The information in this chapter has been adapted from a product tutorial provided by Automated Logic Design Company, Inc. The tutorial presented in this chapter can be performed using software supplied on the companion CD-ROM.*

ALDEC's SUSIE-CAD™ and ACTIVE-CAD™

The SUSIE-CAD and ACTIVE-CAD products are based on what ALDEC calls its Active Schematic™ technology. The products are built around a schematic capture program with a built-in background simulator. This integration means that all schematic symbols (components) behave like the real parts; each new schematic entry is equivalent to adding a new device or wire to the hardware breadboard. The schematic editor also tracks electrical design rules dynamically and warns you about your design errors as they are created.

To observe the behavior of your design, you can assign symbolic LEDs to selected I/O pins directly on the schematic. The color of each LED depends upon the logical state of the assigned pin. By monitoring the color transitions, you can observe the logical states of all signals and device I/O pins.

One of the most important features of the Active Schematic concept is that it allows you to apply your stimuli or test vectors directly at the selected test points on the schematic. This is equivalent to cutting off wires and directly applying probes from a signal generator to selected device pins on a breadboard. And because these operations are controlled by a central design data base, all design changes are precisely tracked as they occur.

When equipped with ALDEC's Virtual Hardware Editor (VHE) option, the Active Schematic can directly control actual hardware operation. Also, hardware generated signals can be directly fed into any schematic test point. This allows for instant functional verification of schematic design with the target hardware. Other applications of this technology include hardware modeling, in-circuit emulation, and direct control of industrial processes from schematics that include ICs and functional blocks described by Boolean equations or VHDL statements.

ALDEC has two basic implementations of the Active Schematic:

- SUSIE-CAD is a very-low-cost design development environment for FPGA and system-level designs, with practically unlimited design size capability. Its performance and price range are designed to fit the professional consultant or start-up company's budget.

- ACTIVE-CAD is a higher-performance design environment intended for established companies.

Both of these EDA environments are supported with large symbol and IC libraries and easy to use VHDL and Boolean IC modeling tools. ALDEC has indicated that analog modeling options will be added to the products in the near future.

Quick Tips

Here are a few things to keep in mind when following the instructions in this tutorial:

- When this tutorial mentions a mouse button, it refers to the left mouse button. Only the right mouse button is listed explicitly.

- All gray-shaded buttons are inactive. You must first select the appropriate element such as file, option, device, and so on to activate the corresponding gray-shaded button(s). Only the black and bright-colored buttons are active, and they allow you to perform an operation on the previously selected items.

- To minimize the number of menus and optimize the screen space, SUSIE has some buttons with multiple operations. Clicking on such a button activates the next in sequence operation assigned to this button. When the last operation is reached, the first button operation is displayed. Examples of such buttons are **Simulation Mode** button (FN, GL, TM) and **Search Mode** button (Errors, Breakpoints, Tags, Milestones).

- ☐ SUSIE operates much like any other Windows-based product; when you are in doubt about some general Windows operation not covered in this tutorial, consult your Windows documentation.

Simulation Basics

If you are a first time digital simulator user or have used only two-state simulators, then you need to know some of the basics of *n*-state digital simulations:

- ☐ The SUSIE simulator accepts, calculates, and outputs many logical states to accurately model the behavior of typical hardware. These states include such things as *high (1)*, *low (0)*, and *3-state (z)*.
- ☐ In addition, SUSIE recognizes the strength of a signal. For example, the simulator may produce on an IC model output a *resistive strong* signal, *resistive weak* signal,or other simulated value. Since IC models have built-in tables for handling such inputs, their simulated responses appear identical to the real hardware devices.
- ☐ Some IC devices, like flip-flops, have a random logical output state on power on. To emulate this case, the simulator also includes an *unknown (x)* logical state. While there is no *unknown* logical state in hardware, this is the only way to account for the random nature of some outputs on power on. You will be warned by SUSIE if any of these random outputs appear in your design.

Functional simulators analyze design behavior without taking into account any timing propagation through the devices. Since the device and layout propagation delays are assumed to be zero, the outputs respond instantly to any and all input changes. The data produced by the functional simulators is easy to understand, and for this reason you should start your design analysis with a functional simulation.

In the real world, of course, the propogation of electrical signals through devices and through wires takes time. ALDEC's ACTIVE-CAD is a timing simulator with a 10 picosecond resolution. This simulator includes timing models for thousands of actual devices.

Starting a New Project

If you have installed the SUSIE program from the CD-ROM correctly, you should have the SUSIE program icons available (Figure 7-1). To start the SUSIE program

1. Double-click on the Schematic icon to invoke the SUSIE schematic editor.

When invoked, SUSIE displays its **Project Manager** window (Figure 7-2). This window is only displayed when there are no projects in the **Project Manager**. Otherwise SUSIE will display the schematic of the last project. You can invoke the

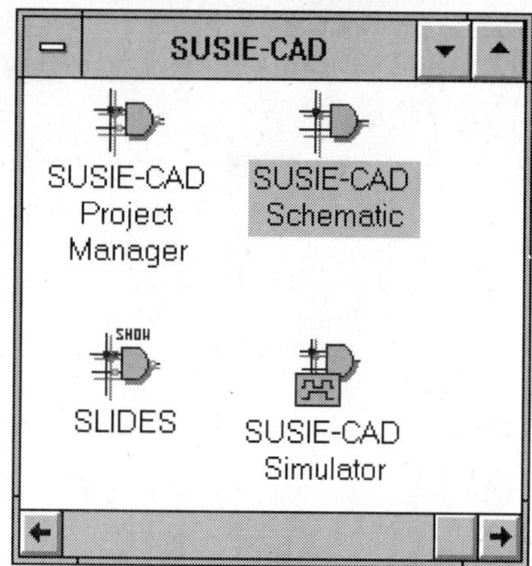

Figure 7-1
To invoke the SUSIE environment, you first launch the Schematic application.

Project Manager at any time by selecting the **Project Manager** option within either the schematic or simulator menu.

Enter the New Project Name

To enter your new project name,

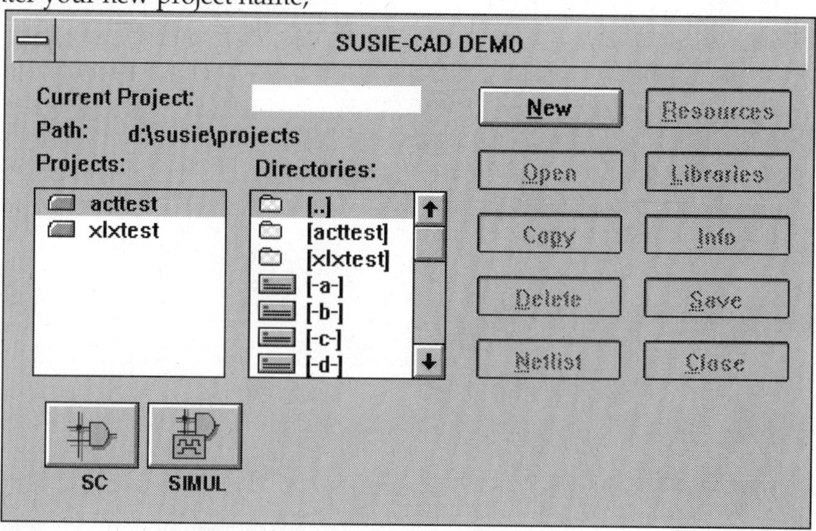

Figure 7-2
SUSIE-CAD's Project Manager helps you keep track of your schematic and library files.

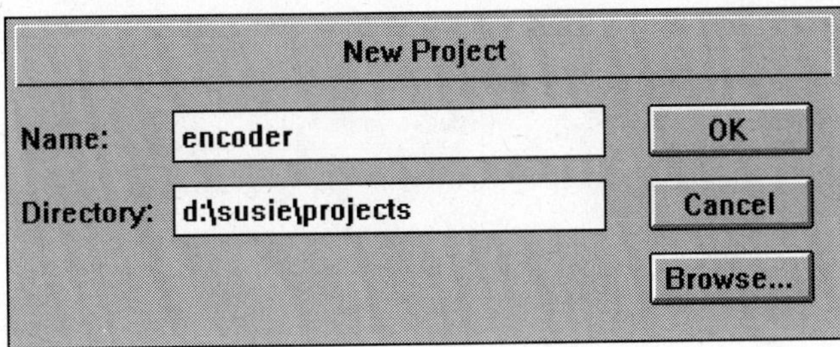

Figure 7-3
Entering the project name in the New Project dialogue box.

1. Click on the **NEW** button (Figure 7-2). In response, SUSIE displays the dialogue box shown in Figure 7-3.

2. Enter your new project name. To follow with this Tutorial, enter **ENCODER** as the new project name.

3. Press the **OK** button in Figure 7-3 and **Close** button in Figure 7-2. SUSIE immediately shows the schematic screen.

The newly entered project name is displayed as the **Current Project** field in the **Project Manager** window.

The Resources Button

The **Resources** button (Figure 7-2) activates the dialogue box in Figure 7-4. This dialogue box allows you to select for your project such supporting files as schematics from other projects, test vector files, JEDEC files, and other files that you may wish to have handy when working on a project. The **Copy** operation moves the selected resources to the current project, and the **Link** operation allows direct use of files located in other directories. Since this operation is not essential for our present exercises, it will be described later on.

Selecting the Project Libraries

The **Project Libraries** option in the Schematic Editor **File** menu allows you to select the desired IC libraries for your project. SUSIE loads the default libraries automatically. If you have additional libraries or want to change libraries used for your project, you will use the **Project Libraries** option. When this option is selected, SUSIE displays the library operations window shown in Figure 7-5.

The **Project Libraries** window lists all the libraries that you can use in your current project. The **Attached libraries** window lists additional libraries that you can add to the current project. If the **Project Libraries** does not list the **DEMOLIB** library that is needed for this Tutorial, you will need to add it:

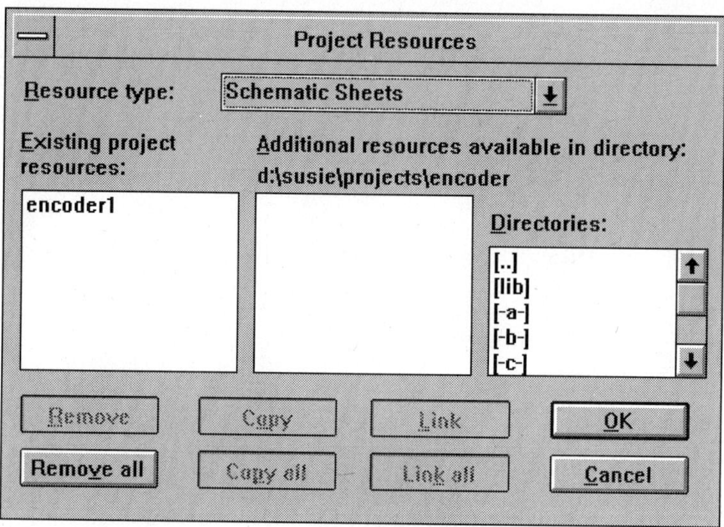

Figure 7-4
The Project Resources dialogue box.

1. Click on the **DEMOLIB** library in **Attached libraries**, then click on the **Add** button. This adds the **DEMOLIB** library to the current project libraries.

The window in Figure 7-5 shows additional options like **Remove**, **Info**, and **Reorder**. The **Remove** option allows you to remove any library from the current project to speed the search for selected devices, the **Info** option displays information about selected library locations on the disk, and the **Reorder** option allows you to change the library search order. For example, if you have parts with the same name, but in different libraries, you can decide which one should be found first and used for your design.

In SUSIE-CAD, each new project has its own library with the same name as the project itself. This library is added to the listing of the current project libraries. This library can be used to create modified versions of the system library parts; for example, you can modify IC pin numbers, timing specification, and other attributes. The project library is also used to store custom IC models created with SUSIE modeling tools. All these new IC models and libraries reside within the current project only. You can, however, select the library containing custom ICs to other projects and use these IC in several different projects.

Drawing a Schematic

After you have created the new project (and selected resources and libraries)

1. Click on the **Close** button in the **Project Manager** window. In response, SUSIE displays a schematic screen (Figure 7-6).

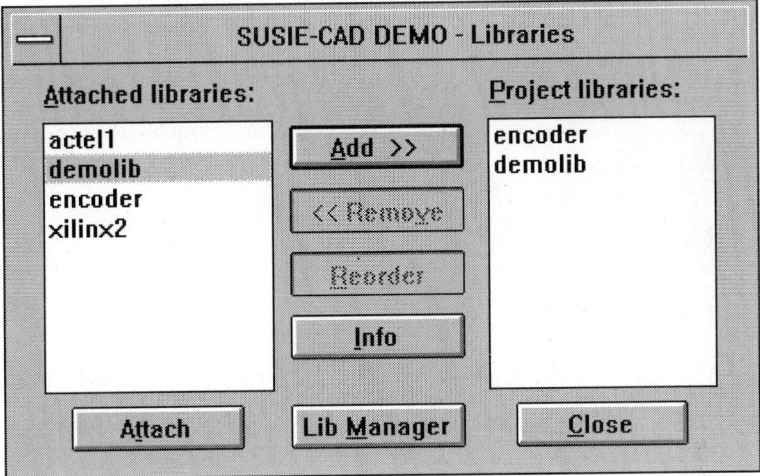

Figure 7-5
The Library dialogue box.

The next time you start the Schematic Editor your project will automatically be loaded without having to use the **Project Manager**. If you need to go back to the **Project Manager** window to create a new project, you need to use the **Project Manager** option located in the Schematic Editor **File** menu.

Selecting Components

To select components for your schematic,

1. Press the **Symbols** button (the button that looks like an AND gate) in Figure 7-6.

In response, a component library listing and the associated toolbox appear (Figure 7-7). You can select any component listed in that window and then drag it directly to any spot on the schematic. (To simplify your search for a component, you can use the icons in the Symbols toolbox to preselect the desired type of components.)

To select a component from the component window and place it on the schematic, place the cursor over the selected part and press the mouse button. Following this action, a highlight bar appears, indicating that the given component has been selected for the schematic display.

Select, for example, the 7400 IC symbol. You can do this in one of three ways:

1. Using the side scroll bar, bring the 7400 component into the window, and then click on it with the mouse device. Or,

2. Place the cursor in the components window in Figure 7-7 and click on any component. When a green bar appears, move it over to the selected component

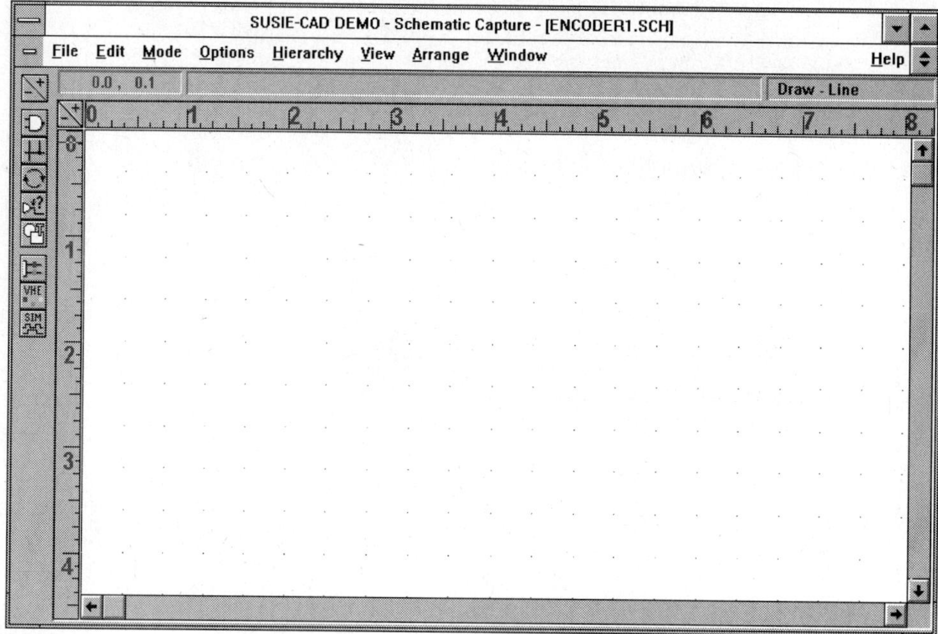

Figure 7-6
The schematic editor main screen.

by scrolling the component listing with the **PgUp**, **PgDn** and the keyboard cursor keys. Or,

3. Place the cursor at the top of the **Symbol** toolbox in Figure 7-7 , click the mouse button, and enter the name of the selected component. For example, entering "7400" will instantly place the highlight bar over the 7400 device.

Placing Components on the Schematic

When a component is selected, you can move it onto the schematic and place it as needed.

1. Using one of methods described in the previous section, select a 7400 device.
2. When a highlight bar appears over the 7400, release the mouse button and move the cursor outside the components window. Note that the component outline follows each cursor movement.
3. When the component is located where you want it placed, press the mouse button. One instance of the component will be placed where you specified.

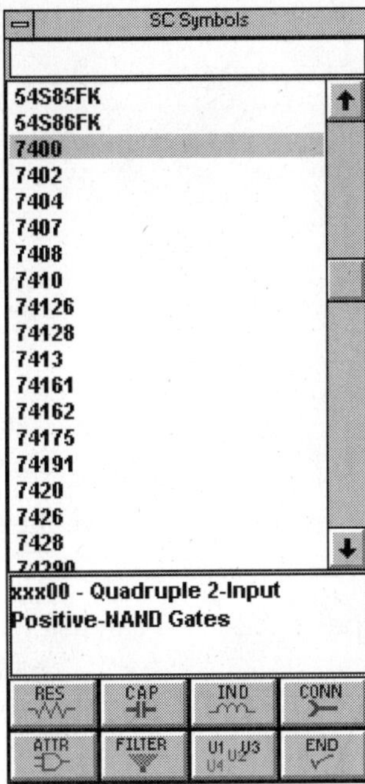

Figure 7-7
The symbol selection window.

4. Now release the mouse button and move the cursor again. As you move the cursor again, an outline of a second 7400 component follows the cursor. Click the mouse button to place a second instance of the 7400 gate to the right of the first as shown in Figure 7-8.

5. To discontinue component placement, press the right mouse button. This leaves the outline of the component at the last cursor location. To get rid of that outline, press the **END** button (Figure 7-6). If you do not press the **END** button, then every time you will click the left mouse button, the cursor will jump back to the outline of the last placed component.

If you want to place a component that is identical to one already on the schematic, just click over that component and watch as its copy follows the cursor. This way you don't need to use the Symbols toolbox for symbol selection.

Speeding Component Search

Since the number of components available in SUSIE is quite large, you may want to narrow your choices by using the **RES**, **CAP**, **IND**, and **CONN** buttons shown in Figure 7-7. These buttons act as filters for discrete components, and limit the search of components to resistors, capacitors, inductors, and connectors, respectively.

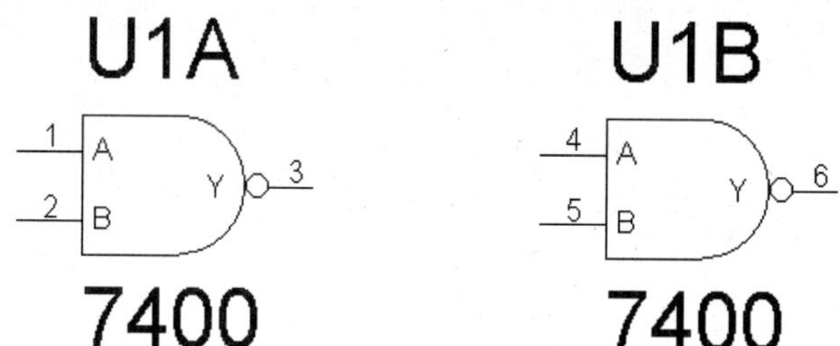

Figure 7-8
Two instances of a 7400 TTL symbol.

1. Click on the **RES** button, and observe the change in the list of symbols. Click on the **RES** button again to deselect it.

To select specific types of ICs, you can use the **FILTER** button.The **FILTER** option allows you to selectively choose for IC technology and type of device or use a component name mask to narrow down the search.

2. Click on the **FILTER** button in Figure 7-7.

Try using this feature to select a flip-flop device. Figure 7-9 shows the **FILTER** option menu. By default, all libraries are enabled.

3. Click on the **Clear** button to disable all libraries.

4. Next, select the **Flip-Flop/Latch** option within the **Attributes** selection field and click on the **OK** button to exit the **Filter** window. In response, SUSIE displays a window similar to Figure 7-7 containing only flip-flops and latches.

5. Search for the 7474 flip-flop in the components window (Figure 7-7) and place it on the schematic as shown in Figure 7-10.

Connecting Components

To connect the components in Figure 7-10,

1. Select the **Connections** button (the button located just below the components button in Figure 7-6). In response, a new toolbox (Figure 7-11) appears.

The first connection tool that you will use is the **WIRE** button. This button controls all single-wire operations and is active when depressed.

2. Click on the **WIRE** button to activate it.

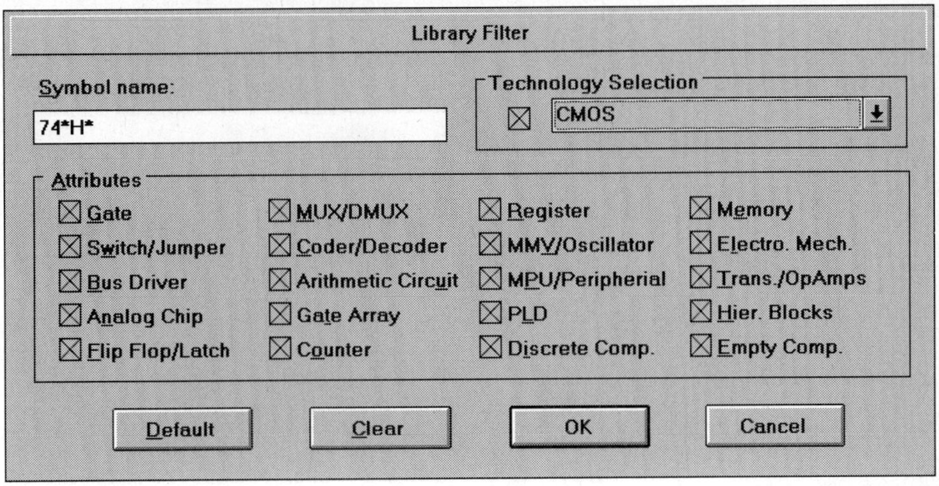

Figure 7-9
The Library Filter.

3. With the **WIRE** button active (depressed), click on the **U1A-3** pin and move the mouse device away from the pin. Note that a black line, anchored at the **U1A-3** pin, is now attached to the cursor and follows all its movements.

4. Move the cursor over the **U1B-4** pin and click the mouse button. Note that a permanent blue line (wire connection) between **U1A-3** and **U1B-4** has been created. SUSIE automatically snaps wires to device pins and assures that all connections are electrically correct.

This is the most basic method of connecting components in SUSIE. You should experiment with the **WIRE** tool at this point and become familiar with the operation of the mouse buttons.

Autorouting Wire Connections

You might have noticed that if you run wires over the top of existing components, SUSIE does not object. Instead, it waits until you make the final connection, and then tries to automatically reroute the wire, so that it does not run over any component.

Try this using the autorouting feature:

1. With the **WIRE** button active, click on the **U1B-5** pin in Figure 7-10 and move the cursor across the **U1B** and **U2A** parts. Notice that a black line now goes across these components.

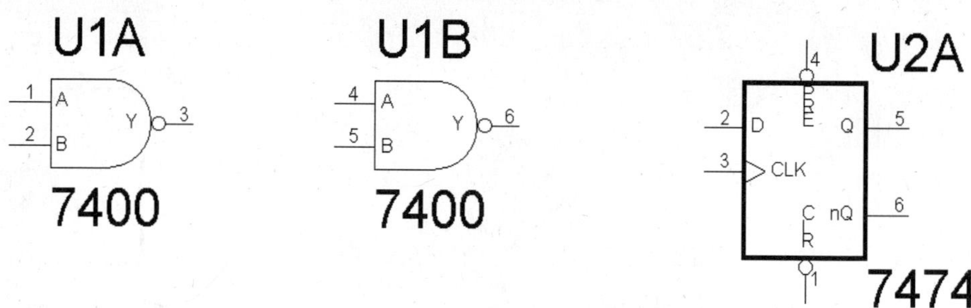

Figure 7-10
Adding a 7474 TTL flip-flop primitive to the circuit.

2. Move the cursor over the **U2A-5** pin and click the mouse button. Since the wiring goes across the components, SUSIE does not create a direct wiring path. Instead, it tries to place the wire connection around these symbols. With complex wiring you may have some messages blinking in the status line (located right above the schematic), informing you about the progress of automatic wire routing.

3. Experiment with the routing of signals until you have a display similar to that shown in Figure 7-12.

Using Table-Driven Autorouting

When a schematic is large and your screen resolution low, wiring a schematic may require a lot of scrolling. To avoid this nuisance, you can wire a schematic by

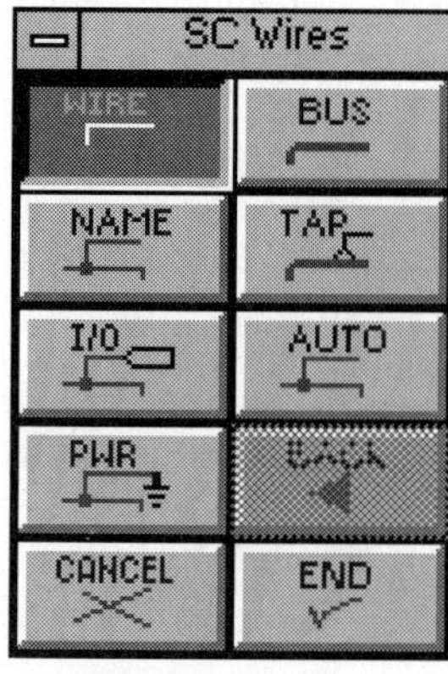

Figure 7-11
The connection toolbox.

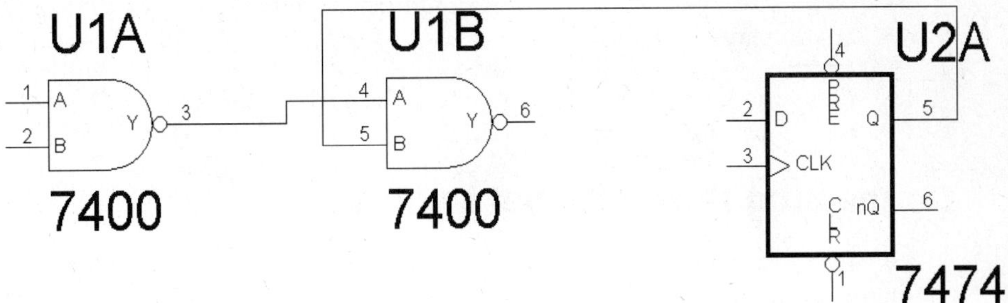

Figure 7-12
Adding wires to the schematic.

directly calling components and their pins from a table. This is usually the quickest way to make all point-to-point connections.

1. Assuming you have a similar schematic to the one in Figure 7-12, press the **AUTO** button in Figure 7-11. SUSIE responds with the auto connections table in the Figure 7-13.

2. Click the mouse button over **U1A-7400**, located within the **Connect From** field. A list of pins for that device appears in the **Pin** column.

3. Select pin 2 by placing the cursor and clicking the mouse button.

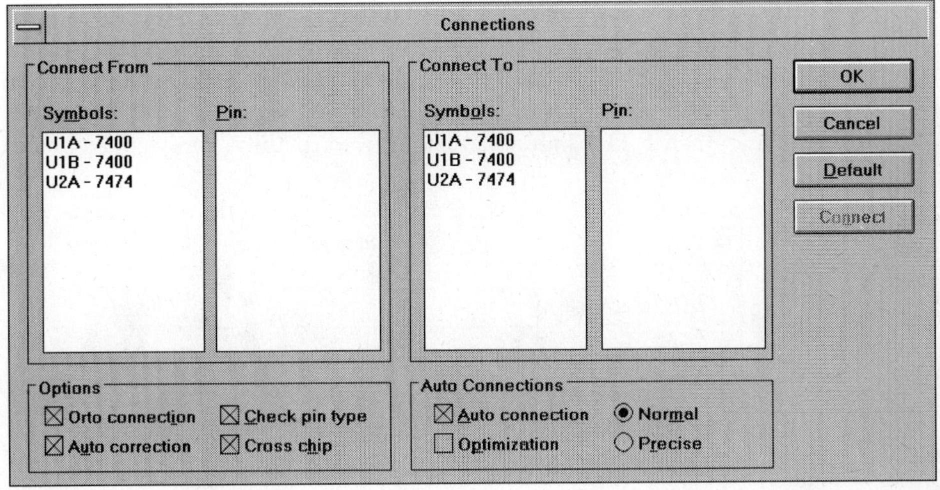

Figure 7-13
The Connections dialogue box.

4. Next, select **U2A-7474** from the **Connect To** field. When the pins of **U2A-7474** are displayed, select pin 6.

5. Press the **Connect** button and then the **OK** button to exit. A newly created wiring connection is displayed.

Connecting Pins with Net Names

SUSIE allows you to connect test points (device pins) by means of net or signal names. This method of device connectivity saves time and is particularly useful when you are creating schematics with multiple sheets. You will use a common net name to create a connection between two pins on this simple schematic.

1. Click on pin **U1A-1** and move the cursor about .5 inches away from the pin. Click the right mouse button to detach this line from the cursor.

2. To select the net (signal) name, click on the **NAME** button (in Figure 7-11). In response, SUSIE displays the window in Figure 7-14.

3. Enter the letter **A** from the keyboard and click on the **OK** button. A display such as that shown in Figure 7-15 appears, showing the **U1A-1** pin connected to the net named **A** .

4. Now repeat this operation to assign the same net name, **A**, to pin **U2A-2**. Because the **U1A-1** and **U2A-2** are connected to the same signal name (net name **A**), both pins are electrically connected (Figure 7-16).

Creating I/O Terminals

Each schematic sheet needs some connections with the outside world. If these connections are to other sheets of the same flat design, then common signal labels are sufficient for inter-sheet connections. If the connections are to other hierarchical schematic, then I/O terminals must be used. If these connections are with other

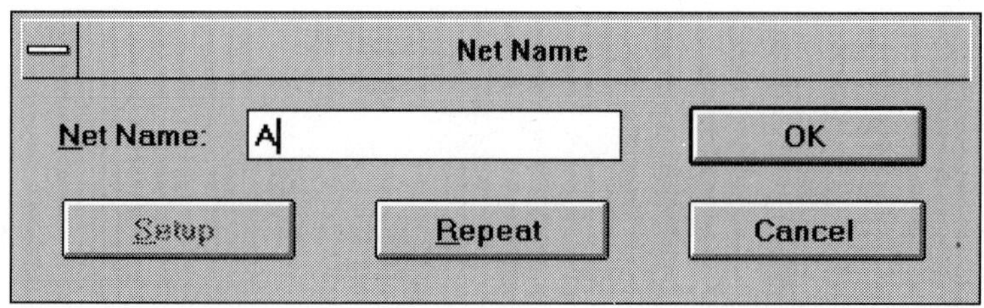

Figure 7-14
The Net Name dialogue box.

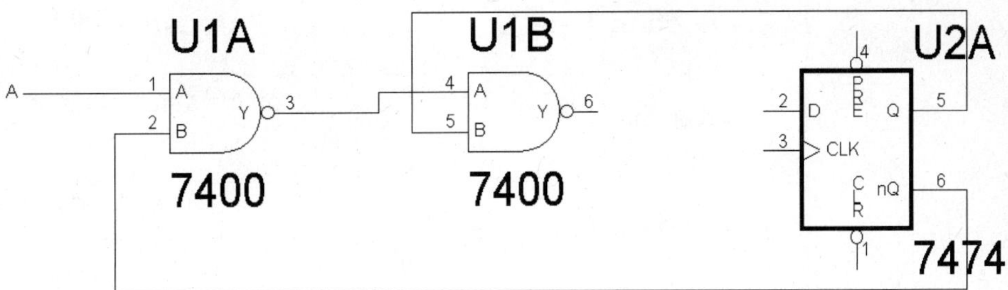

Figure 7-15
Connecting components with wires.

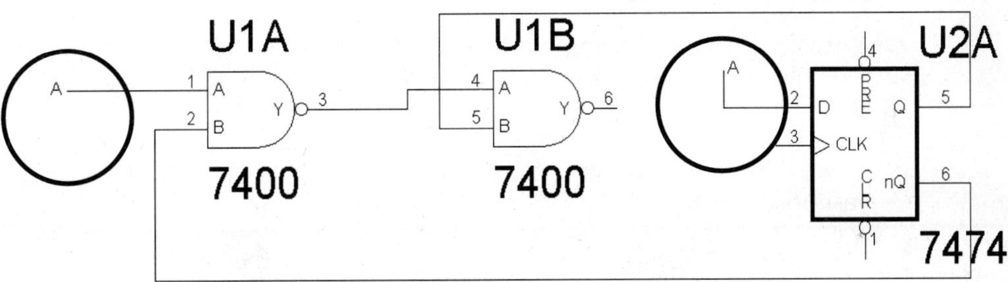

Figure 7-16
Connecting signals by using a common signal name.

types of equipment, then connector pins should be used instead of I/O terminals. The convention of using net names, terminals and connectors is very important and has been summarized in the following table:

Connection Type	Purpose
Net name	To connect pins on the same hierarchical level.
I/O terminal	To connect to higher hierarchical level. To create a hierarchical symbol pin.
Connector	To physically connect with other equipments through real connector.

To create an I/O terminal,

1. With SUSIE set to wiring mode, click on the wire coming out of pin **U1A-2**. When a black line appears, following the cursor, drag it for about .5 inches to the left.

2. Next, click the right mouse button, then click the **I/O** button in Figure 7-11. In response, the window in Figure 7-17 appears.

3. Select **INPUT** as the I/O signal type by clicking on the **Terminal Type** window (arrow) and selecting appropriate terminal type from the selection list.

4. Next, enter **IN1** into the **Terminal Name** field as the name of the new terminal and activate the **OK** button. The **IN1** terminal is displayed as shown in Figure 7-18.

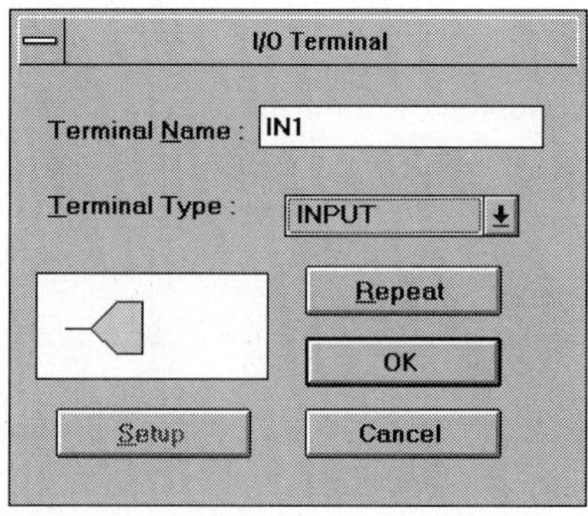

Figure 7-17
Selecting an I/O terminal.

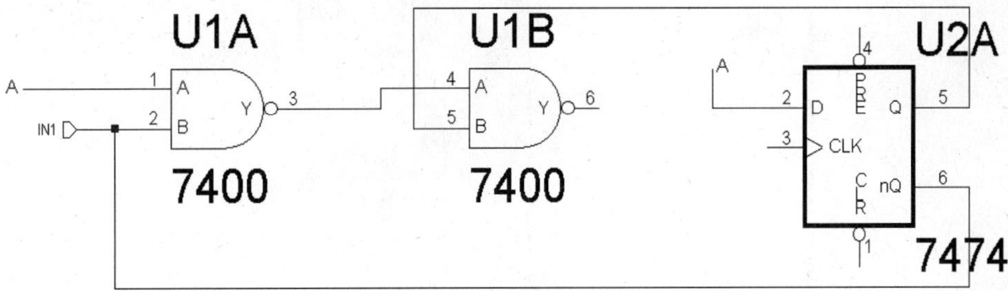

Figure 7-18
Adding an input terminal.

Assigning Power Points

You can assign Ground, Vcc, Reference, and High voltage to any pin or signal line. For this simple circuit, you are going to add a connection to **Vcc** for the preset line of the 7474 flip-flop device. To add the connection to **Vcc**,

1. Click on pin **U2A-4** and drag the resulting wire vertically for about .25 inches. Click the right mouse button to detach the cursor from the wire.
2. Click the **PWR** button in the Figure 7-11. In response, SUSIE displays the window shown in Figure 7-21.
3. Select **1 HIGH** from the **PWR Signal Type** and the arrow graphical shape from the **PWR Shape** window.
4. Click on the **OK** button. Note that pin **U2A-4** is now attached to the **Vcc** voltage supply.

Making Schematic Modifications

All schematic modification tools have been put together in one menu, called **Changes**. You can select this editing mode, shown in the Figure 7-19, by pressing the **Changes** button (the button that looks like two arrows chasing each other) in Figure 7-6.

Deleting Wires

To see how deletion of wires works, delete the two wires that feed back from the outputs of the 7474 symbol.

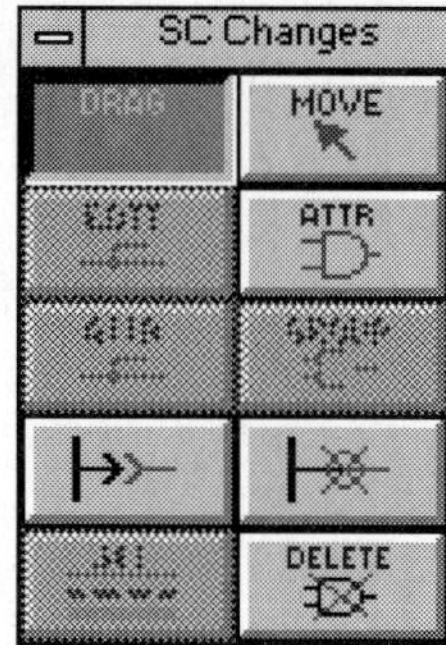

Figure 7-19
Selecting the Drag mode.

1. Click on the **Changes** button, then select the wire coming out of **U2A-5**.
2. The wire will turn red, indicating that it has been selected.
3. To delete the wire, click on the **DELETE** button.
4. Repeat this sequence of operations to delete the wire coming out of **U2A-6**.

Dragging Components and Wires

SUSIE allows you to change the position of components and wires. The most useful of these procedures is dragging, which shifts components, wires, and wire interconnections while maintaining their connectivity. This feature helps when you want to move both wires and components to make the schematic more readable.

1 Click on the **U1A** gate. Note that there has been a red square added around the **U1A** gate.

2. Holding the left mouse button down, drag the gate upward, and then release the mouse button. If there is not enough space for the gate in its new position, SUSIE beeps a warning sound. Try moving the symbol to different locations on the schematic, and observe how the wires remain connected.

3. Now try moving wires. Click on the wire between **U1A-3** and **U1A-4**. The wire turns red. Place the cursor over that red wire and drag it down the schematic while holding the left mouse button depressed. When the wire reaches the desired shape (position), release the mouse button.

Moving Components

Often you need to move a component to a totally new location on the schematic. You cannot do this with the dragging option because dragging does not allow for

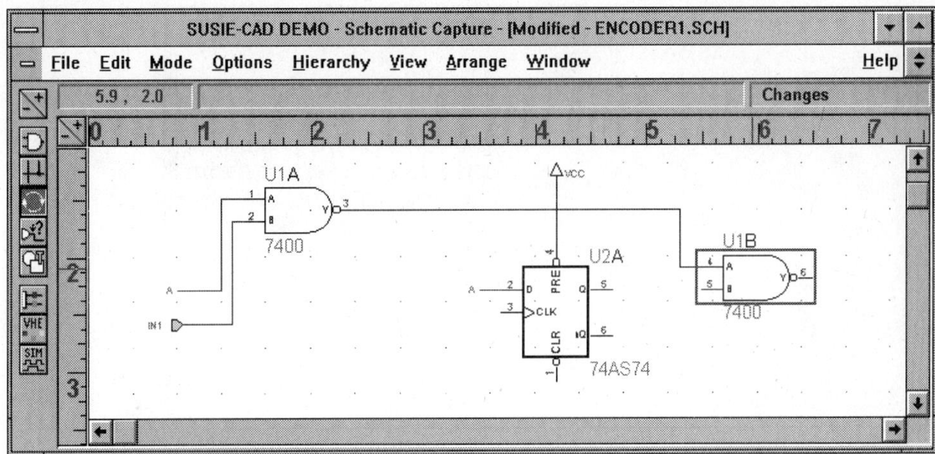

Figure 7-20
Moving a component by dragging.

the movement of components over wires or other components. You can, however, move components to any place on your schematic by using the **MOVE** option.

1. Click on the **MOVE** button in Figure 7-19. Next, click on the gate **U1B** and move it to the right of the **U2A** flip-flop. Notice that as you release the mouse button, SUSIE rewires the moved component.
2. Using the movement and dragging features, modify the drawing so it looks similar to Figure 7-20.

Saving the Schematic File

As in any application, it is important to save your work frequently.

1. To save this schematic, use the **Save As** selection in the **File** menu, and save it with the name **encoder1**.

Using Design Query

SUSIE allows you to quickly trace signal flows, search for device data, review component comments, and perform other query-related tasks. These options are selected by pressing the **Query** button (the button with the question mark symbol) in Figure 7-6.

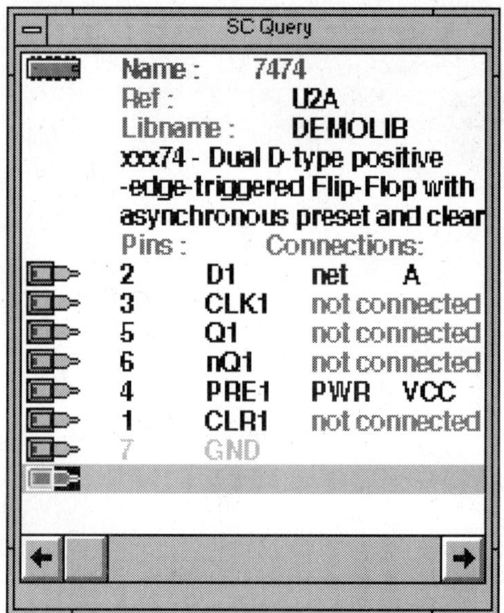

Figure 7-22
The SC Query window.

1. Try out this feature by activating the **Query** button and clicking on the **U2A** device. A display such as the one shown in Figure 7-22 will appear.

2. Next, click on the **IN1** input terminal and note that the window in Figure 7-22 now displays the connectivity for the entire **IN1** node (Figure 7-23).

3. Now click once on the item "pin 2 B1 U1A (In)" in Figure 7-23. Note that a pink blob appears at the selected pin on the schematic.

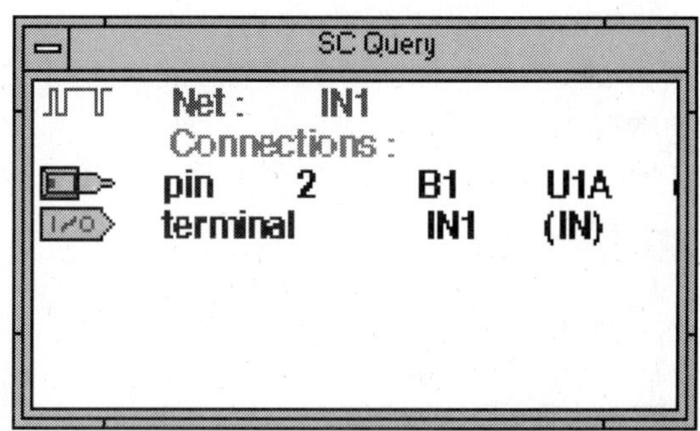

Figure 7-23
Selecting a device pin to query.

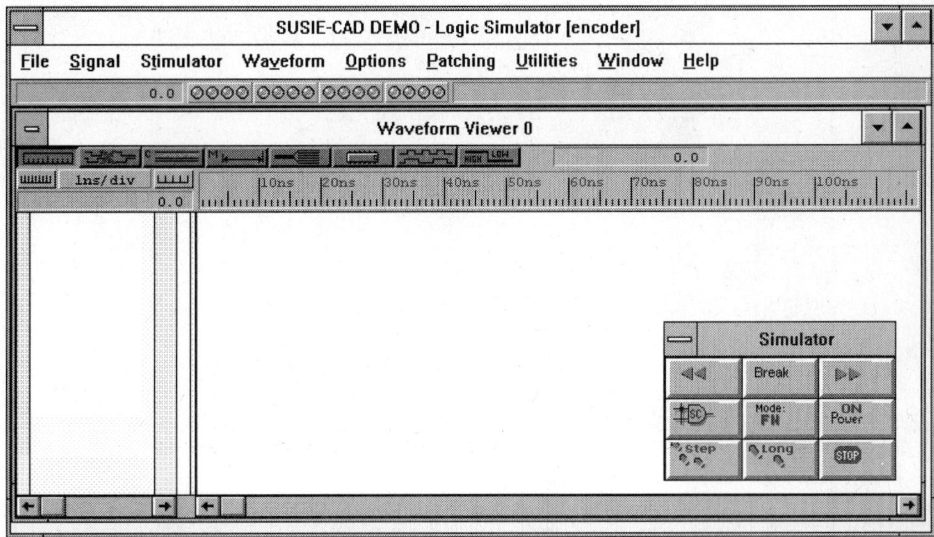

Figure 7-24
SUSIE-CAD simulation waveform window.

4. Double-click on the selected pin and note that SUSIE instantly selects the component associated with the selected pin for viewing.

Working with the Simulator

SUSIE has a built-in background simulator that is closely integrated with the schematic editor. To activate the simulator,

1. Click on the **SIM** button (the one at the bottom of the button bar in the Figure 7-6). In response, SUSIE displays the screen in Figure 7-24.

SUSIE starts the simulator by creating a schematic netlist, then converting that netlist into a set of tables for real-time interaction with the schematic. All schematic modifications, including adding or deleting components, wires, JEDEC files, hex files, etc., will be automatically added to the simulator tables as they are made, so the simulation will run concurrent with your changes.

After you have clicked on the **SIM** button and the design tables have been generated, SUSIE displays the simulator screen.

2. Using standard Windows procedures, shrink the simulator window and place it below the schematic as shown in Figure 7-25.

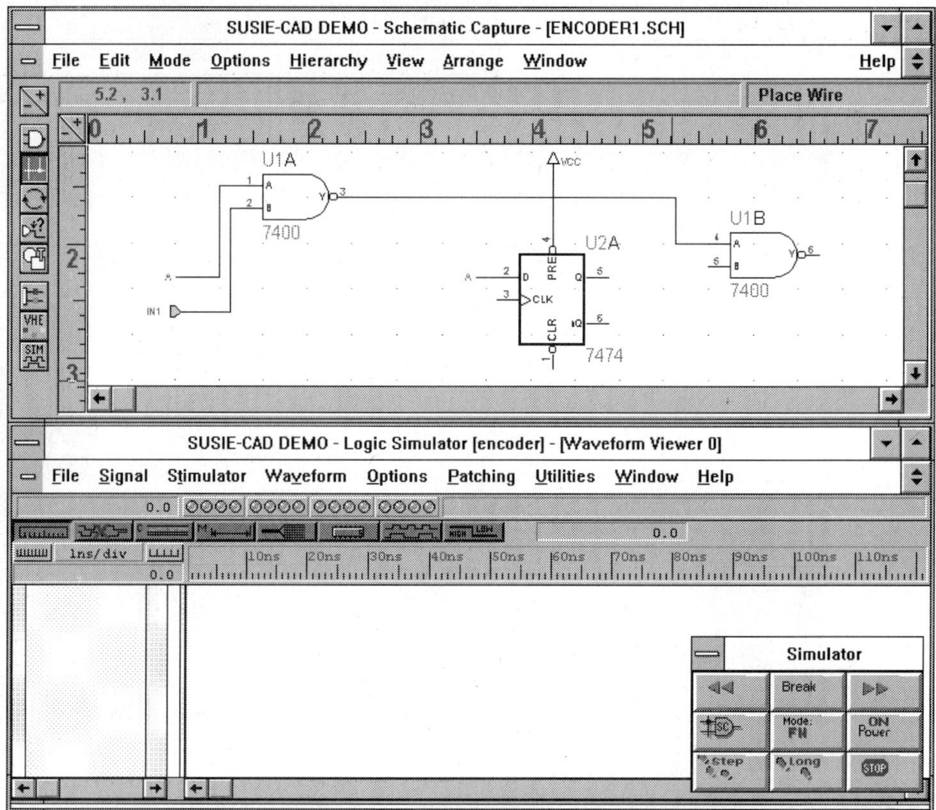

Figure 7-25
Arranging schematic and simulator waveform windows.

About the Simulated Signals

SUSIE simulates all signals in the entire design. However, due to memory limitations only some of these signals are displayed and stored. To save on memory space, the logical states of signals that have not been displayed are overridden with the new simulation data. SUSIE can display and record over 1,000 signals. However, because you can add additional signals to the display at any time, you should keep on the display only those signals for which you have current use. This will help to make your display readable.

You can add new signals to the simulator display both from the schematic and the simulator menu.

Selecting Signals from the Schematic

To select signals from the schematic editor:

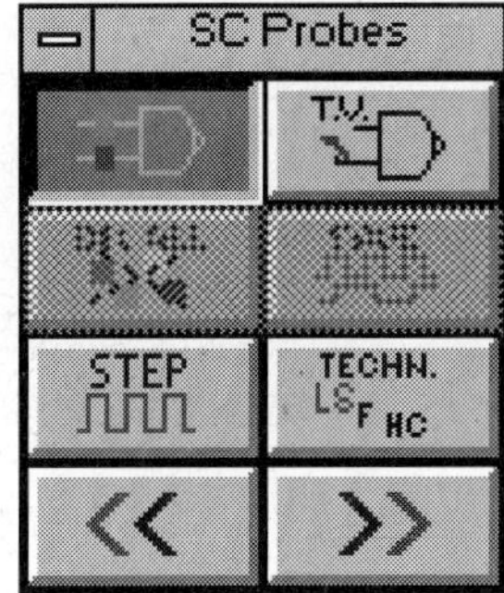

Figure 7-26
The SC Probes toolbox.

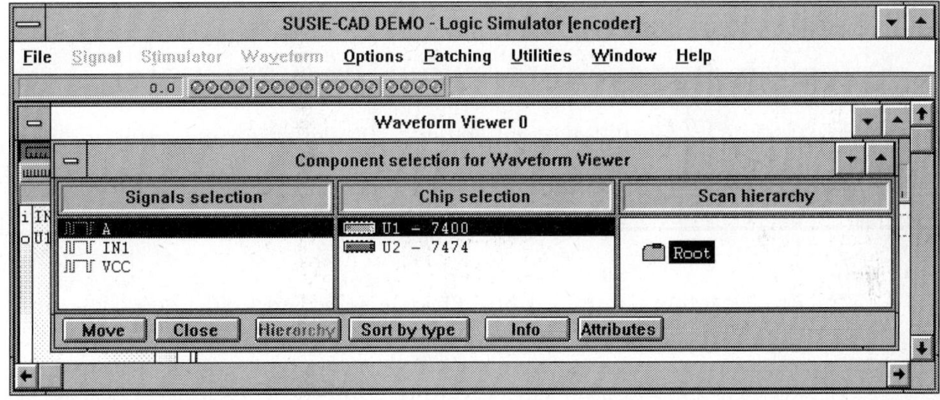

Figure 7-27
Adding signals to the simulation display.

1. Click on the **SC Probes** button (the third button from the bottom, located just above the **VHE** button in Figure 7-6). In response, SUSIE displays the toolbox in Figure 7-26.

2. Activate the **Probes** button, then click first on terminal **IN1** and then on pin **U1A-3**. Note that each time you have clicked, a gray square has appeared at the selected test points. The selected test points have also been added to the list of signals on the simulator screen (Figure 7-27).

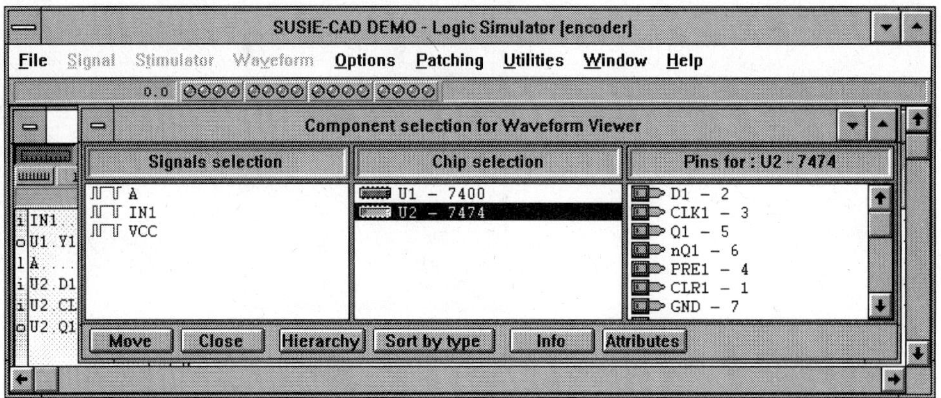

Figure 7-28
Adding pins of selected components to the simulation display.

Selecting Signals from Within the Simulator

To select an I/O terminal or signal name for display from within the simulator,

1. Click on the **Signal** option in the main simulator menu, then select the **Add signals** option. In response, SUSIE displays the **Component selection** table in Figure 7-28.

2. Click on the **A** signal in the **Signals selection** field, then click on the **Move** button at the bottom of this window.

3. To exit the **Component** selection window, click on the **Close** button. In response, the signal **A** is added at the bottom of the signal list.

You can also select pins of selected components for display in the waveform window. To select component pin names for display,

4. Select **Component selection** again (Figure 7-28). This time, double-click on **U2A-7474** in the **Chip selection** field.

5. When a pin list for this device appears to the right, click on the following pins in sequence: **D1**, **CLK1**, and **Q1**. When selected, the marked pins turn dark.

6. Move the selected pins to the simulator display by clicking in sequence on the **Move** and **Close** buttons. The resulting display is shown in the Figure 7-29.

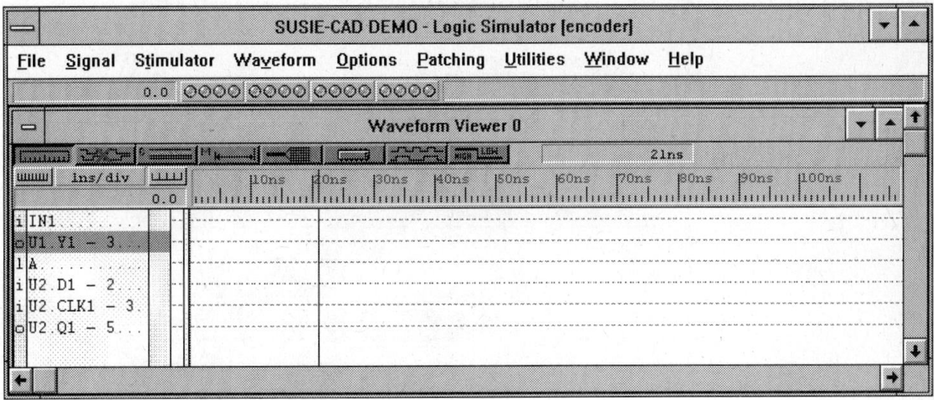

Figure 7-29
Waveform display, with signals selected.

Adding Stimuli

To simulate a design, you need stimuli. SUSIE allows you to develop and apply this stimuli in several ways. The simplest way is to use the ready-made stimuli that SUSIE offers. For example, you can assign any keyboard key to a signal line and toggle that line from the keyboard while the simulation is in progress. SUSIE also has a 16-bit software-driven binary counter that counts with a preset clock speed. You can assign any true and inverted bit of this counter to any schematic test point and provide for automatic toggling of the selected signal lines.

SUSIE also has special options for development of custom test vectors, which are not described here. These test vectors can be tweaked to optimum performance while the simulation is in progress. Some versions of SUSIE allow tweaking of these test vectors with a 10 picosecond accuracy.

Applying Ready-Made Stimuli

SUSIE comes equipped with some ready-made test stimuli called signal stimulators. The stimulators include a 16-bit software-driven binary counter and all alpha keyboard keys, [a] through [z]. These stimulators can be assigned to any schematic test point in real time, without any compilations. The process of assigning stimulators to the schematic test points resembles applying signal generator probes to devices located on a hardware breadboard.

The stimulators are selected from a stimulator window that is activated by selecting the **Add Stimulators** option within the **Stimulator** menu.

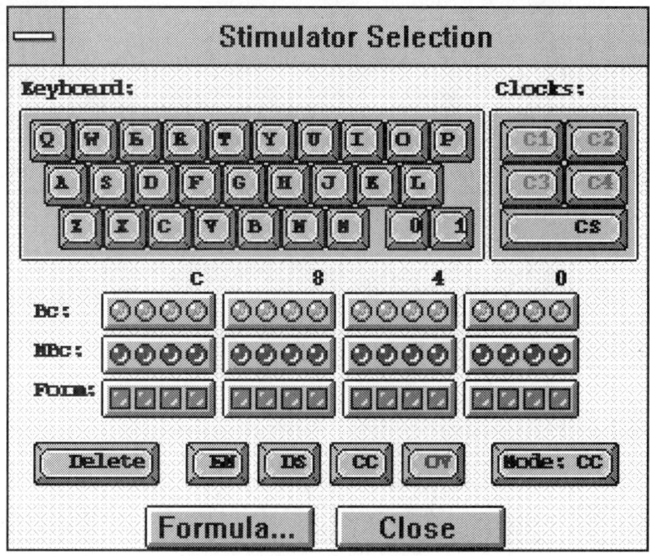

Figure 7-30
Stimulator selection dialogue box.

Applying Binary Counter Bits as Stimuli

To use the built-in binary counter for design stimuli,

1. Click on the **Stimulator** option within the main simulator menu, then select the **Add Stimulators** option. In response, SUSIE displays a window that includes a keyboard with two rows of lamps, placed at the bottom of the keyboard (Figure 7-30).

There are 16 yellow lamps and 16 red ones representing bits **B0-B15** of the 16-bit binary counter. The yellow lamps represent the true counter output and the red ones represent the inverse of the counter output. This screen can be also displayed by clicking directly on the **Stimulator** button shown in Figure 7-24.

2. Click on the third from the right yellow lamp (**B2**), drag it over the **IN1** signal line in the **Signal** field, and then release the mouse button. SUSIE confirms the assignment of **B2** counter bit to the **IN1** signal line by displaying **B2** to the right of the **IN1** signal name (Figure 7-31).

3. Click on the **Close** button in Figure 7-30 to close the **Stimulator** window.

4. To test the effect of stimulator **B2** on the **U1A** gate, you should simulate a few steps by clicking repeatedly on the **Step** button in the Figure 7-32.

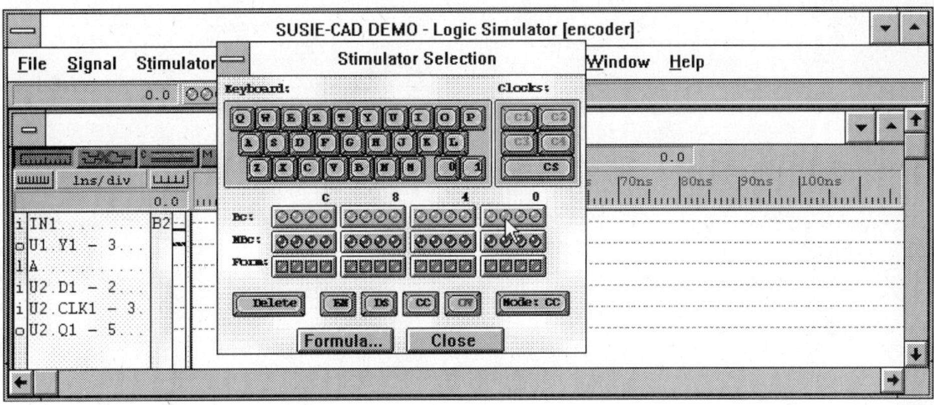

Figure 7-31
Creating stimulus with the built-in binary counter.

Note that SUSIE displays a black square waveform for **B2** and a blue one for the **U1A-Y** output. Signals **A** and **U2.CLK1** have rugged shape, indicating high impedance or z-state. The **U2.Q1** signal waveform is shown as a gray area between two heavy blue lines. This indicates that the **U2** flip-flop is in the unknown or x-state.

Toggling Signal Values with Keyboard Keys

To eliminate the z and x states, add a few more test vectors to the signals in Figure 7-31.

1. Following the previous example, invoke the Stimulator Selection window (Figure 7-30).

2. Click on the signal **A** in the **Signal** field.

3. When signal **A** turns blue, click on the button representing the keyboard key **[A]**. Note that the letter "a" is listed to the right of the signal line **A**, indicating that the keyboard key "a" is in direct control of this signal line. (You can use any keyboard key to control the signal line **A**; the names used in this example are not significant.)

4. When you assign a keyboard key, SUSIE does not know from what logical state it should start the control of signal **A**. For this reason, click with the mouse button on the rugged line just to the right of the letter "a." Note that the rugged line has changed to a solid line.

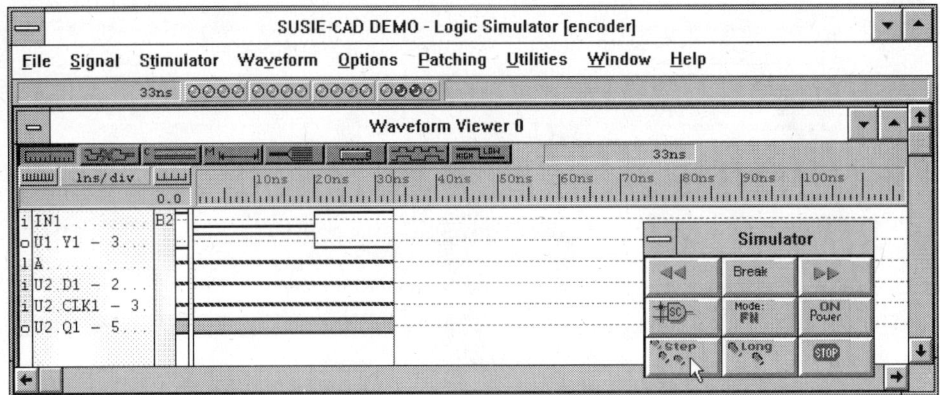

Figure 7-32
Stepping the simulation.

5. Click on the keyboard key "a" a few times and and notice that the new solid line is responding to each keyboard key activation and is toggling signal line **A** between the high and low logical states.

6. To create a waveform of changing values using this method, toggle the keyboard key "a" and then click the **Step** button. Repeat toggling of the keyboard key "a" and clicking on the **Step** button a few times. Notice that the waveform for **A** and the corresponding **U1.Y1** output signal line respond to each keyboard key operation.

Alternately, instead of toggling selected signal lines with the keyboard keys, you can position the mouse cursor to the right of the "a" symbol and toggle the "a" signal line by clicking the mouse button.

Setting the Binary Counter Clock Period

You can control the period of the 16-bit binary counter from 10 ps to 1 ms, thus producing a broad range of design stimulators. To set the clock speed:

1. Select the **Clock settings** option from the **Options** menu. Remember that this clock is symmetrical and that you are entering one half of the clock period; for example, if you want your clock period to be 4.3 ns, you need to enter **2.15 ns** into the clock field.

Setting Simulation Steps

To simplify operations, SUSIE allows you to simulate in short and long steps. These steps are set from the window shown in Figure 7-33. This **Step Setup** window can

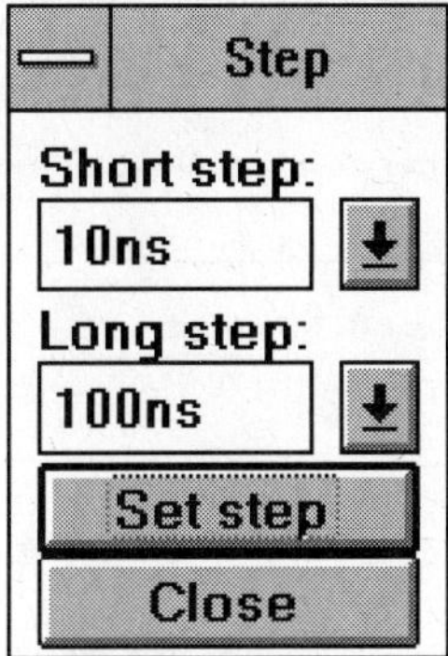

Figure 7-33
Setting simulation step values.

be activated from the **Utilities** menu, using the **View** sub-menu and **Step Setup** option.

To set the simulation step values for this example,

1. Click the mouse button on the **Short step** selection box (Figure 7-33), and when a list of predefined steps appears, select the 10 ns option.

2. Click on the **Close** button.

3. Next, click on the **Step** button and note that the simulation time has changed.

4. Repeat this process again, but this time set the **Short step** to 100 ns. Similarly, set the **Long step** to several different values and simulate them by toggling the **Long Step** button.

You can also set the simulation step by writing its value directly into the window.

5. Repeating the previous procedure, click on the **Short step** window and enter a 25.5 ns value. Next, click on the **Step** button and note that SUSIE has simulated 25.5 ns.

Applying Custom-Made Test Vectors

Custom-made test vectors can be applied by loading appropriate ASCII test vector files. These files can be generated with an enhanced test vector editor provided with the ACTIVE-CAD product or can be developed with the help of the **Waveform** menu.

This menu allows for on-line editing of test vectors while the simulation is in progress. The Waveform menu also allows test vectors to be described using a formula method. This method is particularly useful for repetitive waveforms such as clocks or code generators.

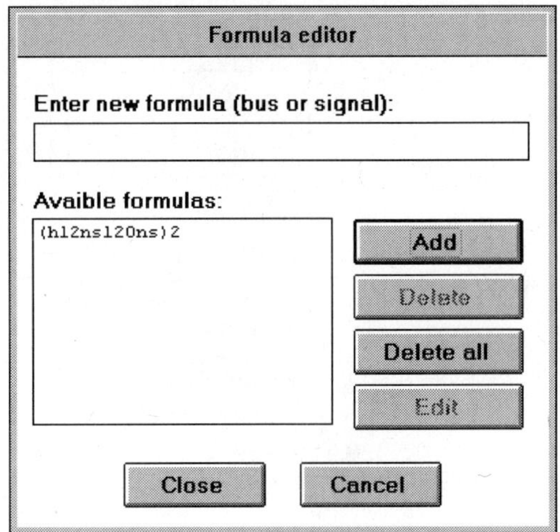

Figure 7-34
Creating stimulus with the formula editor.

1. To create a repeating waveform using a formula, click on the **Formula** option within the **Waveform** menu. In response, SUSIE displays the window shown in Figure 7-34.

2. Select the **Edit** option, and when the dialogue box appears, enter the desired timing. For example, if you want a waveform that is high for 12 nanoseconds, followed by low for 20 nanoseconds, repeated twice, enter **(H12nsL20ns)2**.

3. Press the **Add** and **Close** buttons.

4. To apply this newly created waveform at the selected location on the waveform display, place the cursor and click the mouse button. The signal you selected turns green and a blue cursor is displayed at the selected timescale position.

5. Next, select the **Formula** option within the **Waveform** menu, and when the window shown in Figure 7-34 appears, click on the **Replace** option. When a list of predefined signal waveforms appears, click on the selected formula, then click on the **OK** button.

Note that a green signal waveform of 12 ns high, 20 ns low, repeated twice, is displayed on the screen at the current cursor location overriding the previous waveform at that location.

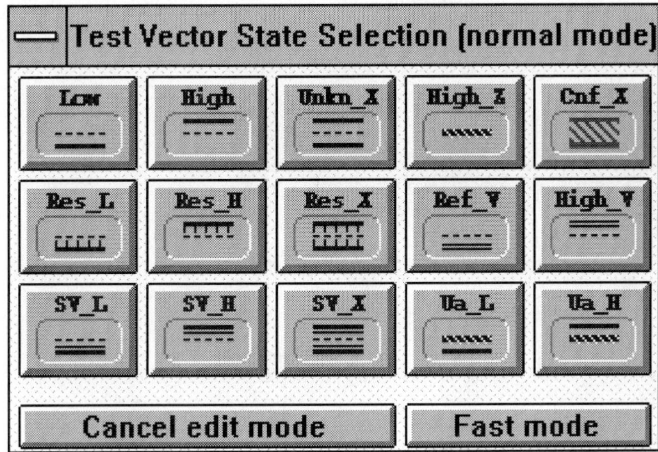

Figure 7-35
Editing the waveform.

Editing Signal Waveforms

Using the SUSIE graphical test vector editor, you can precisely "tweak" each timing waveform to the desired logical state. Since SUSIE allows you to override or emulate any cell output, it also allows you to display such signal states as resistive high, resistive low, unknown resistive, undefined low, etc. You will find this I/O override feature extremely useful when testing various design constraints and error conditions.

To see how waveforms are editied within the waveform editor,

1. Place the cursor over the **Waveform** option of the main simulator menu and click the mouse button.

2. When the menu appears, select the **Edit** option. In response, SUSIE displays a set of buttons with logical states (Figure 7-35). Note that the SUSIE editing cursor has a new shape.

3. Place the waveform editing cursor over the selected signal waveform area and click the mouse button. In response, SUSIE places the blue vertical cursor at the selected screen location.

4. Next, click on the **RES X** (unknown resistive state) button in Figure 7-35 and note that the signal waveform look has changed; it now represents the unknown resistive state. Only the area from the last signal transition to the current cursor location is affected.

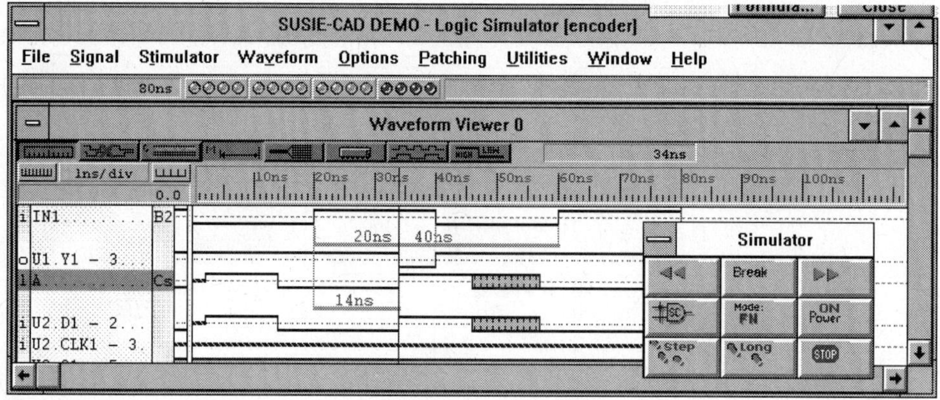

Figure 7-36
Using the measurement features of the waveform window..

Other Simulator Features

Making Timing Measurements

SUSIE-CAD comes standard with a functional simulator. If you need timing information in your simulations, you need to add the timing option that allows you to simulate designs with a 10 ps accuracy. (This feature is standard in ALDEC's ACTIVE-CAD product.) The timing measurement option is provided within the **Waveform** window. To activate this feature, click on the **Waveform** menu and in the submenu select the **Measurement on** option.

1. Select the **Measurement** option, and notice that the cursor has changed. This new cursor is called the *measurement start cursor*.

2. Position the up-pointing arrow of the cursor over the first selected signal transition and click the mouse button. The blue vertical cursor snaps to the selected edge, and the mouse-driven cursor changes its shape again. The new cursor is called the *measurement end cursor*.

3. Position the up-pointing edge of this cursor on the second signal waveform transition and click the mouse button (make sure that the second edge is at least one inch away from the first one so that you can see the numeral value of the timing delay). Note that the measurement data is now displayed at the current blue cursor location. An example of such measurement is shown in the Figure 7-36.

4. If the measurement is not displayed because of the short distance, place the cursor in the ruler area, right above the measurement display. Holding the

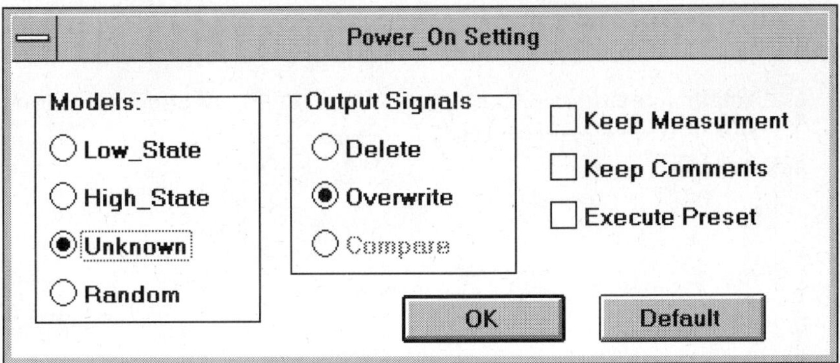

Figure 7-37
Specifying power-on settings.

mouse button down, drag the cursor horizontally. When you release the mouse button, the marked area expands and shows the measurement value.

Specifying Power-On Settings

SUSIE allows you to set such devices as flip-flops, latches, registers, counters, etc. to a preselected logical state during power-on. To force a selected power-on logical state, click on the **Power-On Setting** option within the **Option** menu. In response, SUSIE displays the power-on options table in the Figure 7-37. The standard table setting will generate random or unknown outputs. Should you wish to change it to the high or low logic state, select the appropriate option from the **Models** field shown in Figure 7-37.

Upon resimulation of the design you may get different signal waveforms (due to "random" power-on state or poor system reset practices). Because of this, you need to decide if you wish to keep the old timing waveforms and timing measurements. You can select these power-on conditions by clicking on the appropriate options as shown in Figure 7-37.

Remember that each complimentary flip-flop output has to be set individually. Setting of the flip-flop Q output does not automatically reset its complimentary output to the opposite logical state.

Also remember that if you preset a logical state to any output pin, it does not change until a device produces its own signal upon on input change. If the device does not toggle, the power-on state remains unchanged. This may produce incorrect states on combinational devices.

Resimulating Designs

You will frequently want to resimulate designs with some component changes or new test vector setups. At times, you may also need to return to a condition that existed in your design just prior to an error. Both cases can be handled by the

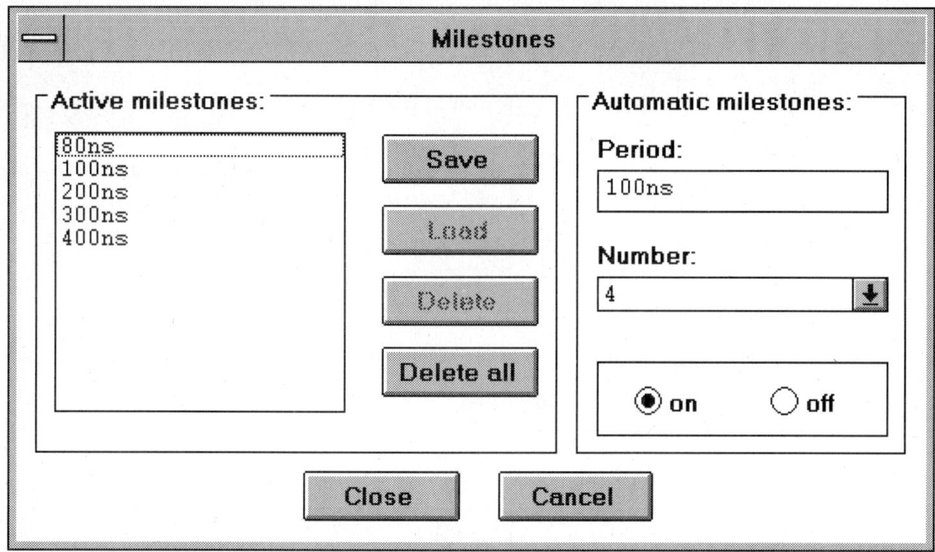

Figure 7-38
Setting milestones.

Milestones option, which automatically saves the state of the entire design for your future reference. Since saving designs takes disk space, you should limit how many milestones SUSIE keeps. You can set the maximum number of milestones or system states by selecting the **Milestone** option from the **Options** menu.

To use the milestone feature,

1. Select the **Milestone** option by clicking on the **Options** menu. When the menu appears, choose the **Milestones** option. In response, SUSIE displays the **Milestones** window shown in Figure 7-38.

2. Enter "100" into the **Period** field as the desired time period between milestones.

3. Next, click on the down-pointing arrow next to the **Number** field, and when a listing of milestones (from 2 to 32) appears, select 4. This will be the maximum number of Milestones saved at any time by SUSIE.

4. To complete your selections, select the **On** option and click the **OK** button. When SUSIE displays the main simulator screen, click at least four times on the **Long** step button in Figure 7-24.

Now notice that some small red squares have appeared on the ruler located right above the signal waveforms. These red squares represent the saved milestones.

Restoring Past Simulation Status

Using the milestones, you can restore past simulation status, including the state of flip-flops and counters, internal state of microprocessors, PLDs, FPGAs, etc.

To restore a milestone, select the **Milestone** option from the **Options** menu. When the window appears, click on the topmost milestone in the **Active Milestone** field and then activate the **Load** button. The red vertical cursor is instantly moved to the selected milestone and all registers in the entire design are automatically restored to the logical states that existed at the selected time (milestone). You can now inquire about the logical state of any test point by selecting it to the display screen and monitoring its behavior during the simulation process.

If you wish to return back to any special design state, save it with the manual milestone save operation for future use. You can have any number of such manual milestones, acting as design reference points. Their number is limited only by the available hard disk space.

1. Click once on the **Step** button, then select the **Milestones** menu shown in Figure 7-38.

2. Click on the **Save** button (Figure 7-38). SUSIE returns back to the main simulation screen and displays a new milestone that has been manually forced by activating the **Save** button.

Since the manual milestones cannot be overridden by automatic milestones, you must delete them manually.

3. Select the **Delete All** button from the Milestones menu. (If you want to delete only a few selected milestones, you can select them individually and press the **Delete** button.)

Presetting Devices to Selected States

You can preset any device output signal line to a selected logical state by means of the **Selective Preset** option, located within the **Utilities** menu. This preset affects the outputs for the duration of the first signal (output) transition. It is not a permanent setup of internal IC model states. To see how devices can be preset:

1. Click on the **Utilities** menu and select the **Selective Preset** option.

2. When the **Selective Preset** window appears, click on the **Add** button. SUSIE displays **Component Selection for Selective Preset** window.

3. Click on signal names and device pins that you want to preset.

4. Click on the **Move** button and then the **Close** button.

5. Now click on the **Edit** button. The **Set Selective Preset** window appears (Figure 7-39).

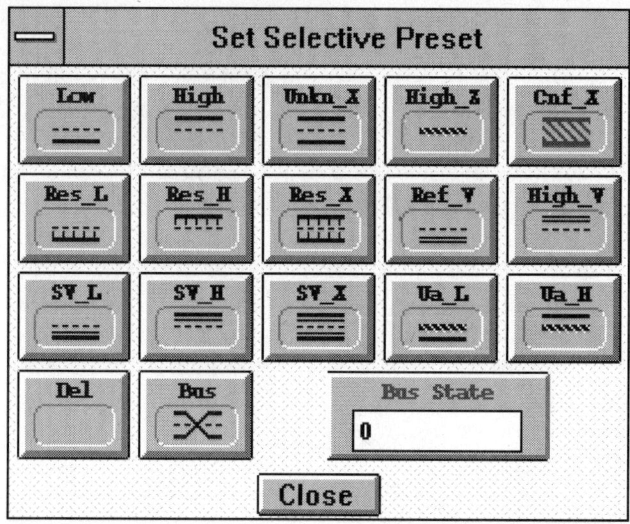

Figure 7-39
Presetting to selected states.

6. Click on the selected signal line in the **Selective Preset** window and then on the selected logical state button. You can assign the selective preset state to any number of signals.

7. To enforce the signal preset, press the **Execute** and **Close** buttons.

8. Simulate a few steps and note that the selected signals have changed their logical state to preset values.

When setting the value of flip-flops, remember that each complimentary flip-flop output has to be set individually. Setting of the flip-flop Q output does not automatically reset its complimentary (**nQ**) output to the opposite logical state.

Replacing Components During Simulation

The SUSIE simulator allows you to modify your design at any time, including in the middle of a simulation session. A particularly useful application of this is replacing parts with their functional equivalents to obtain different timing behavior.

For example, if a part originally specified is too slow and creates a timing violation, you can easily replace it with a faster one and correct the design problem. The component replacement is handled by the **Change Technology** option within the **Patching** menu. To try this out,

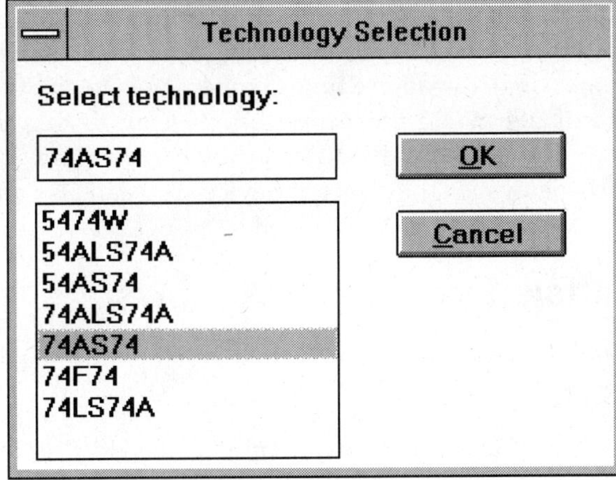

Figure 7-40
Substituting components using the technology selection window.

1. Select the **Change Technology** option from the Patching menu. In response, SUSIE displays the **Change technology** window.

2. To change the **U2** flip-flop device from 7474 to 74AS74, double-click on the **U2** in the **Chip selection** field. SUSIE then displays all available replacements for this parts (Figure 7-40).

3. Click on the 74AS74 and exit the window by clicking on the **OK** button in Figures 7-40 and the **Close** button in the **Change Technology** window.

Note that the schematic now shows the 74AS74 part name. Also, all internal simulator timing tables have been modified to simulate the 74AS74 device instead of the 7474.

Editing Device Timing Parameters

You can also change device timing parameters at any time. This allows you to set critical paths to either min or max propagation delay values. You can also simulate the effect of temperature by modifying the min/max. propagation delays of each device. To change device timing parameters:

1. Click on the **Patching** option, then select **Edit Timing Specifications**. In response, SUSIE displays the **Edit device specification** window.

2. Double-click on **U2-74AS74** in the **Chip selection** field. SUSIE responds with a list of the U2-74AS74 timing parameters.

The **Set** column displays parameters that have actually been used by the simulator. Note that they have been set to the average propagation delays.

You can change the device timing parameters to any value by specifying it as a percentage of the maximum propagation delay in the **% of Max.** window. For example, entering 124 will automatically calculate 124% of the maximum propagation delays for the selected device. You can also click over any data in the **Set** column and edit its value.

Using Multiple Simulation Windows

SUSIE allows you to display simulation data in multiple windows. To invoke extra Windows:

1. Click on the **Waveform Viewer** option in the **Utilities** menu. SUSIE returns you to the main simulator menu and displays a new simulation Window. Notice that the windows (Waveform Viewer 0 and Waveform Viewer 1) are positioned one behind the other.

2. To arrange these windows next to each other, select the **Tile** option from the **Window** menu. You can set a separate time scale for each **Waveform Viewer** window by clicking on the scale icons, placed to the left and right of the scale resolution display, which is located right above the signal name listing.

Since SUSIE makes all signals available to each window, to display any special signal arrangement, you need to select and move signals in each window so that they are shown in the required order. The easiest way to move signals is to position the cursor over the selected signal, press the mouse button and drag the selected signal to the new screen position. When the mouse button is released, the signal is dropped at the new position. The signal that has been previously residing at this position, is moved down by one location.

Saving Design Results

As in most Windows programs, loading and saving SUSIE designs is accomplished through the **File** menu. The schematic **File** menu has provisions for saving schematic design and the simulator **File** menu handles saving of the simulation results. The **Project Manager** has a **Save** option that saves the new project configuration (new resources and libraries).

Moving On

This Hands-On chapter has given us an opportunity to try out a representative low-cost digital simulation product. Digital simulators like SUSIE-CAD and ACTIVE-CAD can be a powerful addition to your design tool suite, and are ideal tools for debugging complex digital ciruits.

Although digital simulation is the most common way to analyze a complex digital circuit, it is by no means the only way. In the next chapter, we are going to examine an alternative method of digital circuit analysis, using timing analysis tools.

CHAPTER 8

FOCUS ON TECHNOLOGY: DIGITAL TIMING ANALYSIS

In electronic system design, there are two things that you can count on: circuits are getting faster, and they are getting smaller. Sub-micron ASICs that operate at 400 MHz internally, multichip modules (MCMs) and boards that operate with system clock speeds in excess of 200 MHz; high-speed connectors that put scores of pins into spaces unheard of in the past—all these factors and more place new demands on you as a designer. To work effectively in such an environment, you must take a cross-disciplinary approach to the problem of circuit analysis. If you are a digital system designer, then you must not only focus on problems such as signal delay, clock skew, and set-up and hold; you must return to your roots and re-learn the concepts of capacitance, inductance, and loading. You must be prepared to perform complex DC and AC analyses on your designs and to calculate the impact of point-to-point delays, undershoot, overshoot, crosstalk and other transmission line effects in the circuits you create.

In this chapter, and in the chapter that follows, we will survey some of the tools available to analyze problems such as these in high-speed digital circuits. In doing so, we will focus on three broad classes of analysis tools: static timing analyzers, timing diagram analysis tools, and signal integrity analysis tools. These three classes of design tools provide quite different capabilities and can all be used to improve the reliability of complex digital systems.

Timing Analyzers

A timing analyzer is a software package that can identify timing problems—specifically register-related problems like setup and hold violations—without the need to perform a comprehensive simulation or create test vectors. Timing analysis can uncover problems that might never be found during simulation, since the number of test vectors required to test every path in a complex system can be impossible to generate. Timing analysis can be used to analyze a design at the design level (using a functional representation such as a netlist of primitives) and at the printed circuit board level (using back-annotated delay information), and are also finding increasing use for ASIC- and FPGA-based designs.

Static timing analyzers work by exhaustively tracing every signal delay path in the system being analyzed. Worst case interconnect and component delays are considered, and the resulting analysis can pinpoint problems such setup and hold and pulse width violations. Unlike a simulation environment, in which you are only informed that such violations occurred, a timing analyzer will tell you exactly which component or interconnects delays resulted in the violation. High-end static timing analyzers such as Quad Design's MOTIVE report such violations and the paths delays that resulted in the violations, using combinations of digital waveform and tabular displays.

Because not every potential violation in a large circuit is actually critical to that circuit's correct functional operation, it is important that a timing analyzer allow you to add modify the constraints and tailor the analysis to your circuit's functional requirements.

Timing Models and Delay Data

To perform accurate timing analysis of a digital system, a timing analyzer must be provided with information about the timing characteristics of every component (or, in the case of an ASIC, every gate or cell primitive) used in the design. These models are typically provided as libraries of delay data expressed as functions of parameters such as capacitive loading, input delay, and input rise time. In addition, timing analysis software must accept back-annotated delay data from sources such as ASIC vendor place-and-route or layout software. For PCB designs, the interconnect delay data may be derived from the actual Gerber photoplot (or other) PCB data files.

Timing Diagram Analysis Tools

Timing diagram analysis tools are programs for creating and analyzing digital timing diagrams. These tools are relatively new to the EDA market and are not yet well known or widely used. Timing diagram analyzers are used in the design process as the graphical equivalent of a spreadsheet, and allow you to quickly assess the effect of a change in a timing parameter on their overall design. Because these tools include timing diagram drawing features, they can also be used to document the detailed operation of a circuit.

A timing diagram analyzer can be used as a stand-alone design verification tool, or it can be used in conjunction with a digital simulator to analyze simulation results. Using the timing diagram representation that these tools are based on, and by using the analysis features that they provide, it is easier to see timing relationships between signal transitions than with a traditional simulator. (This is evidenced by the fact that many engineers still draw timing diagrams by hand even when they have access to powerful digital simulators.) Timing diagram analyzers are especially useful for analyzing system-level timing where simulation models for complex parts are often not available or parts have not yet been specified.

Timing diagram analyzers can be used at both ends of the design cycle. As a design tool they are particularly useful for up-front analysis when simulation is not an option. As a documentation tool, they allow the generation of detailed timing diagrams that are vastly easier to create and maintain than those that can be generated using conventional drawing packages. One of the most useful benefits of using a timing analyzer in the design process is that circuit documentation can be generated automatically as a by-product of the design analysis process.

So what do these tools look like? Figure 8-1 shows one such tool, The Timing Diagrammer produced and sold by SynaptiCAD, Inc. of Blacksburg, VA.

Note: *The companion CD-ROM includes evaluation versions of two timing diagram analysis products: Chronology Corporation's Timing Designer® and The Timing Diagrammer™, which is sold by SynaptiCAD, Inc. You are encouraged to try out both of these products, and to contact the vendors directly for more detailed information. Much of the information in this section was provided courtesy of SynaptiCAD, Inc.*

Drawing Waveforms

The primary function of a timing diagram analyzer is to provide a specialized CAD environment for drawing and analyzing waveforms and the timing relationships between events in different waveforms. The analyzers allow you to work with waveforms that represent the common multistate logic such as you would find in digital simulators or in data books. These values include such things as high, low, tristate, valid (known), and invalid (unknown). For more demanding applications, additional values (such as strong and weak values) may be needed. Some timing analyzers meet this requirement by having special signal segments display numerical values in either hexadecimal or binary. These value segments can be used to model an almost unlimited number of logic states.

To simplify complex designs, you may want to combine multiple signals into a bus, or represent commonly used or repeating signals (such as clocks) in your diagram. Buses and clocks are two kinds of specialized signals that automate the drawing of timing diagrams. Just as in a schematic, buses allow you to edit or draw

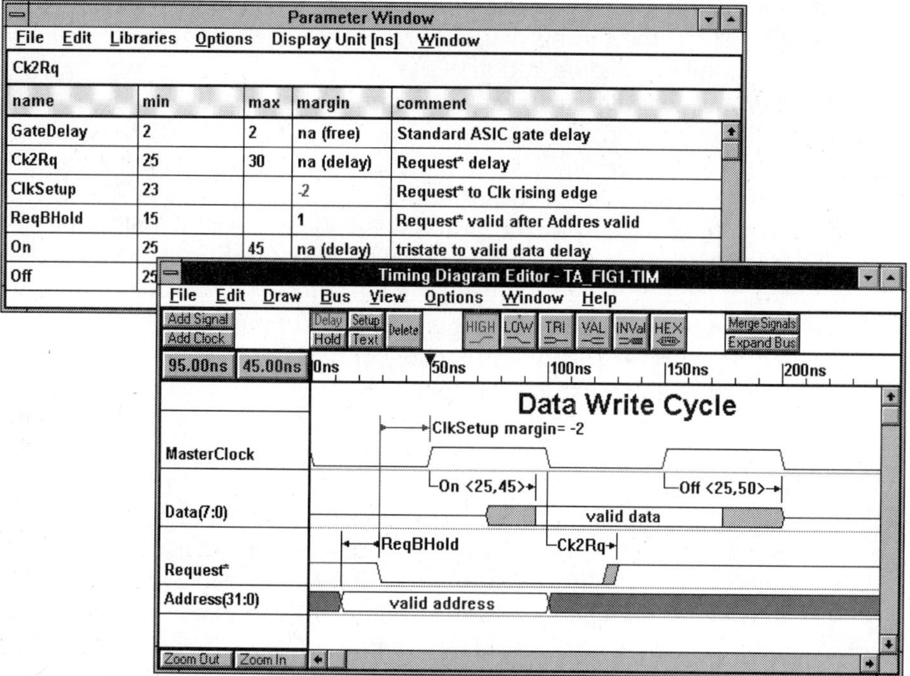

Figure 8-1
A timing diagram analysis tool. (SynaptiCAD's The Timing Diagrammer.)

many signals at the same time, and to view the timing values in a variety of forms, such as binary or hexadecimal.

Clocks are periodic signals that can be set up to draw themselves based on their attributes: period or frequency, duty cycle, edge jitter, offset, and other parameters. Clock signals allow you to assess the effect of a different clock frequency by just entering a new value, with the change being automatically propagated through the timing diagram.

To model circuits that modify the system clock (like a *divide by 2* circuit or a clock distribution scheme), a timing diagram analyzer may have features that allow clocks to be related to other clocks. These features are typically implemented using clock formulas. Clock formulas allow clock attributes to specified using algebraic formulas (such as a clock with a period of one-half of the period of another clock). Depending on the implementation, clock parameters may also be referenced in parameter formulas.

The ability to edit waveforms is just as important as simplified design entry, since a timing diagram analyzer will frequently be used as a primary form of design entry. Windows-based timing analyzers typically use the Windows drag and drop methodology to move signal transitions. Other typical features include the ability to insert, delete, or modify the state of a signal segment or transition. Most analyzers also offer the capability of entering exact time coordinates at which an edge is to be placed.

Entering Timing Parameters

The true power of timing analyzers comes from the ability to relate different signal transitions through timing parameters. There are three basic types of timing parameters used in analysis of digital circuits: *delays*, *setups*, and *holds*. These functions may be called by different names, but are essentially the same in all analysis tools. A timing parameter either actively forces signals to be specified distances between each other (acting as a *constraint*) or passively monitors the distance between two signal transitions.

A delay constraint between two signal transitions will force those transitions to be a specified distance apart. This keeps you from having to specifically place signal transitions at exact times. For example, to make two signal transitions exactly 15 ns apart, you would roughly sketch the two waveforms, add a delay parameter and specify min/max delay as 15 ns. The second signal transition would then move to that exact location. Because the two signal transitions are related, if either is moved then the other will follow to keep the correct timing. This is how changes in timing are propagated through the diagram.

Setups and holds monitor the relative position of two signal transitions. Setups and holds are closely related: a setup time monitors a transition on the data signal before the control signal transition, while a hold monitors a transition on a data signal after the control signal transition. These timing parameters allow you to try different "what if" scenarios on the design. If a timing change forces a signal transition to violate the setup or hold time, the timing parameter will flag an error.

Minimum and maximum values can be associated with timing parameters to reflect variations in propagation delays of parts. Algebraic expressions may also be used to specify minimum and maximum values (Figure 8-2).

Measurement Features

Virtually all analyzers offer the ability to measure absolute locations of edges. Many analyzers also offer the ability to approximately measure events using the mouse cursor, but these measurements are not as precise when viewing diagrams at low zoom levels. Another common feature is the ability to measure relative distances between edges.

Advanced Features

The more advanced features of timing diagram analysis tools help you to manage large timing diagrams and complex timing relationships. Three of the most important advanced functions are multiple delay resolution, reconvergent fan-out, and library creation and management facilities.

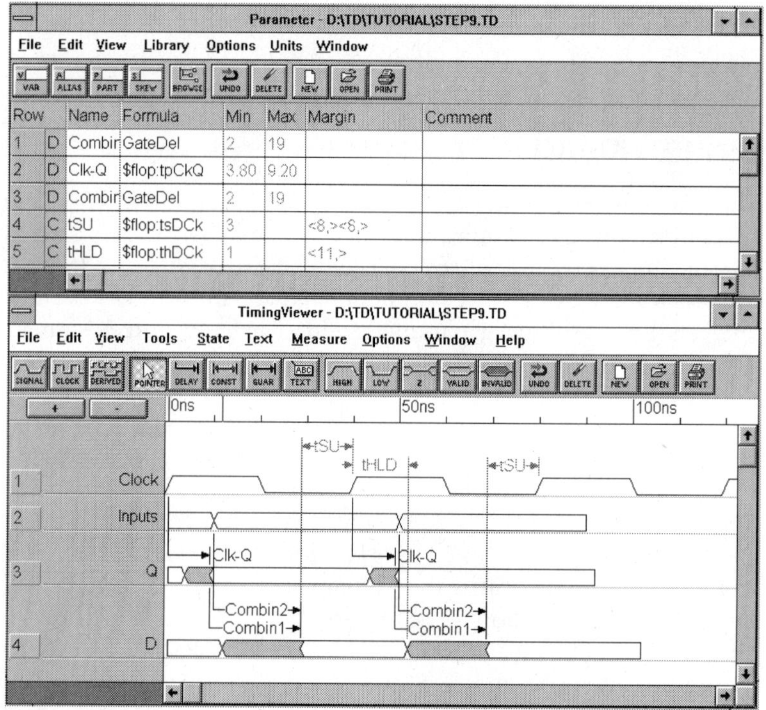

Figure 8-2
Setting timing parameters in a diagram. (Chronology Corporation's Timing Designer.)

Multiple delay resolution is useful for situations in which a transition is triggered by multiple events. For example, data output from a ROM will become valid after the chip select becomes active (first event) and the address lines stabilize (second event). This situation can be modeled using two delays: one from the chip select to the data valid transition and another from the address bus transition. In this case, the delay which causes the data valid transition to happen latest should dominate. In other cases, however, it may be desirable to have the transition occur as soon as possible (when any of several events can cause the transition). To model this ambiguity, you can select how multiple delays are reconciled for each transition. There are four different ways that this ambiguity can be resolved:

- *Earliest transition*: The earliest min edge and the earliest max edge will determine the uncertainty region of the delayed edge. Use this method when a transition occurs after one of several transitions has occurred.

- *Latest transition*: The latest min edge and the latest max edge will determine the uncertainty region of the delayed edge. Use this method when a transition occurs only when all of a set of transitions have occurred.

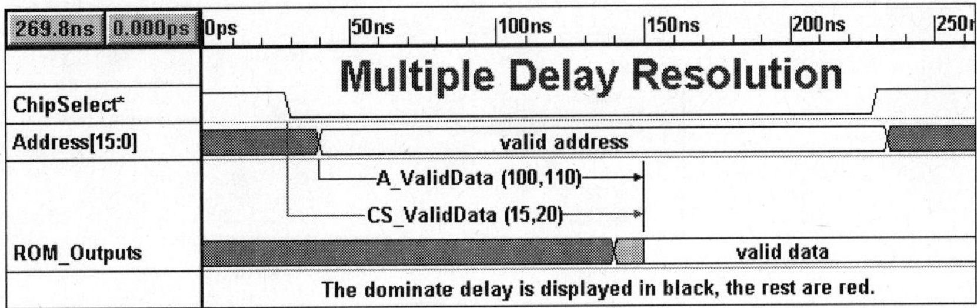

Figure 8-3
Using multiple delay resolution. (The Timing Diagrammer.)

- *Max uncertainty*: The earliest min edge and the latest max edge will determine the uncertainty region of the delayed edge (maximizes the uncertainty from forcing edges).
- *Min uncertainty*: The latest min edge and earliest max edge will determine the uncertainty region of the delayed edge.

Some analyzers also allow you to choose a default reconciliation method for all transitions not specifically set. Figure 8-3 shows an example of multiple delay resolution.

Reconvergent Fan-out analysis can be used help with overly pessimistic margin calculations in cases where uncertainty times are included in the calculations. Specifically, if two signals are derived from the same signal source then the margin calculation between the two signals should not include the uncertainty of the signal source, because no matter when the source transitions it will occur at the same time for both signals. When this happens the circuit is said to have reconvergent fan-out, because the two signals diverge from a common source and reconverge at the inputs of a gate. Reconvergent fan-out is sometimes referred to as common delay removal, because the source delay common to the two timing paths is removed. The ability of a timing analyzer to recognize and remove the pessimistic effects of reconvergent fan-out is important especially for circuits whose timing is very tight. Without this feature the designer might be deceived in to thinking that the design would not function properly when in fact it would. Some timing analyzers optionally allow removal of uncertainty between multiple edges of the same clock signal, but this option is turned off by default as removal of jitter uncertainty is not generally desirable between two different edges. Figure 8-4 shows an example of reconvergent fan-out.

Libraries

The ability to create and maintain your own libraries of timing parameters is important for the efficient use of a timing diagram analyzer. Most timing analyzers go a step further and offer standard libraries to help you get started in developing

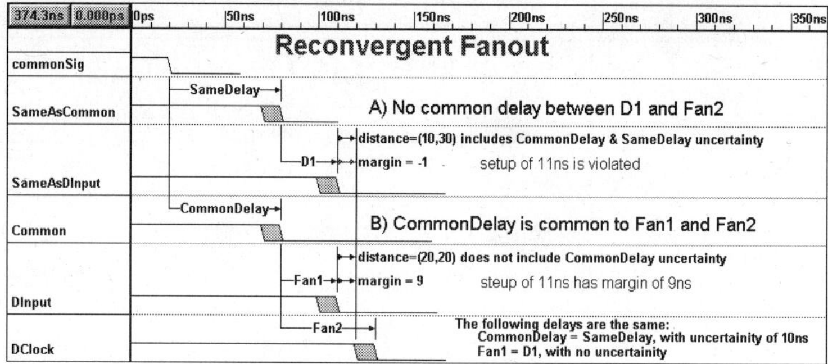

Figure 8-4
Reconvergent fanout analysis. (The Timing Diagrammer.)

your own libraries. The library features may also include the ability to specify standard parts such as TTL devices, PLDs or other more complex components such as RAM devices.

Documentation Features

Timing analyzers provide a multitude of documentation features for customizing a timing diagram. Most timing analyzers contain the basic documentation features contained in normal drawing programs. These features include text annotation, the ability to insert blank spaces, and the ability to move objects around. In addition to these basic drawing features, timing diagram tools typically include more advanced documentation features specific to timing diagrams. For example, almost all timing analyzers let the user choose which parameter attribute is displayed for a timing parameter (e.g., name, min/max, margin, or comment). Some even allow fully customizable strings to be displayed with embedded control codes to represent parameter attributes.

The ability to control the appearance of a signal is also important. The most obvious feature necessary for signals is whether or not edges are sloped. For accurate printing and for general readability, the ability to control the line thickness and color used to draw signals is also helpful.

And finally, the ability to export timing diagrams to other software packages (such as word processors and desktop publishing programs) is important. In Windows-based software, the Windows clipboard is typically used to allow timing diagrams and parameter data to be exported. Another common method is to use postscript files as a common format between different tools.

Future Directions for Timing Diagram Analyzers

Perhaps the most important ability that we can look for in the near future for timing diagram analyzers is the ability to exchange data with conventional simulators, allowing timing diagram analyzers to function as stimulus generators and specialized waveform viewers.

Another feature we can expect before long is in-place editing of diagrams embedded in word processor and desktop publishing programs (using technologies such as OLE 2).

Moving On

This completes our look at timing analysis tools. In this chapter you have seen how timing diagram analysis tools can be used to get better visibility of the most common timing-related problems in digital circuits. In the next chapter, we will be looking at another class of design analysis tools, and see how how signal integrity-related problems can be tackled.

CHAPTER 9

FOCUS ON TECHNOLOGY: SIGNAL INTEGRITY ANALYSIS

There are many electromagnetic effects that must be taken into consideration when you are designing high-performance digital and analog systems, and many tools are now appearing that help in the analysis of these effects. These tools typically combine SPICE or equivalent modeling (described in the next chapter) with electromagnetic (EM) analyzers and solvers to provide specialized analysis for signal integrity problems.

In this chapter, we will survey some of the tools available to analyze signal integrity-related problems in high-speed digital circuits. Unlike the analysis tools covered in the previous chapter, which dealt only with the timing of idealized digital signals, signal integrity analysis tools apply methods of analog simulation to detect problems in high-speed circuits. These tools model actual signal parameters such as voltage, capacitance, and inductance and can therefore be applied to problems of analog and mixed signal designs.

In a typical signal integrity analysis tool, parasitic parameters are extracted from the physical interconnections of the circuit. These parameters are determined using complex formulas that model such things as the inductance and capacitance effects of connectors and device pins. These parameters are then converted into a SPICE-like equivalent subcircuit. These equivalent circuits are then combined with the I/O buffers and loads of the system to form a composite circuit that can be simulated over time.

Actual geometries of the circuit (the traces on a board, for example, and the relationships between board layers) are handled using numerical methods that include the finite difference method (FDM), finite element method (FEM), boundary element method (BEM), multipole expansion, or asymptotic waveform evaluation. This information is then used by EM simulators to solve complex matrix equations that model the parasitic parameters of the circuit.

Each method used by a signal integrity analysis tool is intended to attack a specific problem in signal integrity, and each method operates from its own assumptions about the circuit. The most full-featured signal integrity tools offer a variety of analysis methods and are capable of reading and extracting circuit information from sources such as Gerber or GDSII files.

The core of the simulator (sometimes called the solver) must include sufficient numerical algorithms to handle arbitrary geometries, non-homogeneous material, and frequency-dependent parameters that range from DC to very high frequencies. The simulator must also handle both trace (wire) and plane conductors.

IBIS Models for Signal Integrity

As in other types of simulation that we have covered in this book, signal integrity analysis depends on having accurate models for each component type being simulated. Unlike the models discussed in earlier chapters, though, the models required for signal integrity analysis do not need to include information about the actual function of a device. Instead, a model for signal integrity analysis purposes is intended to provide information about the EM characteristics of each pin (or, more precisely, the I/O buffers) on the component being modeled. No information about the device's actual function is required for this analysis. This means that the same model can be used to represent a wide variety of actual devices (perhaps within the same device family) that have the same EM characteristics on their buffers.

Increasingly, models for signal integrity analysis are being provided in an industry standard format first developed at Intel. This format, called the *I/O Buffer Information Specification*, or *IBIS*, includes such information as slew rates and clamping values, in addition to providing voltage/capacitance tables for each I/O buffer. A new version of the IBIS specification (version 2.0) adds data for sharing of output pins, parasitics, and differential drivers. Additional information about power and ground pins is also provided to help in ground noise evaluations.

The difference in model requirements for simulation and for signal integrity analysis has had a useful side effect for component vendors: rather than release detailed SPICE models for their components (which would reveal everything about the components to potential competitors), component vendors can now provide models that are specifically intended for signal integrity analysis and keep information about the detailed internal operation of the devices proprietary.

Using a Signal Integrity Analysis Tool

To understand how a signal integrity analysis tool operates, we'll take a quick look at an analysis tool produced by HyperLynx, of Redmond, Washington. The

BoardSim for Windows software is a postlayout signal integrity simulator intended specifically for the analysis of printed circuit boards and accepts data directly from PCB layout packages such as those sold by Protel, OrCAD and Allegro.

The general process for analyzing a board design using HyperLynx is as follows:

1. Use a custom translator (either provided by HyperLynx or built into the selected board layout tool) to generate a HyperLynx data file (a **.HYP** file).
2. Load the **.HYP** file into BoardSim.
3. If desired, edit the board's *stackup* (the arrangement of conductive and dialectric layers on the board) to modify the analysis or to isolate a layer of interest.
4. Select *nets* (a specific trace, plus all its branches) to simulate.
5. Select driver and receiver ICs for the simulated net and, if necessary, modify passive-component (resistor, capacitor and inductor) values.
6. Attach simulated oscilloscope probes to points of interest on the net.
7. Open the oscilloscope display and start the simulation.

Creating a .HYP File

BoardSim reads special HyperLynx-format ASCII files (**.HYP** files) that contain the information about a board's layout relevant to signal-integrity analysis. This information includes data relating to the metal segments and geometries of the board layers, information about the components and IC devices used in the design (listed by reference designator), information about the stackup of layers on the board, and other data relevent to calculating electromagnetic (EM) effects.

There are several ways to create a .HYP file, depending on which PCB-layout package was used to created the board being analyzed. For boards created using OrCAD's layout package, for example, a DOS-based translator is provided to convert the OrCAD layout data into **.HYP** format. For designs created in Protel, you would select the **Export HyperLynx** command from within Advanced PCB's **File** menu. Each PCB layout package has its own method of dealing with third-party tools such as BoardSim, but all methods result in the same **.HYP** format file.

Setting Up for a Simulation

After a design has been loaded into BoardSim, you have the option of editing its stackup. In PCB layout packages, the stackup information is not written to the **.HYP** file, and you must created it manually using the stackup editor provided in

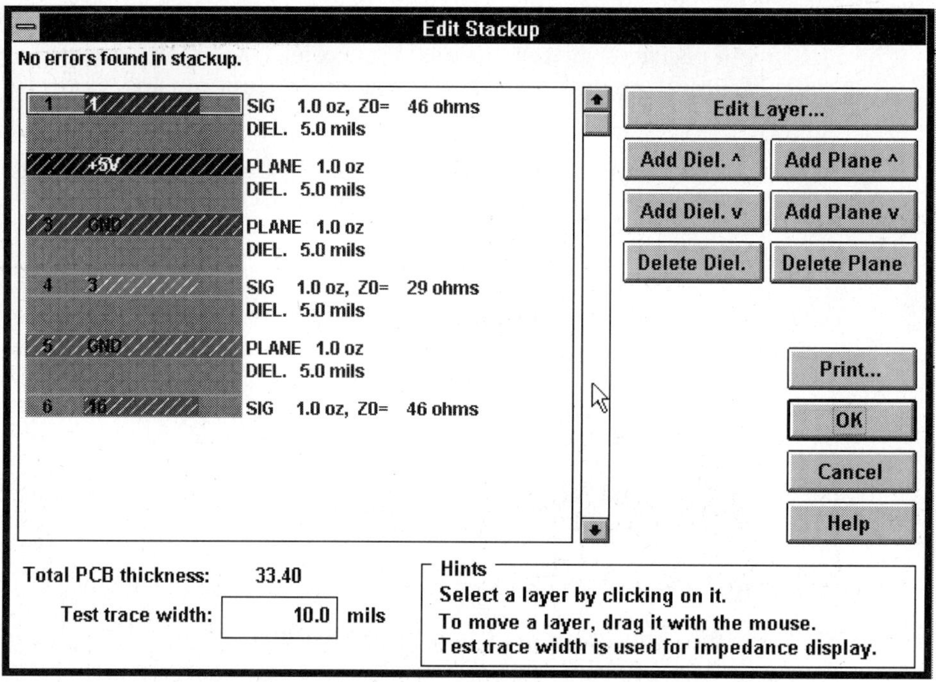

Figure 9-1
Modifying the stackup of a board. (HyperLynx BoardSim.)

BoardSim (Figure 9-1). When editing the board's stackup, you can use buttons to add, edit, or delete layers and move layers by dragging them with the mouse.

Before simulating, you must select a net and specify drive and receiver ICs for the simulation. To select a net for simulation, you can either choose the net by selecting its name (from a list box) or by selecting a reference designator associated with the net.

When selecting driver and receiver ICs, you choose a reference designator and pin combination from a list box, then choose a library and device model for each IC. The model libraries supported in HyperLynx include both a proprietary, user modifiable format and the industry standard IBIS format.

To help analyze the effects of changing circuit elements such as pull-up resistors and terminators on traces, you have the option of modifying the values of passive components (resistors, capacitors, and inductors) before running a simulation. This is particularly useful when you are trying to tweak a net that shows marginal results (fails to stabilize quickly enough or may induce false clocking or glitches). You can often solve such problems by simply increasing the size of a capacitor or modifying

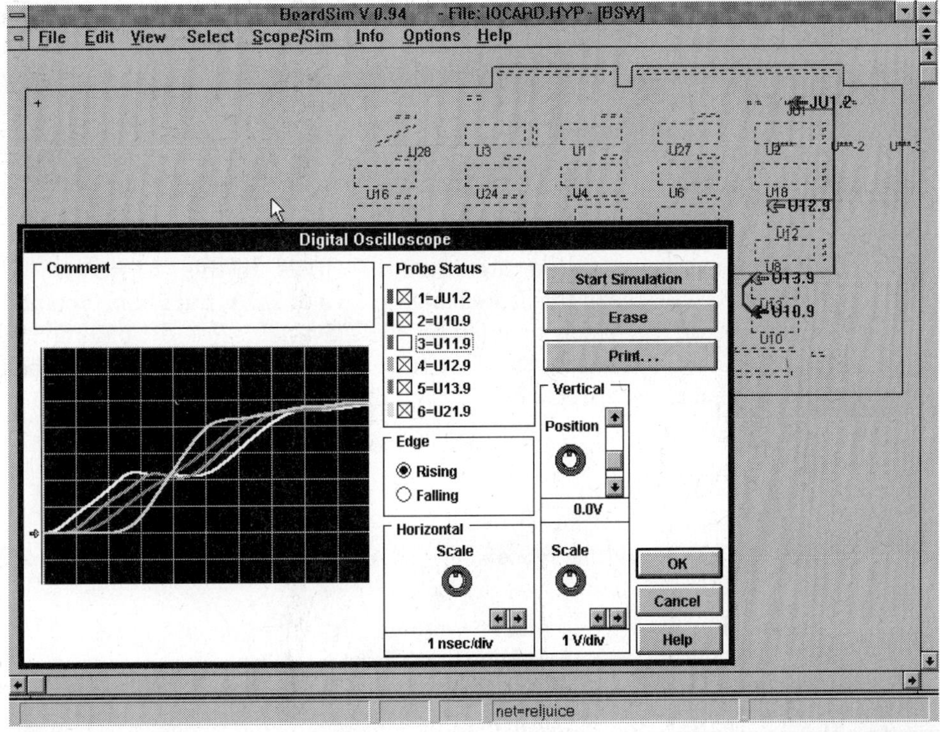

Figure 9-2
Analyzing a signal. (HyperLynx BoardSim.)

the value of a resistor and having the ability to instantly see the results of such changes can be a real time-saver.

Simulating a Net

Before running a simulation, you must attach probes to the net at each location (node) that you wish to observe. You do this by highlighting a reference designator and pin combination in the list box, and then clicking on a channel button to select which channel of the simulated scope you wish to assign to the selected node.

To open the simulated scope and start a simulation, you choose the **Run Scope** command from a menu, select the driver edge direction that you want to simulate, and then begin the simulation by clicking the **Start** button.

A sample output is shown in Figure 9-2. In the waveform shown, you can see how different points on the net respond over time to the driver signal being applied. Notice how one of the nodes being graphed rises only halfway up to its maximum value, settles back briefly, and then continues up. If the circuit being simulated uses

CMOS devices, there is a potential for a false clock (or other glitch behavior) because the signal does not rise cleanly through the switching threshold region. This is precisely the kind of problem that signal integrity analysis tools are intended to identify.

Moving On

This completes our look at circuit analysis tools. In this chapter, we have only skimmed the surface of this fast-changing area of EDA, but I hope you now have a better idea of the kinds of analysis tools available for debugging high-speed circuits. In the next few chapters, we're going to leave the digital world behind and explore the analog aspects of the design process.

Other Resources

Chou, Tai-Yu, *Signal Integrity Analysis in ASIC Design*, ASIC & EDA, May 1994.

Johnson, Howard W., and Martin Graham, *High-Speed Digital Design, A Handbook of Black Magic*, Prentice Hall, Englewood Cliffs, NJ, 1993.

Rosenstark, Sol, *Transmission Lines in Computer Engineering*, McGraw-Hill, New York, 1994.

CHAPTER 10

FOCUS ON TECHNOLOGY: ANALOG SIMULATION

Analog design tools and methods have experienced something of a renaissance in recent years. This new interest is due to a number of factors, including increased densities and speeds of board and chip-level circuits, new emphasis on signal processing applications (such as wireless communications and multimedia), and new requirements for product reliability and conformance.

Circuit analysis, in the form of analog simulation, is an important aspect to electronic product design, and in this chapter we'll be examining its basic concepts. In the two chapters that follow, we'll be looking at how two representative low-cost analog simulators operate.

What Is Analog Simulation?

Analog simulation allows you to model the electrical characteristics of a circuit and analyze its behavior under various conditions before you build any actual hardware. An analog simulator applies mathematical modeling and numerical analysis to the known characteristics of circuits and semiconductors to produce an approximation of signal values at given points in time.

The difference between digital and analog simulation lies primarily in how the values of the various signals within the circuit are modeled in the computer, and in the types of analyses performed. As we learned in the previous two chapters, most digital simulators represent signal values using a small number of possible values, with each value representing a logical state of the signal (high, low, disabled, unknown, etc.) and its signal strength.

An analog simulator, on the other hand, is capable of calculating and storing actual voltages and currents for selected signals in the circuit, using complex numerical algorithms and formulas. Analog simulators can precisely characterize the behavior of high-speed circuits composed of discrete components and transistor-level logic, as well as higher-level circuits composed of behavioral or system-level descriptions. Advanced analog simulators allow you to build very accurate models of your analog circuits, and provide the tools necessary to analyze the effects of operating temperature, capacitance and inductance, transmission line effects, and many other important factors.

Modeling all these factors and making an accurate prediction of the circuit's behavior as actual hardware can require many iterations of simulation to be run. These iterations will typically include a wide range of operating conditions and component tolerances, as well as differing input stimulus, and can result in a large amount of data being generated. Most analog simulators therefore include advanced statistical analysis facilities to help with the interpretation of large amounts of test data. Statistical analysis is an extremely powerful tool for predicting the behavior of complex circuits under a wide variety of operating conditions.

Another factor in the increased use of analog simulation is the increasing power of simulation computing platforms, including the newest generation of 32-bit personal computers and higher-capability operating systems such as Microsoft's 32-bit Windows products. Analog simulation can require many thousands of complex mathematical calculations to produce an accurate representation of a circuit; the more accuracy that is required from simulation, the more processing power is required, it has been only recently that such power has been available on low-cost personal computers.

Circuit Analysis Programs

Circuit analysis programs such as SPICE (described in the next section) analyze the voltages at selected nodes in a circuit by iterating toward a solution from an initial estimate. Each iteration is based on results obtained from the previous iteration, and the iterations continue until the successive difference in the computed node voltages of the circuit is less than some threshold value (typically less than .1%). The calculations required for this analysis are first-order, nonlinear ordinary differential equations which describe the circuit and its associated signal sources.

Figure 10-1 shows a flow diagram representing a typical circuit analysis program. To begin the analysis, the program sets the time to zero and chooses an initial voltage for the nodes in the circuit. The initial voltage is usually zero (unless otherwise specified) for nodes not directly driven by voltage or current sources. Next, the program begins iterating. To begin the iteration, nonlinear device models are evaluated to obtain matrix and righthand side values for subsequent calculations. Contributions from linear elements (such as resistors, capacitors and time-invariant voltage and current sources) are loaded into the matrix at the same time.

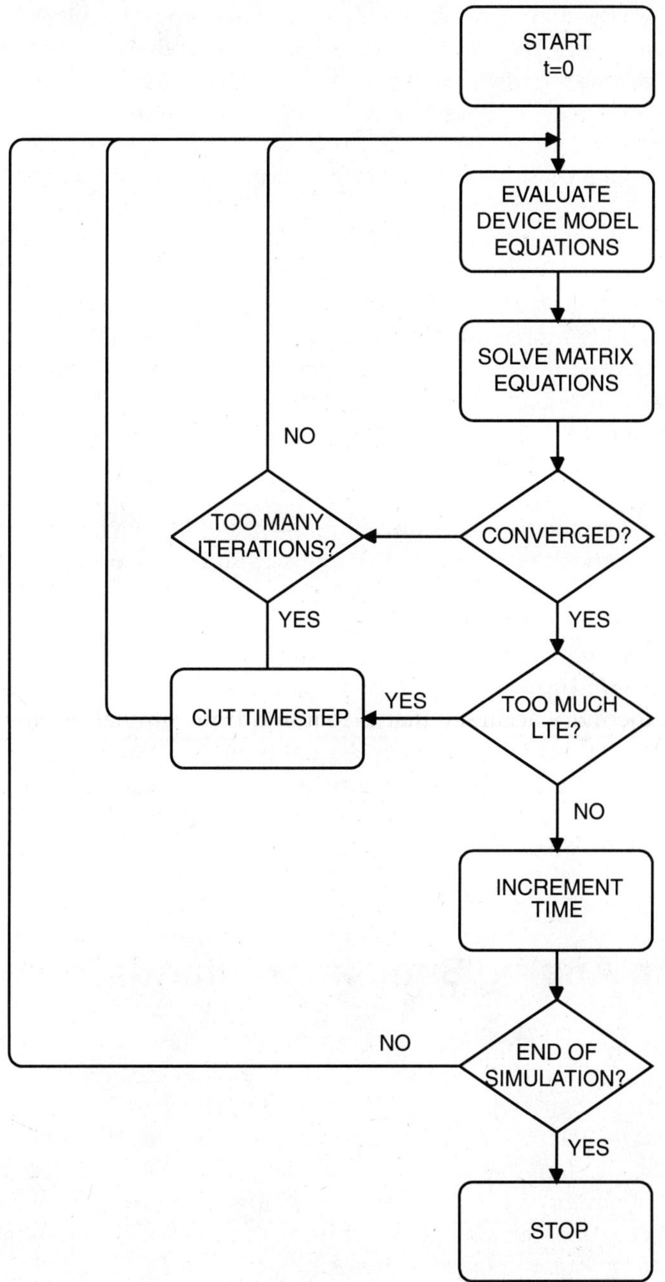

Figure 10-1
Flow diagram for circuit analysis.

When the matrix has been populated, the program solves the resulting linear equations using an efficient sparse matrix algorithm. The resulting voltages are compared to the previous estimate (or to the result of the previous iteration) to determine if the analysis has converged on a solution. The typical number of iterations performed per time point is three to five. If the program does not converge in a reasonable number of iterations, it reduces the time step and tries again.

Once the analysis has converged, the program attempts to determine if the solution is satisfactory. This determination can be performed in many ways, including a local truncation error (LTE) scheme, or indirectly by counting the number of iterations through the loop required for convergence.

If the program determines that the solution is not satisfactory for the current time point, it reduces the time step added to the time point and tries again. This middle loop is repeated until an acceptably small error (or number of iterations until convergence) is obtained for the current time point.

To continue solving the circuit over time, the program increments the current time point by the time step and starts iterating once again toward a solution. This repeating process (the outer loop in the diagram) continues until the circuit analysis is complete.

There are many steps in this analysis process where alternate strategies can be attempted, and vendors of analog circuit analysis tools typically place a great deal of effort into improving the speed and accuracy of the analysis. The differing amounts of time and effort put into such improvements is reflected partially in the wide range of prices for analog simulation tools. While it is possible to purchase commercial SPICE-based simulation tools for as little as a few hundred dollars, analog simulation tools that are appropriate for large-scale analysis (such as might be needed for analysis of a large board or custom IC) can cost many thousands of dollars.

SPICE: An Analog Simulation Standard

Virtually all analog simulators available today (on either personal computers or workstations) are based on the SPICE technology developed at the University of California at Berkeley. SPICE is a general purpose circuit analysis tool originally intended for the modeling of transistor-level circuits, but which has grown into a simulation system that can operate at virtually any level of circuit abstraction. The SPICE program can analyze the operating or quiescent behavior of simple or complex circuits, calculate the response (over time) of both static and active circuits, and perform other detailed analyses.

SPICE is, at its most basic level, a nonlinear equation solver; to determine the response of a circuit to a given stimulus at any point in time, SPICE iteratively solves for Kirchoff's laws (stating that the sum of all voltage drops around a circuit loop equals zero, and that the sum of all currents entering a node also equals zero) for the entire circuit. This method can produce a highly accurate simulation of the circuit, assuming the circuit has been correctly modeled.

For many years, SPICE was available only to users of high-end engineering workstations and mainframes, and was confined largely to academic or ASIC development environments. Since the mid-1980s, however, SPICE has been made available by a variety of vendors on personal computer platforms. Very-low-cost (sometimes free) versions of SPICE are widely available for use by students of electrical engineering, and this has resulted in a new generation of engineers who rely on SPICE to help them solve complex circuit design problems.

History of SPICE

SPICE is the product of a research project begun at the University of California at Berkeley in the late 1960s. SPICE (which stands for *Simulation Program with Integrated Circuit Emphasis*) was first released in 1972. Development of SPICE during this period was spearheaded by D. Pederson and R. Rohrer of U.C. Berkeley, and the actual implementation was carried out by a number of graduate students from the Department of Electrical Engineering and Computer Science.

Initial efforts at creating a circuit analysis tool were focused on development of an accurate and efficient numerical method for circuit representation, solution of nonlinear equations, integration algorithms, sparse matrix solutions, and modeling of nonlinear semiconductor devices. The result of this research was a system of analysis that involved a Newton-Raphson solution for nonlinear equations, coupled with various limiting techniques, implicit integration methods using fixed time steps, and reordering schemes for sparce matrices.

SPICE was one of many analysis programs developed during the 1970s. Some of these programs were offshoots of SPICE, while others were developed independently. These analysis programs were targeted primarily at bipolar device technologies, diodes and transistors. These were, of course, the important emerging technologies of the time. Another factor in the evolution of circuit analysis programs was the computing platforms available. In the early 1970s, circuit analysis was very much a batch-oriented process, in which a circuit analysis program and circuit model were loaded via punched cards into a computer (such as an IBM or CDC mainframe) and executed. (This method of program and circuit data entry is the origin of the term *SPICE deck*, which is still in common use today.)

SPICE1 was first released in the public domain in May 1973. This first public version included improved semiconductor device modeling capabilities and other enhancements. Soon after the release of SPICE1, an efficient method of modeling large circuits (called *macromodeling*) was developed that eliminated the need to describe circuits such as operational amplifiers at the transistor level. This macromodel approach to modeling remains in use today.

The next major release of the program, SPICE2, was released by Ellis Cohen in 1975. This version offered significant improvements over the first version, including a new circuit representation (called *modified nodal analysis*) and a memory management feature that allowed the program to use the entire available memory during analysis. Additional improvements were made by adding a time-step control and a stiffly stable multiple-order integration method called the Gear method.

Commercialization of SPICE began in earnest in the late 1970s and throughout the 1980s, as computing platforms for engineering (such as the PDP 11 and VAX minicomputers available from Digital Equipment Corporation) became prevalent in industry. In the mid-1980s, versions of SPICE began appearing on personal computer platforms, beginning with PSPICE which was released by MicroSim in 1984. Workstation EDA vendors who prospered in the early 1980s (most notably Daisy, Mentor, and Valid) also added a large number of SPICE users. These companies demonstrated that SPICE could be an integral part of system-level design, by linking SPICE-based simulation with graphical design tools such as schematic entry and waveform editors.

Important enhancements made to SPICE in the 1980s included improvements in the program's ability to converge on a solution for problematic circuits. A major rewrite in the C language produced SPICE3, which supports interactive operation. SPICE3 forms the basis of much of the current research taking place in advanced simulation algorithms and models, and has been adopted by several vendors as the core of their commercial SPICE programs. Additional work on proprietary versions of SPICE (and intense competition between by EDA vendors such as Cadence, Mentor, Intergraph, Viewlogic, and many others) has led to increased power and reliability for these SPICE-based analysis tools.

There are many activities going on in the 1990s in relation to analog simulation and SPICE. Efforts are underway to standardize an analog simulation language (based on VHDL) to replace current schematic or circuit file representations. Additional SPICE-based analysis features related to high-speed signal integrity and electromagnetic field effects are being developed and marketed. A longer-term goal for many researchers is the development of analog synthesis tools, with SPICE acting as an analytical engine in a system that will automatically generate circuitry. At the same time, hardware platforms (most notably low-cost personal computers) are gaining in power and availability to the point where mainstream electrical engineers can perform simulations of very large circuits right on their desktops.

SPICE Features

SPICE provides a number of analysis features that can be used to accurately determine the behavior of a circuit under different input parameters and operating conditions. In addition to the standard features of SPICE, vendors of SPICE-based products often add their own analysis options as well. These additional features, coupled with bug fixes, speedups and general optimizations, and comprehensive component libraries, are what distinguish higher-priced SPICE-based simulators from low-cost (or free) versions of the software.

SPICE2, as supplied by the University of California at Berkeley, supports the following types of circuit analysis:

- ☐ DC analysis functions, including sweeps of input voltages, currents, and temperatures.
- ☐ Sensitivity analysis for DC voltages or currents.
- ☐ Small-signal transfer function, or Thevenins equivalence, reported as a small-signal gain value and values for input and output resistance.
- ☐ Transient analysis, including time-domain response and Fourier analysis.
- ☐ Distortion analysis, which computes the steady-state harmonic or the intermodulation products for small input signal magnitudes.

SPICE3 addes the following features:

- ☐ Temperature analysis, allowing the entire circuit, or individual devices, to be simulated with specific temperature gradients.
- ☐ Pole-zero analysis, which computes the poles and/or zeros of a small-signal AC transfer function from any input to any output.
- ☐ AC sensitivity, which extends the DC sensitivity analysis to AC signals
- ☐ AC analysis, including small-signal frequency response and noise analysis

DC Analysis

DC analysis is one of the most basic types of analysis performed by SPICE. During DC analysis, the frequency is assumed to zero, and all inductors and capacitors in the circuit are therefore assumed to be short and open circuits, respectively.

The steps performed by SPICE during DC analysis are:

1. Start with all circuit voltages at zero, except those specified by **.ic** or **.nodeset** statements.
2. While the voltage or current change from the previous iteration is larger than the user-specified error tolerance,
   - a. Form equations by determining the currents through the devices at the current voltage guess.
   - b. Solve the resulting linear system to get a new guess for the node voltages.

The *operating point* of nonlinear devices (such as diodes and transistors) is important for analysis, and this value (which is also known as the *bias point*, or *quiescent point*) can be specified to SPICE during DC analysis. When the operating point is provided, SPICE can calculate and display the currents and power dissipations throughout the circuit, as well as the voltages.

Sensitivity analysis is used by SPICE to calculate the sensitivity of output voltages or currents with respect to every circuit and device parameter. During its operation, a sensitivity operation calculates the bias point and the linearized parameters around the bias point. The sensitivity is then determined by either a perturbation or adjoint technique. The effect on the entire circuit of a change in one or more component values can then be observed.

The *small-signal transfer function*, or *Thevenins equivalence*, can also be computed by SPICE. SPICE calculates the small-signal transfer function by linearizing the circuit around the operating point. The results of this analysis are reported as the small signal DC gain, input resistance, and output resistance of the circuit.

DC sweeps are performed by calculating the DC operating point and small-signal DC gain for a range of input values. DC sweeps can be nested, and SPICE provides commands allowing values to be swept using linear or nonlinear ranges.

AC Analysis

AC analysis is used to calculate the response of a circuit over a range of frequencies. Before AC analysis is performed, SPICE performs the DC solution to determine the large signal characteristics of the circuit and the bias point information. Small signal parameters must be calculated for any circuit containing nonlinear devices (such as diodes and transistors) prior to AC analysis.

AC analysis calculates the small signal characteristics of the circuit as a function of frequency. The basic steps performed during an AC analysis are,

1. Perform DC analysis to obtain the operating point.
2. For each frequency point from the starting frequency to the ending one,
   a. Form a complex linear system at the operating point.
   b. Solve the system and output the results.

Noise Analysis

Noise analysis can be performed in conjunction with AC analysis. Each noise generating element in the circuit is propogated by superposition to an output node for each frequency specified in the AC analysis. The propagated noise contributions are combined and reported for each frequency.

Transient Analysis

Transient analysis is used to analyze the response of a circuit over time. Unlike DC analysis, inductors and capacitors are assumed to be part of the system at each step. The basic steps performed during transient analysis are

1. Initialize the circuit.
2. Perform a DC analysis.
3. While the time step is not accepted,
    a. Choose a new time step.
    b. Integrate all capacitors, using (I = C * DV/DT), G = I/V = C/V * DV/DT, where DV/DT is computed using the integration method.
    c. While voltages or currents have not converged,
        1. For each device, determine current and conductance contributions for each component based on the voltages from the previous iteration. Load conductance into the matrix and current into the right-hand side.
        2. Factor the matrix.
        3. Back solve to determine the new voltage values.
    d. Accept or reject the step based on local truncation error and number of iterations.

Initial values can be specified for nodes, and step values allow the response to be analyzed over time for changing node values. Fourier analysis performed after transient analysis generates a frequency domain analysis of data collected during the transient analysis.

Temperature Analysis

Temperature analysis is used to examine the effects of differing operating temperatures on the performance of a circuit. SPICE allows temperature effects to be reported for a range of temperatures and can be used to evaluate the effects of thermal mismatch in a circuit.

During temperature analysis, the characteristics of semiconductor devices are calculated and applied to the model of each device. The results of subsequent analyses are then calculated and the results reported.

More advanced *thermal analysis* features available in higher-performance analog simulation tools allow different temperatures to be assigned to each device in the circuit. This provides accurate modeling of the thermal characteristics of a board, for example, and is a useful tool for reliability analysis.

Monte Carlo Analysis

Monte Carlo analysis is a method used to perform statistical analysis of a circuit. In a typical Monte Carlo analysis (whether DC, AC, or transient), multiple runs of the analysis are performed with variations (based on the statistical tolerances) being made on the parameters of the model for each run. The first run is performed with nominal values for all components, and subsequent runs are performed with variations as specified in the model definition. Options available in the Monto Carlo analysis include,

- ☐ Finding the greatest difference in each waveform from the initial (nominal) run
- ☐ Finding the minimum and maximum value for each waveform
- ☐ Finding the first occurrence of a waveform that exceeds or crosses below a specified threshold

Convergence

Convergence (or lack of convergence) is a common problem faced by users of SPICE-based simulators. SPICE operates by applying iterative algorithms to the circuit, starting with an initial estimate of the final solution. Each iteration starts with a set of node voltages, and subsequent iterations calculate new sets of voltages (based on the previous results) that are expected to be closer to the actual solution. For certain analysis operations (DC sweeps, bias point calculations and transient analyses), it is possible that the iterative approach will fail to converge on a solution.

An example of a circuit analysis that may fail to converge is a DC analysis of a Schmitt trigger. A Schmitt trigger is a circuit with a regenerative feedback, and is not appropriate for DC analysis because of discontinuities in the solution at the circuit's crossover point.

SPICE simulation vendors use a variety of methods to improve the ability of SPICE to converge on a solution for a wide variety of circuits. These methods are usually proprietary and are an important characteristic of more expensive (and traditionally workstation-based) SPICE derivatives.

SPICE Circuit Files

SPICE reads circuit information and simulation commands from a user-created file called the *circuit file*. This circuit file consists of a sequence of SPICE statements describing the circuit elements (transistors, capacitors, etc.) and their interconnections, as well as information about voltage and current sources, and commands instructing the SPICE simulator how to analyze the circuit (and what reports or other resulting outputs to create). The following SPICE circuit file describes a very simple circuit composed of a resistor, a capacitor, and an inductor. The circuit file also includes a voltage source and SPICE commands specifying a simple transient analysis:

```
RLC CIRCUIT
R1 1 2 1K
L1 2 3 100UH
C1 3 0 30PF
V1 1 0 PULSE (0 1 2NS 2NS 2NS 50SN 100NS)
.TRAN 5N 1U
.PRINT TRAN V(3) V(2) V(1)
.PLOT TRAN V(3)
.END
```

Reading from the top of the SPICE circuit file, we see,

- A title line (in this case "RLC Circuit").
- An element line representing the resistor (**R1**), including a resistance parameter.
- An element line representing an inductor (**L1**) with a value of 100 uH.
- An element line representing a capacitor (**C1**) of 20pf.
- An element line defining a pulsed source (**V1**). The parameters of the pulsed source include the initial voltage, pulsed voltage, delay, rise and fall times, pulse width and period.
- A **.TRAN** statement instructing SPICE to perform a transient analysis of the circuit for a given step and stop time.
- A **.PRINT** statement instructing SPICE to print the values of the indicated signals at each step of the analysis.
- A **.PLOT** statement instructing SPICE to prepare a graphic plot of signal **V(3)** over time.
- A **.END** statement.

When processed by SPICE, this circuit file will result in two output formats: a tabular format showing the value of the indicated signals for each step of the analysis and a graphical plot of signal **V(3)**.

SPICE Models

The accuracy of a simulation is dependent to a large extent on the accuracy of the *device models* provided to the simulator. (Other factors include the algorithms used to iterate toward a solution, the time step used during simulation, and the accuracy and power of the computing platform being used.)

SPICE models may be provided by the simulation vendors, provided by component vendors (often under a nondisclosure agreement), or created by the SPICE user. Simulation vendors often promote their products by advertising the number of models provided in their libraries, but the level of detail provided in each component model is just as important as the number of models offered. Passive devices (resistors, capacitors, and inductors), for example, may include information about tolerances and parasitics in addition to the standard component values needed for DC analysis. Active devices (such as diodes, transistors, and switches) may include very complex model data, and this data may be considered proprietary by component vendors who provide the models.

For models of complex semiconductor devices (such as op-amps), the model developer must trade off the accuracy and speed of simulation. As models get larger and more complex, the time required for the simulation to solve the entire circuit grows dramatically. When using complex SPICE models, particularly in combination with large circuits, it may become necessary to use more powerful computing hardware (such as a hardware accelerator) to obtain a solution.

Moving On

Although SPICE was originally developed as a batch-mode circuit analysis tool, it has been successfully used as the basis for a number of interactive simulation products. These products, like the digital simulation products we looked at in the previous chapter, allow a design entered in the form of a schematic to be simulated and the results to be viewed in a graphic representation such as a waveform. Most interactive SPICE-based tools also allow you to enter and modify input values and to observe results right on the schematic (using software probes or meters) as if you were working with an actual breadboard of your circuit.

The SPICE tools that we will look at in subsequent tutorials both use this interactive approach to SPICE-based analysis.

Other Resources

Antognetti, Paolo, and Guiseppe Massobrio, *Semiconductor Device Modeling with SPICE*, McGraw-Hill, New York, 1988.

Deutsch, Jeffrey T., *Algorithms and Architecture for Multiprocessor-Based Circuit Simulation*, Doctoral Dissertation, University of California at Berkeley, 1985.

Muller, Karl Heinz, *A Spice Cookbook*, Intusoft, San Pedro, CA, 1991.

Newton, Richard, *The Simulation of Large Scale Integrated Circuits*, Electronics Research Laboratory, College of Engineering, University of California at Berkeley, 1978.

Quarles, T. L., *SPICE3 Version 3C1 User's Guide*, University of California at Berkeley, 1989.

Rashid, Muhammad H., *Spice for Power Electronics and Electric Power*, Prentice Hall, Englewood Cliffs, NJ, 1993.

Tuinenga, Paul, *SPICE: A Guide to Circuit Simulation and Analysis Using Pspice*, Prentice Hall, Englewood Cliffs, NJ, 1992.

Vlach, J., and Singhal, K., *Computer Methods for Circuit Analysis and Design*, 2nd ed., Van Nostrand Reinhold, New York, 1994.

Vladimirescu, Andrei, *The SPICE Book*, John Wiley & Sons, New York, 1994.

CHAPTER 11

HANDS-ON EDA: INTERACTIVE SPICE

To give you an idea of how analog simulation can be used, I'll present examples using two representative SPICE-based analog simulators. While both of these simulators are based on SPICE, they have quite different feature-sets and philosophies. The first is a very low-cost package intended for small-scale or educational projects, while the second is a more full-featured package that supports a very high level of interactivity, includes more comprehensive libraries of devices, and includes more advanced analysis options.

Note: *Information in this chapter is based on a product tutorial provided by Beige Bag Software. The companion CD-ROM includes an evaluation version of the B²Spice simulator that you can use to follow along with this tutorial.*

Beige Bag Software's B²Spice

In this chapter I'll be using a low-cost SPICE simulation package produced and sold by Beige Bag Software of Ann Arbor, Michigan. This simulator is primarily intended for small-scale projects or educational use and sells for less than $150. If you have never used an analog simulator and want to learn the concepts quickly and with little risk, the B²Spice simulator is a good choice. B²Spice lacks many of the advanced features of its more expensive kin, but the features it has are implemented very well and provide enough power for most small projects.

Analyzing a Circuit with B^{2}Spice

In this tutorial, we'll go through one of the sample circuits included with the B^{2}Spice simulator. This sample circuit is a differential amplifier and is shown in schematic form in Figure 11-1.

A differential amplifier circuit accepts a voltage waveform as input and amplifies the magnitude of that waveform while preserving its shape. A differential amplifier could be used, for example, to amplify the strength of weak radio signals or could be one stage of an operational amplifier.

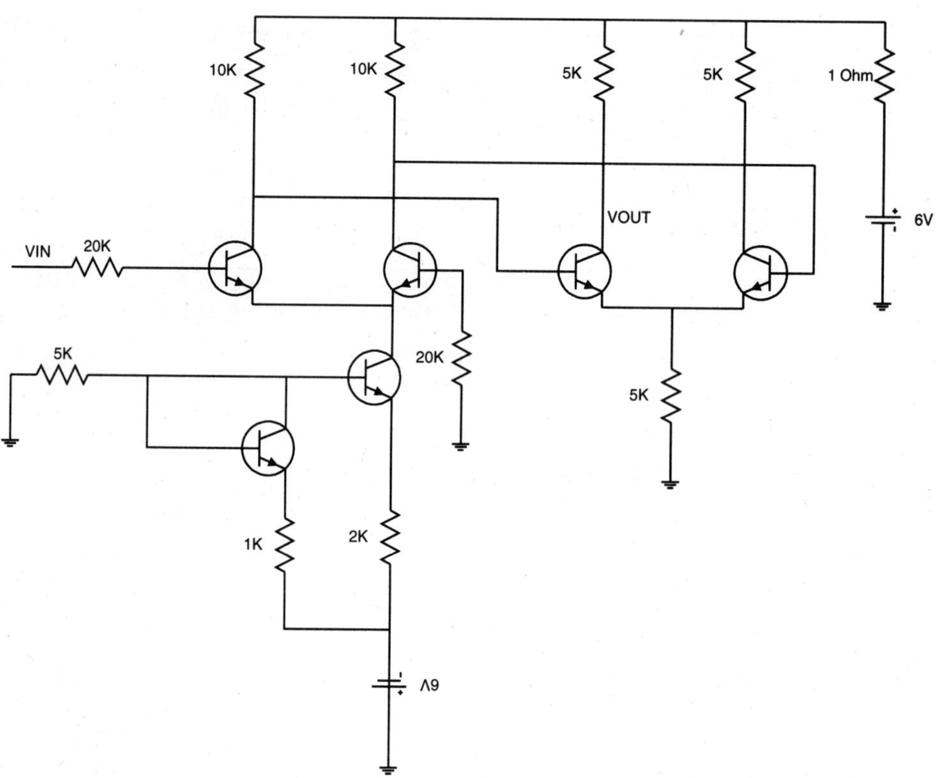

Figure 11-1
A differential amplifier circuit.

Entering a Circuit

B^2Spice has a menu of discrete devices, ranging from resistors and transistors to various types of voltage and current supplies. The devices you can use are limited to those that are available in the menus, and there is no facility for adding your own components. The device menu also includes meters of various types; we'll see how those are used in a moment.

1. Double-click on the application icon to invoke B^2Spice. The program will begin with a blank circuit window, and the cursor will appear as a selection arrow.

The B^2Spice main window is sparse, with a somewhat primitive tool bar, but there is a fair amount of power hidden behind the simple interface. If you are familiar with other Windows drawing tools, you will have no trouble learning how to draw circuit diagrams with B^2Spice. The program has a well-designed set of fundamental drawing features.

2. To add a component to the circuit window, select the **Devices** window and click on a device name.

3. Select a resistor device to place in the circuit by clicking on the device name **Resistor**. Move the component into place on the left side of the circuit, then click the mouse button again to drop the device symbol.

After you click to place the component, the corresponding device remains selected, so you can quickly create multiple component instances of the same device, or rotate the component as needed to fit your circuit diagram.

4. Continue selecting devices and placing them in the circuit window to create the basic component placements shown in Figure 11-2.

Drawing Wires

Although the drawing features of a simulator front-end are one of the least important aspects of a simulation package, a well-designed drawing interface can speed up the design entry process tremendously. In this area, the B^2Spice program does a good job. For example, it's obvious that a lot of thought went into the way that wires are handled. The program allows you to move wires around by grabbing them on either end and repositioning them, by moving symbols and letting the wires stretch and reshape accordingly, or by dragging the corners of multisegment lines to adjust their shape and routing. Connectivity rules (the way that wires automatically snap to symbols, and the rules for connecting intersecting wires) are intuitive, and the program rarely does anything unexpected.

Continue entering the sample circuit by connecting the components with wires. To draw wires on the diagram,

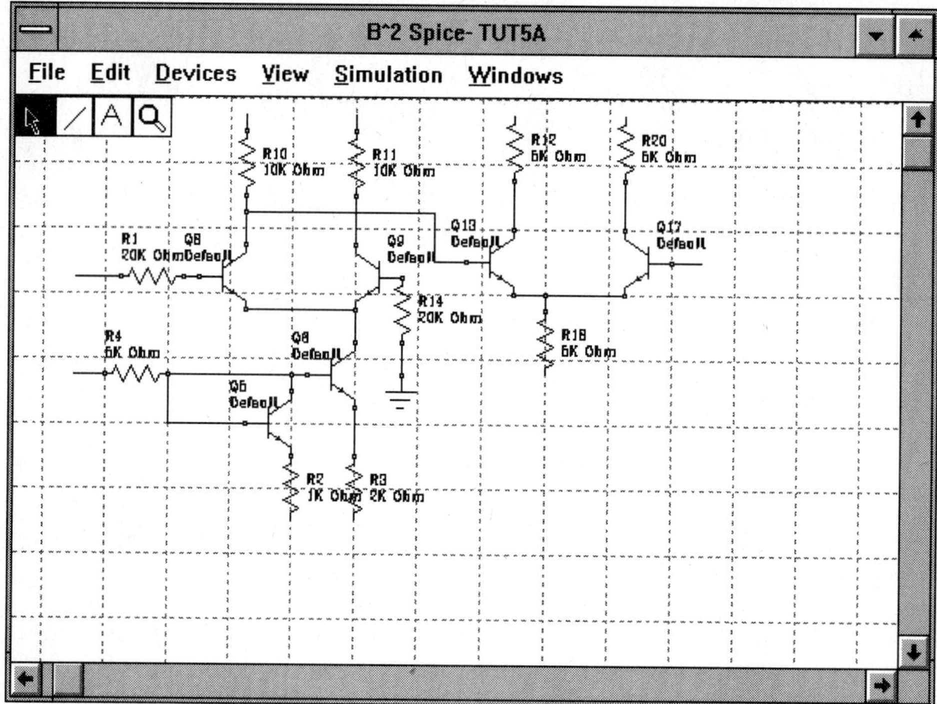

Figure 11-2
The B²Spice schematic editor.

1. Click on the line drawing tool (the button that looks like a "/" character) to change the drawing mode. The cursor will change.

2. To draw a wire, click on the end of a component input or output terminal, then release the mouse button and move the mouse to the point at which you will either want to end the wire (the terminal of the destination device) or where you will want to change the direction of the wire (in the case of a multiple-segment wire). If you are drawing a single-segment wire (one with no bends), then you should simply double-click the mouse button at the device terminal you are connecting the wire to. If you are creating a multiple-segment wire, then you should click the mouse button once each time you want to change direction, and double-click when you have reached the destination terminal and want to end the wire.

Modifying drawings or simply making them more "pretty" is easy with B²Spice. Selecting and moving entire areas works as you would expect, and the program interfaces well with the Windows clipboard for copying drawings or portions of drawings.

3. If you want to modify a line (move it to a new location, etc.), you can use the selection arrow button in the toolbar. With the selection arrow active, you can select components, line segments or line vertices and move them to new locations. When you want to move one of these objects, you must press and hold the mouse button while you drag the item to its new location.

   To delete an object, select it using the selection arrow, then choose the **Clear** item from the **Edit** menu.

4. Continue drawing wires and connecting components to create the circuit as shown earlier.

Setting Component Properties

The last step in creating a circuit for simulation is to modify the properties for each component. Each device supported in B^2Spice has a unique set of properties that can be set. Resistors, for example, have a resistance value, while power sources have specific AC or DC voltages and phases.

To modify the properties of a component,

1. Click on the selection arrow button on the tool bar.

2. Use the selection arrow to select a device. For this example, select the rightmost resistor component.

3. Double-click on the component to bring up a property editing window.

4. Enter the name of the component (in this case **R24**) and its resistance value (1 ohm) in the editing window.

5. Click **OK** to exit the property editing window.

Repeat the property editing procedure to modify the values of each component as shown in the earlier diagram.

Adding Power Sources and Voltmeters

After the circuit has been entered, it needs to be provided with various power sources. The differential amplifier requires a 6V DC power source, so you will need to add power source symbols to the drawing. To simulate the circuit, you will also need to supply an input waveform to **VIN**, and provide a way of monitoring the resulting waveform at various points in the circuit.

The first test of this circuit, however, will be a static test using a constant voltage. For this test, you will add a constant power source to the input (Figure

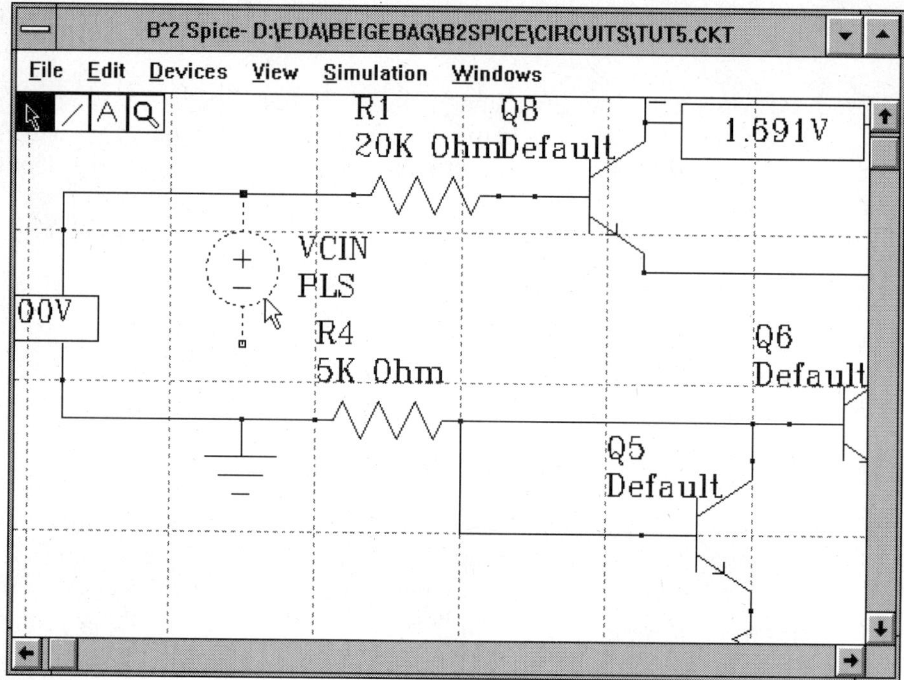

Figure 11-3
Adding a power source to the circuit.

11-3). Performing a static test is a good idea, because it will quickly uncover mistakes (such as reversed components) in how the circuit was drawn.

To add a constant power source to the circuit,

1. Using the **Devices** menu, select the device named **Constant** and place it on the diagram in the three locations shown. Use the **Rotate** commands from the **Edit** menu to orient the power supply devices as shown.

2. Use the previously described method to modify the properties of each constant power supply component, giving them the DC voltage values shown in Figure 11-4.

3. Connect the constant power supply components to the circuit with wires, and add **Ground** components (from the **Devices** menu) as shown.

After you have added the constant power source components to the circuit and connected them via wires, you will need to add some voltmeters to the circuit so you can observe the behavior of the circuit during simulation. Like other kinds of devices, voltmeters are accessed from the **Devices** menu:

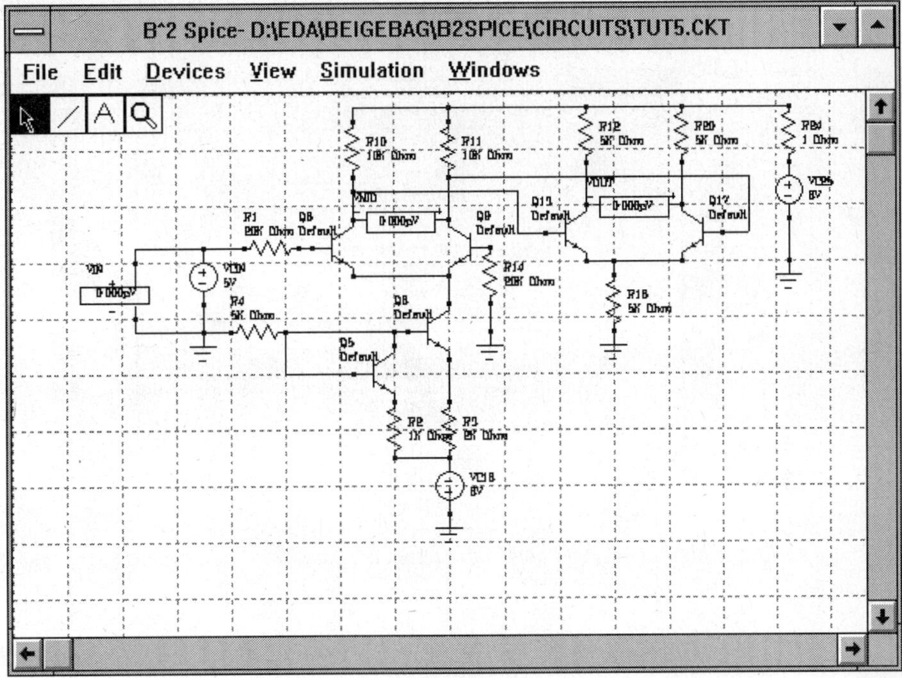

Figure 11-4
The complete differential amplifier circuit, as entered in B^2Spice.

4. Select the **Voltmeter** device from the **Devices** menu, and place it on the diagram to create three unique voltmeter components at the locations shown in Figure 11-4. Use the **Rotate** commands from the **Edit** menu to orient the voltmeters as shown, and use the wire tool to connect the voltmeters to the indicated points in the circuit.
5. Double-click on each voltmeter component to give them unique names (**VIN**, **VMID**, and **VOUT**) as shown.

The circuit is now ready for the first test.

Analyzing Steady-State Response

To perform the static test, you will initiate what, in SPICE terms, is called a *DC sweep*. The DC sweep function will apply a sequence of constant values that that you specify to the **VIN** input, and graph the resulting output values.

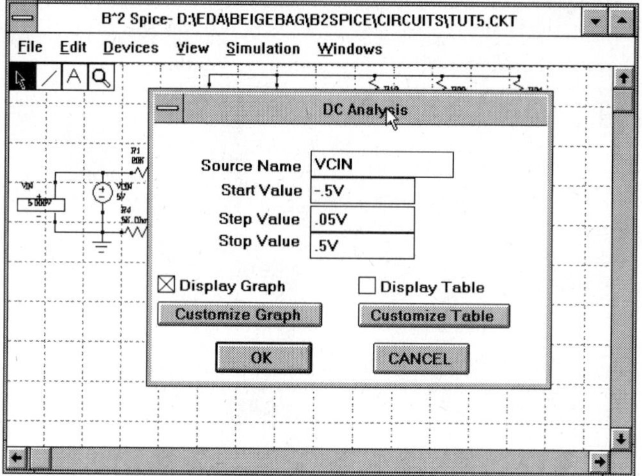

Figure 11-5
To set up a static analysis, you must supply starting and ending values, and a step value.

1. To set up for a DC sweep operation, select **Set Up DC Sweep** from the **Simulation** menu.
2. Set a starting, ending, and step value in the **Set Up DC Sweep** dialogue box as shown in Figure 11-5. Set the start value to -.5V, the step value to .05V, and the stop value to .5V. These values will result in a total of 21 separate tests being performed, with values ranging from -.5 to .5 volts.
3. Check the **Graph** option, then click **OK** to exit the window.
4. Choose the **Run DC Sweep** item from the **Simulation** menu.

When the sweep is completed, the results are displayed as a graph, as shown in Figure 11-6. The graph shows that the circuit correctly amplifies input values, and also shows the range of input values in which you can expect to have a linear amplification (approximately -0.05V to +0.05V).

Analyzing Transient Response

Once you have determined that the circuit works for steady input values, you will want to know whether the circuit maintains the waveforms of high-frequency signals. For this test, you will replace the constant voltage source with a pulse source and will define a high-speed pulse that will be applied to the circuit.

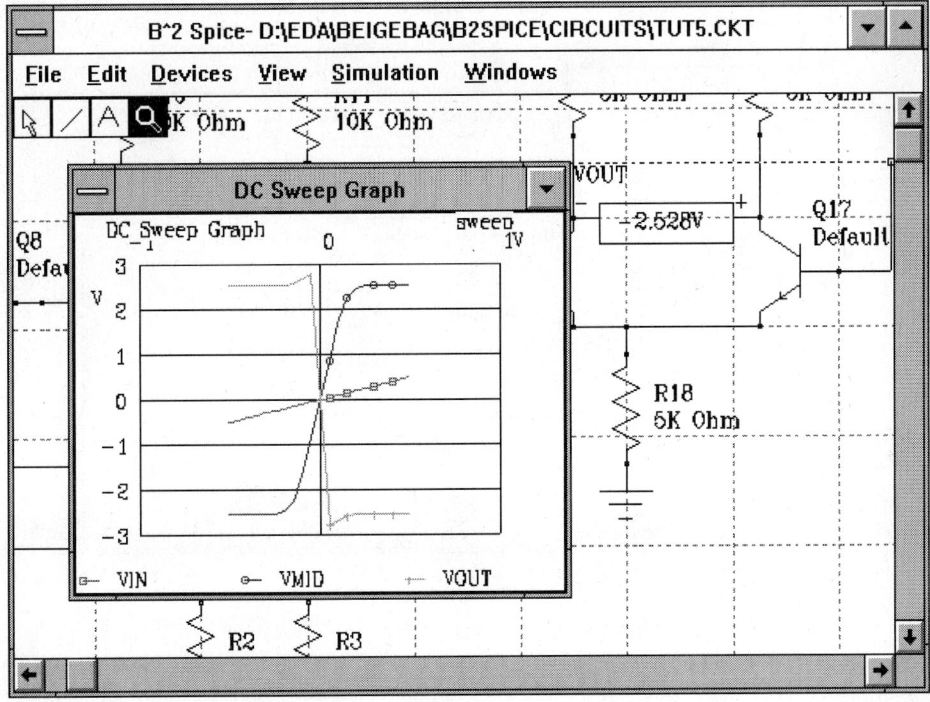

Figure 11-6
The DC sweep results are displayed as a graph.

1. Delete the constant voltage source component at **VCIN** by selecting the component and choosing **Clear** from the **Edit** menu.

2. Replace the constant voltage source with a **Pulse** voltage source using the **Devices** menu. Rotate the pulse voltage source using the **Rotate 180** command from the **Edit** menu.

3. To set up the pulse, double-click on the pulse source symbol, and fill in the dialogue box that appears. Specify an initial value of 0, and characterize the pulse by supplying a pulsed value of 1 mV, rise time, delay and fall times of 100ns, a pulse width of 1 us, and a period of 2 us (Figure 11-7).

4. Choose **Set Up Transient Analysis** from the **Simulation** menu, and specify 2 us for the end time, .1 us for the step time, and .1us for the maximum step.

5. Check the **Graph** option, click on **OK**, then choose **Run Transient** from the **Simulation** menu.

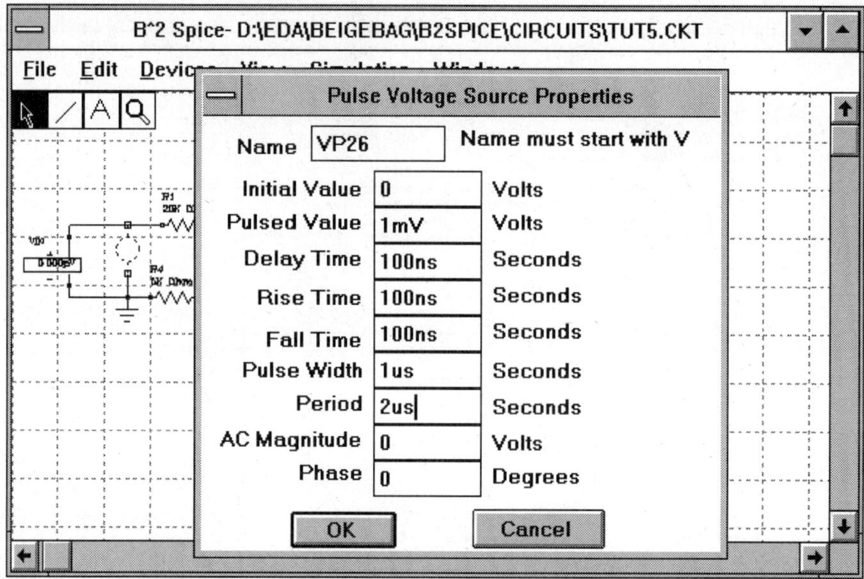

Figure 11-7
Specifying pulse source properties.

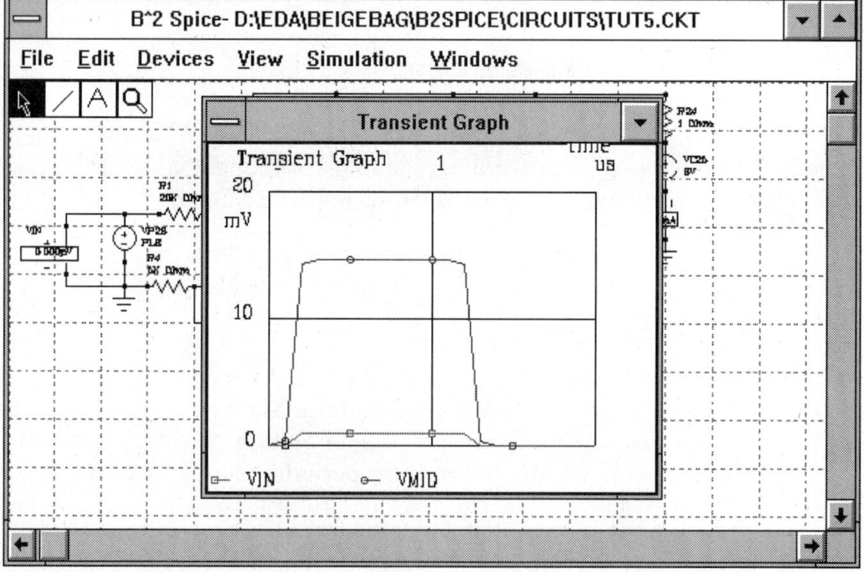

Figure 11-8
The transient analysis graph.

After the transient simulation run has completed, a graph is again displayed. By plotting only the **VIN** and **VMID** signals, and by customizing the graph display somewhat with graphing options, you can see a waveform similar to that shown in Figure 11-8. This graph shows that the input pulse has been translated properly by the amplifier circuit.

Analyzing Power Requirements

The next analysis you will perform is a calculation of power consumption. B^2Spice includes an ammeter symbol that can be added to the circuit diagram (Figure 11-9) to probe the current used at the two power supply points.

1. Make room for the ammeter symbols by use the selection tool to move the Ground and Constant voltage supply components at locations **VC16** and **VC25**.

2. Choose the **Ammeter** device from the **Devices** menu, and place two ammeter components in series with two power supplies as shown in Figure 11-9. Use the **Rotate** commands from the **Edit** menu to orient the ammeters properly.

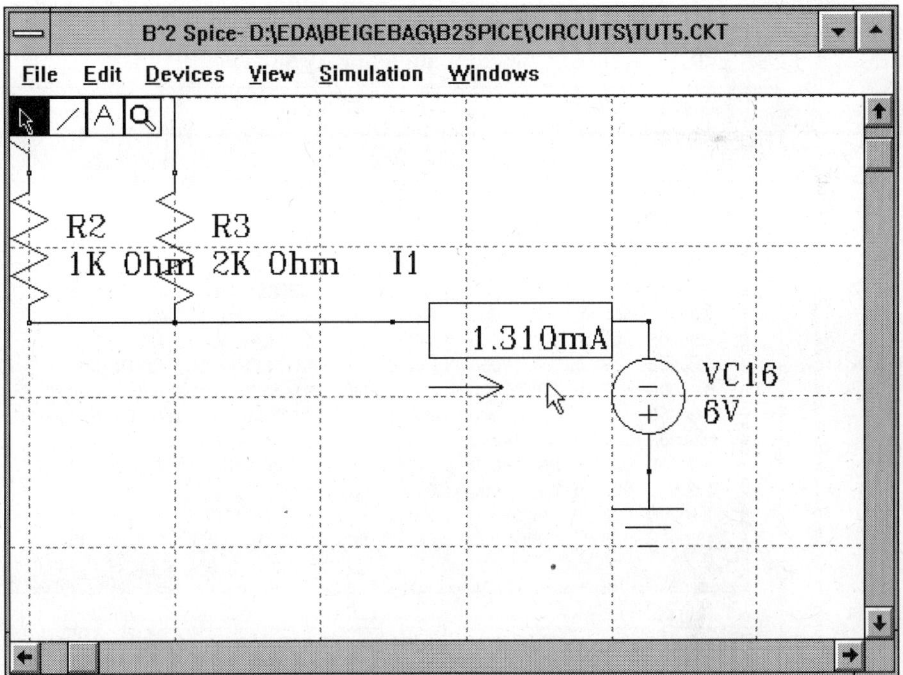

Figure 11-9
Adding ammeter symbols at each power supply point.

3. Double-click on each of the ammeter components, and give them names of **I0** and **I1**.

If you add up the two current values indicated by the ammeters and multiply the result by 6 (the supply voltage), you can obtain the total power usage at any given time. This power usage can either be graphed or displayed in tabular form. To see the power usage in tabular form,

4. Select the item **Set Up Transient Analysis** from the Simulation menu.

5. Check the **Display Table** option, then click on **Customize Table**.

6. Now click on **Add Expression**, and enter the expression **(I0 + I1) * 6** into the expression field.

7. When you click on **OK** to exit the window, you will see the power displayed in a table similar to the one shown in Figure 11-10.

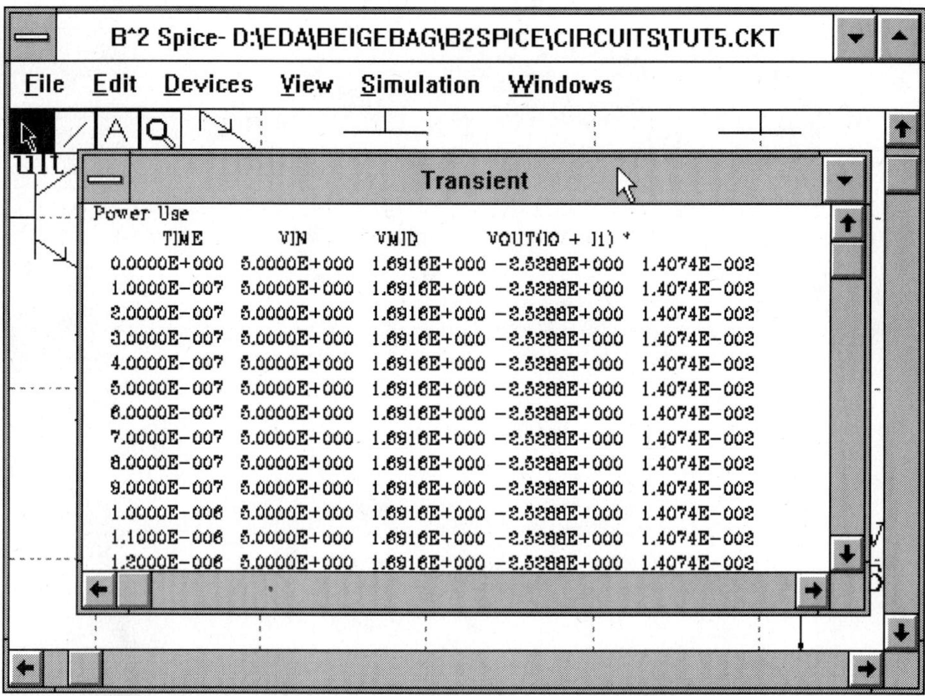

Figure 11-10
Power usage displayed in tabular form.

Moving On

This quick tutorial has only skimmed the surface of what is possible using SPICE simulation and using the B^2Spice software. The B^2Spice package supports many more advanced features, and its companion simulator, B^2Logic, adds digital simulation capabilities as well. In the next tutorial we're going to be examining some of the more advanced features of SPICE while trying out the ICAP/4 tools offered by Intusoft.

CHAPTER 12

HANDS-ON EDA: MORE SPICE SIMULATION

The tutorial presented in the previous chapter showed only the basics of SPICE-based simulation. SPICE provides additional options such as temperature and noise analysis, and most SPICE-based simulators (including B^2Spice) support some or all of these options in their DC and AC sweep analysis. When large numbers of test conditions are performed in a sequence of sweeps, more comprehensive data analysis tools may be provided to allow test results to be interpreted meaningfully. These more advanced tools also offer broader SPICE model support, making them more appropriate for system-level design.

To demonstrate some of the more advanced features of SPICE-based simulators and to show a more full-featured analog simulation product, we're going to switch gears and try out the analog simulation tools produced by Intusoft, of San Pedro, California. Intusoft specializes in SPICE-based simulation tools, and produces a suite of tools that are among the best available for the Windows platform.

Note: *The information in this chapter is based on a tutorial example provided by Intusoft with their ICAP/4 product. An evaluation version of the Intusoft ICAP/4 simulator has been provided on the companion CD-ROM. Note, however, that not all features of ICAP/4 shown in this chapter are available in the evaluation software.*

Intusoft's ICAP/4

ICAP/4, produced and sold by Intusoft of San Pedro, California, is a package based on SPICE version 3F.2, an updated SPICE program released by the University of California at Berkeley in 1993. The ICAP/4 program is completely interactive and allows long simulations to be paused and resumed as needed while providing many interactive views of the simulation data. Parameters (and even components) can be changed "on the fly" and output data such as waveforms can be displayed at any time. Cross-probing between the IsSpice program and the ICAP/4 schematic editor (SpiceNet) is also provided. The IntuScope program included with ICAP/4 is intended for detailed waveform analysis and includes many complex graphic and reporting functions.

The following tutorial, which has been adapted from two examples provided in IntuSoft's Getting Started manual, demonstrates some of the more advanced interactive analysis features that are provided in comprehensive packages such as ICAP/4.

The ICAP/4 Environment

ICAP/4 consists of four primary Windows applications that communicate with one another as you use them to enter your design, perform SPICE analysis, and view the results. For design entry, a schematic editor (SpiceNet) is provided that includes symbol libraries for a huge number of discrete components.

A context-sensitive text editor is also provided for those times when you need to enter SPICE statements and commands directly. The text editor has a built-in help facility that recognizes SPICE keywords and commands and can display comprehensive help information at any time.

The IsSpice simulator is an interactive SPICE-based simulation program that allows precise control over circuit stimulus and result reporting and communicates directly with the SpiceNet schematic editor to provide cross probing of simulation results from the schematic itself.

The IntuScope application takes debugging and analysis a step further, by providing many detailed analysis functions. IntuScope accepts data from the IsSpice simulator, or can accept data from other sources, such as externally-generated laboratory test data.

Creating a Circuit

The first step in the design process is entering the design. You can do this by creating a SPICE circuit file directly, or you can enter a schematic that will be automatically translated to a circuit file. To enter a schematic using SpiceNet, you launch SpiceNet from the ICAP/4 main application window (Figure 12-1) and begin drawing the diagram.

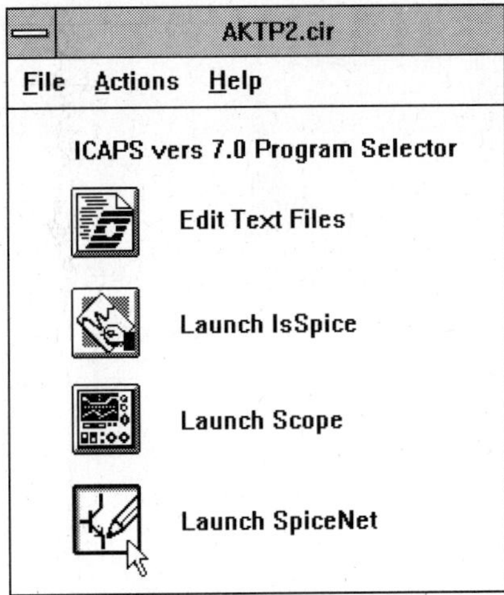

Figure 12-1
ICAP/4's main program selection screen.

Rather than walk through the creation of a new schematic, we'll just load up an existing schematic from the Intusoft examples directory. The first circuit that we will examine is a relatively simple low-pass filter and is named **AKTP2.D1**. To load the schematic,

1. Invoke the ICAP/4 application from the Windows Program Manager.

2. Launch SpiceNet from the main ICAP/4 application windows by clicking on the SpiceNet icon.

3. Load the sample schematic by choosing **Open** from the **File** menu. Navigate to the ICAP/4 examples directory, and select the schematic name **AKTP2**.

The SpiceNet schematic editor, with the schematic loaded and ready to process, is shown in Figure 12-2.

The schematic for the low-pass filter consists of three resistors, three capacitors, one transistor, and three power sources. Two of the power sources are DC sources, while the third, and leftmost, source is an AC source that represents the test input. The special Y-shaped symbol on the right side of the schematic is a test point. This symbol will generate a .PRINT statement in the circuit netlist so we can view the results of the simulation. (Later we will see how test points can be dynamically inserted using probes.)

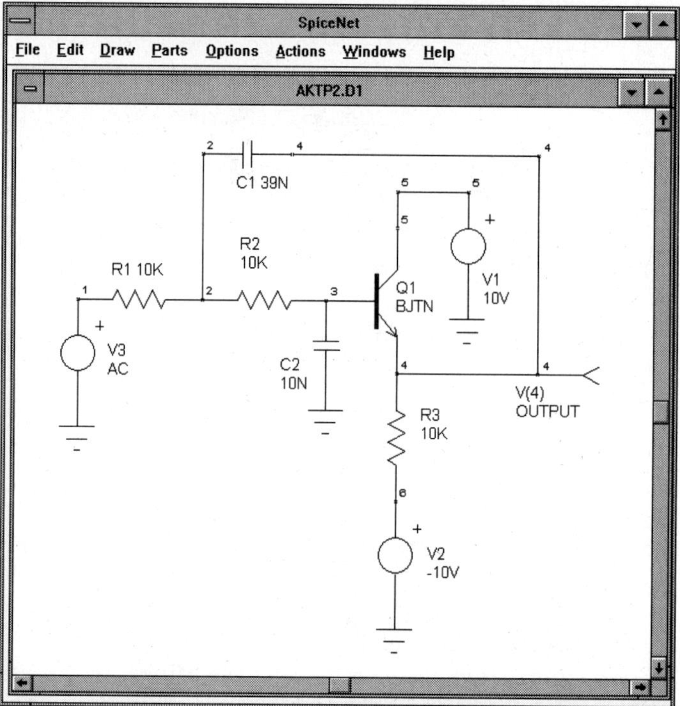

Figure 12-2
The SpiceNet schematic editor, with a sample circuit loaded and ready to go.

Examining the SPICE Circuit File

Generating a SPICE circuit file from a schematic is easy in ICAP/4; in fact, the program automatically generates the circuit file any time a modification is made and you exit the application or save the schematic, so you never have to explicitly request that the file be generated. To examine the circuit file generated from this circuit,

1. Save the schematic by selecting **Save** from the SpiceNet **File** menu.

2. Select the **Text Edit** function from the **Actions** menu, or double-click on the **Edit Text Files** icon in the ICAP/4 main application window.

The complete SPICE circuit file (netlist) for this design is listed in Figure 12-3. Notice the transistor (BJTN) is represented as a model in the circuit file, since there is no primitive element for a BJTN transistor in SPICE. This particular transistor model is an *ideal model*, meaning that it can be used to represent many different NPN BJT diode transistors. An ideal model was used in the demonstration circuit to help

```
AKTP2
*SPICE_NET
.AC DEC 50 100HZ 100KHZ
.PRINT AC VDB(4) OUTPUT_PHASE
.CONTROL
OP
SAVE ALL ALLCUR
ALIAS OUTPUT_PHASE PH(V(4))*1
.ENDC
*ALIAS  V(4)=OUTPUT
.PRINT AC  V(4)  VP(4)
R2 2 3 10K
C1 2 4 39N
C2 3 0 10N
Q1 5 3 4 BJTN
.MODEL BJTN NPN
R3 4 6 10K
V1 5 0 10V
V2 6 0 -10V
V3 1 0 AC 1
R1 1 2 10K
.END
```

Figure 12-3
SPICE circuit file generated by the SpiceNet program.

keep things simple; for more acurate simulation, you will probably want to use more accurate models that represent specific devices. These device-specific models are usually provided (either by the simulation vendor or by a component vendor) in the form of SPICE model libraries.

Models libraries very important for doing large-scale analog simulations. Since there are literally thousands of discrete components available today, it is important to have access to a large number of high-quality simulation models. Comprehensive model libraries are therefore one of the key factors that distinguish the higher-capability (and higher cost) analog simulators from lower-cost educational tools.

Invoking the IsSpice Simulator

With the schematic loaded and ready to go and a circuit file generated, you can invoke the IsSpice simulator to analyze the design. You can do this by either returning to the main application window and launching IsSpice or by selecting the **Simulate** item from the **Actions** menu.

1. Return to the main ICAP/4 application window and click on the **Launch IsSpice** icon, *or* select **Simulate** from the SpiceNet **Actions** menu.

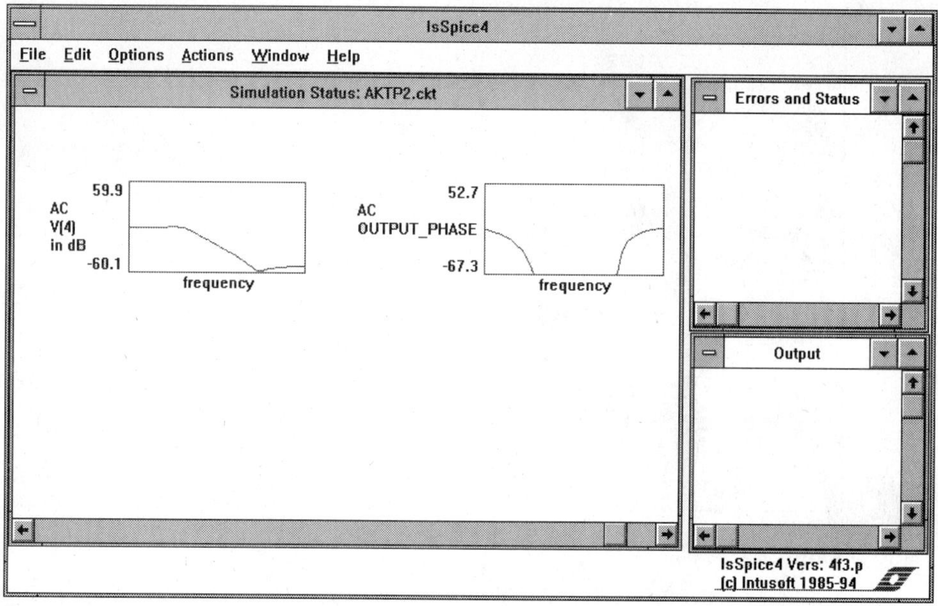

Figure 12-4
IsSpice simulator display.

When the simulator is invoked, it reads the circuit file, builds the circuit from the netlist information, and calculates the values on each node for the entire circuit. The initial display is created (based on the **.PRINT** statements in the circuit file) and appears as shown in Figure 12-4.

The Simulation Display

The window containing the two waveforms is called the real time display, and shows the values of circuit nodes as they are simulated. Two smaller windows display error status messages and textual output (for capturing data during interactive simulation), and a large floating window (Figure 12-5) is provided for controlling simulation flow, specifying additional stimulus data, and accessing previously generated simulation data.

The initial simulation you will perform is an AC test, as indicated in the **Mode** section of the simulation control panel. The **Start**, **Pause**, **Resume** and **Abort** buttons can be used to re-run the simulation at any time, and to stop it at any point to examine intermediate results. (For a small circuit like this one, the simulation may run too fast to allow you to pause it midrun.) To begin the simulation,

1. Click on the **Start** button in the Simulation Control window.

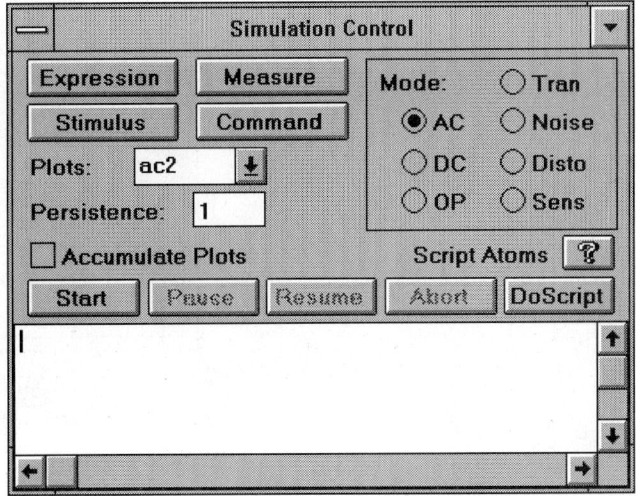

Figure 12-5
The IsSpice Simulation Control window.

The simulation will begin, and the waveforms will update as the simulation progresses.

Waveform Scaling

Depending on how the program has been set up, the waveforms displayed in the initial real time display may not be scaled the way you want them. To correct this, the program includes a waveform scaling function that is accessed by double-clicking on a waveform.

1. Double-click on the left-most waveform display. A dialogue box appears that lets you enter a new base (bottom) value for the waveform and a total height.

2. To have the waveform automatically scaled to fit, select the **Auto** button as shown in Figure 12-6.

3. Repeat the above procedure to scale the remaining waveform.

Adding Waveforms

To add a new waveform to the real time display, you just double-click in any blank area of the waveform display area. This brings up the same waveform scaling window, but without a node name in the **Node** entry field (Figure 12-7).

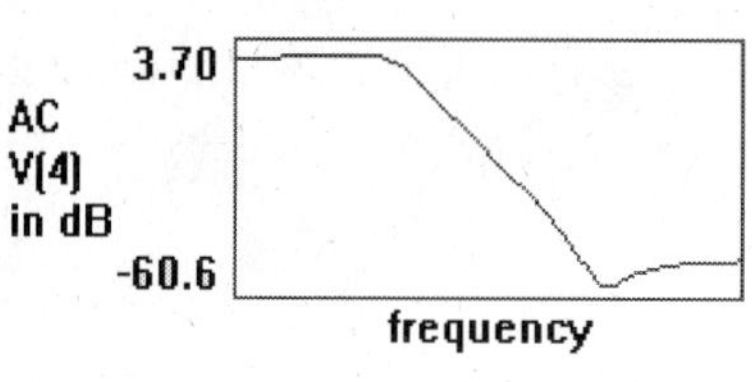

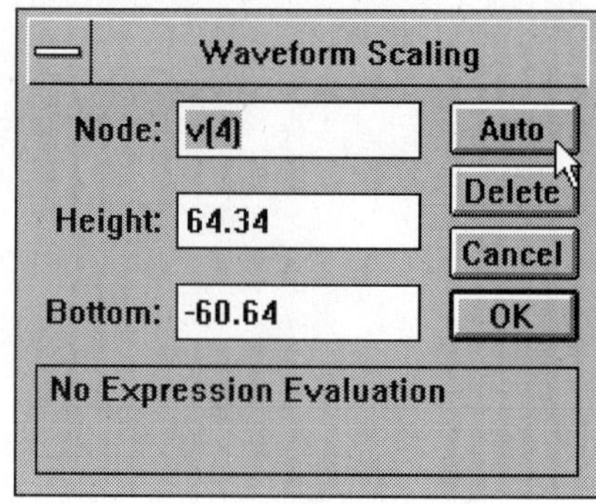

Figure 12-6
Scaling a waveform to fit.

1. Click the mouse button with the cursor in the blank area below the two existing waveforms. The waveform scaling window appears.

2. To add a new node, type in the node name **V(2)**, select appropriate scaling values (or click the **Auto** button), and click **OK**. The new waveform will be added to the display (Figure 12-8).

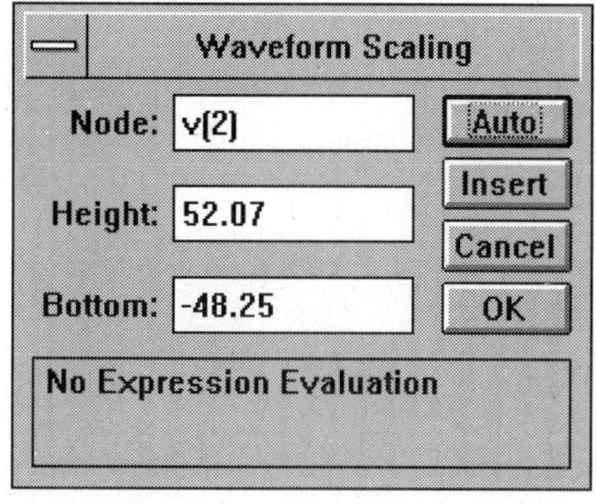

Figure 12-7
To add a new waveform, you double-click on the display area and a scaling dialogue box appears.

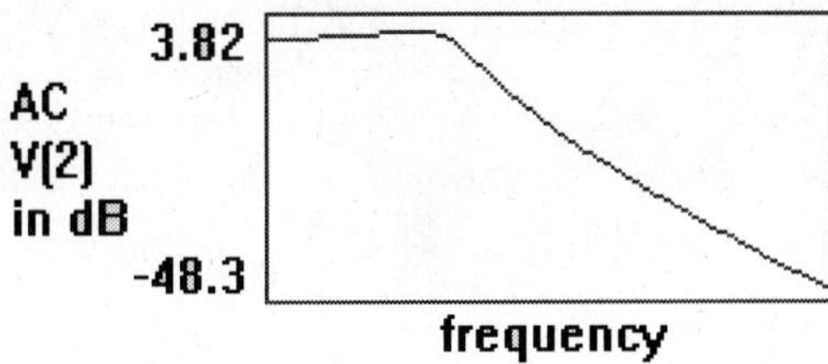

Figure 12-8
The new waveform is added to the display.

Schematic Cross-Probing

ICAP/4 allows simulation results to be viewed not only in the real time display of IsSpice, but directly on the schematic as well. The simulated values of nodes are displayed, and using a feature called *cross-probing*, you can even select nodes and create probes that display the actual waveforms right on the schematic.

To use cross-probing, the IsSpice application must be running while you are viewing the schematic. With the simulator running and the schematic in the foreground,

1. Select the **Probe** option from the **Actions** menu and place a probe on the schematic at the node location shown in Figure 12-9.

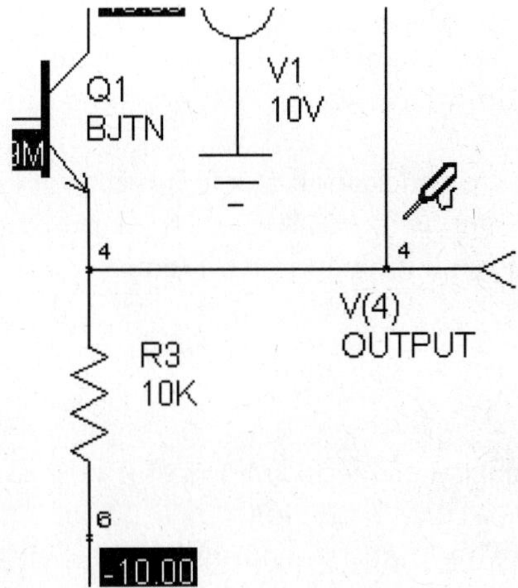

Figure 12-9
Adding a probe to the schematic.

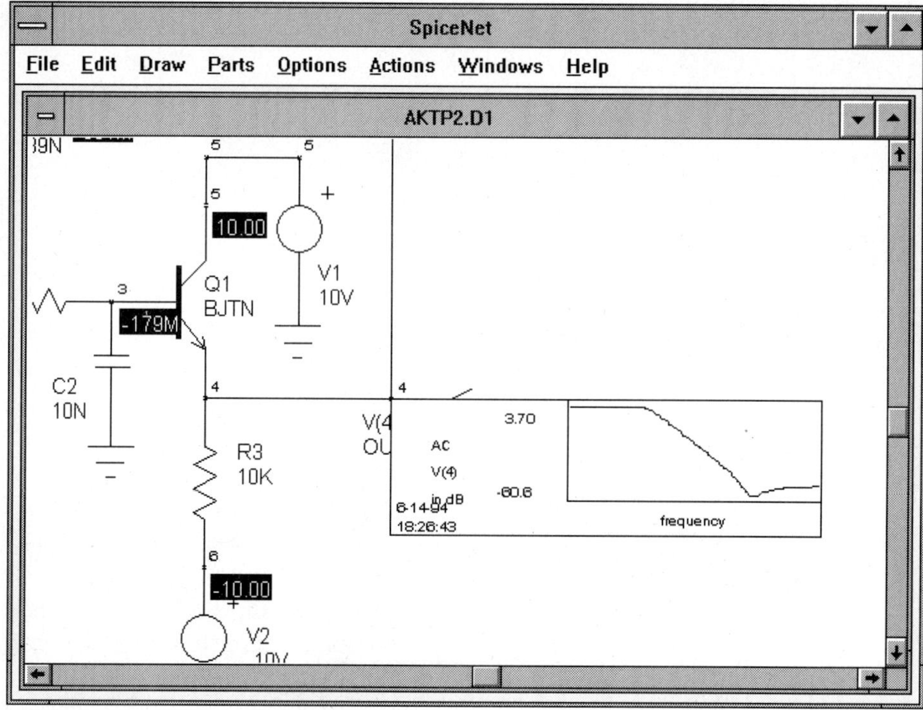

Figure 12-10
Displaying a voltage graph on the schematic.

When you place a probe on the schematic, a waveform display appears on the schematic (Figure 12-10) containing the waveform generated during simulation for that node.

Cross-probing is useful for a quick look at the internal operation of a circuit. The real analysis power, however, is found back in the simulation display, and in the IntuScope application that we'll look at a little later.

Performing Sweeps

As we saw in the previous chapter, sweeps are a useful way to capture data and quickly generate analyses of a circuit's behavior for a range of input conditions and component parameters. IsSpice has many sweeping features, including DC and AC sweeps and parameter sweeps. The display options of the program allow the results of sweeps to be displayed as overlaid graphs, or captured in other forms.

Sweeping Circuit Parameters

Sweeping circuit parameters (such as component values) can be a valuable way to analyze how a circuit will behave when components are out of tolerance, or to "tweak" a design and find the optimum values for components. To analyze this circuit, we'll start by sweeping this circuit with a range of values for the **C2** capacitor.

To view a series of sweeps concurrently, you must first set the persistence value in the Simulation Control window, and then select the component and parameters to sweep:

1. Enter a value of 5 in the **Persistence** field of the Simulation Control window (Figure 12-11). This value will allow you to view five waveforms overlaid on the same waveform display before the graph is erased and redrawn.

2. Click on the Stimulus button in the Simulation Control window. A Stimulus Picker window will appear.

You are now going to sweep the capacitor value for component **C2**, and watch what happens in the waveform window.

3. In the Stimulus Picker window, select the component **C2**, then click on the capacitance parameter in the rightmost list box (Figure 12-12).

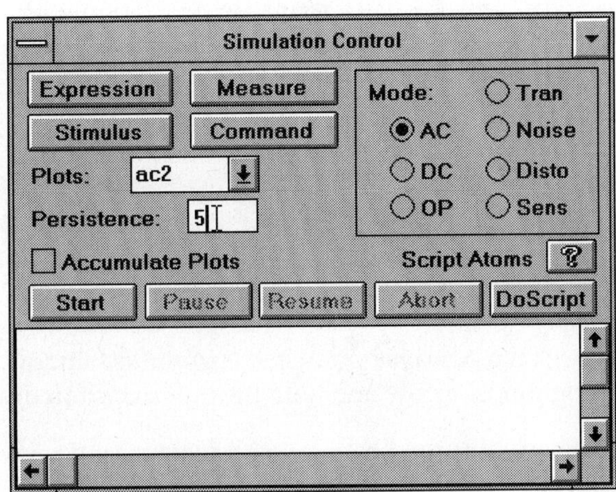

Figure 12-11
Setting the persistence value.

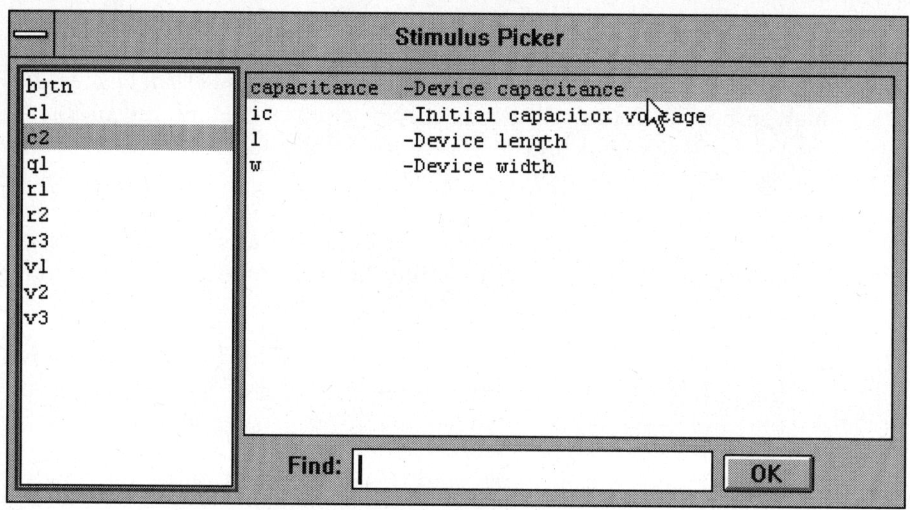

Figure 12-12
The stimulus picker dialogue box.

4. Close the Stimulus Picker window by clicking on **OK**. At this point, a stimulus dialogue box appears (Figure 12-13).

The stimulus window for **c2:capacitance** has a sequence of arrows that increase in size from the center of the sequence to the largest arrows on the outsides. These arrows provide a quick way to rerun the simulation with increasing or decreasing values. (The bigger the arrow, the more the value changes.) Alternately, you can enter a new value directly in the parameter value field.

5. Place the mouse cursor on the rightmost (largest) arrow and click once. Note that the value has changed.

6. To rerun the simulation with the new value, click on the **Set** button. The simulation is rerun and a new waveform is added to the waveform (Figure 12-14).

7. Now check the **Always** option in the stimulus window. Place the mouse cursor on the rightmost arrow and hold the mouse button down.

The simulation will run repeatedly with increasing parameter values. Experiment with the different stimulus change arrows and watch the results in the waveform display.

8. Reset the capacitance parameter of **C2** back to its original value by clicking on the **Revert** button before exiting the Stimulus Picker window.

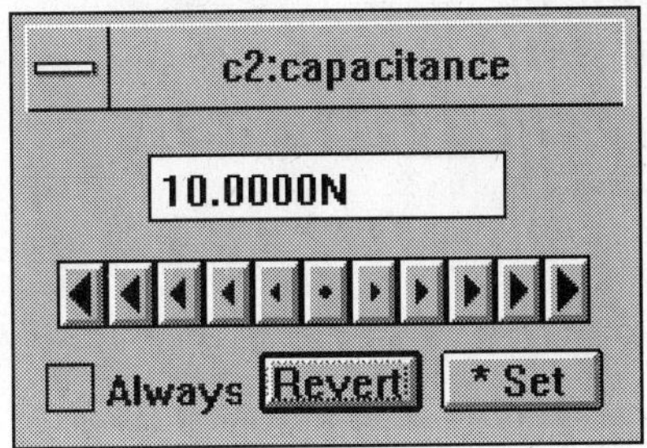

Figure 12-13
The stimulus dialogue.

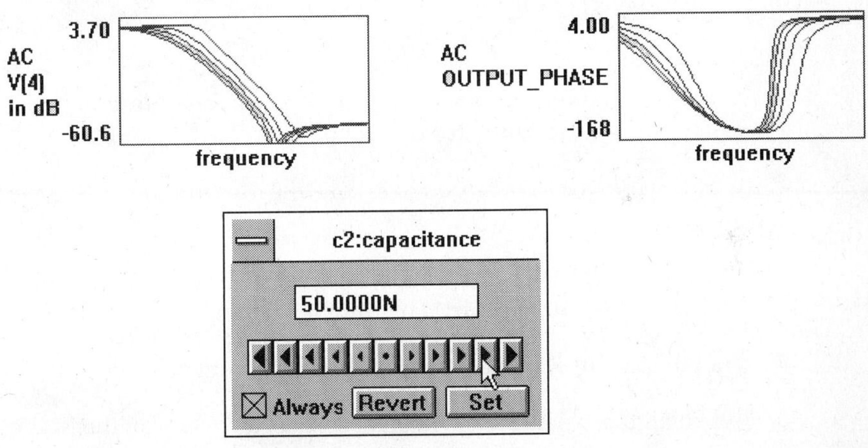

Figure 12-14
Multiple waveforms representing different stimulus values are graphed in the display window.

Viewing Operating Point Changes

Next, you'll combine the interactive stimulus that you just performed with the interactive measurements used earlier to thoroughly evaluate the operating point of the circuit for changing conditions.

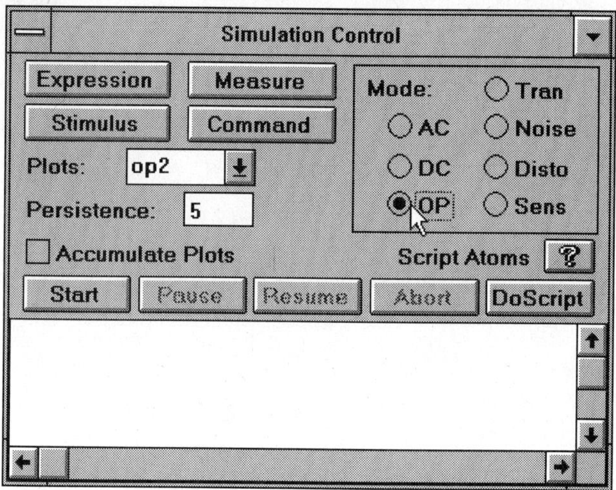

Figure 12-15
Setting the operating point option.

1. Change the analysis mode of the simulator to **Operating Point** by selecting the **OP** button on the simulator control panel (Figure 12-15).
2. Click on the **Measure** button to invoke the Measurements dialogue box (Figure 12-16).
3. For component **Q1**, select the **ib- current at base node**, **P-power dissipation**, and **vbe- B-E voltage** entries by double-clicking.
4. For component **R3**, select the **p - Device power** entry.
5. When all these parameters have been selected, click on the **Make** button.
6. Click on the **Stimulus** button in the simulator control panel.
7. Select component **R3** and click on the **resistance** entry, then click **OK**.
8. Select the **Always** option, then change the value of the resistance as shown in Figure 12-17.

As you change the value of **R3**'s resistance, you can see the values of the operating point for each selected parameter get updated in the Measurement dialogue box (Figure 12-18).

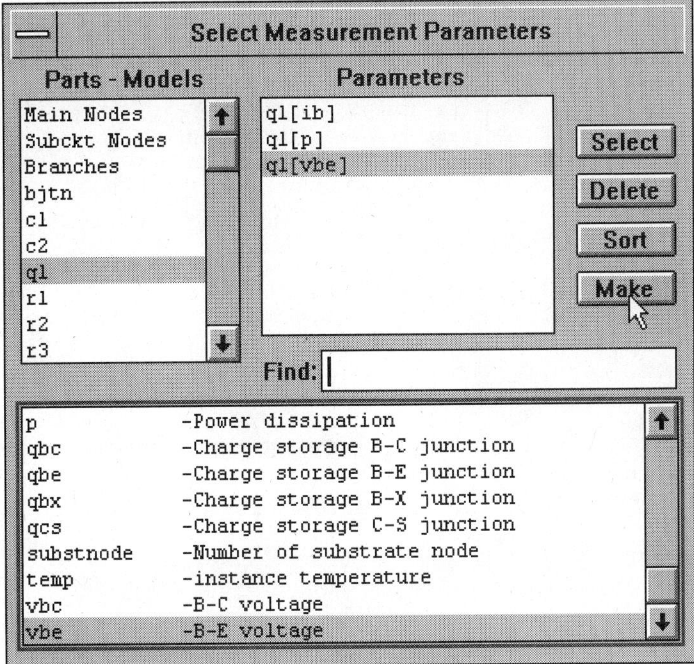

Figure 12-16
Each component has a number of parameters that can be measured or modified.

9. Reset the parameters back to their original values by clicking on the **Revert** button before exiting the Stimulus Picker window. Click the **Set** button and close the stimulus window.

Other Sweeping Options

There are many types of sweeps that you might want to perform on a circuit, and the preceding examples have touched on only the most basic sweeping operations. Interactive sweeps such as this are good for performing a quick analysis of a circuit for a small number of parameters or values, but more complex sweeps may require that arithmetic expressions be used to define values, or the complete sweep may require a long series of test cases and parameter changes. For these types of sweeps, it is often more useful to describe the sweep directly in the circuit file (as a set of SPICE statements) or by using a scripting language.

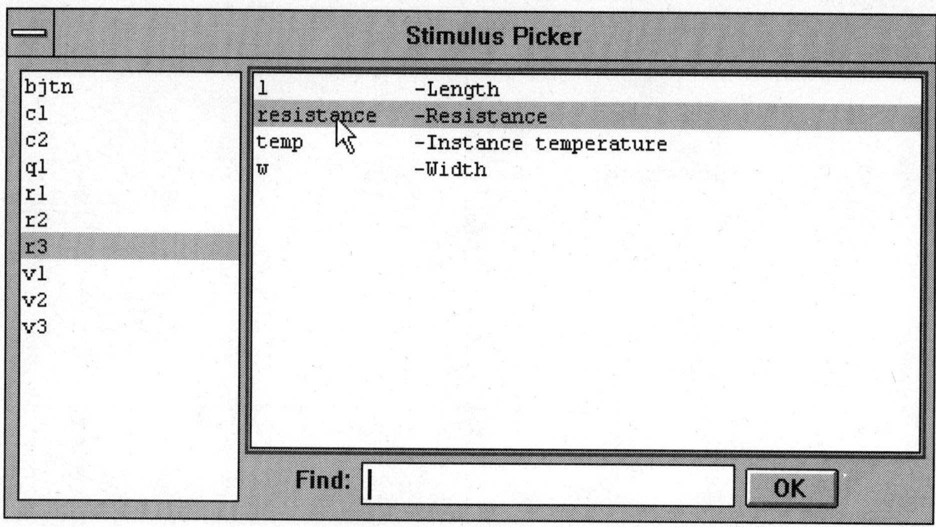

Figure 12-17
Selecting the resistance value for a component.

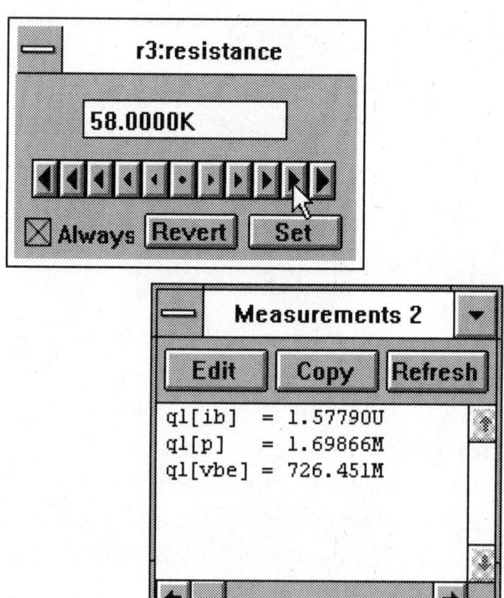

Figure 12-18
By changing the resistance value of a component, you can view the operating point for each selected parameter.

Scripting

IsSpice provides a script language (called *Interactive Command Language*, or *ICL*) that is useful for defining complex or lengthy circuit stimulus and analyses, and for generating large sweeps. Scripts can be entered in ASCII files and invoked, or can be typed directly into the Script Window of the simulator control panel and executed immediately (Figure 12-19).

Figure 12-20 shows the script language being used interactively to set up and run a noise analysis for the low-pass filter circuit. The three statements create waveforms for the analysis and invoke the noise analysis function with respect to **v(3)**.

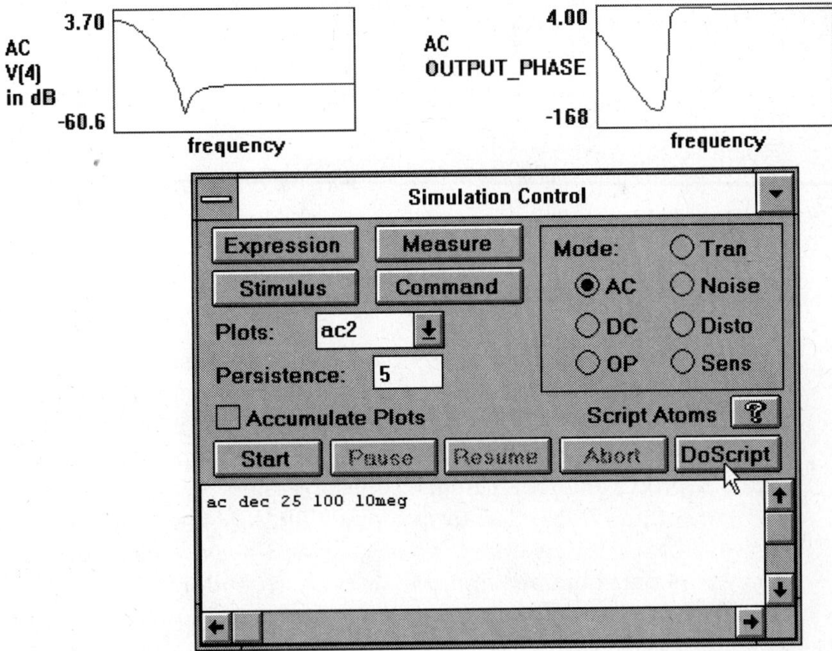

Figure 12-19
Using the script language to set up a sweep.

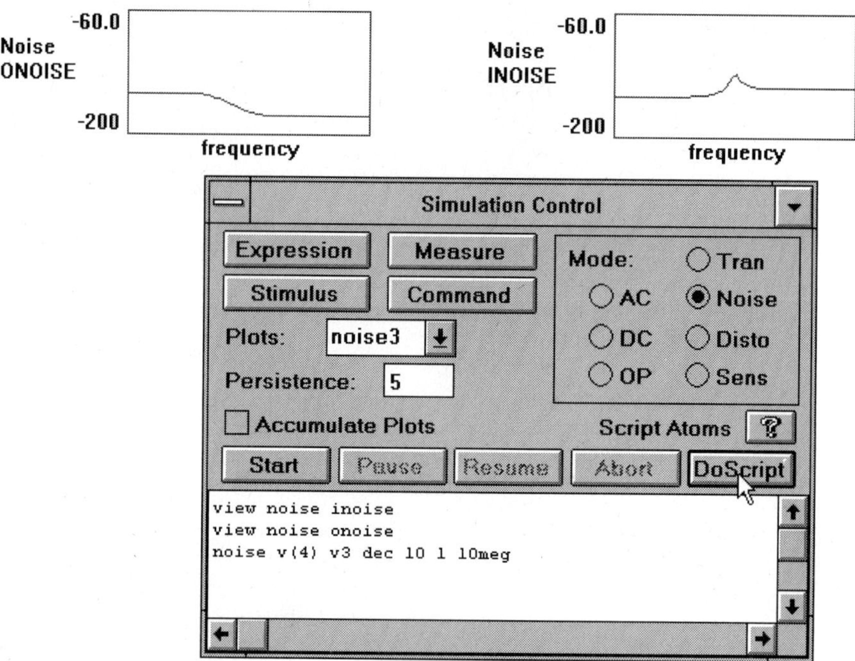

Figure 12-20
Using the script language to analyze noise characteristics of a circuit.

Waveform Analysis

While the ICAP/4 simulator, IsSpice, provides quite a lot of power for interactive circuit analysis, there are times when additional analysis must be performed on circuits that can only be done after the data has been collected. Analyzing tabular and waveform data for statistical purposes is a common task for analog designers, and postprocessing tools can make the job easier.

Intusoft provides an analysis tool with ICAP/4 that can help with the analysis of waveform data generated by IsSpice, and is an integral part of the statistical analysis of data obtained from Monte Carlo (pseudorandom) tests.

The features of this tool (IntuScope, shown in Figure 12-21) are too detailed and complex to cover here; the tool provides many features to assist in the analysis of one or more waveforms, and to analyze relationships between waveforms. IntuScope even includes a specialized calculator for detailed manual analysis work.

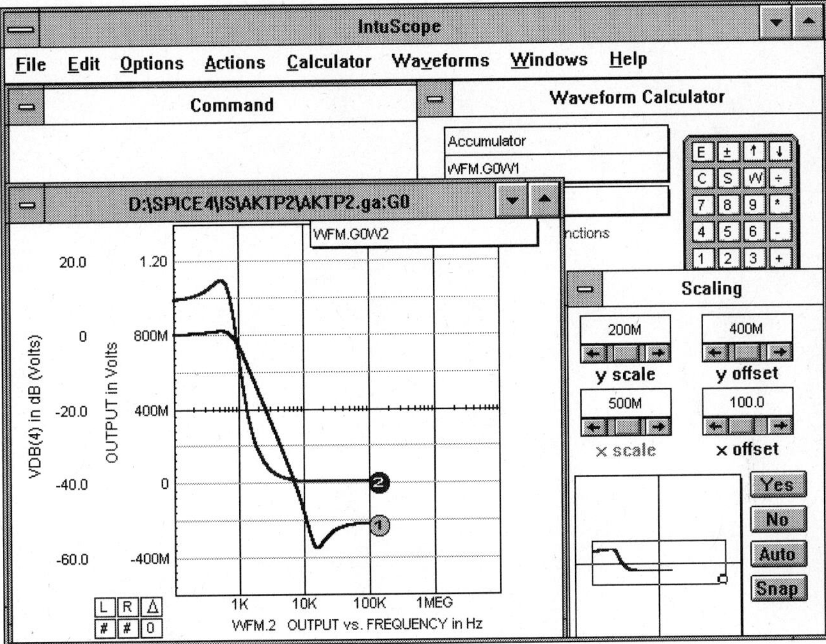

Figure 12-21
The IntuScope analysis tool can be used to perform advanced analyses of waveforms.

Moving On

This tutorial concludes our look at analog simulation. For more complete information on the design tools and techniques, you are encouraged to contact the vendors of analog design tools listed in Appendix A.

CHAPTER 13

FOCUS ON TECHNOLOGY: HARDWARE DESCRIPTION LANGUAGES

Hardware description languages are becoming increasing popular as a way to capture complex designs in a form that is conscise, understandable, and portable. Designs that are captured using HDLs can be easily simulated, are more likely to be synthesizable into multiple technologies, and can be archived for later modification and reuse.

What Is An HDL?

An HDL is a programming language that is intended for the specification of hardware or, more precisely, for specification of the *observable behavior* of hardware. Like high-level software programming languages (such as C, C++, or Pascal), HDLs have features that allow designs to be entered in a modular fashion, and are ideal for designs that will be developed in team environments. HDLs differ from software programming languages in that they are primarily intended to describe systems that have a high level of *concurrency*—systems that are parallel rather than sequential.

VHDL and Verilog HDL

The two predominant HDLs in use today are VHDL and Verilog HDL. (PLD languages such as ABEL, CUPL, and PALASM can also be considered HDLs, and these languages are described in detail in a later chapter.) VHDL and Verilog HDL each provide similar features and can be used for the same basic applications: digital systems design.

An HDL can be used to completely describe a design, or a schematic or some other graphic representation can be used in concert with an HDL to completely specify the system. Hierarchy features provided in both VHDL and Verilog HDL make it possible to mix alternate circuit representations in a large design as needed.

Multiple Levels of Abstraction

The primary benefit of an HDL-based approach to design is that the *level of abstraction* is raised. Rather than designing at the level of transistors, logic gates or other lower-level primitives, you can can design at a higher-level, working directly from a circuit specification. The most efficient level of abstraction will vary from project to project, and HDLs provide features that allow you to describe your circuit at very high levels, or closer to the physical implementation (Figure 13-1).

There are three primary levels of abstraction that are used in HDL-based design. At the lowest level are designs expressed as a structural representation: transistors, gate-level primitives, and other fixed-function components that are connected using a netlistlike representation. The use of structure in a design doesn't necessarily mean that the design is not abstract, however; structural HDL may also be used to connect higher-level components that are themselves described at a higher level of abstraction.

At the next higher level of abstraction, *data flow*, you will find designs that are described using common datapath elements such as comparators, multiplexers, adders and register elements such as flip-flops and latches. This level of abstraction is sometimes refered to as RTL, for register transfer logic. RTL design methods assume that the designer of the circuit has an understanding of the registers used in the system, and is describing the combinational logic that moves data between those registers. As we will see in the next chapter, most synthesis tools being sold today operate on designs that are described at the data flow level of abstraction.

The highest level of abstraction is called *behavioral*, and is typically used for writing HDL models for simulation, rather than for synthesis. A behavioral description differs from a data flow or structural description in that the hardware—specifically the registered portions of the hardware—are implied by the design description, rather then being specified. To describe a registered (sequential) circuit, a behavioral HDL description describes how the circuit operates *over time*, given various input stimulus.

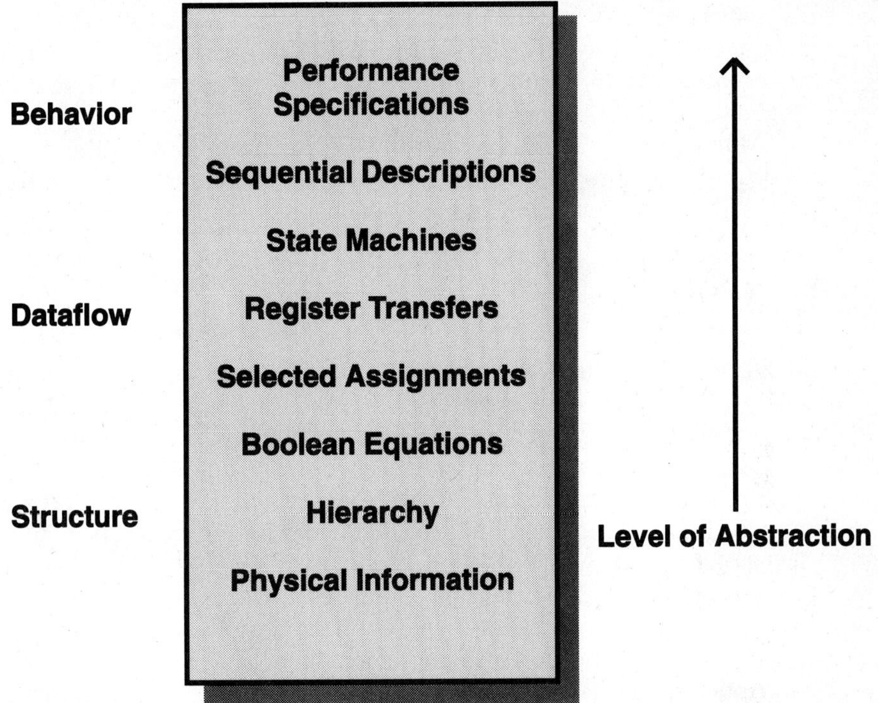

Figure 13-1
HDLs allow designs to be described at varying levels of abstraction.

Where Can HDLs Be Applied?

While there are proposals in existence for a standard HDL for analog circuit design, the primary purpose of today's HDLs is for digital system design. As such, HDLs can be directly applied to the areas of

- Digital system design capture
- Modeling for digital simulation
- Automatic synthesis of digital circuits
- System-level and device-level testing
- Documentation and configuration management

In addition to their use as design capture languages—languages used for design entry—HDLs have also been used, with increasing frequency, as a replacement for proprietary and standard netlist languages, and as a replacement for proprietary simulation model or stimulus and control languages. In fact, it is not unusual to find design tools that use VHDL or Verilog HDL as the primary underlying data format (for both netlists and simulation models) even without supporting either of these languages as a design entry option.

Although these additional uses of HDLs are important, in this book I'm going to focus on the more visible aspects of HDL use. I'll be showing how HDLs are used for design entry, simulation and, in later chapters, synthesis.

VHDL History

VHDL (VHSIC hardware description language; how's that for a nested abbreviation?) was developed in the early 1980s as a spin-off of a high-speed integrated circuit research project funded by the U.S. Department of Defense. During the VHSIC program, researchers were confronted with the daunting task of describing circuits of enormous scale (for their time). With only gate-level design tools available, it soon became clear that better design methods would need to be developed.

To meet this challenge, a team of engineers from three companies—IBM, Texas Instruments and Intermetrics—were contracted by the Department of Defense to complete the specification and implementation of a new, language-based design description method. The first publicly available version of VHDL, version 7.2, was made available in 1985. In 1986, the IEEE was presented with a proposal to standardize the language, which it did in 1987 after substantial enhancements and modifications were made by a team of commercial, government and academic representatives. The resulting standard, IEEE 1076-1987, is the basis for virtually every VHDL simulation and synthesis product sold today. An enhanced and updated version of the language specification, IEEE 1076-1993, has recently been released, and VHDL tool vendors have been responding by adding these new language features to their products.

So Many Standards, So Little Time

Although IEEE 1076-1987 (or the newer IEEE 1076-1993) defines the complete VHDL language, there are aspects of the language that make it difficult to write completely portable designs (designs that can be simulated identically, for example, using different vendors' tools). The problem stems from the fact that VHDL supports many different abstract data types, but does not address the simple problem of characterizing different signal strengths or commonly used simulation conditions such as unknowns and high impedence states. Soon after IEEE 1076-1987 was adopted, simulator companies began enhancing VHDL with new signal types (typically through the use of syntactically legal, but nonstandard enumerated types) to allow their customers to accurately simulate complex electronic circuits. This caused problems because designs entered using one simulator were often incompatible with other simulation environments. VHDL was quickly becoming a nonstandard.

IEEE 1164: Standardized VHDL Data Types

To get around this problem, another standard was pushed through the IEEE. This standard, IEEE 1164, defines a standard *package* (a VHDL feature that allows commonly used declarations to be collected in an external library) containing definitions for a standard nine-valued data type. This standard data type is called *std_logic*, and the IEEE 1164 package is often referred to as the standard logic package, or MVL9 (for multivalued logic, nine-values).

The combination of IEEE 1076-1987 and IEEE 1164 form the complete VHDL standard in widest use today. Sometime soon you should expect to see the IEEE 1164 and 1076-1993 standards merged into a "grand unified standard" VHDL. But don't hold your breath; IEEE 1076-1993 (finally released to the public at the start of 1994) was originally to be named the IEEE 1076-1992 specification. So it goes.

Verilog HDL History

The Verilog hardware description language was first introduced by Gateway Design Automation in 1985. The new language was a departure from the gate-oriented simulation modeling languages of the past and allowed the same format to be used for specifying the simulation model and the test environment. This new language was a primary factor in the success of Gateway's simulation products and caught the attention of the industry.

Verilog: The De Facto Standard for ASIC Modeling

Verilog was quickly accepted by leading-edge simulator users, and soon became a de facto standard modeling language for ASICs. ASIC vendors were soon providing Verilog libraries for their customers, and the 1988 release of Verilog became, in essence, the industry standard simulator used by ASIC companies and ASIC users alike.

Another key factor in the acceptance of Verilog among ASIC users was its use in the Synopsys logic synthesis products. Verilog is a good language for writing synthesizable descriptions of circuits, and the combination of the Verilog language and Synopsys synthesis was (and remains) a powerful combination.

The next step in the evolution of Verilog was the 1989 merger of Gateway Design Automation with Cadence Design Systems. This merger, and a later merger of Cadence and another major EDA vendor, Valid, indirectly resulted in the opening up of the Verilog language as a standard. A major factor in the decision by Cadence to promote an open Verilog was the increasing popularity of VHDL, which threatened to replace Verilog in the industry. Although VHDL was not widely used for ASIC modeling, the fact that it was a standard language endorsed by the IEEE and required by the Department of Defense made it clear that the Verilog language would have to be placed in the public domain and standardized in order to compete.

Open Verilog International

In May 1990, Open Verilog International (OVI) was formed as an independent organization dedicated to the promotion of the Verilog language and Verilog-related technologies. OVI has since published a number of important standards documents, including the OVI Verilog Language Reference Manual, the Programming Language Interface (PLI) specification, and the specification for the Standard Delay Format (SDF). The new standard, while not endorsed by the IEEE or any other traditional standards organization, has made it possible for many small companies to compete in the Verilog HDL simulation and synthesis marketplaces. This recent activity has also led to an increase in activity in the VHDL community, where there are now efforts underway to incorporate standards such as SDF, and to resolve the disparities between the features available in the two languages.

VHDL and Verilog HDL provide an interesting comparison between a language designed by commitee, under government contract, and one created commercially, by a small group of dedicated (and profit-motivated) engineers. Although VHDL has more features useful for large projects (such as its many useful features for configuration management), it is actually inferior in many respects to Verilog HDL, which was able to advance more quickly in response to customer needs, without the tedious commitee meetings and balloting processes that were required to improve VHDL. It remains to be seen, of course, how the two languages will evolve in the future, under similar standards-derived constraints.

The HDL Wars: Are They Over?

Not likely. Although broad-line EDA companies, and even some smaller simulation and synthesis vendors, have seen the light and are providing solutions that address the needs of both VHDL and Verilog users, there are still design tool vendors and other long-time VHDL or Verilog language supporters who consider any challenge to their beliefs worth fighting over. And why shouldn't they? Many of the companies peddling HDL-based tools have invested (*gambled* might be a better word) millions of dollars in tools and applications oriented toward one of these languages. The cost of adding a second language is enormous, both in terms of the technology required and in terms of the user education. (There is also a public relations cost that can be involved: when Viewlogic Corporation, a long-time champion of VHDL, purchased Chronologic Simulation, a maker of Verilog-based simulation tools, there were many grins and comments of "I told you so" among members of the Verilog community.)

But is all the debate necessarily bad? I don't think so; competition, after all, has resulted in advancements in both languages. It is unlikely that the Verilog language would have been placed in the hands of the EDA public by Cadence without the threat of a VHDL takeover. And it is also unlikely that the VITAL initiative (which has been dubbed "the initiative to steal Verilog models" by at least one observer) would have moved forward so quickly without the threat of Verilog becoming the defacto standard—if it isn't already—for ASIC timing models.

How should you, as an EDA user, respond to the rantings of EDA "language bigots"? It's easy: just ignore them. Select your design tools based on important features such as synthesis support for the devices you will use, on the availability of simulation tools and simulation models, and on overall speed and cost.

Whatever you do, don't base your decision simply on which language looks easist to write (both are easy to learn but hard to master) or rely exclusively on the opinions of someone (or some company) who may have little or no experience with the alternate language. Choose your tools based on what they can do, then use whichever language is supported by the tools that you have selected.

Moving On

In this chapter, I have presented the basic concepts of HDLs, and have described in general terms where HDLs fit into the design process. In the next two chapters, you will learn more about VHDL and Verilog HDL and will see how these languages are used to enter and simulate designs.

In the later chapters, I'm going to continue discussing HDLs and show how they fit into the world of synthesis.

Other Resources

Armstrong, James R. and F. Gail Gray, *Structured Logic Design with VHDL*, Prentice Hall, Englewood Cliffs, NJ, 1993.

Berge, Jean-Michel, Alain Fonkoua, et al., *VHDL '92*, Kluwer Academic, Hingham, MA, 1992.

Bhasker, Jayaram, *A VHDL Primer*, Prentice Hall, Englewood Cliffs, NJ, 1992.

Bhasker, Jayaram, *The VHDL Primer Revised*, Prentice Hall, Englewood Cliffs, NJ, 1995.

Carlson, Steve, *Introduction to HDL-basedDesign Using VHDL*, Synopsis, Inc., Mountain View, CA, 1990.

Lipsett, Roger, Carl Schaeffer and Cary Ussery, *VHDL: Hardware Description and Design*, Kluwer Academic, Hingham, MA, 1989.

Perry, Douglas L., *VHDL (second edition)*, McGraw-Hill, New York, NY, 1993.

Sternheim, Singh, Trivedi, Madhavan, Stapleton, *Digital Design and Synthesis With Verilog HDL*, Automata, San Jose, CA, 1992.

Thomas, D. and P. Moorby, *The Verilog Hardware Description Language*, Kluwer Academic, Hingham, MA, 1992.

Standards Documents

The VHDL standards documents (IEEE standards 1076-1987 and 1076-1993, and IEEE standard 1164) can be obtained from the IEEE at

IEEE Computer Society Press
IEEE Service Center
445 Hoes Lane
P.O. Box 1331
Piscataway, NJ 08855-1331
(800) 678-IEEE
(908) 981-9667 fax

The Verilog Language Reference Manual, Programming Language Interface (PLI) manual and Standard Delay Format (SDF) manual are all available from Open Verilog International. Contact OVI directly for more information at

Open Verilog International
15466 Los Gatos Blvd.
Suite 109-071
Los Gatos, CA 95032
(408) 353-8899
(408) 353-8869 fax
ovi@netcom.com

HDL User Groups

The following two groups have been formed to promote their respective languages, and to provide forums for HDL users and industry representatives to exchange information. Both organizations publish regular newsletters, and hold conferences periodically.

Open Verilog International
15466 Los Gatos Blvd.
Suite 109-071
Los Gatos, CA 95032
(408) 353-8899
(408) 353-8869 fax
ovi@netcom.com

VHDL International
407 Chester Street
Menlo Park, CA 94025
(800) 554-2550
(415) 329-0758
(401) 324-3150 fax

CHAPTER 14

HANDS-ON EDA: USING VHDL SIMULATION

To help you understand where HDLs fit into the design process, I'll walk through a design session in which a small circuit is entered and simulated using VHDL. In the chapter that follows, I'll show how the same design can be entered and simulated using Verilog HDL.

VHDL: A First Look

VHDL is a large and complex language, so I'm not going to attempt to present all aspects of the language in this chapter. Instead, I'm going to introduce some of the more important concepts of the language, and present a few simple examples. (I'll be presenting somewhat more complex examples in a later chapter, when I describe VHDL synthesis.)

Perhaps the most important concepts to understand in VHDL (and Verilog HDL, for that matter) are the concepts of *concurrency* and *hierarchy*. Since these topics are so important, I'm going to be introducing both concepts in the design examples I present. First, though, let's look at a simple, nonhierarchical VHDL design file, and see what a minimal VHDL source file consists of.

Figure 14-1 shows a simple VHDL design (a shifter/comparator circuit that I'll be describing a bit later) and diagrams the important elements of a VHDL source file. Reading from the top of the VHDL file, we see

- ☐ **Library** and **use** statements that reference an external library (the IEEE 1164 library mentioned in the previous chapter).

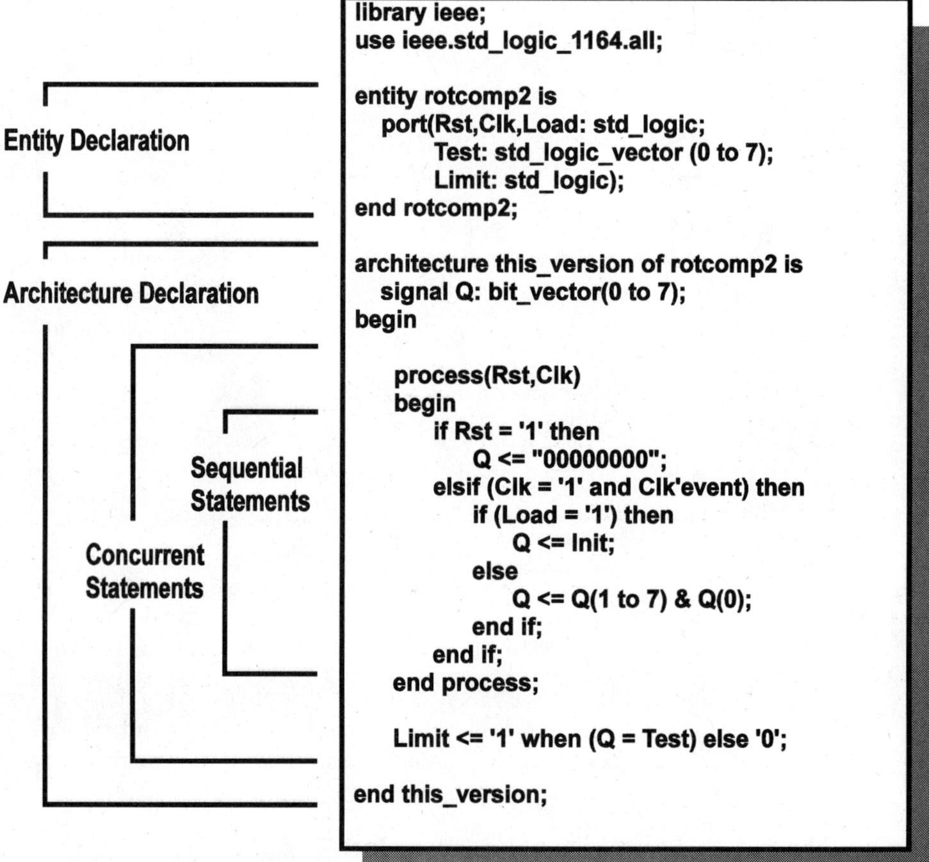

Entity Declaration
Architecture Declaration
Concurrent Statements
Sequential Statements
library ieee;
use ieee.std_logic_1164.all;
entity rotcomp2 is
port(Rst,Clk,Load: std_logic;
Test: std_logic_vector (0 to 7);
Limit: std_logic);
end rotcomp2;
architecture this_version of rotcomp2 is
signal Q: bit_vector(0 to 7);
begin
process(Rst,Clk)
begin
if Rst = '1' then
Q <= "00000000";
elsif (Clk = '1' and Clk'event) then
if (Load = '1') then
Q <= Init;
else
Q <= Q(1 to 7) & Q(0);
end if;
end if;
end process;
Limit <= '1' when (Q = Test) else '0';
end this_version;

Figure 14-1
A minimal VHDL design file consists of an entity declaration, a corresponding architecture declaration, and one or more concurrent statements describing the design's function.

- ☐ An **entity** declaration that defines the inputs and outputs—the ports—of this design
- ☐ An **architecture** declaration that defines what the design actually does, using a combination of sequential and concurrent statements
- ☐ Within the **architecture** declaration, a **process** describing the behavior of the registered (sequential) portion of the design
- ☐ A concurrent signal assignment that defines the operation of the combinational portion of the circuit

Entities and Architectures

Every VHDL design consists of at least one entity/architecture pair. In VHDL, an *entity declaration* describes the circuit as it appears from the "outside"—from the perspective of its input and output interfaces. If you are familiar with schematics, you might think of the entity as being analogous to a block symbol on a schematic.

The second part of a minimal VHDL source file is the *architecture declaration.* Every entity in a VHDL design must be *bound* with a corresponding architecture. The architecture describes the actual function—or contents—of the entity. In the schematic view of things, you can think of the architecture as being roughly analogous to a lower-level schematic that is pointed to by a higher-level functional block symbol.

Within the architecture there are a sequence of statements, some of which I have labeled *sequential,* while the remainder are *concurrent.* Sequential and concurrent are very important concepts to understand when using HDLs: unlike software programming languages (such as C and Pascal) HDLs allow the inherently parallel operation of digital circuits to be precisely described. Concurrency in the language is what makes this possible; every statement in a VHDL architecture declaration can be considered to be operating in parallel—concurrently—and the order in which statements are entered is unimportant. There are exceptions to this, of course; both VHDL and Verilog provide language features that allow inherently sequential behaviors (such as state machine or other sequential circuits) to be described. In VHDL, the language feature that is provided for this is called a **process** statement. Statements within a process statement "execute" in sequence (Figure 14-2) although the process as a whole operates concurrently with other statements in the architecture.

Confused? Don't worry; I'll be presenting examples using both concurrent and sequential VHDL, and you'll soon understand enough about VHDL to get started.

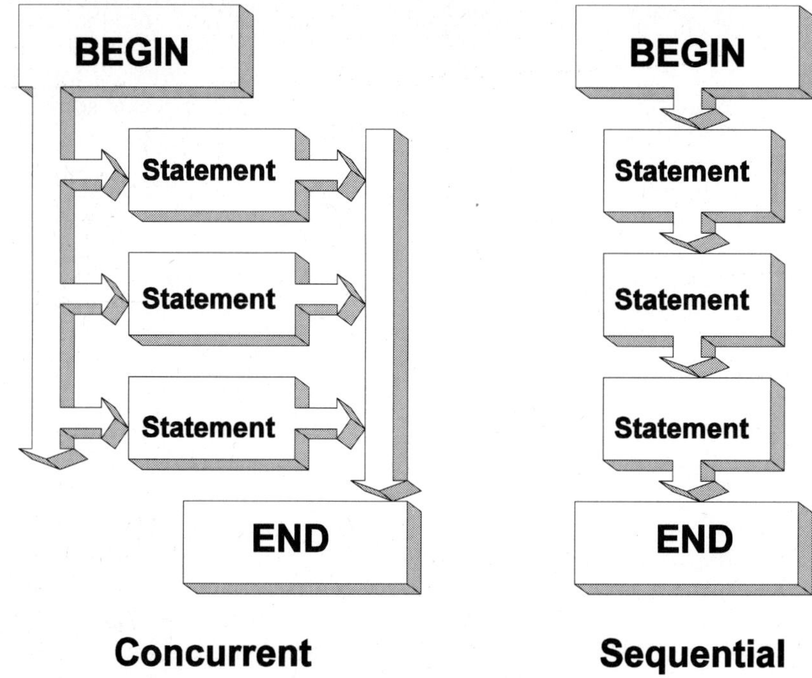

Figure 14-2
Concurrent statements in VHDL "execute" at the same time, while sequential statements (within a process) execute in sequence.

A Sample Circuit

The circuit that we're going to be entering and simulating using VHDL is the barrel shifter coupled with a comparator shown in Figure 14-3. This simple design will help to demonstrate some of the more important aspects of VHDL, and yet is simple enough that lengthy descriptions of its function won't be required. The circuit simply compares an 8-bit input value (**Test**) to another 8-bit value that is stored in a shift register (**Q**) and sets its output to high if the two values are identical. Although small, this circuit is useful because it will allow us to see how both combinational and registed circuits are described in VHDL, and will also allow us to understand the concept of VHDL hierarchy, both in the language itself and in the simulation environment.

Writing Modular Designs

Modularity is an important consideration when you are creating large designs. Designs that are entered using modular design techniques are much easier to develop in a team environment and tend to promote design reuse, because

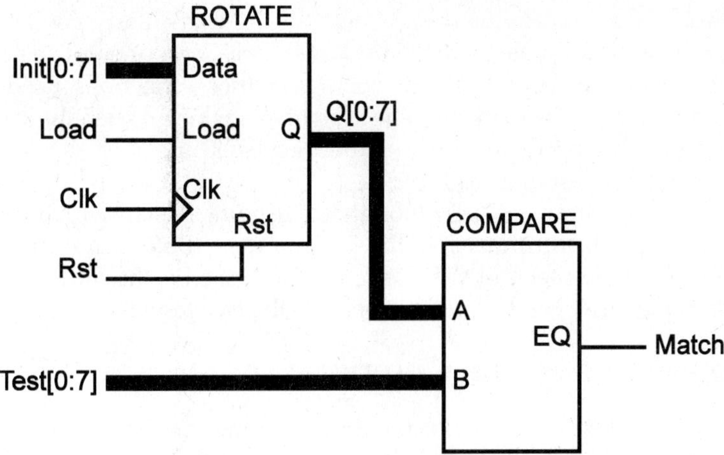

Figure 14-3
The shifter and comparator design.

individual components of a circuit may be applicable in other circuits as well. Modularity can also make a design easier to manage during the simulation and synthesis phases of the design process. The component parts can be simulated individually, and the synthesis step can be performed one piece at a time (this is important for many synthesis tools).

VHDL has many features that allow designs to be entered in a modular fashion. The language supports hierarchy in much the same way hierarchy is supported in schematic editors, and other, more software-oriented modular features (such as procedures and functions) are also provided. The shifter and comparator design that we will be examining could be entered as a single VHDL module (as shown earlier), but we'll enter it as two lower-level VHDL designs to see how the hierarchy features of VHDL work. we'll simulate each of the lower-level components of the design, then combine them using hierarchy and test the complete system. This approach will allow you to see how a modular approach to design is possible using HDLs.

Top-Down Versus Bottom-Up

Of course, the design method I just described—in which lower-level modules are designed first—is not the only way to create a modular design and may not actually be the best way for most projects. Since I will be entering and simulating the lower-level design components (the barrel shifter and comparator) first, I'll be using what's called a *bottom-up* design process. In most large projects, a top-down approach is prefered, in which the top-level system and the interfaces between components in that system are described before the details of each component are worked out. Top-down design methods are particularly good for use with HDLs, because it is possible to model the lower-level components of a sytem at a high level of abstraction (perhaps only including those functions needed for a minimal simulation) while designing the system as a whole. When the system interfaces are completely specified, you can then go back and add detail to the lower-level component descriptions.

For this simple design, though, we're going to start with the simplest of the two lower-level components, the comparator, before moving on to the more complicated aspects of VHDL such as those used in the shifter portion of the design or in the top-level design that connects the two lower-level designs together.

Component 1: The Comparator

The comparator portion of the design (shown in Figure 14-4) is a combinational function that accepts two 8-bit inputs, **A** and **B**, and produces a 1-bit output (**EQ**) indicating whether the two input values were of equal values. To describe this design in VHDL, we first write a specification for the design's interfaces in the form of an entity declaration:

```
LIBRARY ieee;
USE ieee.std_logic_1164.ALL;

ENTITY compare IS
    PORT(a, b: IN std_logic_vector(0 TO 7);
         eq: OUT std_logic);
END compare;
```

This entity declaration corresponds directly to the block diagram of the comparator shown previously and defines the inputs and output for the entity by assigning

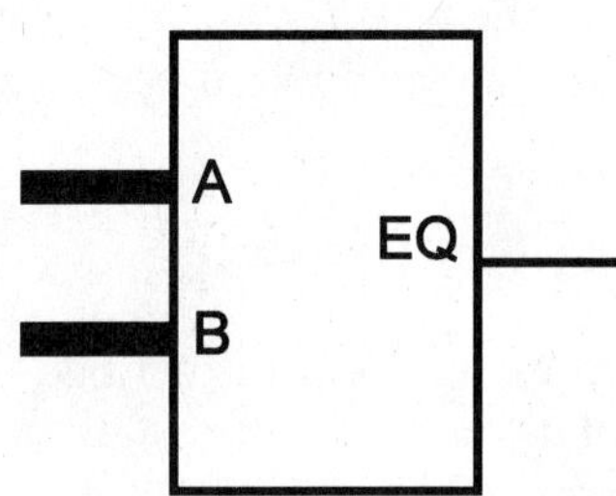

Figure 14-4
The 8-bit comparator.

them names, directions and types. Starting from the top of this source code fragment, we see

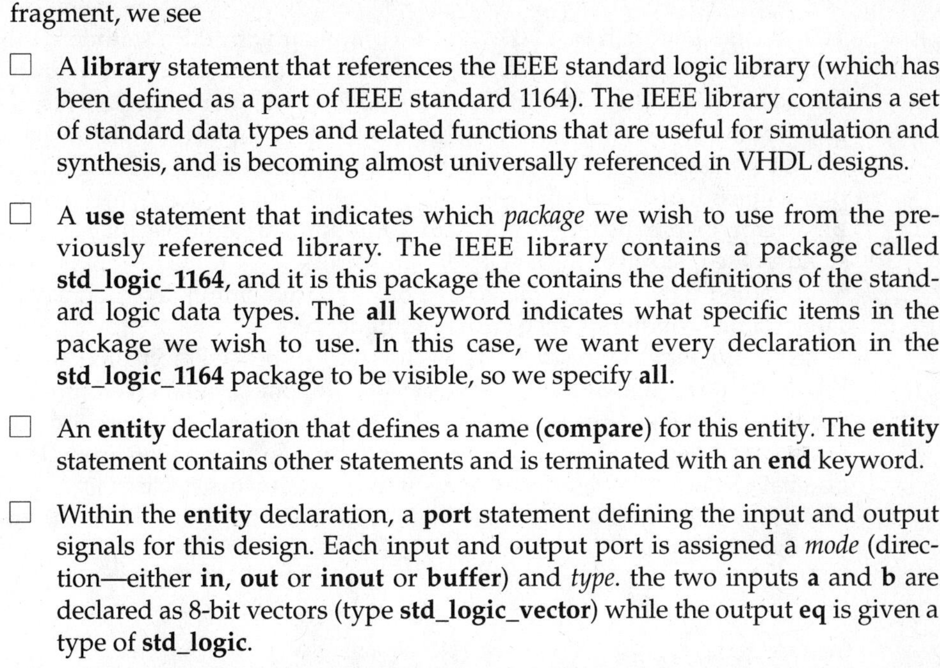

- A **library** statement that references the IEEE standard logic library (which has been defined as a part of IEEE standard 1164). The IEEE library contains a set of standard data types and related functions that are useful for simulation and synthesis, and is becoming almost universally referenced in VHDL designs.

- A **use** statement that indicates which *package* we wish to use from the previously referenced library. The IEEE library contains a package called **std_logic_1164**, and it is this package the contains the definitions of the standard logic data types. The **all** keyword indicates what specific items in the package we wish to use. In this case, we want every declaration in the **std_logic_1164** package to be visible, so we specify **all**.

- An **entity** declaration that defines a name (**compare**) for this entity. The **entity** statement contains other statements and is terminated with an **end** keyword.

- Within the **entity** declaration, a **port** statement defining the input and output signals for this design. Each input and output port is assigned a *mode* (direction—either **in**, **out** or **inout** or **buffer**) and *type*. the two inputs **a** and **b** are declared as 8-bit vectors (type **std_logic_vector**) while the output **eq** is given a type of **std_logic**.

As you can see from this simple entity declaration, VHDL can be a little verbose. But don't worry; you will soon catch on to the syntax, and you might even begin to appreciate the power of the language. For now, though, to help you read this and other VHDL source listings in this chapter, I will enter the designs using all lowercase characters and highlight the VHDL keywords with uppercase characters. This should make it easier to understand the purpose of each statement.

VHDL Data Types

Before moving on to discuss the internal workings of the comparator, let's take a moment to discuss VHDL data types. Like a high-level programming language (but unlike most PLD-oriented languages) VHDL allows data to be described in terms of high-level data types. These data types can represent individual wires in a circuit (normally using type **bit** or type **std_logic**) or can represent collections of wires (type **bit_vector** or **std_logic_vector**). In addition to these hardware-oriented data types, VHDL also includes more abstract data representations, such as integers, characters, real numbers, and records. VHDL even allows you to define your own data types, using what are called *enumerated types*. All these different data types can seem confusing at first, but they begin to make much more sense when you start to work with them.

The Std_logic Data Type

This design is written in VHDL that is compliant with IEEE statndard 1076-1987, and uses the **std_logic** and **std_logic_vector** data types defined in a later standard—IEEE 1164. The IEEE 1164 standard was developed in response to a growing need for a data type that would represent a signal (or group of signals) that could be of multiple values for simulation purposes instead of being limited to the two values (0 and 1) of the existing data types for signals, which were **bit** and **bit_vector**. Before the nine-valued **std_logic** and **std_logic_vector** data types were standardized, simulation developers and users were forced to invent their own multivalued data types to make use of advanced simulation techniques and to model signal conditions such as high impedence.

The **std_logic** and **std_logic_vector** data types were created to solve this problem, and to allow VHDL designs written for one simulation environment to be transported without change to any other simulation environment. **Std_logic** is an enumerated data type found in the IEEE library and represents a single wire that can have nine possible electrical values. These values include 0, 1, unknown, high-impedence, and other values useful in simulation. The complete list of values is shown in Figure 14-5.

Signal Value	Meaning
U	Uninitialized
X	Forcing unknown
0	Forcing 0
1	Forcing 1
Z	High impedence
W	Weak unknown
L	Weak 0
H	Weak 1
-	Don't-care

Figure 14-5
The std_logic data type has nine values.

The Architecture

Now that you have seen some of the basic concepts of data types, and we have our entity declaration with its input and output specification, we can move on to the next part of this design: the *architecture*.

The entity declaration that we just saw describes an external view of the comparator. This external view (including the names, directions, and types of each port) provides all the information needed to wire the comparator circuit into a higher-level circuit.

In some sense, you can think of an entity declaration as being analogous to a socket on a board. To complete this design, we need to provide some additional information about what goes on *inside* the component that we are going to plug into that socket—we need to define how our comparator actually functions. This is where the *architecture declaration* comes in. An architecture declaration (usually just called the *architecture*) is used for this purpose. The following statements constitute the complete architecture declaration for the comparator circuit:

```
ARCHITECTURE compare1 OF compare IS
BEGIN
     eq <= '1' WHEN (a = b) ELSE '0';
END compare1;
```

That's all there is to it; for this design, the architecture just contains a single statement that defines the function of output **eq** as a comparison operation on inputs **a** and **b**. Looking at these statements in a little more detail, we see

- An **architecture** statement that gives a unique name (**compare1**) to this architecture and associates (or *binds*) it with the previously defined entity (**compare**)
- Within the architecture statement, a *conditional signal assignment* statement that describes a comparator operation

If we combine the entity and architecture declarations (and the **library** and **use** statements) into a single source file as shown in Figure 14-6, we have a complete design that can be simulated and, if required, synthesized into actual circuitry.

The Dataflow Style

This simple example demonstrates the most straightforward kind of VHDL that can be written. This style of VHDL, in which *concurrent signal assignments* are made within an architecture body, is called *data flow*. Designs that are described using the dataflow style are very much like designs that are written in a traditional Boolean equation language such as PALASM, ABEL, and the other PLD-oriented languages. In these languages, every equation that is entered in the design is independent of the other equations, and there is no significance to the order in which the equations

```
----------------------------
-- Eight-bit comparator
--
LIBRARY ieee;
USE ieee.std_logic_1164.ALL;

ENTITY compare IS
    PORT(a, b: IN std_logic_vector(0 TO 7);
         eq: OUT std_logic);
END compare;

ARCHITECTURE compare1 OF compare IS
BEGIN

    eq <= '1' WHEN (A = B) ELSE '0';

END compare1;
```

Figure 14-6
The comparator's operation is described using a single concurrent assignment statement.

are entered because *they all operate in parallel*. This inherent parallelism is called *concurrency*.

But what about designs that include registers? In PLD languages, the Boolean equations are often annotated with special assignment operators or signal name extensions that imply a registered function for the associated output. In VHDL, however, things are done quite differently. Rather than having registers or other memory elements built into the language, VHDL requires that you describe a registered, or *sequential*, function in terms of its actual behavior *over time*. This is what is called the behavioral style of VHDL and is how we will enter the next portion of the design.

Component 2: The Barrel Shifter

The second component of this circuit is the barrel shifter, **rotate**. This component (diagrammed in Figure 14-7) accepts and stores an 8-bit data value and, when there is a rising edge on the clock input, rotates the data by one bit. The operation of the barrel shifter is summarized in Figure 14-8.

The barrel shifter source file is shown, complete with its entity and architecture declarations, in Figure 14-9. Like the comparator design, this design uses the IEEE 1164 library and ***std_logic/std_logic_vector*** data types for all its signals. The architecture for this design, however, will look quite different than the comparator with its simple signal assignment.

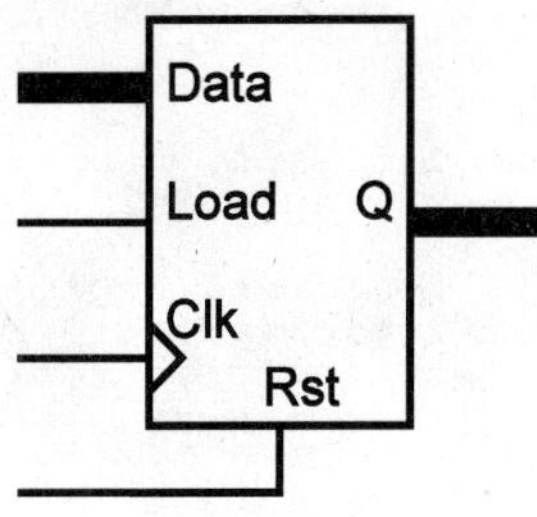

Figure 14-8
The barrel shifter accepts 8-bit data, and shifts the data on each rising clock edge.

Clk	Rst	Load	Operation
X	1	X	Clear shift register
rising edge	0	1	Load Data into register
rising edge	0	0	Rotate one bit

Figure 14-7
The asynchronous reset takes priority.

The Behavioral Style

There are many ways to describe a sequential circuit such as this in VHDL, but all of the possible methods have one thing in common: they all must describe the relationship of the circuit's operation to the transient (edge- or level-triggered) behavior of the clock input and asynchronous reset. In the barrel shifter design shown here, a special VHDL statement called a **process** is used to describe the behavior of the circuit as it relates to the **Clk** and **Rst** inputs.

A **process** statement is, in itself, a concurrent statement within the architecture body. (If there are multiple processes in an architecture, they operate concurrently.) Inside the **process** statement, however (between the **begin** and **end** statements of the process), there are other statements, including signal assignments, that are sequential—they have order dependence. Since hardware that is registered (and synchronized to a clock) has a sequential behavior, it makes some sense to describe it using a sequential programming language, and this is exactly what the **process** statement is designed for.

```
--------------------------------
-- Eight-bit barrel shifter
--
LIBRARY ieee;
USE ieee.std_logic_1164.ALL;

ENTITY rotate IS
    PORT(Clk, Rst, Load: std_logic;
         Data: std_logic_vector(0 TO 7);
         q: INOUT std_logic_vector(0 TO 7));
END rotate;

ARCHITECTURE rotate1 OF rotate IS
BEGIN
      PROCESS(Rst,Clk)
      BEGIN
            IF Rst = '1' THEN                  -- Asynchronous Reset
                  q <= "00000000";
            ELSIF (Clk = '1' AND Clk'EVENT) THEN
                  IF (Load = '1') THEN
                        q <= Data;
                  ELSE
                        q <= q(1 TO 7) & q(0);
                  END IF;
            END IF;
      END PROCESS;
END rotate1;
```

Figure 14-9
The barrel shifter source file is written using a process statement to describe the clocked behavior of the design.

In the barrel shifter's process, you can easily determine how the shifter operates by reading the statements one line after another, keeping in mind the dependencies that are implied by the **if**, **elsif**, and **end if** statements. First, in the **process** statement itself, there is a list of inputs that will cause the process to "execute"; this list of signals is called the *sensitivity list* of the process. In this barrel shifter, the sensitivity list contains two signals, **Clk** and **Rst**. This tells us right away that there are only two signals that have the potential of effecting the output of the circuit immediately when they change. One of them, as we will see, is the clock, while the other is an asynchronous reset.

After the sensitivity list, a sequence of **if-then** statements is used to define the operation of the circuit for various input conditions. The first **if** statement defines an asynchronous reset function; no matter what else happens (even if there is no clock edge occurring) the **q** output register will be cleared if **Rst** goes high. The next **else** clause in the sequence defines the clock function, using a special VHDL signal attribute to describe a signal edge and resulting next value (a change on the **Clk** input resulting in a high value). This statement defines the basic behavior of an edge-triggered flip-flop.

Incidentally, this method of describing clocked behavior is not defined by the VHDL language; it is only a convention. Fortunately, this convention makes sense and is supported by all the VHDL simulator and synthesis tools in common use today. There are other ways of describing clock edges using VHDL, though, that may not translate well to some VHDL tools (particularly synthesis tools), so it is wise to stick with universally supported conventions such as this one.

After the clock is defined, there is an **if-then-else** statement describing the operation of the shift register; when **Load** is high, the new value is loaded in from input **Data**, and when **Load** is low, the register is rotated by one bit. Since this **if-then-else** statement is located within the **Clk'event and Clk = '1'** clause, the function of **q** is dependent on the clock; **q** is therefore a registered output.

Simulating the Components

Before completing the entire design by writing a VHDL description of the interconnections between these two components, let's take a few minutes to simulate both of the component parts. This will allow us to verify that the individual components actually perform the way they are supposed to, as well as giving us an opportunity to learn the basics of VHDL simulation.

Model Technology's V-System Simulator

The simulator we're going to use is the V-Systems simulator sold by Model Technology of Beaverton, Oregon. This simulator is a full-featured VHDL simulation system that operates in the Windows environment. It supports the full 1076-1987 and 1076-1993 standards, as well as IEEE 1164.

Note: *The V-Systems simulator is not included on the companion CD-ROM. An educational version of a VHDL simulator produced by Green Mountain Computing Systems of South Ryegate, Vermont, is provided on the CD-ROM, however. For more information about either of these products, contact the vendors directly. Information about how to contact Model Technology, Green Mountain Computing Systems, and other VHDL simulation vendors can be found in Appendix A.*

Invoking the Simulator

Before we can simulate the comparator and shifter components, we need to set up the simulator and compile the VHDL source files that we have generated.

1. Using a text editor, create the two VHDL source files (**compare.vhd** and **rotate.vhd**) in a directory on your system (in this tutorial, I have used the directory named **\vhdl\rotcomp**).

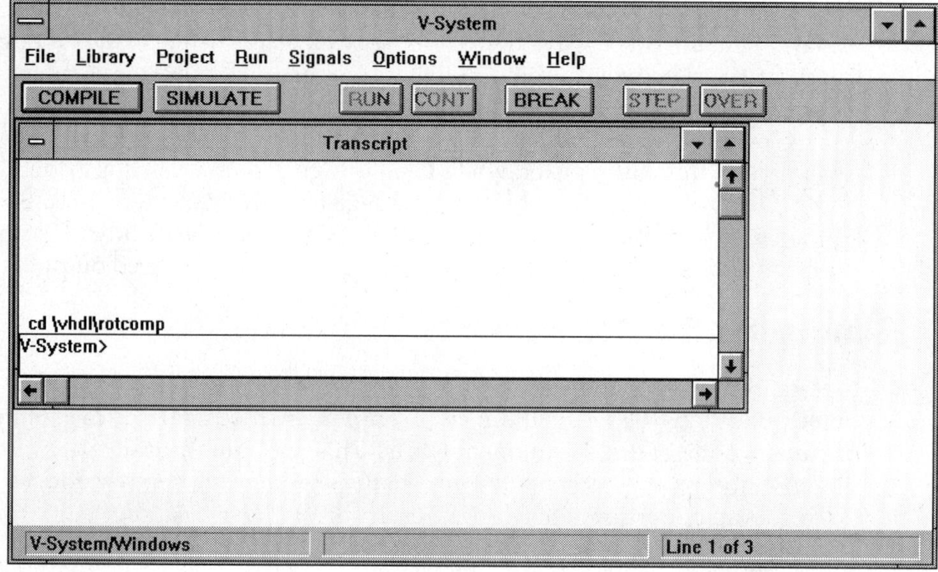

Figure 14-10
Starting the V-System application and changing the current directory.

2. To set up the simulator in that directory, invoke the V-System simulator from Windows and enter a change directory (**cd**) command into the simulator's transcript window as shown in Figure 14-11.

Creating a New Project

The next step is to create a project file. The project file is where the simulator stores information about this project, such as the simulator options (window placement and sizing, waveform display options, timing resolution, and many other parameters) that will be used whenever we return to this project.

1. Create the project file by selecting **New** from the **Project** menu (Figure 14-3).

Creating the Work Library

In a VHDL simulation environment, all the *design entities* (entities, architectures, packages, and configurations) are compiled into special storage areas called *libraries*. We have seen already how the **std_logic** data types are kept in a special library named **IEEE** and referenced in a VHDL source file using the **library** and **use** statements. In most VHDL environments, **IEEE** is a precompiled library; we just reference it in our designs and it is immediately available for use. (There is also a precompiled library called **std** that contains the definitions for data types such as

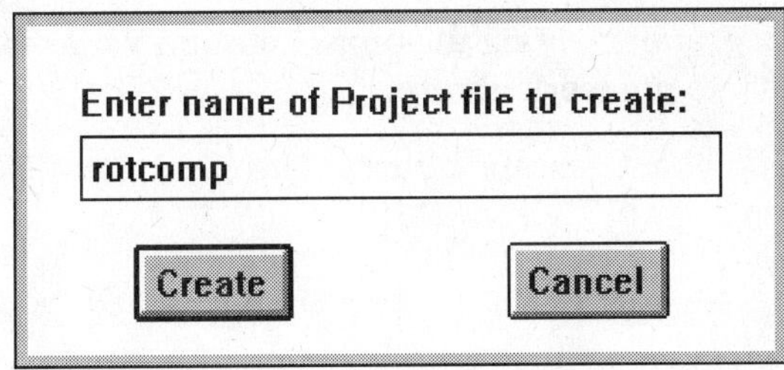

Figure 14-11
*Specifying **rotcomp** as the project name.*

bit, bit_vector, integer, and all the other types that we have seen. **Std** is a standard library defined in the VHDL specification, and we do not have to specify it with a **library** or **use** statement.)

The **work** library is a specialized library that is defined in the VHDL standard. This library is the *default library*, meaning that it is the place where the VHDL simulator (or synthesis tool, as appropriate) will attempt to find any design entity that is not referenced from some other library. The result of all this is that you will usually want to compile all your design units (the entities, architectures and other items) into a library called **work**, and in the V-System environment, you must begin by creating the **work** library in your project directory.

1. To create the **work** library, use the **New** command from the **Library** menu in the V-System simulator, and type in the name **work** as shown in Figure 14-12.

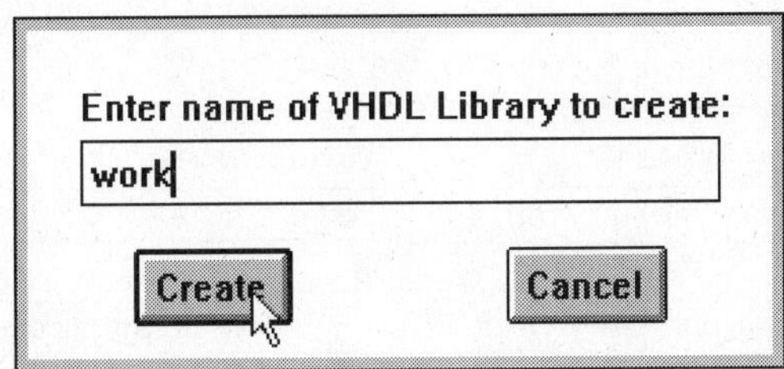

Figure 14-12
*All design units will be compiled into the **work** library.*

Compiling the Source Files

The next step, after creating the project file and **work** library, is to compile the two source files into the **work** library.

1. Click on the **Compile** button. The Compile VHDL Source dialogue box appears.

2. Highlight a source file in the Compile VHDL Source dialogue box (Figure 14-13).

For each source file in the list,

3. Highlight the name of the source file in the selection box, then click on the **Compile** button as shown.

If there are any errors during compilation, the error messages are displayed in the simulator's transcript window (Figure 14-14). Use this procedure to compile both the **compare** and **rotate** source files.

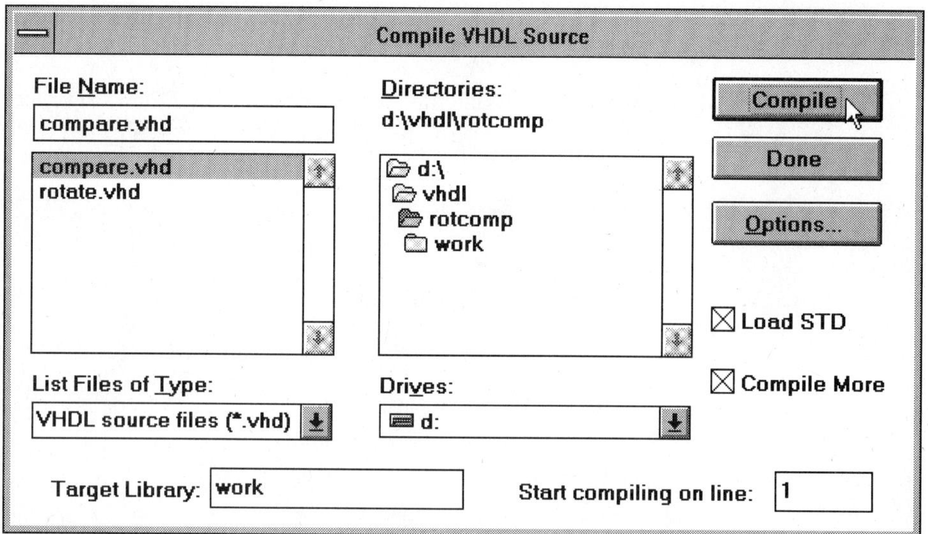

Figure 14-13
Each source fie is compiled into the ***work*** *library by highlighting the file name and clicking on Compile.*

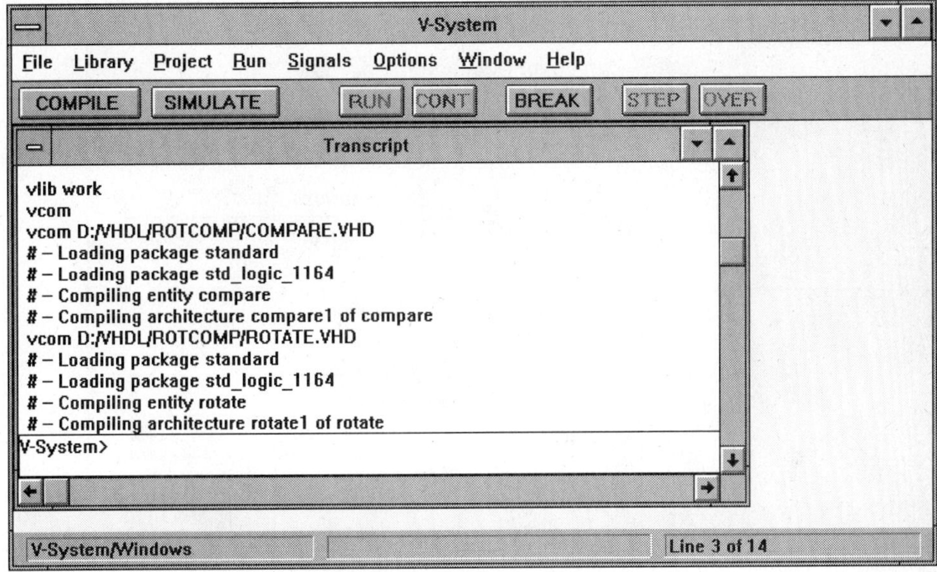

Figure 14-14
The transcript window displays any errors or messages generated during the compile operation.

Simulating the Comparator

Now that the two designs (the comparator and shifter) have been compiled into the **work** library, we're ready to simulate. We'll simulate the comparator first.

1. Click on the **Simulate** button to to invoke the Simulation Parameters dialogue box.

2. Select the **compare** entity from the list of design units in the Simulation Parameters dialogue box.

Notice that the dialogue box asks not only for the entity to simulate, but the architecture as well. This is why VHDL architectures have unique names (**compare1** in this case). This unique name makes it possible to have multiple architectures written for the same entity, a useful capability if you require different architectures for simulation and synthesis, or have different architectures for different implementation technologies or test requirements. In this design, we have only provided one architecture declaration for each of the entities, so the correct architecture is selected for us.

3. Click on the **OK** button to exit the Simulation Parameters dialogue box.

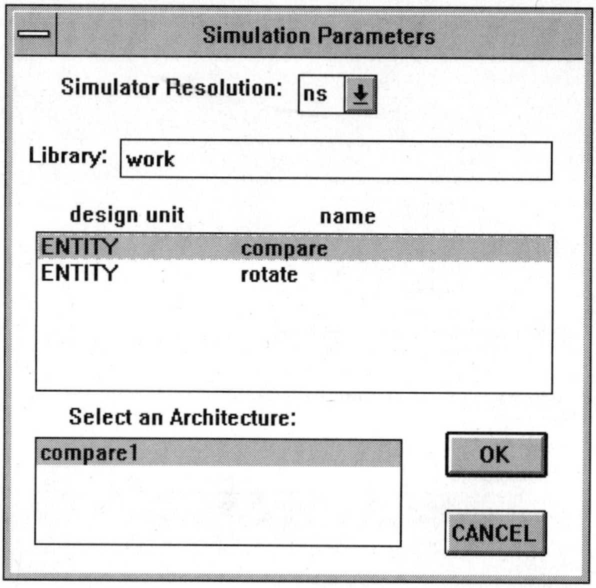

Figure 14-15
To select a design unit to simulate, you highlight the name of the entity. If you have provided multiple architectures for the entity, you must also select the architecture to use.

The simulator reads any simulation options that we have set previously in the project file, and opens up the various simulation windows as shown in Figure 14-16. Since we haven't set any options for window display for this project, all eight simulation windows are opened.

What are all these windows? Here are brief descripions of each window displayed:

- ☐ List Window: This window provides you with customizable view of your simulation results, using a tabular format.

- ☐ Process Window: This window displays information about all processes used in a design and is useful for analyzing the behavior of designs that have multiple processes that operate concurrently.

- ☐ Signals Window: This window displays the current value of each signal in the design. If the signal is of a vector or *aggregate* type, you can double-click on the small box to the left of the signal to expand the signal into its component parts.

- ☐ Source Window: This window displays the currently executing source file (or the source file that you select via the **File/Select Source File** menu item) and is where you can debug your design by setting breakpoints and watching the control flow in sequential designs.

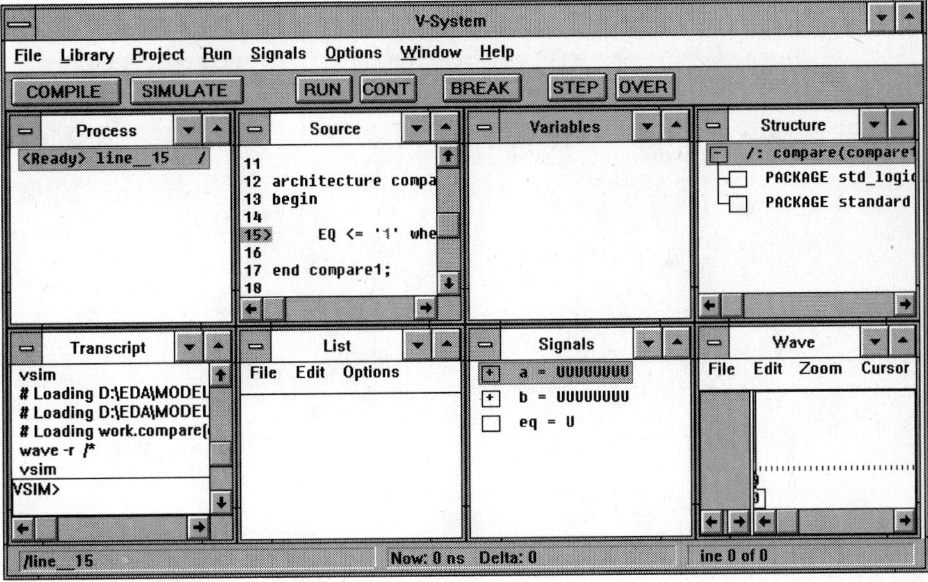

Figure 14-16
The V-System simulator provides many ways to observe a simulation.

- ☐ Structure Window: This window shows how the design is constructed from the point of view of hierarchy. (In the comparator design, the only lower-level design entities are the **std_logic** and **standard** packages, which provide definitions of the data types being used.)

- ☐ Transcript Window: This window displays a history of the simulator commands issued either directly on the transcript command or via the menus. Error messages from compilation are also displayed in this window, as are messages that are generated during simulation.

- ☐ Variables Window: The Variables window is exactly like the Signals window, but displays the values of all variables used in the design. This design does not use any variables, so this window is empty.

- ☐ Wave Window: The Wave window displays the simulation results in a logic analyzerlike format. The Wave window has a menu of options that allow you to customize the display of the waveform as needed.

We don't need all these windows to simulate this simple comparator, so we're going to rearrange the screen to display only the Source, Wave, and Transcript windows. We'll also need to add some signals to the waveform display.

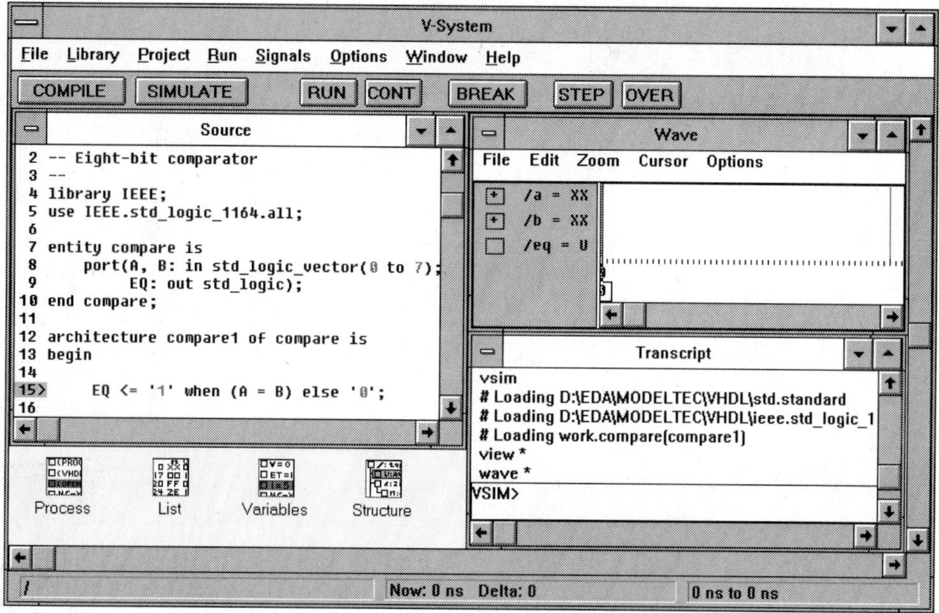

Figure 14-17
More useful arrangement of windows

4. Using standard Windows procedures, close the unwanted simulator windows and resize the remaining windows to make things easier to see.

5. Add **A**, **B**, and **EQ** to the Wave window by typing the command **wave *** in the Transcript window.

The new arrangement is shown in Figure 14-17.

Specifying Stimulus

Now we are ready to see how the comparator works. To actually simulate the design, we need to supply some stimulus to the circuit and view the results. To perform a quick test with two pairs of input values for **A** and **B**, we'll use the command line located in the simulator's Transcript window to type in the values and run the simulation for a brief period.

1. Type the following simulator commands into the simulator's Transcript window (Figure 14-18):

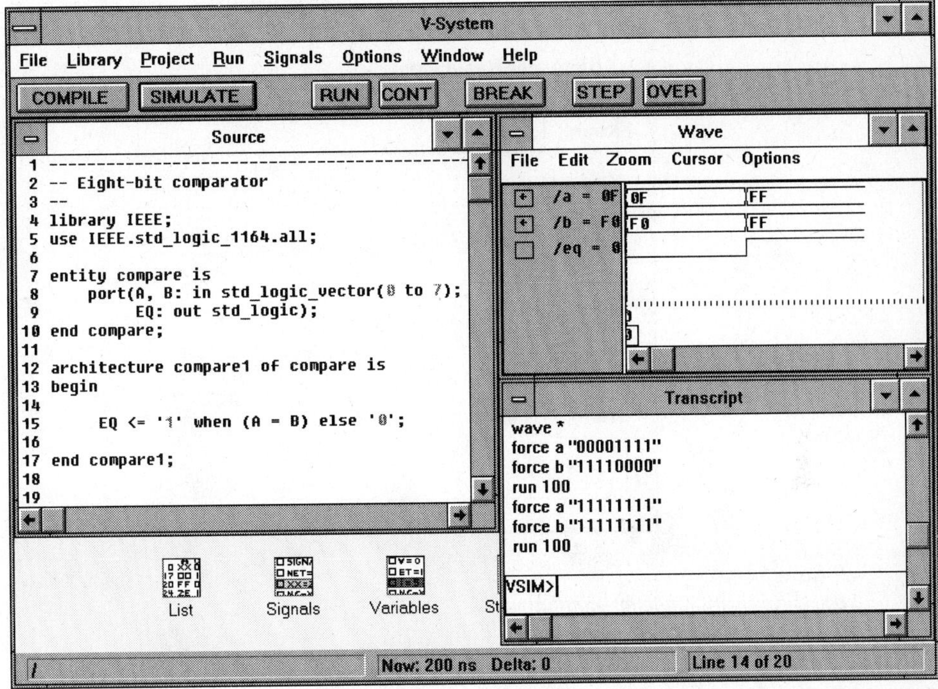

Figure 14-18
The ***force*** *and* ***run*** *commands can be used to control an interactive simulation.*

```
force A "00001111"
force B "11110000"
run 100
force A "11111111"
force B "11111111"
run 100
```

These commands apply stimulus to the circuit (the **force** command) and instruct the simulator to run for 100 ns of simulated time for each pair of values. We can see the results in the simulator's Wave window; when the pair of values are unequal, the output is low; when the values are equal, the output is high.

Simulating the Barrel Shifter

Now we'll simulate the barrel shifter. Before doing so, we must first end the simulation.

1. Selecting **End Simulation** from the **File** menu.

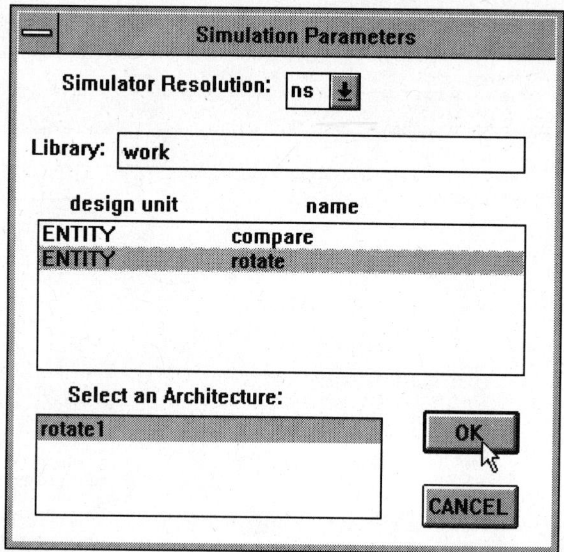

Figure 14-19
Selecting entity rotate for simulation

2. After the comparator simulation parameters have been cleared, click on the **Simulate** button and select the **rotate** entity for simulation (Figure 14-19).

We'll use a similar arrangement of windows for this simulation; Figure 14-20 shows the simulation windows, ready to go with all the design signals displayed in the wave window.

3. Use the **wave** * command to add all signals from the **rotate** module to the waveform display.

The default display format for signals in the Wave window is hexadecimal. Since it is more convenient to view the bits of the shift register directly, we'll change the format of **Data** and **Q** to binary. To change the format of a signal,

4. To select the signal you wish to modify, click on the signal name **Data** in the Wave window.

5. Select the **Options/Signal** command in the Wave window. This command brings up a dialogue box like the one shown in Figure 14-21.

6. To view the signal in binary format, select the **Binary** radio button.

7. Click the **Apply** button, then click the **Done** button.

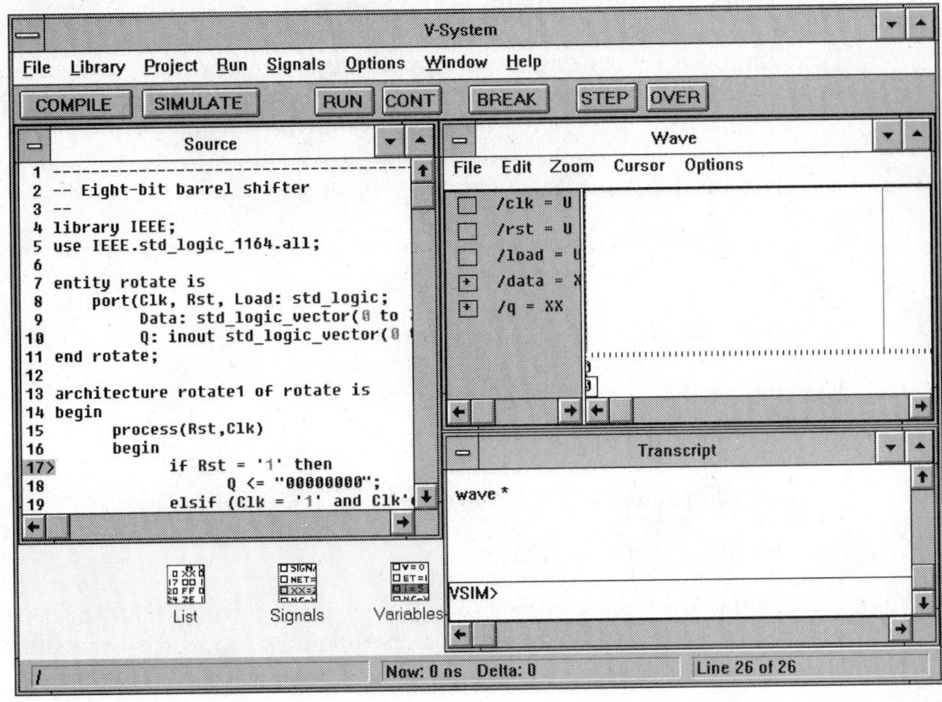

Figure 14-20
Ready to simulate the shifter.

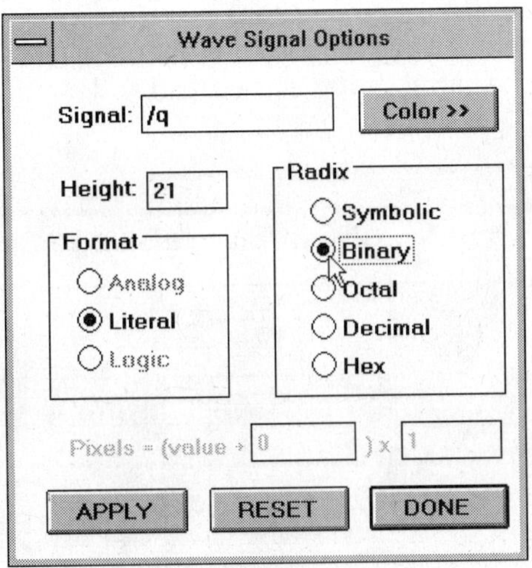

Figure 14-21
Setting the display radix to binary.

Specifying the Stimulus

The stimulus for this design will be a bit more complex than for the comparator circuit. The major difference is that this design is a sequential function and therefore needs a clock. Fortunately, the simulator command language provides commands for setting up cyclic events, so we can describe a clock function without having to type in values for every change in the clock's value.

1. Type the following simulator command into the Transcript window to create a repeating clock with a period of 100 ns:

```
force Clk 1 50, 0 100 -repeat 100
```

This command tells the simulator to

- ☐ Force **Clk** to a value of 1 at 50 ns after the current time, then
- ☐ force **Clk** to a value of 0 at 100 ns after the current time, and
- ☐ repeat the cycle every 100 ns.

To make sure the clock is cycling properly, we can type run 100 (or click on the **Run** button) to observe the first transition from unknown to 1, and the transition (at 100 ns) back to 0.

2. Type **run 100** into the Transcript window.

Next, we will want to test the reset and load functions of the shifter, and then let it run for a few clock cycles to make sure data is shifted properly.

3. Type the following sequence of commands into the Transcript window to exercise the barrel shifter's reset, load and shift functions:

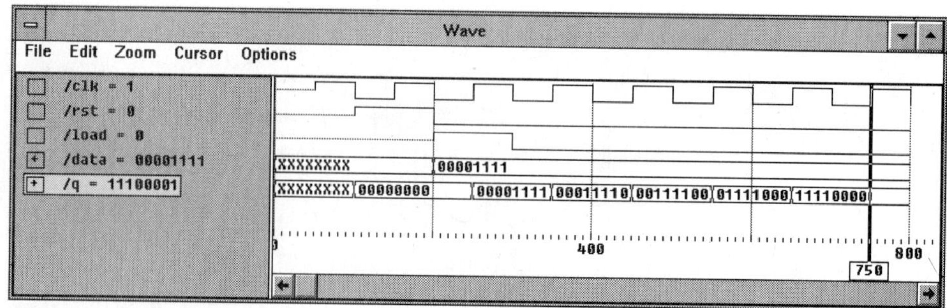

Figure 14-22
The operation of the shifter is displayed for eight clock cycles.

```
force Rst 1
run 100
force Rst 0
force Load 1
force Data "00001111"
run 100
force Load 0
run 400
```

The resulting Wave window display (expanded to show the entire simulation run) is shown in Figure 14-22.

Putting Together the Components

Now that we have entered, compiled and simulated the two component parts, it's time to put them together to form the larger circuit. To do this, we'll use VHDL's hierarchy language features to create a top-level netlist connecting the **compare** and **rotate** components.VHDL provides a number of ways to map higher- and lower-level names to one another; in this design we will use what is called *positional association*, in which the order of ports in the entity declaration and component instances are the only indicators of the proper mapping.

The complete top-level VHDL source file for this design is shown in Figure 14-23. Starting from the top of the file, we have:

- **Library** and **use** statements to make use of the **std_logic** data types, just as in the lower-level **compare** and **rotate** source files.

- A top-level entity declaration defining the inputs and outputs of the entire circuit.

- An architecture for the **rotcomp** entity containing

  - *Component declarations* for the compare and rotate components. (Compare these component declarations to the entity declarations for **compare** and **rotate** that we saw earlier. The syntax for entity and component declarations is nearly identical.)

  - A signal declaration for **Q**, which is an internal signal in the top-level module. This signal will be used to carry the output of the shift register to the **A** input of the comparator, and is not visible as a port outside of the **rotcomp** design unit.

  - Within the **begin** and **end** statements of the architecture, *component instantiations* for the two lower-level design units **compare** and **rotate**. The names **COMP1** and **ROT1** are unique *instance names* that identify each component instance. (This is necessary because there may be more than one instance of a given lower-level component in a hierarchical design.) The

```
---------------------------------
- eight-bit rotate and compare
-
LIBRARY ieee;
USE ieee.std_logic_1164.ALL;

ENTITY rotcomp IS
    PORT(Clk, Rst, Load: std_logic;
          Init: std_logic_vector(0 TO 7);
          Test: std_logic_vector(0 TO 7);
          Match: OUT std_logic);
END rotcomp;

ARCHITECTURE structure OF rotcomp IS
    COMPONENT compare
        PORT( a, b: IS std_logic_vector(0 TO 7);
              eq: OUT std_logic);
    END COMPONENT;
    COMPONENT rotate
        PORT( Clk, Rst, Load: std_logic;
              Data: std_logic_vector(0 TO 7);
              q: INOUT std_logic_vector(0 TO 7));
    END COMPONENT;
    SIGNAL q: std_logic_vector(0 TO 7);
BEGIN
    comp1: compare PORT MAP (q, Test, Match);
    rot1:  rotate PORT MAP (Clk, Rst, Load, Init, q );
END structure;
```

Figure 14-23
*The **rotcomp** top-level design file.*

port map statements positionally associate the top-level signal names with corresponding signals in the lower-level components.

Compiling the Top-Level Module

Now that we have a top-level file connecting the two lower-level files, we are almost ready to simulate the entire design. First, though, we'll need to compile the top-level design (**rotcomp**) into the **work** library, just as we did for the compare and rotate modules.

1. Select the **Restart Simulation** command from the **File** menu to clear the previous simulation run.

2. Select the **Compile** button, then select the rotcomp source file for compilation as shown in Figure 14-24.

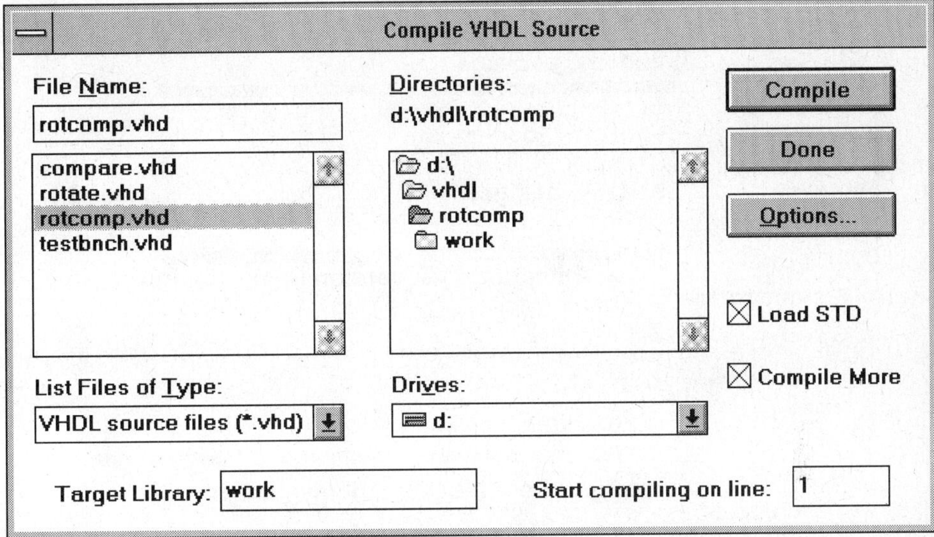

Figure 14-24
*Compiling the top-level design file into the **work** library.*

A Quick Note on Configurations

We now have a design that includes three modules—the comparator, the barrel shifter and the top-level module, **rotcomp**, that connects the two lower-level modules together. I mentioned in the previous chapter that VHDL provides some configuration management features that are useful for large designs, and we should spend a few moments talking about those features before going on.

The primary mechanism that VHDL provides for configuration management is called, quite naturally, a *configuration*. A configuration is a special kind of design unit (like an entity or architecture) that allows you to specify how a hierarchical design is put together. This is an important feature to have in VHDL, because VHDL allows you to have any number of design units compiled into your **work** library (or other libraries) that you can select at the time that you simulate, synthesize or otherwise process your design. You might, for example, have two or more architecture declarations that you use for different types of simulation, or you may have a different architecture that you use for synthesis. You might have a very simple, high-level architecture that was developed as a *stub* (or dummy architecture) for simulating the interfaces, but that is to be replaced at a later date with a real architecture, perhaps one that is synthesizable.

```
package my_package is
  . . .
end my_package
```

```
entity my_design is
    port( . . . );
end my_design;
```

```
architecture this_version of my_design is
begin
    .
    .
    .
end this_version;
```

```
configuration this_build of my_design
is
    . . .
end this_build;
```

Figure 14-25
The four primary design units are entities and architectures (required in any design), packages and configurations (optional).

Design Units

Figure 14-25 illustrates the relationship between the four primary types of design units in VHDL. For each entity, there may be any number of architectures available for use, and a configuration statement (or the default configuration, if there is no configuration) provides the information needed to put the design together. The figure also shows a type of design unit that I have mentioned in passing, but have not described in detail: the **package**. Packages are simply blocks of shared declarations (such as the standard declarations for **std_logic** and **std_logic_vector**) that may be used in your design. Packages can be provided for you by the simulation or synthesis tool vendor (as is the case for the **std_logic_1164** package), or you can create them yourself as needed.

What does a configuration statement look like? Figure 14-26 shows a configuration statement that defines the design unit relationships for our sample design. This configuration can be compiled into the **work** library and selected for simulation just as we have selected the design units **compare** and **rotate**, and as we could select the top-level design unit **rotcomp**.

Configurations can also be useful at the component level. Let's say, for example, that we were going to be implementing our shift and compare circuit in some sort

```
-------------------------
-- configuration for rotcomp default binding
--

CONFIGURATION this_build OF rotcomp IS
    FOR structure
        FOR comp1: compare USE entity work.compare(compare1);
        FOR rot1: rotate USE entity work.rotate(rotate1);
    END FOR;
END this_build;
```

Figure 14-26
Configuration statements specify how a design is put together.

of FPGA, and the FPGA synthesis vendor had provided a comparator function for us (in the form of a lower-level hard macro) that was preoptimized for the FPGA architecture we were targeting. To use this externally provided module, we could use a configuration statement to change the *default binding* of the **comp1** component to a different **compare** entity or lower-level architecture.

Although I've shown a configuration statement for this design, we're not going to use this configuration to perform the simulation; the default binding is exactly what we want, and no configuration statement is required.

Creating a Test Bench

When we simulated the **compare** and **rotate** modules, we interacted directly with the V-System simulator to apply stimulus to the circuits, and we observed the results in the Wave window. This is a fine way to debug small circuits that don't require large amounts of stimulus, but is impractical for designs that are large and complex. Although most simulators (including V-Systems) include a command language for writing loop functions, tests, and other important tasks, it is more useful to test your design by developing a conceptual circuit called a *test bench*.

Perhaps the easiest way to understand how a test bench (or *test fixture*, if you like) works is to think of it as a breadboard into which you will plug your design. Just like a breadboard, your test bench will need to have things like clock generators to create input stimulus and some sort of circuitry allowing you to observe the result and to detect and report failures. Depending on the complexity of the design, you may want your test bench to do things that a simple breadboard can't do, such as reading in an ASCII file containing test vectors.

The test bench that I have generated for this design is shown in Figure 14-27. This test bench uses VHDL's record and array data types to define a sequence of test vectors, and uses a VHDL process to set up a clock and loop through each vector checking the results. Looking at this file in detail, we see

Figure 14-27
Test bench source file.

```
————————————————————
— testbench for eight-bit rotate and compare
—

entity testbnch is
end;

library IEEE;
use IEEE.std_logic_1164.all;

architecture fixture of testbnch is

    component rotcomp
        port(Clk, Rst, Load: std_logic;
             Init: std_logic_vector(0 to 7);
             Test: std_logic_vector(0 to 7);
             Match: out std_logic);
    end component;

    signal Clk   : std_logic;
    signal Rst   : std_logic;
    signal Load  : std_logic;
    signal Init  : std_logic_vector(0 to 7);
    signal Test  : std_logic_vector(0 to 7);
    signal Match: std_logic;

    type test_record_t is record
        Rst  : std_logic;
        Load : std_logic;
        Init : std_logic_vector(0 to 7);
        Test : std_logic_vector(0 to 7);
        Match: std_logic;
    end record;

    type test_array_t is
        array(positive range <>) of test_record_t;

    constant test_patterns : test_array_t := (
    —   Rst Load    Init         Test       Match
        ('1', '0', "00000000", "00000001", '0'),
        ('0', '1', "00100010", "01000100", '0'),
        ('0', '0', "00000000", "01000100", '1'),
        ('0', '1', "10101010", "01010101", '0'),
        ('0', '0', "00000000", "01010101", '1'),
        ('0', '1', "01010000", "00000101", '0'),
        ('0', '0', "00000000", "00000101", '0'),
        ('0', '0', "00000000", "00000101", '0'),
        ('0', '0', "00000000", "00000101", '0'),
        ('0', '0', "00000000", "00000101", '1'),
        ('0', '1', "00001111", "11110000", '0'),
        ('0', '0', "00000000", "11110000", '0'),
        ('0', '0', "00000000", "11110000", '0'),
        ('0', '0', "00000000", "11110000", '0'),
        ('0', '0', "00000000", "11110000", '1')
    );
```

```
begin
    — instantiate the component
    uut: rotcomp
    port map(Clk => Clk,
             Rst => Rst,
             Load => Load,
             Init => Init,
             Test => Test,
             Match => Match);

    — provide stimulus and check the result
    testrun: process
        variable vector : test_record_t;
        variable found_error : boolean := false;
    begin
    for i in test_patterns'range loop
        vector := test_patterns(i);

        — Apply the input stimulus...
        Rst <= vector.Rst;
        Load <= vector.Load;
        Init <= vector.Init;
        Test <= vector.Test;

        — Clock (low-high-low) with a 100 ns cycle...
        Clk <= '0';
        wait for 25 ns;
        Clk <= '1';
        wait for 50 ns;
        Clk <= '0';
        wait for 25 ns;
        — Check the results...
        if (Match  /= vector.Match) then
            assert false
            report "Did not match!";
            found_error := true;
        end if;
    end loop;

    assert not found_error
        report "There were ERRORS in the test."
        severity note;
    assert found_error
        report "Test completed with no errors."
        severity note;
    wait;
    end process;
end;
```

- ☐ An **entity** declaration. Note that there are no ports required in this test bench; it is entirely self-contained and will not "plug into" any other circuit.
- ☐ **Library** and **use** statements, again to provide access to the **std_logic** data type.
- ☐ An **architecture** (**fixture**) containing:
    - A component declaration for our **rotcomp** design.

- Signal declarations that will provide us with a set of top-level signals with which we can either force values into our circuit or observe the resulting outputs.
- A *type declaration* that defines a record (**test_record_t**) and its component fields.
- Another type declaration that defines an unbounded array of **test_record_t** records.
- A constant declaration that creates an array of test vector records.
- After the **begin** statement, a component instantiation (instance name **uut**) for the **rotcomp** module, with a **port map** statement associating the top-level signals with the matching signals in the **rotcomp** component
- A process (**testrun**) that repetitively applies the input portions of each vector (consisting of record fields **vector.Rst**, **vector.Load**, **vector.Init**, and **vector.Test**) to the corresponding top-level signals, sets up a 100 ns clock using **wait** statements, and checks the resulting values of **Match** against record field **vector.Match**.

The file uses **assert**, **severity**, and **report** statements to generate output to the screen (in the V-Systems transcript window, in this case) during the simulation.

Confusing? Perhaps; in fact it is not unusual for a test bench to be more complex and lengthy than the actual description of the circuit it is intended to test. This doesn't mean that you are going to have to spend all of your time writing test benches, though. Since the requirements of most test benches are virtually identical, you will probably create one basic test bench that serves your purposes (perhaps by copying a sample test bench like this one) and simply modify that test bench as needed for new designs.

Simulating the Design

The real beauty of test benches is how much they simplify the testing and debugging process. Once you have compiled your test bench into the **work** library (Figure 14-28) and selected it for simulation (Figure 14-29) all you need to do is start the simulator running (by specifying however much simulated time you want to observe) and view the results when it has finished. If the simulator you are using supports source-level debugging, you can even set breakpoints in your source code and observe the values of internal signals as the simulation progresses.

1. To view the results of the simulation for this circuit, set up the waveform with the top-level signals using the following Transcript window commands:

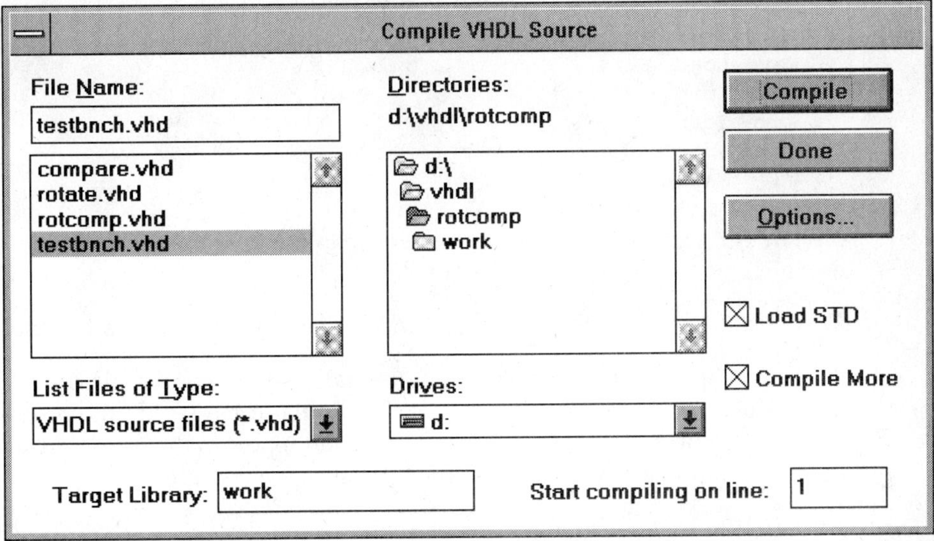

Figure 14-28
The test bench is compiled into the work library.

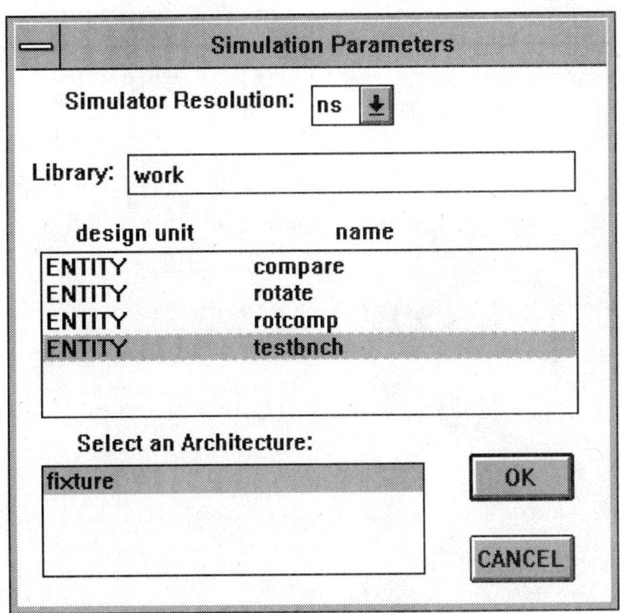

Figure 14-29
The test bench is selected for simulation, just like any other design unit.

```
Wave Clk
Wave Rst
Wave Load
Wave Init
Wave Test
Wave uut/Q
Wave Match
```

(The **uut/Q** signal is a hierarchical reference to the **Q** shift register in the **rotcomp** module.)

2. Start the simulator by selecting **Run Forever** from the **Simulate** menu.

When you specify **Run Forever**, you are really telling the simulator to run until there is no more stimulus. This causes the simulator to execute the process in the test bench, loop through all the test vectors, and report to the transcript window if there are errors. The completed simulation is shown in Figure 14-30.

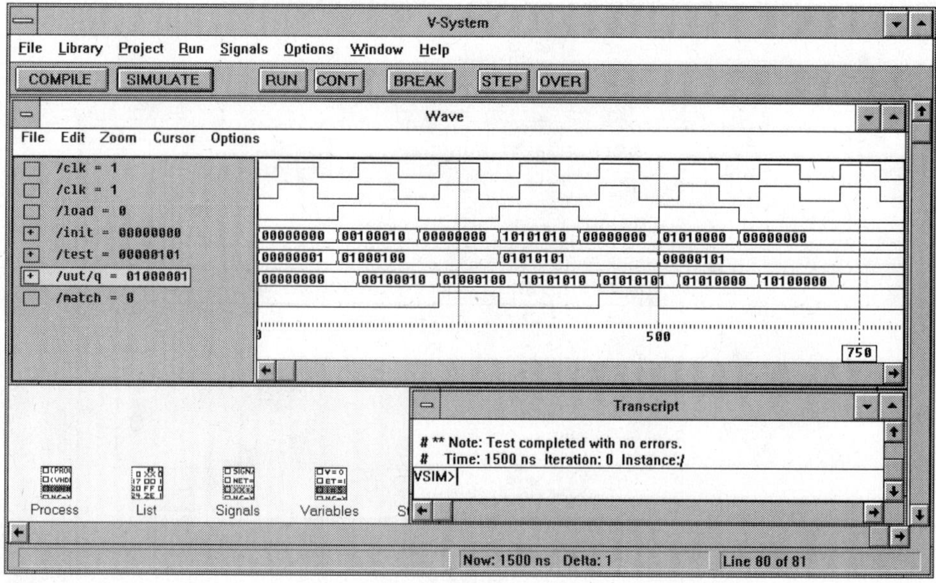

Figure 14-30
Running the simulation using the test bench.

Moving On

There is much more to VHDL—and VHDL simulation—than I could possibly show in a simple example such as this one. The language includes modular coding features such as functions and procedures and allows compile-time values to be passed into design units through the use of special types of parameters called *generics*. There are also useful features for text input and output contained in a standard package called *textio*. All these features combine to make VHDL a powerful language for design entry and testing.

In the next chapter we'll be looking at another widely used hardware description language, Verilog HDL, and see how it compares to VHDL both in terms of language features and in terms of simulation tools. In a later chapter, we'll see how VHDL applies to the problem of synthesis and will be looking at the language in more detail as learn about synthesis conventions and subsets.

CHAPTER 15

HANDS-ON EDA: USING VERILOG SIMULATION

In this section, we're going to see how the same simple circuit presented in the previous chapter (a barrel shifter and comparator) can be entered and simulated using Verilog HDL and a common PC-based Verilog simulator. The simulator I have chosen to use, FrontLine Design Automation's BaseLine system, is a popular simulator that supports all of the Verilog language specification (as published by Open Verilog International), including the PLI (Programming Language Interface), UDP (User Defined Primitive), and SDF (Standard Delay Format) sections of the language standard.

This tutorial presents a very simple circuit and therefore does not include descriptions of Verilog's more advanced features. It is only intended to show the basics of the language and the general operation of Verilog simulation tools.

Note: *Evaluation versions of three Verilog simulation products, including FrontLine's BaseLine simulator, have been provided on the companion CD-ROM. You are encouraged to install this evaluation software and follow along with tutorial.*

Describing the Sample Circuit in Verilog HDL

To describe this design using Verilog HDL, we'll follow the same basic procedure as in the previous chapter and enter the design from the bottom up. Like VHDL, Verilog provides features for entering a design as a hierarchy of components, so this circuit can be entered in much the same way as in VHDL. Verilog also allows test stimulus to be entered using the same concepts of hierarchy and test bench circuits used in VHDL designs. (In Verilog parlance, however, the test bench is normally called a *test fixture.*)

Describing the Comparator

As you'll recall from the earlier example, the first part of our circuit is an eight-bit comparator. Using VHDL, I entered this design module using a simple form of VHDL called dataflow and described the logic of the circuit with a single signal assignment statement. In Verilog HDL the syntax is a bit different, but the method is essentially the same. Figure 15-1 is a complete Verilog HDL description of the 8-bit comparator design. Looking closely at this source file, we see

- ☐ A **module** statement declaring the comparator module by name and specifying its ports (inputs and/or outputs).
- ☐ Declarations specifying the direction (either **input**, **output** or **bidir**) and width of each port.
- ☐ A single *continuous assignment* statement that defines the logical behavior of the **EQ** output.
- ☐ An **endmodule** statement.

That's it, there isn't anything else needed to compile and simulate this simple design. If you compare this module with the VHDL version of the comparator design presented in the previous chapter, you will notice the following differences:

- ☐ There are no types specified for the signals. While VHDL provides a large number of different data types and requires that you assign a type to every signal in the design, Verilog HDL has only two fundamental types: nets and registers. These two types can be either single bit (*scalar*) data elements like **EQ**, or take the form of vectors (with width) such as **A** and **B**.
- ☐ This module is completely self-contained, and there is no equivalent to the architecture declaration in VHDL. This is one reason why Verilog designs tend to look more compact than the equivalent designs written in VHDL. If you don't need the configuration management features of VHDL, then you won't miss the extra typing that VHDL often requires.
- ☐ Finally, there is no reference to an external library or package such as **IEEE.std_logic_1164**. Verilog's signal data types are predefined to have the nonbinary values required for simulation.

If you have done any programming in the C language, Verilog HDL may look somewhat familiar to you. Many of the operators and statements are the same as you would use in C, and the basic format of the modules is very similar to the

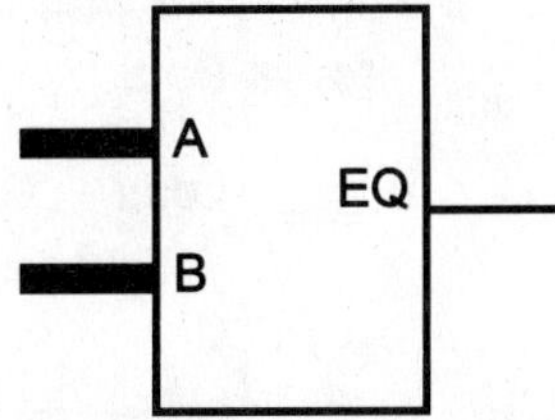


```
/*************************************
* Eight-bit comparator
*/

module compare (A,B,EQ);
    input   [0:7] A;
    input   [0:7] B;
    output EQ;

    assign EQ = (A == B);

endmodule
```

Figure 15-1
A comparator described with Verilog HDL.

format of a C subroutine. The real difference between C and Verilog HDL, of course, is that C describes software, which is inherently sequential, while Verilog HDL describes hardware, which is inherently concurrent. This difference can cause some confusion for those who have coded extensively in C.

Describing the Barrel Shifter

The next part of this small circuit is the barrel shifter. In the VHDL implementation, you might recall that I used a **process** statement to describe the behavior of the shifter in terms of events occurring on the **Clk** and **Rst** inputs and used a sequence of **if-then-else** statements to describe how the data load and shift operations occur at the rising edge of a clock.

In the Verilog HDL version of this design (Figure 15-2) the description is similar, in that the **Rst** and **Clk** inputs are the only inputs that can cause a change in the value of the **Q** output. Let's step through this source file and see how it works. Starting at the top, we see

- ☐ A **module** statement that names the current module (**rotate**) and defines the list of ports.
- ☐ Input and output declarations for **Clk**, **Rst**, **Load**, **Data** and **Q**.

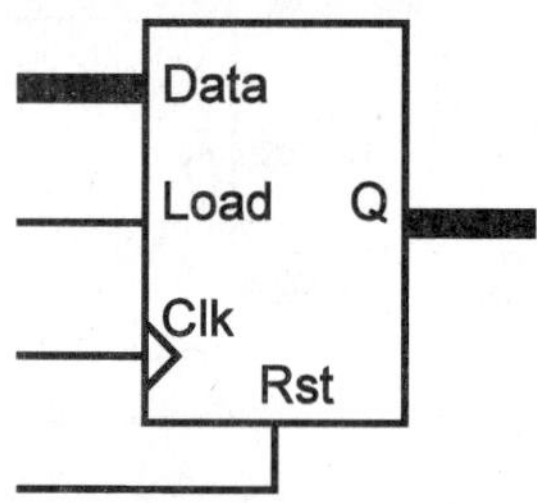


```
/*************************************
* Eight-bit barrel shifter
*/

module rotate (Clk,Rst,Load,Data,Q);
    input  Clk, Rst, Load;
    input  [0:7] Data;
    output [0:7] Q;
    reg    [0:7] Q;

    always @(Rst)
        Q = 'h00;
    always @(posedge Clk)
    begin
        if (Load)
            Q = Data;
        else
            Q = {Q[1:7], Q[0]};
    end
endmodule
```

Figure 15-2
The barrel shifter module written in Verilog HDL.

- ☐ A **reg** declaration for output **Q**. This declaration defines **Q** to be a register type signal. This means that the **Q** signal will be capable of holding a value over time. A net signal type, on the other hand, is only capable of providing a connection between elements in the circuit.

- ☐ An **always** statement (or *always block*) defining the asynchronous reset behavior of the circuit. In the context of simulation, you can think of always blocks as being very much like a process in VHDL. Always blocks contain statements that operate sequentially, and the block of statements is executed whenever the conditions in the event expression are true. In the first always block, **Q** is assigned a value of **0** whenever the **Rst** input is high.

- ☐ A second always statement that defines the behavior of the circuit when there is a rising edge on the **Clk** input. The **if-else** statement pair describes the load and shift behavior of the circuit, and is almost identical to the same function described in VHDL.

- ☐ An **endmodule** statement.

Describing the Connections

To create a top-level design connecting these two lower-level circuits, we'll write a Verilog module that looks quite a lot like the top-level design I entered earlier using VHDL. The top-level module, **rotcomp**, will reference one instance each of **compare** and **rotate** and will connect these two modules together using an intermediate signal, **Q**. The complete top-level design file is shown in figure 15-3. The source file consists of

- ☐ A **module** statement declaring the name of the module, **rotcomp**, and the module's ports
- ☐ **Input** and **output** declarations for the ports
- ☐ A **wire** declaration creating an intermediate net type signal **Q**
- ☐ Component instantiation statements that define the components **ROT1** and **COMP1**, and define their connections using positional association
- ☐ An **endmodule** statement

Pretty simple, isn't it? Of course, there are more advanced features of Verilog HDL that can make a hierarchical design like this one appear to rival VHDL's level of complexity, but for most designs, the straightforward syntax of Verilog HDL is much easier to read and comprehend than the equivalent design written in VHDL.

To be fair to VHDL, however, once you have written a few designs in either language, you will have little trouble remembering the rules and will find designs written by others to be quite easy to read and understand. The choice of whether to use VHDL or Verilog HDL should not be based on how easy it is to type in a design. The real issues surrounding these two languages are such things as design tool costs and simulation model availability.

Simulating a Verilog Design

Now that we have the entire design expressed in Verilog HDL, it's time to simulate it. We're going to see how a Verilog design is simulated by creating a Verilog HDL test fixture, just we did using VHDL, executing the test fixture using the BaseLine simulator produced by FrontLine Design Automation.

Creating a Test Fixture

The test fixture for this circuit will look similar in some respects to the one we entered earlier using VHDL. Rather than writing the test stimulus in the form of test

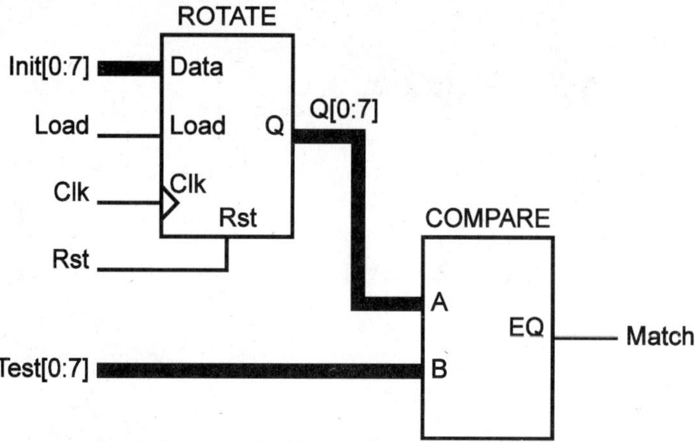


```
/************************************
* Eight-bit rotate and compare
*/

module rotcomp (Clk,Rst,Load,Init,Test,Match);
    input  Clk, Rst, Load;
    input  [0:7] Init;
    input  [0:7] Test;
    output Match;

    wire   [0:7] Q;

    rotate ROT1    (Clk,Rst,Load,Init,Q);
    compare COMP1 (Q,Test,Match);

endmodule
```

Figure 15-3
Top-level Verilog file for the rotate/compare design.

vectors (using an array of records) as we did earlier, though, we're going to create a test fixture that sets up a background clock, and then write the stimulus using a sequence of signal assignments within a type of Verilog statement called an *initial block*. (We'll be doing this just to see an alternate way of writing stimulus; like VHDL, Verilog HDL provides features that allow complex tabular data such as test vectors to be described.)

The complete test fixture is shown in Figure 15-4. The source file contains,

- ☐ A **module** statement declaring the name of the test fixture (**trotcomp**), but with no ports.

```
module trotcomp;

    reg  Clk, Rst, Load;
    reg  [0:7] Init;
    reg  [0:7] Test;
    wire Match;

    rotcomp uut (Clk,Rst,Load,Init,Test,Match);

    parameter period = 100;
    parameter setup  = 20;

    // Set up the system clock
    initial Clk = 1;
    always #(period/2) Clk = ~Clk;

    initial
    begin
        $waves($group=ID_1,"Clk",Clk,"Rst",Rst,
               "Load",Load,"Init",Init,"Test",Test,
               "Q",uut.Q,"Match",Match);
        #(period-setup)  Rst = 1;
                         Test = 'h01;
        #(period)        Rst = 0;
                         Load = 1;
                         Init = 'h22;
        #(period)        Load = 0;
                         Test = 'h44;
        #(period * 2)    Load = 1;
                         Init = 'haa;
        #(period)        Load = 0;
                         Test = 'h55;
        #(period * 2)    Load = 1;
                         Init = 'h50;
        #(period)        Load = 0;
                         Test = 'h05;
        #(period * 4)    Load = 1;
                         Init = 'h00;
        $finish;
    end

endmodule
```

Figure 15-4
Test fixture for rotate/compare design.

- ☐ **Reg** declarations creating top-level signals for the five inputs **Clk**, **Rst**, **Load**, **Init** and **Test**. These signals must be of type **reg** because we will be forcing values onto them during simulation.

- ☐ A **wire** declaration for the top-level output signal **Match**. This signal does not have to be of type **reg** because it simply carries the value of the output out of the lower-level component (the *unit under test*, or *UUT*).

- A component instantiation statement that creates one instance of the **rotcomp** module and associates the top-level signals with the corresponding signals in the lower-level module (using positional association).
- Parameter statements assigning constant values to the identifiers **period** and **setup**. This is simply a convenience, and allows these parameters to be easily changed to simulate a design at different speeds.
- An **initial** statement setting the value of the **Clk** registered signal at simulation time zero.
- An **always** statement describing the operation of the **Clk** signal over time. The **#*nn*** parameter of the **always** statement indicates a timed event, and in this case causes the **Clk** signal's value to toggle at a rate of twice the desired clock cycle time.
- An initial block containing a sequence of statements and delay specifications, including,
- A directive (**$waves**) instructing the simulator which signals are to be captured in the waveform viewer. (Verilog directives are usually installation specific, and may differ depending on the simulator being used.)
- Delay specifiers, beginning with the # character, that indicate how much simulated time should elapse before the next statement occurs.
- Signal assignment statements that force values onto the circuit inputs.
- A **$finish** directive instructing the simulator to end its simulation after the desired sequence of input values has been applied. This is important because we have set up a clock that will run forever and will therefore result in the simulation running indefinitely.

When this test fixture is executed by the simulator, the always block and the two initial blocks are executed concurrently, so the clock operates independent of the stimulus being applied to the other circuit inputs. Let's fire up the BaseLine simulator and see how the design simulates.

FrontLine's BaseLine Simulator

The BaseLine simulator used in this tutorial is produced and sold by FrontLine Design Automation of San Jose, California. BaseLine is a popular Verilog simulator that supports all of theVerilog language specification (as published by Open Verilog International), including the PLI, UDP, and SDF sections of the language standard. We won't be using these more advanced features of the language, however.

Running the Simulation

The first step is to invoke the BaseLine simulator and open the design file. Although the BaseLine simulator—like all Verilog simulators—allows multiple source files to be used, it is easier to run this small example by placing all the design elements, including the three design modules and the test fixture, into a single source file. In this example, the four design modules (**compare**, **rotate**, **rotcomp**, and the **trotcomp** test fixture) have been combined into a single source file named **rotcomp.v**.

To prepare the design for simulation, it must first be compiled:

1. Invoke the BaseLine simulator from Windows by double-clicking on its icon.
2. Open the source file using the **Open** command in the **File** menu (Figure 15-5).

When the simulator opens and reads a source file, it checks the syntax, compiles the design into a form ready for simulation, and begins execution of the initial blocks. Any errors during this process are reported to the transcript area of the main application window (Figure 15-6).

During this initial compilation, the BaseLine simulator determines the hierachy of all the elements of the design by examining which modules are referenced in which higher-level modules. The resulting map of the design hierarchy can be viewed in the Browser window:

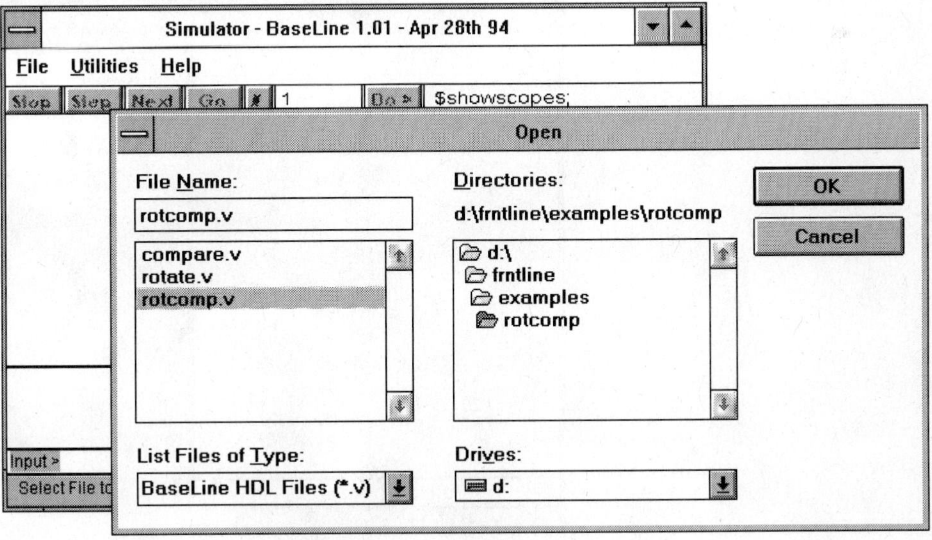

Figure 15-5
Compiling a source file in BaseLine.

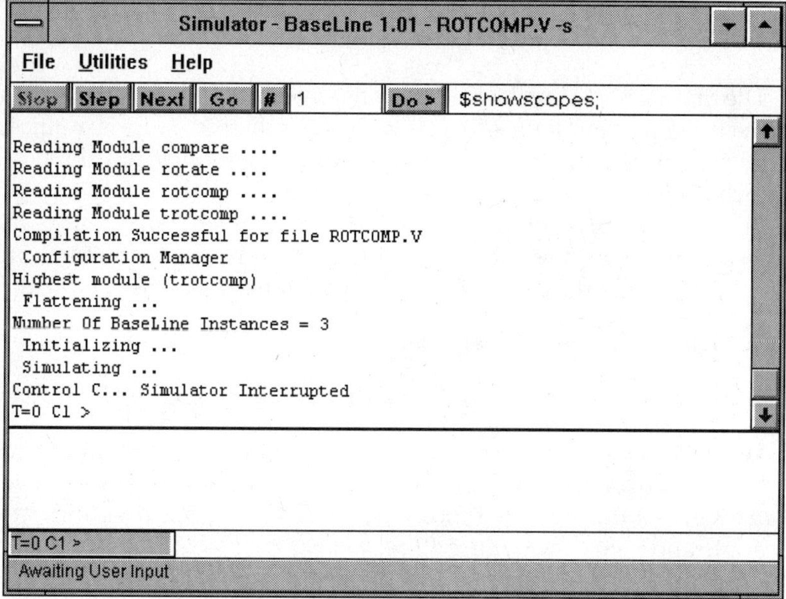
Simulator - BaseLine 1.01 - ROTCOMP.V -s
File Utilities Help
Stop Step Next Go # 1 Do > $showscopes;
Reading Module compare ....
Reading Module rotate ....
Reading Module rotcomp ....
Reading Module trotcomp ....
Compilation Successful for file ROTCOMP.V
Configuration Manager
Highest module (trotcomp)
Flattening ...
Number Of BaseLine Instances = 3
Initializing ...
Simulating ...
Control C... Simulator Interrupted
T=0 C1 >
T=0 C1 >
Awaiting User Input

Figure 15-6
The BaseLine message window reports errors and status during compilation.

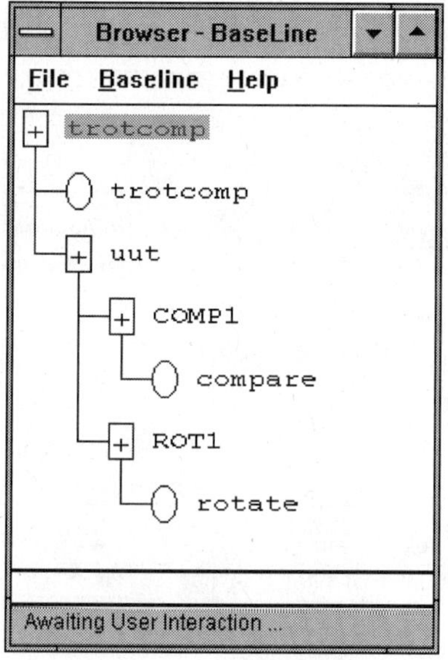
Browser - BaseLine
File Baseline Help
trotcomp
trotcomp
uut
COMP1
compare
ROT1
rotate
Awaiting User Interaction ...

Figure 15-7
The Browser window provides a graphic view of a design's hierarchy.

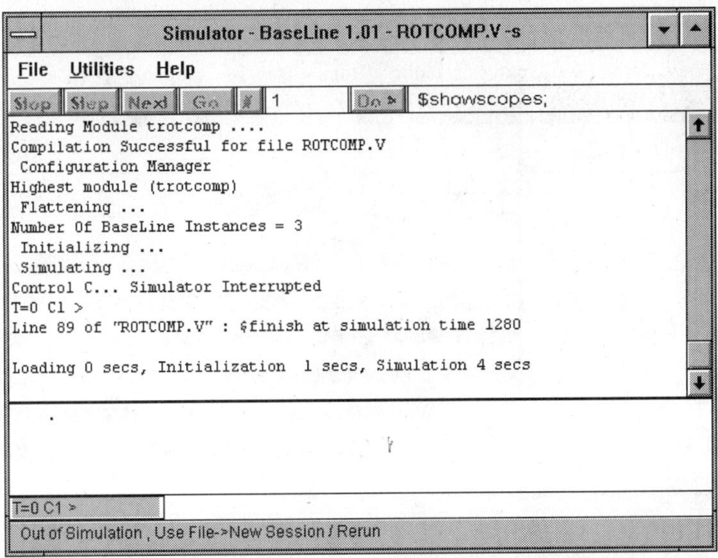
Simulator - BaseLine 1.01 - ROTCOMP.V -s
File Utilities Help
Stop Step Next Go 1 Do $showscopes;
Reading Module trotcomp ....
Compilation Successful for file ROTCOMP.V
Configuration Manager
Highest module (trotcomp)
Flattening ...
Number Of BaseLine Instances = 3
Initializing ...
Simulating ...
Control C... Simulator Interrupted
T=0 C1 >
Line 89 of "ROTCOMP.V" : $finish at simulation time 1280
Loading 0 secs, Initialization 1 secs, Simulation 4 secs
T=0 C1 >
Out of Simulation , Use File->New Session / Rerun

Figure 15-8
The simulation reports status information as the simulation progresses.

3. Select the Browser command from the Utilities window. A hierarchy display will appear (Figure 15-7).

In addition to giving you a clear picture of how your design is structured, this window also allows you to control which part of the design you are currently working with, so you can, for example, simulate a lower-level module independent of the larger design.

After the design has been compiled and the simulation initialized, you can view the initial simulation values in the Waveform window (Figure 15-8). The waveform window displays the values of unknown or unitialized signals as solid bars, as shown. Unlike the VHDL simulation we performed in the last chapter, the Verilog simulator's waveform window is already set up with the signals of interest. This is because the appropriate signals have been specified in the Verilog test fixture using the **$waves** directive. Verilog provides a number of directives that you can use to control the simulation run. Some of these directives are are specific to certain simulation environments, while others (such as **$waves** and **$finish**) are defined in the Verilog HDL standard.

To run the entire simulation up to the point at which the **$finish** directive takes effect, we just need to click the **Go** button in the main application window (Figure 15-9).

4. Click the **Go** button in BaseLine's main application window.

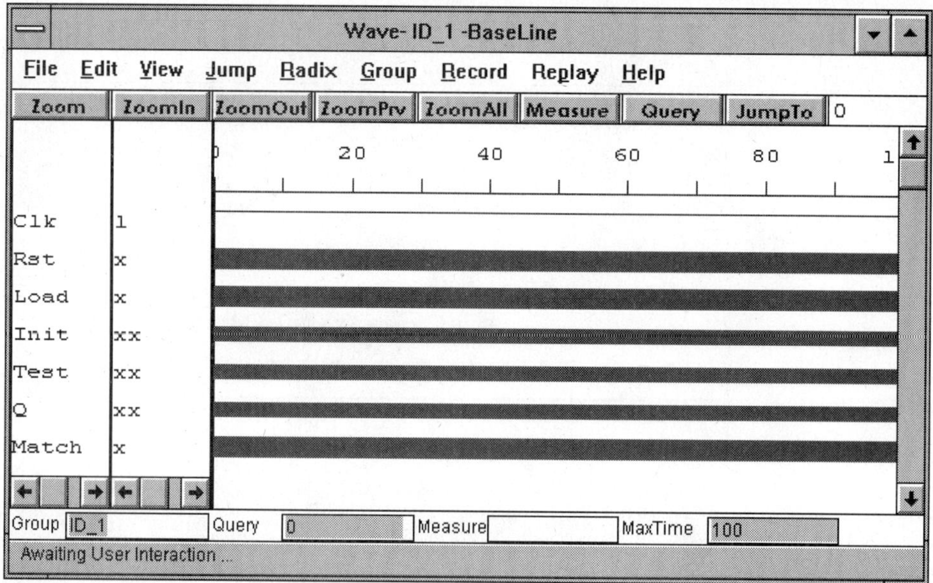

Figure 15-9
The Waveform window showing the initial simulation values prior to running the simulation.

As the simulation runs, the waveform window is updated. When the simulation completes, you can zoom out the waveform display and view the entire sequence of events (Figure 15-10).

5. Click on **Zoom All** to view the entire waveform.

Notice that the values in the waveform are displayed as hexadecimal values. The BaseLine waveform viewer will also display waveform values using binary, octal and decimal values. (No matter which radix you choose, however, the simulator trims off the leading zeros. This can make results—particularly binary ones—somewhat difficult to analyze.)

Source-Level Debugging

A nice feature of many HDL-based simulators is their capability for source-level debugging. The V-System VHDL simulator we used in the previous chapter supports this feature, as does the BaseLine Verilog simulator. Source-level debugging is particularly nice when you are describing sequential circuits (such as state machines) or are performing detailed debugging of your simulation results. Figure 15-11 shows the BaseLine debugging window. This windows allows you to step through your Verilog program, select signals for display on the waveform window, and perform other useful analysis tasks.

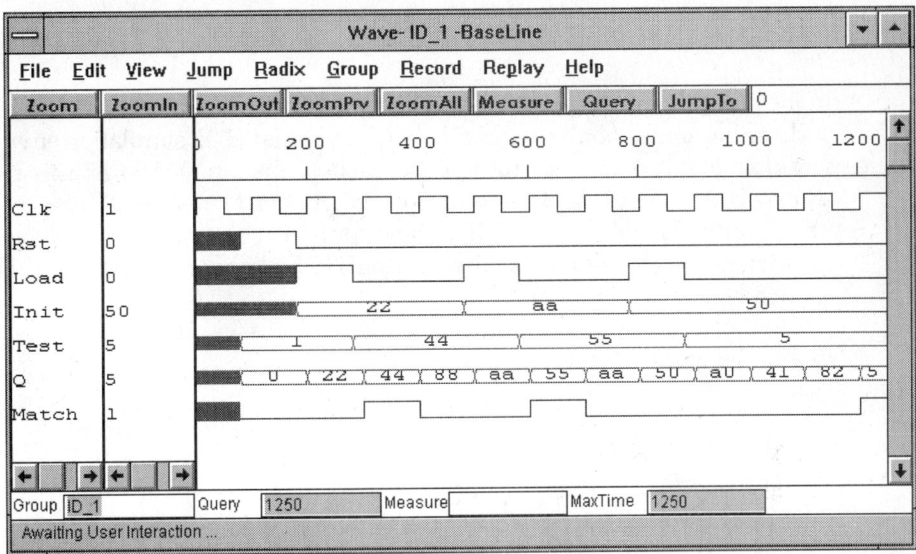

Figure 15-10
The complete simulation results are displayed in the waveform window.

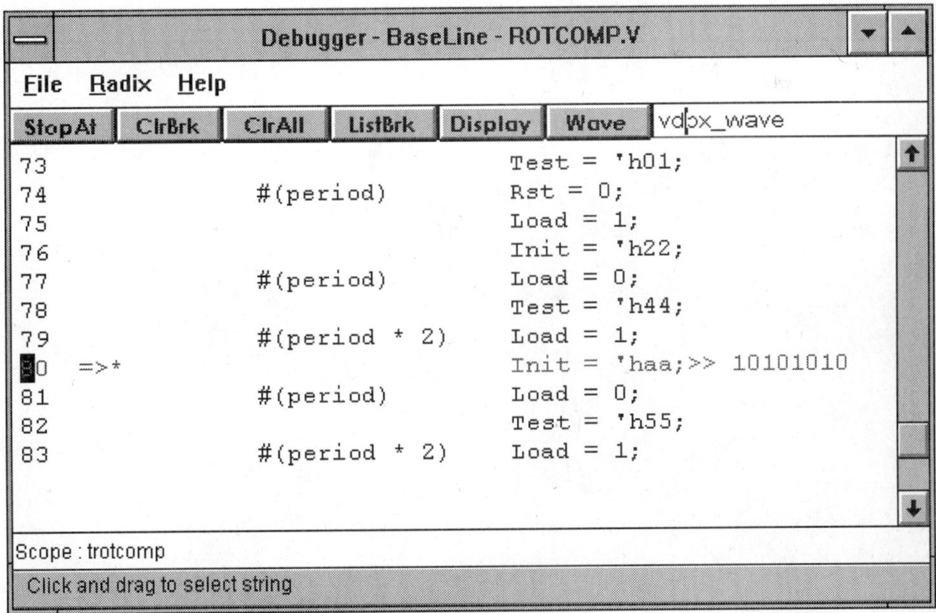

Figure 15-11
Most HDL simulators, including BaseLine, provide a source-level debugger.

Moving On

In the preceding three chapters, you have been presented with the basics of VHDL and Verilog simulation, have seen how two popular HDL simulation environments work, and have had basic tutorials in each of the languages. At this point, you should have enough knowlege of both languages to read HDL source files and understand the essence of what they contain. You should also have enough understanding of the issues surrounding HDLs to evaluate whether they make sense for your particular application.

In the next chapter, I'm going to continue discussing HDLs and show how they fit into the world of synthesis.

CHAPTER 16

FOCUS ON TECHNOLOGY: LOGIC SYNTHESIS

Synthesis, according to my 1937 edition of *Webster's Dictionary*, is "composition, or putting of two or more things together." That definition of synthesis, untainted by any jargon of technology, provides a good insight into what synthesis is all about. Synthesis is a process of automated composition, putting your design specification together with the constraints of a target technology to create a result that is practical, efficient, and ready for implementation.

Synthesis is not a new technology; it has been in widespread use for at least two decades in the areas of ASIC and programmable logic design. Synthesis has been growing in importance—and in use—as designs have become more complex and as synthesis technologies have become more mature and more accessible to mainstream designers.

While it is common to think of synthesis as being synonymous with high-priced ASIC development tools, this is actually not the case. If you have ever used a PLD design language to describe and implement a design, then you have already used synthesis technology.

What Is Synthesis?

In broad terms, synthesis can be described as an automated process in which a design description is made less abstract by converting it to a form more closely matching the form of the target implementation technology. Those last three words, *target implementation technology,* are the key to understanding what synthesis does and where it can help. When you enter a design using some abstract description method (such as an HDL or a schematic of higher-level functions), you are probably less concerned with the details of the implementation (the types of flip-flops to be used, how the logic is arranged, and so on) than you would be if you were entering the design at a gate or transistor level. Because the design is entered in an abstract form, it should be possible to translate the design—synthesize it—for different target technologies. That translation process is where synthesis technology fits in.

It is useful to think of synthesis as being much the same process for hardware as compilation is for software. The same ideas apply; in software development, you enter your design using a high-level language (Pascal, C, C++) and compile that design into a form that is optimized for a particular type of hardware (such as an Intel or Motorola microprocessor, a workstation or mainframe system, or an embedded DSP system). In both hardware synthesis and software compilation, there are different types of optimization that can be performed by the software. Software compiler tools and hardware synthesis tools are both intended to insulate you from the grubby details of the target technology, so you can get your job done faster.

But there is another parallel between software compilation and hardware synthesis that you need to be aware of. No matter how powerful a hardware synthesis tool is, you cannot ignore the underlying hardware requirements and capabilities if you want to create a competitive application. The same rules hold true for software development and hardware synthesis: if you do not take the underlying hardware or, in the case of software, the operating system or user interface framework into consideration during the design process, you are not likely to achieve an efficient implementation of your product concept. We'll be exploring examples of this in the chapters that follow.

How Does Synthesis Work?

In the previous section, I described synthesis as the conversion of an abstract design description into a less abstract form. What forms can that abstract design description take? Like software, it could take the form of a text-based description of the design's intended behavior. We looked at two popular hardware description languages in the previous two chapters. Textual design entry forms, in which VHDL, Verilog HDL or some other language is used to describe the design, are becoming more common as language-based synthesis and simulation tools are becoming more affordable. Synthesis does not automatically imply a language-based entry method. Some synthesis tools also accept netlists of schematic primitives or higher-level functions (such as TTL equivalents) that can be used as building blocks to describe a design. In some design entry systems, a combination of graphical blocks, lower-level primitives, and HDL source files can be used to describe a design for synthesis.

Reaching a Higher Level of Abstraction

When you use synthesis tools, you are able to create complex circuits more rapidly because you are able to raise the level of abstraction at which you design. This can be a great time-saver, but can also lead to confusion when you try to understand the circuitry implemented in the target hardware. In all of the possible ways of describing a design for synthesis, including those that are based on simple gate-level primitives, the design concept as entered into the system may have little or no relationship to the actual arrangement of circuit elements (gates, flip-flops or simple transistors) that are available in the target technology (be it a custom chip, gate array, FPGA, or some other technology). If fact, by the time a synthesis tool finishes chewing on your design, changing or deleting whole sections of logic and generally making a mess—from your perspective—of things, you may have a very hard time relating the resulting output back to the design you entered. This can make debugging the circuit quite a challenge.

The preceding comments are not intended to scare you away from synthesis technology; quite the contrary, as designs get larger and larger, you will find it impossible to deal with the overwhelming complexity of the gate-level details of the circuit and will find that synthesis is the only practical way to deal with your designs. At some point in the not-too-distant future, you might begin to feel about gates and flip-flops the same way a software application developer might feel about machine language.

The actual mapping of a netlist of synthesized primitives, for both the random logic and structured logic parts of the design, is known as *technology mapping* or, in some products, *device fitting*. Technology mapping and device fitting algorithms are highly specific to the target technology and result in a form of the design that is ready for implementation in a specific device type.

This description of synthesis technology is, of course, a gross oversimplification. There are many ways that synthesis tools can approach the problem of converting an abstract design description into a form appropriate for the target technology. In some environments, different sections of the design may be synthesized individually, and will not be merged together until it is time to actually map the design, section by section, into the device. In other environments, the intermediate form may may be a Boolean logic representation of the circuit.

Do You Need Synthesis?

The answer to this question depends, naturally enough, on the application and target technology. If you are using PLDs, you are almost certainly already using a form of synthesis. PLD design environments usually have some form of front-end synthesis (logic optimization, translation of state diagrams into Boolean logic, etc.) coupled with a primitive technology mapper such as a fuse pattern generator.

If you are intending to design for larger programmable devices such as the Altera MAX and AMD MACH series of complex PLDs, then you will either have to obtain some kind of more advanced synthesis tools for automatic device routing or suffer the pain of routing the chips by hand. (In the Altera devices, the latter option is not even available.)

If your target is an FPGA such as those sold by Xilinx, Actel, and Quicklogic (among others) and your designs are relatively small (less than a few thousand gates or so), you can probably get away with using the manual placement and routing tools provided by the vendors, use schematic capture to design with the various macros and gate-level symbols provided, and forgo higher-level synthesis technology for the time being.

If you are intending to migrate your designs out of complex PLDs and FPGAs into more complex devices (such as gate arrays) or expect to increase the complexity of your designs beyond the point at which schematic-based design methods are practical, synthesis is your only option, and you should become familiar with the process before you are faced with an impossible schedule on a large design.

What it boils down to is this: the only digital circuit designers who can afford to ignore synthesis tools are those who are only developing small-scale designs using discrete (TTL or equivalent) components or who are designing system interfaces that are outside the bounds of today's synthesis technology.

What Are the Limitations of Synthesis?

Today's synthesis technology is reasonably good at converting a well-defined segment of an overall circuit—the random logic, control functions and, to some extent, the data path elements—into an efficient form that can be implemented in a single PLD, FPGA, or larger ASIC. Synthesis tools do tend to have problems, however, when they are presented with nonregular problems such as I/O circuitry or clock distribution trees and when the implementation for a particular segment of the design clearly maps directly to a hardware feature (such as a clock generator, RAM block, or other device-specific feature) that is not generally available in a wide variety of devices. Synthesis tools today also do a poor job of crossing device boundaries (automatic partitioning tools—where they exist—are immature and only work for a limited number of devices) and often fall to pieces (or run forever) when presented with overly large designs—or even relatively small designs, if you don't follow the proper design rules and synthesis conventions.

Because of this, it is helpful to think of today's synthesis tools as module generators—not in the device-specific sense that the term was used earlier, but in the sense that you should use synthesis technology for relatively small portions of the design (perhaps even the same size that you, yourself would be comfortable working with) and combine the synthesized design modules later in the process. There are two benefits to this philosophy: first, you will have a better chance of getting the smaller design segments through the synthesis tools and, second, you will have a much easier time debugging the circuit when the synthesized version does not perform the way you expect.

What Does Synthesis Cost?

Synthesis tools, being relatively new to the market, are changing rapidly in both their feature contents and in their costs. Prices for "universal" synthesis technology that is full-featured enough to do serious work with complex PLD or FPGA-class devices, or small-scale gate arrays, is probably going to cost you somewhere between $3,000 and $15,000. (If you will be doing more advanced ASIC synthesis, you can expect to pay many times that amount and will be outside of the realm of the tools described in this book.) Prices are often confusing, with some synthesis vendors selling basic synthesis technology that is of no use without one or more technology libraries or "device kits." Synthesis tools that are specific to a single family of devices (and are supplied by device vendors) may be significantly cheaper than their "universal" counterparts. If you plan on using a small number of device families, you may find that it's less expensive to purchase the basic synthesis tools from device vendors rather than from third-party synthesis tool vendors.

One thing to keep in mind for the future is that the proliferation of LPM (Library of Parameterized Macros—see the end of this chapter for details) in synthesis tools may exert a significant downward pressure on the cost of synthesis tools. Since LPM allows the decoupling of front-end synthesis from back-end synthesis, and many device vendors view back-end synthesis tools as give-away technology that they should be producing themselves, it is quite possible that front-end synthesis vendors will soon be engaged in a price war to maintain their share of the somewhat smaller front-end synthesis market. It is also quite possible that new, low-cost synthesis tools will appear on the market, since the cost of developing LPM-based synthesis tools is much lower than the cost of developing complete, front-to-back synthesis tools that include technology mapping components for a wide variety of target technologies.

Synthesis and Optimization Strategies

As we will see in the next chapter, synthesis tools can make use of a variety of optimization routines and strategies to generate a circuit that is compact and/or fast. One strategy that is sometimes employed in synthesis tools is to apply multiple synthesis algorithms to the design so the best result can be chosen. This strategy of trying a sequence of seemingly random synthesis algorithms might appear a little arbitrary, and in some sense it is. The fact is, synthesis tools today do not have the power to know in advance which strategy will produce the "best" circuit, or which strategy will result in a circuit that comes even close to meeting your worst-case timing and area constraints.

To fully utilize synthesis technology, you must be aware of the strategies that can be employed—both in the synthesis tools and in the design description itself—and take the approach of *designing for synthesis*, rather than expecting synthesis to take care of everything for you. The larger your designs get, the more this is true: synthesis is a powerful tool, but you have to learn how to operate it effectively.

Writing "Good" Synthesizable Designs

Before you even consider pushing your thousand-line VHDL design through a synthesis program, you must spend some time thinking about what synthesis results you expect to see. While it isn't necessary to know in advance what every complex VHDL expression you have written will become, in terms of actual gates (after all, if you knew what the logic was going to look like, why would you need synthesis?), it is important that you consider the general type of logic that is likely to be produced. If you don't know in advance whether your synthesized design should result in a few dozen flip-flops with resets, clock enables, and a lot of combinational logic, or should instead synthesize into a hundred or so latches with a few AND gates, then you are going to be in trouble right from the start.

The Importance of Registers

Registers are the key to synthesis, because the synthesis technology in widespread use today is *register transfer level* (RTL) synthesis. This means that even if you are describing a design at a relatively high, behavioral level of abstraction, the synthesis tool will assume that your design can be decomposed into a set of flip-flops or latches fed by a collection of combinational logic elements. Your job, as the designer of the circuit and as the synthesis operator, is to describe your design in such a way that you get the types of registers you want, and that the combinational logic is correctly expressed, with no redundant expressions or unwanted feedback loops.

Note: *There have been many industry announcements and other press reports about higher-level synthesis products. These products are often described with words like "behavioral synthesis" or "algorithmic synthesis" and are intended to raise the level of abstraction by crossing automatically determining such things as the number of register levels, the timing of events in those registers, and so on. While these tools may mature into widely available—and affordable—products at some point in the future, I'm not going to spend any time describing them here. Such technology is only available at a very high price, and has not yet been proven for a wide range of applications.*

When you describe a registered circuit using either VHDL or Verilog HDL, you are describing the behavior of the circuit over time, rather than describing the physical structure of the circuit. This is the primary difference between higher-level behavioral languages (such as VHDL or Verilog HDL) and lower-level languages intended only for PLD design (such as PALASM). Describing a circuit behaviorally can be faster (and more fun) than describing it structurally, but can also result in ambiguities, since there can be many different hardware realizations of the same behavioral description. This is the primary reason that there are *synthesis conventions* that you should adhere to.

Register Conventions

In both VHDL and Verilog HDL, there are certain ways of describing registered circuits that have been promoted for synthesis. These conventions have not been published as a standard, but have instead evolved over time as the synthesis tools have matured. The VHDL convention for synthesis is to use the conditional **if-then-else** sequence to describe the behavior of a registered circuit. Nowhere in the VHDL specification does it say that this sequence of statements describes an edge-triggered flip-flop with a reset—it is only a convention of synthesis tools that makes it possible for you to predict the kind of circuitry that will result. This is true whether you are using VHDL or Verilog.

The lesson? Read your synthesis documentation carefully and examine any design examples supplied with the package. Learn the synthesis conventions, and design with synthesis in mind. If you only enter your design with the narrow goal of creating a successful simulation, don't expect that design to synthesize into a meaningful or efficient circuit.

Combinational Logic

The creation and optimization of combinational logic has traditionally been one of the most tedious aspects of digital design. Fortunately, today's logic synthesis tools can do a very good job of generating large amounts of combinational logic, thereby saving you vast amounts of time. It is important, however, that you consider the impact of using different types of combinational logic descriptions. If you fail to take synthesis into consideration when describing your design, then you will probably waste combinational logic, and may even create a design with serious testability problems. Once again, consult your synthesis tool documentation and try to understand the impact of using different kinds of language statements. Will a chained **if** statement generate more logic than a **case** statement? What about that divide operation—will it really map into a simple shift operation, or will there be additional logic generated? It's best to find these things out before you begin, rather than have to go back and rewrite a large design that doesn't meet your design constraints.

Synthesis Options

Synthesis tools tend to have many options and controls, and it is important to understand what these options are, and when they can be used for the most benefit. Since synthesis of a large circuit can be quite time consuming, you don't want to be faced with the task of running every combination of synthesis options to determine the best set of options for your particular design. Instead, spend some time up-front thinking about your design and about your target technology. Does the design have a large state machine with many transitions? Perhaps a one-hot encoding (a common synthesis option) would be most appropriate. Are there standard data flow elements such as comparators used in the design? Perhaps some minor design changes, followed by a module generation strategy would be best for the architecture you have chosen. Check the specific features available in the target architecture. If there are predefined hard macros available in the device that you will be using, see if the synthesis tool allows you to use these building blocks directly, or is capable of inferring them from your high-level descriptions.

Module Generation

Device-specific synthesis tools that include extensive module libraries containing information about each target device often do a better job of mapping higher-level functions to a unique architecture. This is because the synthesis vendor can "tune" the optimization algorithms to meet the needs of the target device. In reality, the gains in efficiency that you get from this kind of synthesis technology are actually much less than you will get from a careful examination of your design, from having a general understanding of the strengths and weaknesses of the target architectures, and from developing a "design-for-synthesis" mind-set. Much of the device-specific synthesis can actually be deferred to the device vendor's technology mapping and place-and-route software, anyway, lessening the need for device-specific front-end synthesis. There are some significant gains that can be made, however, by preserving higher-level functions and allowing the back-end synthesis tools (normally provided by the device vendors themselves) to do the work of mapping these functions directly onto the device.

Accessing Device-Specific Modules

The area where this kind of device-specific, library-based synthesis can really help is in the use of device-specific higher-level functions provided by the vendors of the devices themselves. These higher-level functions, which are often called *macrocells*, are predefined blocks of logic usually representing commonly used data path functions such as adders and comparators. The device vendor creates these macrocells by hand, either out of the standard gates and registers available in the device or by implementing them directly in silicon. The vendors then publish information about how to access these special macrocells, providing the name of the netlist symbols and other data needed to use them. To use these features in a synthesis-oriented design flow, you either have to somehow include the functions into your design without confusing the synthesis tools (typically by using hierarchy in your design to invoke one or more external macrocells) or have a synthesis tool that is aware of the existence of the higher-level macrocells and can generate references to them as needed.

The Xilinx 4000 series devices, for example, feature a number of these software-accessible features. The Xilinx 4000 series *soft macros* include functions ranging from 7400 series TTL equivalents (74138, 74154, etc) to generic data path functions such as barrel shifters, counters, comparators and decoders. These preoptimized, high-level functions can be used to advantage for large circuits—particularly large data path circuits—if the synthesis tool is aware of them. Synthesis tools that are optimized for the Xilinx 4000 architecture can provide access to these features using both user-specified methods (using hierarchy) and through automatic module generation features, in which high-level operators (such as '=' and '+') are automatically mapped to the corresponding soft macro functions.

LPM: Library of Parameterized Macros

In the preceding description of synthesis technology, I described how the design description is mapped from an abstract form (an HDL or other functional representation of the design) into a form that more closely resembles hardware (a netlist of primitives). I also described how the primitives that result from synthesis may be simple primitives such as gates and flip-flops, or more complex primitives such as counters, comparators, and multiplexers. Developers of front-end synthesis tools, together with creators of back-end technology mapping software developers (who are usually, but not always, employed by device vendors), have recently realized that the entire world of synthesis tools could be simplified if there was some attempt to standardize both the netlist format that is used to connect front-end and back-end tools and, more important, to specify the actual primitives that can be represented in that netlist format. This is the role of LPM, Library of Parameterized Macros. LPM, which is built upon a standard EDIF netlist, has been defined by a consortium of FPGA and complex PLD vendors and defines a standard set of intermediate logic primitives (adders, comparators, and the like) that can be parameterized to arbitrary input and output widths.

The LPM standard holds a great deal of promise for the EDA industry in general, and for users of programmable logic and ASICs in particular. With a standard format like LPM in the middle (Figure 16-1) it will finally be possible to choose design entry and synthesis tools based on their merits as high-level design tools, rather than on their support for specific device architectures and netlist formats.

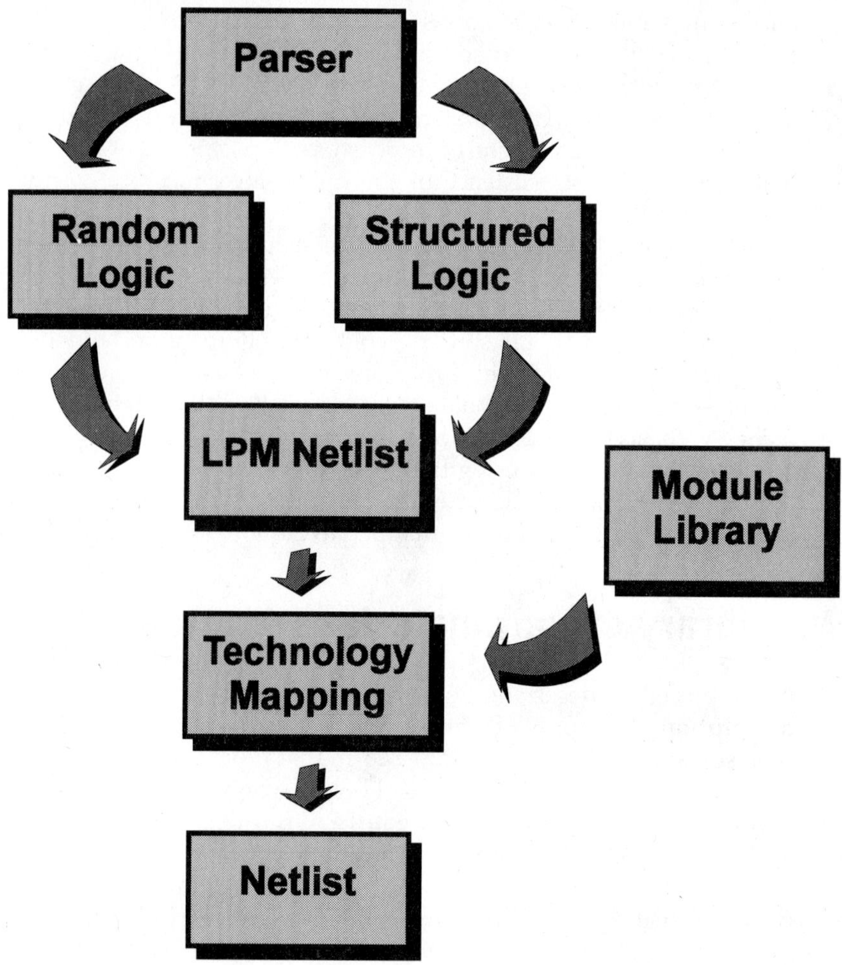

Figure 16-1
Synthesis processing flow using LPM

Moving On

Now that we have discussed the basic philosophies and capabilities of today's synthesis tools, it's time to synthesize some examples. In the next chapter, we're going to try out a synthesis package and see how various designs are processed into forms ready for implementation into actual devices.

Other Resources

Airiau, Roland, *Circuit Synthesis with VHDL*, Kluwer Academic, Hingham, MA, 1993.

Armstrong, James R. and F. Gail Gray, *Structured Logic Design with VHDL*, Prentice Hall, Englewood Cliffs, NJ, 1993.

Carlson, Steve, *Introduction to HDL-Based Design Using VHDL*, Synopsys, Mountain View, CA, 1989.

Perry, Douglas L., *VHDL, (2nd ed.)*, McGraw-Hill, New York, 1993.

Sternheim, Singh, Trivedi, Madhavan, Stapleton, *Digital Design and Synthesis with Verilog HDL*, Automata, San Jose, CA, 1992.

CHAPTER 17

HANDS-ON EDA: USING SYNTHESIS

To understand how the the synthesis process works, we're going to take a close look at a synthesis product produced and sold by Exemplar Logic of Berkeley, California. Exemplar's CORE is representative of a small number of tools that are specifically intended for logic synthesis and are relatively accessible to cost-sensitive design engineers.

Note: *This chapter uses Exemplar Logic's CORE to demonstrate synthesis concepts. Exemplar Logic has provided an evaluation version of their software on the CD-ROM, as have other synthesis vendors. Because synthesis technology is advancing rapidly, however, you are encouraged to contact the synthesis vendors listed in Appendix A for the most current information about synthesis features and support for specific devices and other implementation technologies.*

Exemplar's CORE

Exemplar's CORE (Complete Optimization and Retargeting Environment) package is a collection of synthesis programs and libraries that allow designs entered in a variety of formats (including VHDL, Verilog HDL, and various netlist formats) to be processed into a form appropriate for a selected type of hardware. The types of hardware supported by CORE range from complex PLDs (such as those offered by Altera Corporation) to high-capacity FPGAs and gate arrays. CORE includes optimization routines that are optimized for each type of hardware target and is intended to be used in conjunction with place and route software provided by programmable logic and gate array device vendors.

In the CORE design flow (Figure 17-1), VHDL or Verilog HDL source files are the primary input to the synthesis tool (which also accepts various forms of netlists) and are processed into two basic forms. The first form of the design is what might be called the "random logic" section of the design, and includes abstract descriptions of combinational logic and RTL functions (functions with well-defined register requirements). This segment of the design is what is going to be synthesized—using circuit optimization algorithms—into a form more closely approximating hardware.

The second segment of a design, which might be called the "structured logic" segment, includes those parts of the design that are described using blocks of predefined circuitry that already map reasonably well into hardware. This portion of the design might include high-level blocks (such as counters, comparators and multiplexers), or lower-level circuit elements that are specific to the target device (such as specialized clock buffers, I/O macrocells or other technology-specific items). This segment of the design will probably not be synthesized in the same way as the random logic section of the design, since the blocks of circuitry are already in a form that is reasonably close to a hardware representation. Instead, the synthesis tool will perform what is called *module generation*, which is a fancy term for a library lookup function; each block of circuitry in the structured logic section of the design will be mapped into a technology-specific equivalent module, and these technology-specific modules will then be combined with the optimized netlist representing the synthesized random logic before the entire design is mapped into the target hardware.

We'll walk through a few simple examples to show how synthesis tools such as Exemplar's CORE can be used. Since we're going to be synthesizing the circuit using Exemplar's CORE, we could use either VHDL or Verilog HDL to enter these designs. We are going to use VHDL, though, because there are currently more synthesis tools available that operate from the VHDL language than from Verilog HDL.

In the first example, we'll be taking the VHDL version of the shifter/comparator design presented in Chapter 14 and use CORE to create an optimized, device-specific netlist ready for implementation in an Actel FPGA. Although synthesis technology is most useful for larger, more complex designs, the simplicity of this design will allow us to explore the synthesis process in detail. After finishing with the simple circuit, we'll go on to try two somewhat more complex examples, target them to a Xilinx 4000 series LCA, and learn how different synthesis strategies can affect the synthesis results.

Determining a Synthesis Strategy

Before beginning the synthesis process, we have to spend a moment thinking about the design and considering the various synthesis strategies possible for the selected

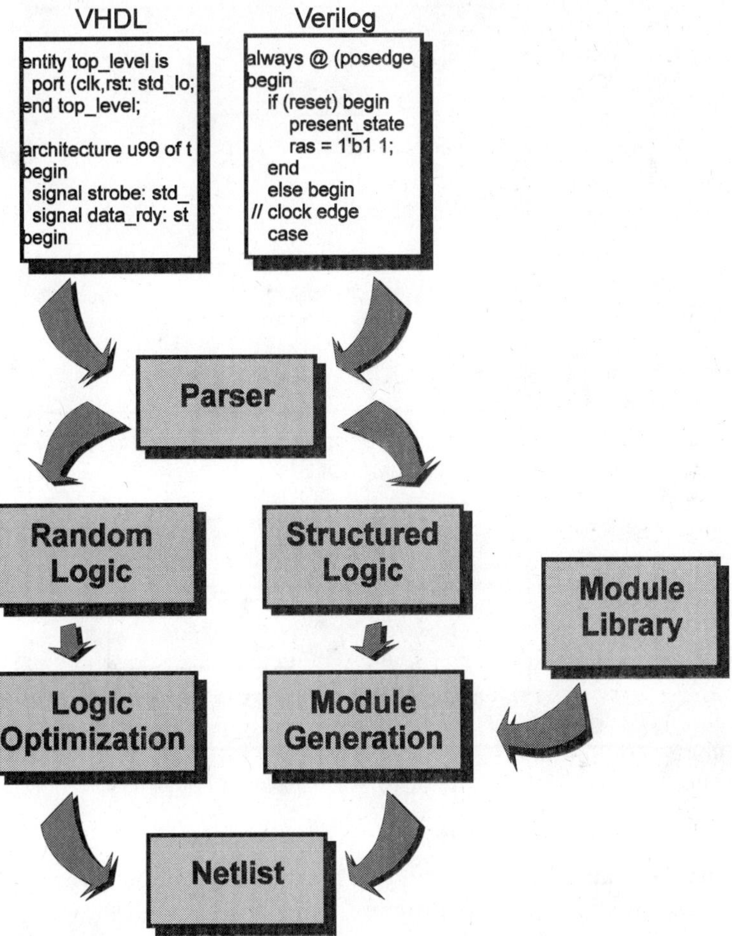

Figure 17-1
CORE synthesis processing flow.

device. When you have a design that is modular (such as the shifter/comparator) you have the option of either combining, or *flattening*, the entire design prior to synthesis, or leaving it modular until the final phases of placement and routing.

If you want to take advantage of global optimization, and have the best chance of your design being optimized to its minimum area or delay measurements, then you will probably want to try, at least initially, to flatten the design during the synthesis process. If the design is hierarchical (as is our sample design) you will simply combine the entire design into a single file or use some other HDL feature (such as Verilog HDL's 'include directive) to present the synthesis program with the entire design. (In most tools, including Exemplar's CORE, the synthesis program

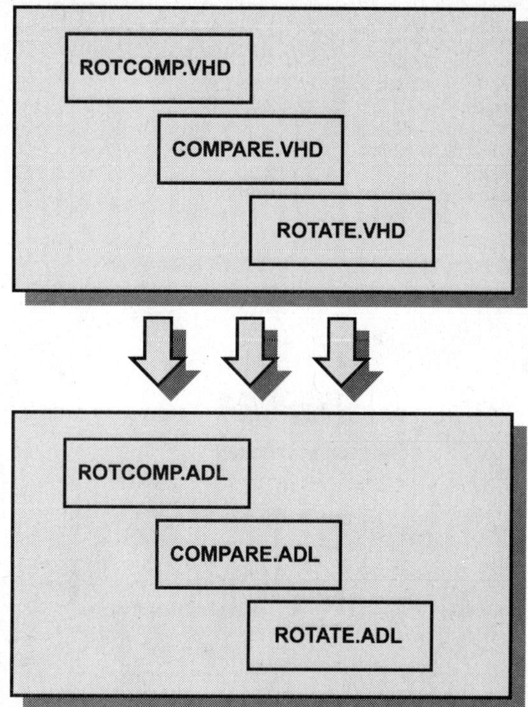

Figure 17-2
Synthesizing each module separately results in a hierarchical netlist.

can be also given a list of input files that will be combined during synthesis.) During processing, the synthesis program will analyze the design's hierarchy and flatten the design into a single layer, collapsing all component instances into higher-level modules before continuing with the synthesis process. The result will be a large mass of logic representing the design, in the form of a single netlist format output file.

The primary disadvantage to this approach is one of practicality. All synthesis tools today (including Exemplar's) have serious difficulty digesting very large, flat designs. If you attempt to feed the CORE software a design—or portion of a design—that greatly exceeds a few thousand gates in size, you had better be prepared to wait for a long time before anything useful is generated. Instead, it is better to enter your design in a modular way (using either hierarchy or a multi-sheet approach) and process the circuit one module at a time. Later, when you are ready to map the design into the device, you will merge the synthesized modules together to form the complete circuit.

The shifter/comparator design is in a hierarchical form, so we're going to preserve its hierarchy through the synthesis process. The CORE tools don't directly support hierarchy (all designs are flattened when processed) so we'll maintain the hierarchy by running CORE three times, once for each of the three entity/architecture pairs. We'll follow the same ordering of processing as we did during simulation in earlier chapters, beginning with the simplest module, the comparator.

Processing the Comparator

The CORE software runs from within Windows, but is actually a 32-bit DOS program that runs in a DOS box.

1. To start CORE, invoke the application from Windows by double-clicking on its icon.

2. Open the **compare.vhd** design file using the **Open** command in the **File** menu (Figure 17-3).

Before beginning the actual synthesis, you can select compile options from a small number of dialogue boxes. You then select the **Run** button to synthesize your design. For this design, we'll just select the device type (an Actel ACT 1 family device) and run the synthesis with the default options.

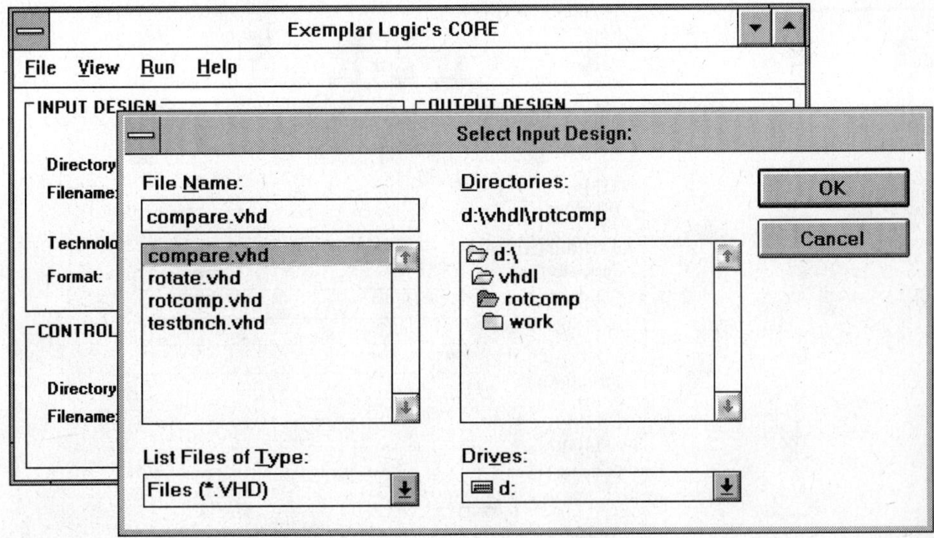

Figure 17-3
Opening a source file with Exemplar's CORE.

During its operation, CORE translates the input file (which may be VHDL, Verilog HDL, or one of a variety of netlist formats) into a technology-independent internal form. CORE then applies one or more synthesis and optimization algorithms to the design, based on the device architecture and the synthesis options selected. Before running this synthesis and looking at the results, let's spend a moment exploring the synthesis options that are available.

Global Options

The CORE software allows you to select certain optimization options before running the synthesis. Global options that you can select (Figure 17-4) include the number of optimization passes to run, and maximum delay or area values. The area values you will specify depend on the method of area estimation used for the chosen architecture. For Actel devices, the unit of measure is a Logic Module, which is a multiplexer-based structure that may or may not include a register, depending on the family of Actel devices being used.

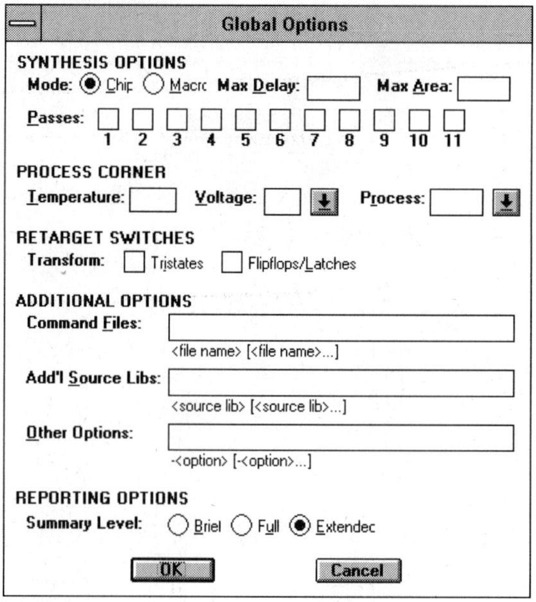

Figure 17-4
Setting global optimization and synthesis options.

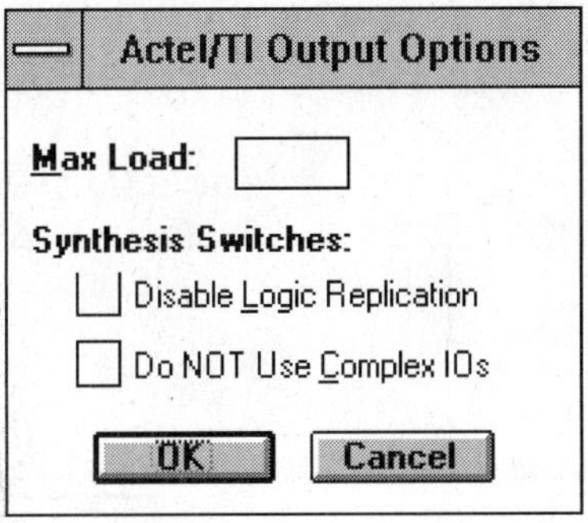

Figure 17-5
Actel synthesis output options.

Retargeting Options

For device retargeting, CORE also allows you to remap registers and latches, and to specify how three-state outputs are to be handled. One example of register re-mapping is the treatment of register reset and preset. The software will remap asynchronous resets to synchronous resets (and generate a warning) if you specify the register retarget option. The software can also eliminate unused registers or registers that are fixed at a constant value after optimization. If two or more registers have identical input logic, the software will combine the registers by merging them.

One of the most important options is the Chip/Macro selection. This option specifies if the target netlist is to be generated as a complete design (with I/O ports mapped to input and output pins) or will be a part of a larger design that will be merged when it is mapped into the device. For our sample design, we might want to specify Macro for the two lower-level modules **compare** and **rotate**, but specify Chip for the top-level module, since we expect to map the top-level ports of the design to actual I/O pads in the chip.

Many of the optimization and synthesis options are specific to certain classes of devices. For the Actel FPGAs, there are additional options available in the Output Options dialogue box (Figure 17-5). These options include a **Max Load** option, which limits the fan-out from logic modules, a **Disable Logic Replication** option, which disables the use of replicated logic to meet fan-out constraints, and an option for disabling the use of complex I/O macrocells (typically macrocells that have both I/O buffers and register logic) in the final circuit.

Optimizing for the Target Architecture

After the design has been read into CORE and translated into the technology-independent internal representation, CORE reads in a technology-specific library corresponding to the target architecture. The content of

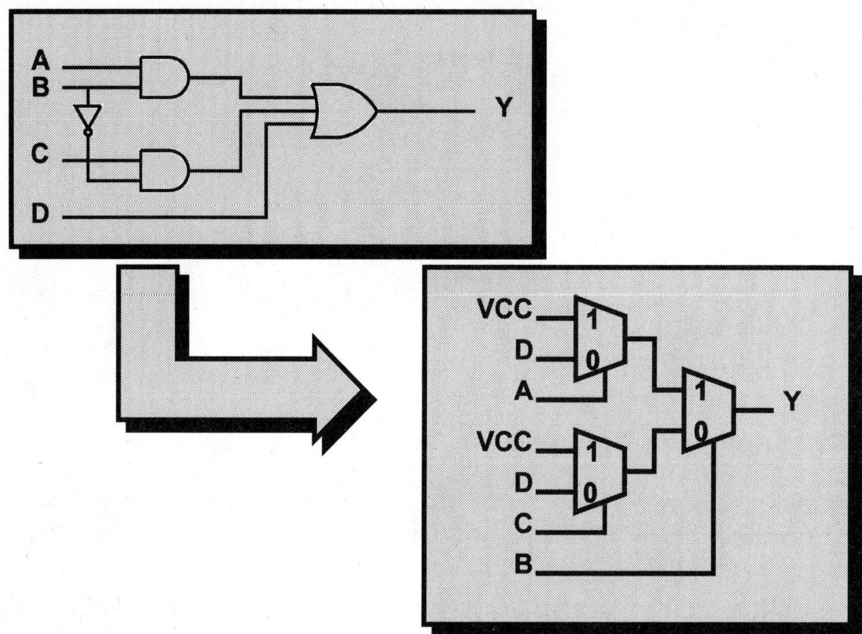

Figure 17-6
AND/OR logic is converted into multiplexer logic appropriate for the Actel logic modules.

this library differs depending on the architecture, but generally includes information about the type and size of logic blocks and other primitives available in the device, as well as information about the type of optimization algorithms to be applied to the circuit. For a Xilinx LCA, for example, the optimization strategy may be based on the lookup table architecture of a configurable logic block (CLB), while for a Toshiba gate array the optimizer may attempt to reduce the logic using a different strategy based on AND/OR/Invert logic. Every type of target technology has different requirements, and technology-specific synthesis is invoked as needed for each.

For the Actel devices, a multiplexer-based approach to optimization is used, since the Actel logic modules are composed of multiplexer circuits. CORE's Actel-specific optimization algorithms understand how multiplexer-based logic modules can be configured to create inverters, AND gates and OR gates, as well as being used as simple multiplexers. Since the multiplexer is the most efficient structure for implementation in the Actel logic module, the software attempts to convert AND/OR functions into multiplexer logic as a part of the overall optimization strategy (Figure 17-6).

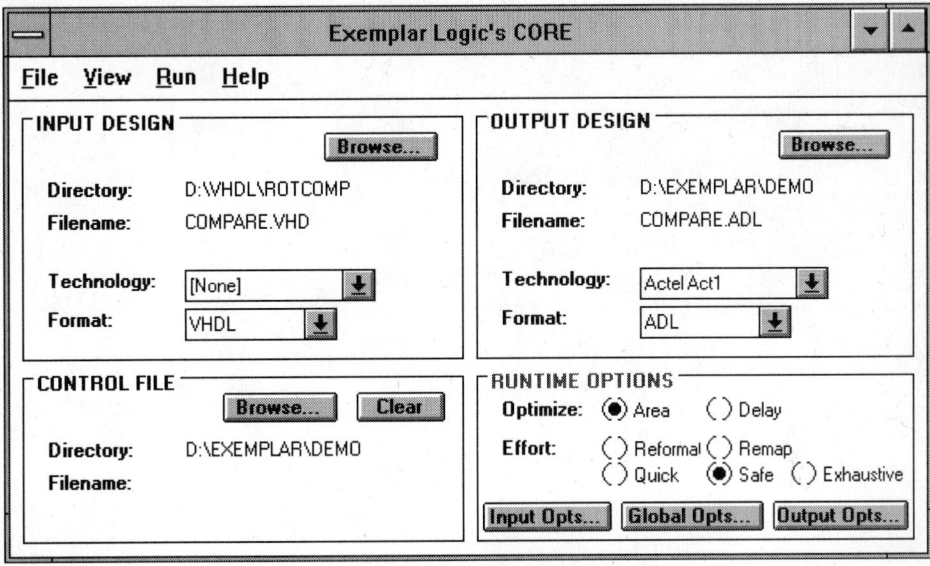

Figure 17-7
*The **rotcomp** module will be translated into a hierarchical ADL netlist.*

Technology Mapping

For most device technologies, the optimization phase is followed by (or combined with) a technology mapping phase, in which higher-level primitives (such as multiplexers, adders and registers) are mapped to lower-level primitives in the target device. This technology mapping phase may also be deferred for the final synthesis step, which is the mapping of the design into the device through the use of device-vendor supplied software. In the CORE tools, the technology mapping process for the Actel architecture is combined with the optimization phase. During this phase, the optimizer selects and configures logic modules by applying a weighted cost function that involves area, speed, number of signals used and other factors. The area and speed figures are obtained from an Actel-specific technology library, while the other numbers are derived from the optimized design. The weighting of the area and speed numbers are changed depending on how you choose to optimize the design.

Repetitive Optimization

Many synthesis tools, including the CORE software, perform optimization iteratively using different optimization strategies for each pass. This allows you (or the synthesis software) to select the best combination of area and speed from the results. The CORE software, in addition to providing predefined optimization and

```
Reading library file 'd:\exemplar\lib\act120.syn'...
Library version = 1.14
Delays assume: Temp= 25.0 C  Voltage=5.00 V
Process=typical

Exemplar Logic's CORE  Sun Jun  5 14:32:46 1994


Pass    Area      Delay      Io              -CPU-
     (modules)     (ns)  (modules)          min:sec
1          9        22        17             00:14
2          9        22        17             00:14
3          9        29        17             00:14
4          9        29        17             00:11
5          9        22        17             08:57
6          9        22        17           1:21:30
7          9        22        17             02:03
8          9        22        17             02:20
9          9        22        17             02:21
10         9        29        17             02:16
11         9        22        17             02:22
map pass 1:
```

Figure 17-8
Running the CORE program.

synthesis passes specific to each device, allows you to further tailor the synthesis process by specifying various levels of "effort." These effort levels range from **Quick** (in which only one optimization pass is invoked) to **Exhaustive**.

Synthesizing the Comparator

To synthesize the rotate/compare design into an Actel ADL netlist, ready for implementation in a device

1. If you have not already done so, load the **compare.vhd** source file into CORE using the **Open** command in the **File** menu.

2. Select the **Actel ACT 1** family of devices by clicking on the **Technology** field in the main application window (Figure 17-7).

```
                    Resource Use Estimate

    Design:            COMPARE
    Technology:        act1
    File:              D:\VHDL\ROTCOMP\COMPARE.VHD
    Area:              9 modules
    Critical Path:     22 ns
    Io modules:        17 modules


                         Delay Summary

    Node:    Slack       Arrival         Required       Load
                       rise    fall    rise    fall
    EQ   :   0.00    21.90   21.90   21.90   21.90    1.00


                      Cell Usage Summary

 Cell                  Uses              Cost                 Total

  AND4B             1 uses(s)     1.00 modules      1.00 modules
  XA1A              2 uses(s)     1.00 modules      2.00 modules
  XNOR              2 uses(s)     1.00 modules      2.00 modules
  XO1               2 uses(s)     1.00 modules      2.00 modules
  XOR               2 uses(s)     1.00 modules      2.00 modules
                                                   -----
                                       Total =     9.00
```

Figure 17-9
Core's Summary Report provides statistics that help estimate device utilization.

3. Select the ADL netlist output design format by clicking on the **Format** field in the **Output Design** section of the main application window.

4. Click on the **New Run** command in the **Run** menu to begin synthesizing the design module.

The CORE application starts running in a DOS window, and reports the results of each optimization pass as it runs (Figure 17-8).

Looking at the Results

When the CORE program finishes running, it produces a summary report, a log file, and the complete netlist (or other format) required to map the design into the target device. Figure 17-9 shows a portion of the summary report produced for this design. The report lists useful information such as estimated worst case path delays and the number and type of logic modules that will be required. This report is useful for determining if the design is likely to meet its speed and area constraints and can help in the device selection process.

The netlist itself (Figure 17-10) contains references to the Actel-specific logic primitives, and is ready for use with Actel's ALS device mapping software. Notice

```
; PROGRAM D:\EXEMPLAR\BIN\PC\FPGA.EXE
 D:\VHDL\ROTCOMP\COMPARE.VHD D:\EXEMPLAR\DEMO\COMPARE.ADL
 -COMMAND_FILE=D:\EXEMPLAR\DEMO\TMP3.$$$
; VERSION V2.1.4
DEF COMPARE; A_0_, A_1_, A_2_, A_3_, A_4_, A_5_, A_6_, A_7_,
 B_0_, B_1_, B_2_, B_3_, B_4_, B_5_, B_6_, B_7_, EQ.
USE ADLIB:XOR; $1I17.
USE ADLIB:XO1; $1I18.
USE ADLIB:XOR; $1I19.
USE ADLIB:XO1; $1I20.
USE ADLIB:XNOR; $1I21.
USE ADLIB:XA1A; $1I22.
USE ADLIB:XNOR; $1I23.
USE ADLIB:XA1A; $1I24.
USE ADLIB:AND4B; $1I25.
NET A_0_; A_0_, $1I23:B.
NET A_1_; A_1_, $1I24:B.
NET A_2_; A_2_, $1I17:B.
NET A_3_; A_3_, $1I18:B.
NET A_4_; A_4_, $1I19:B.
NET A_5_; A_5_, $1I20:B.
NET A_6_; A_6_, $1I21:B.
NET A_7_; A_7_, $1I22:B.
NET B_0_; B_0_, $1I23:A.
NET B_1_; B_1_, $1I24:A.
NET B_2_; B_2_, $1I17:A.
NET B_3_; B_3_, $1I18:A.
NET B_4_; B_4_, $1I19:A.
NET B_5_; B_5_, $1I20:A.
NET B_6_; B_6_, $1I21:A.
NET B_7_; B_7_, $1I22:A.
NET $0; $1I17:Y, $1I18:C.
NET $1; $1I18:Y, $1I25:A.
NET $2; $1I19:Y, $1I20:C.
NET $3; $1I20:Y, $1I25:B.
NET $4; $1I21:Y, $1I22:C.
NET $5; $1I22:Y, $1I25:C.
NET $6; $1I23:Y, $1I24:C.
NET $7; $1I24:Y, $1I25:D.
NET EQ; $1I25:Y, EQ.
END.
```

Figure 17-10
ADL netlist for the comparator module, as generated by CORE.

that the primitives **XOR**, **XO1**, **XNOR**, **XA1A**, and **AND4B** are referenced only once each and given unique instance names such as **$1I17**. This is also how an ADL netlist is used to represent hierarchy, as we will see when we examine the synthesized top-level netlist for the **rotcomp** design module.

The Synthesized Circuit

The netlist representation of this synthesized design may not seem very interesting, but let's take a look at it anyway. First, consider the most likely representation for an 8-bit comparator like this one. You might expect such a comparator to be composed of a set of eight XNOR gates feeding one or more AND gates. If you were to draw the circuit described in the synthesized netlist, however, you would see that the CORE software has used a variety of different Actel logic primitives to map the design efficiently into the device. This is the essence of device-specific synthesis: the software has traded off size and speed, and has made use of device-specific primitives to achieve the desired result with a minimum cost.

Synthesizing the Barrel Shifter

What about the barrel shifter? This design module has been described using a higher-level form of design description, and we would expect it to result in the generation of a set of flip-flops and perhaps some additional logic to create the load function. Let's run the synthesizer on this portion of the design and see what we get.

1. Open the **rotate.vhd** source file using the **Open** command in the **File** menu.

2. Keeping the same optimization options as in the previous run, select **New Run** from the **Run** menu.

When CORE has finished, you can see that the summary report (Figure 17-11) does, indeed, report that there are eight flip-flop primitives (the **DFM3** primitives) required, but there are no other logic gates required, other than some buffers. This is because the Exemplar synthesis program has correctly determined that the load function can be implemented directly in the **DFM3** flip-flop primitives. (The ADL netlist for the rotate module is shown in Figure 17-12.) The **DFM3** primitives have both asynchronous reset inputs and built-in load functions, so no additional combinational logic is required to implement the shift and load functions.

Synthesizing the Top-Level Module

Now that we have the two lower-level modules synthesized into ADL netlists, we will need to create the top-level netlist that connects them. This step is a simple translation of the top-level VHDL module **rotcomp** into a corresponding ADL format netlist. This translation will be performed by CORE when we process the top-level module.

1. Open the **rotcomp.vhd** source file, using the **Open** command in the **File** menu.

Before running the synthesis program, there is one more option that we will need to set. Because this top-level module represents our entire design, and the ports of the module will be connected to actual pins on the device, we will need to set the **Chip** option described earlier.

2. Open the **Global Options** dialogue box and set the **Chip** option as shown in Figure 17-13. This option instructs the CORE program to add the appropriate

```
                 Resource Use Estimate

   Design:          ROTATE
   Technology:      act1
   File:            D:\VHDL\ROTCOMP\ROTATE.VHD
   Area:            20 modules
   Critical Path:   12 ns
   Io modules:      19 modules


                 Delay Summary

   Node:      Slack      Arrival          Required        Load
                      rise    fall     rise    fall
   Q(0)   :    4.20   7.30    7.30    11.50   11.50     1.00
   Q(1)   :    4.20   7.30    7.30    11.50   11.50     1.00
   Q(2)   :    4.20   7.30    7.30    11.50   11.50     1.00
   Q(3)   :    4.20   7.30    7.30    11.50   11.50     1.00
   Q(4)   :    4.20   7.30    7.30    11.50   11.50     1.00
   Q(5)   :    4.20   7.30    7.30    11.50   11.50     1.00
   Q(6)   :    4.20   7.30    7.30    11.50   11.50     1.00
   Q(7)   :    4.20   7.30    7.30    11.50   11.50     1.00


                  Cell Usage Summary

 Cell             Uses            Cost               Total

 BUF            4 uses(s)     1.00 modules      4.00 modules
 DFM3           8 uses(s)     2.00 modules     16.00 modules
                                               -----
                                   Total =     20.00
```

Figure 17-11
The Summary Report for the barrel shifter.

input and output buffers so that the design can be mapped directly to the device pins in the Actel chip.

3. Select **New Run** from the **Run** menu to begin the synthesis process.

When the synthesis runs, CORE prints two warning errors (Figure 17-14) to tell us that the design is incomplete. This is fine, since the lower-level modules have been previously synthesized and will be combined during processing by the Actel software. The resulting ADL netlist (Figure 17-15) is hierarchical, and includes references to the lower-level modules **compare** and **rotate**. The netlist also references the **INBUF** and **OUTBUF** primitives, which correspond to I/O pads in the completed design.

Ready for Implementation

Now that we have a technology-specific netlist (in this case a netlist of Actel primitives represented in Actel's ADL format) we are ready to map the design into

```
; PROGRAM D:\EXEMPLAR\BIN\PC\FPGA.EXE
; VERSION V2.1.4
DEF ROTATE; CLK, RST, LOAD, DATA_0_, DATA_1_, DATA_2_, DATA_3_,
 DATA_4_, DATA_5_, DATA_6_, DATA_7_, Q_0_, Q_1_, Q_2_, Q_3_,
 Q_4_, Q_5_, Q_6_, Q_7_.
USE ADLIB:BUF; $1I68.
USE ADLIB:BUF; $1I69.
USE ADLIB:BUF; $1I70.
USE ADLIB:BUF; $1I71.
USE ADLIB:DFM3; $1I72.
USE ADLIB:DFM3; $1I73.
USE ADLIB:DFM3; $1I74.
USE ADLIB:DFM3; $1I75.
USE ADLIB:DFM3; $1I76.
USE ADLIB:DFM3; $1I77.
USE ADLIB:DFM3; $1I78.
USE ADLIB:DFM3; $1I79.
NET CLK; CLK, $1I68:A, $1I69:A.
NET RST; RST, $1I70:A, $1I71:A.
NET LOAD; LOAD, $1I72:S, $1I73:S, $1I74:S, $1I75:S, $1I76:S,
 $1I77:S, $1I78:S, $1I79:S.
NET DATA_0_; DATA_0_, $1I72:B.
NET DATA_1_; DATA_1_, $1I73:B.
NET DATA_2_; DATA_2_, $1I74:B.
NET DATA_3_; DATA_3_, $1I75:B.
NET DATA_4_; DATA_4_, $1I76:B.
NET DATA_5_; DATA_5_, $1I77:B.
NET DATA_6_; DATA_6_, $1I78:B.
NET DATA_7_; DATA_7_, $1I79:B.
NET Q_0_; $1I72:Q, Q_0_, $1I79:A.
NET Q_1_; $1I73:Q, Q_1_, $1I72:A.
NET Q_2_; $1I74:Q, Q_2_, $1I73:A.
NET Q_3_; $1I75:Q, Q_3_, $1I74:A.
NET Q_4_; $1I76:Q, Q_4_, $1I75:A.
NET Q_5_; $1I77:Q, Q_5_, $1I76:A.
NET Q_6_; $1I78:Q, Q_6_, $1I77:A.
NET Q_7_; $1I79:Q, Q_7_, $1I78:A.
NET $48; $1I68:Y, $1I72:CLK, $1I73:CLK, $1I74:CLK, $1I75:CLK.
NET $49; $1I69:Y, $1I76:CLK, $1I77:CLK, $1I78:CLK, $1I79:CLK.
NET $50; $1I70:Y, $1I72:CLR, $1I73:CLR, $1I74:CLR, $1I75:CLR.
NET $51; $1I71:Y, $1I76:CLR, $1I77:CLR, $1I78:CLR, $1I79:CLR.
END.
```

Figure 17-12
ADL netlist for the barrel shifter.

the target device. From this point on, the design process is the same as if we had entered the design in schematic form, using a schematic editor and the appropriate Actel primitive symbols. Because this final mapping process is unique to each type of target architecture (be it an FPGA, gate array or a simple PLD) I'll defer the descriptions of this process for later chapters.

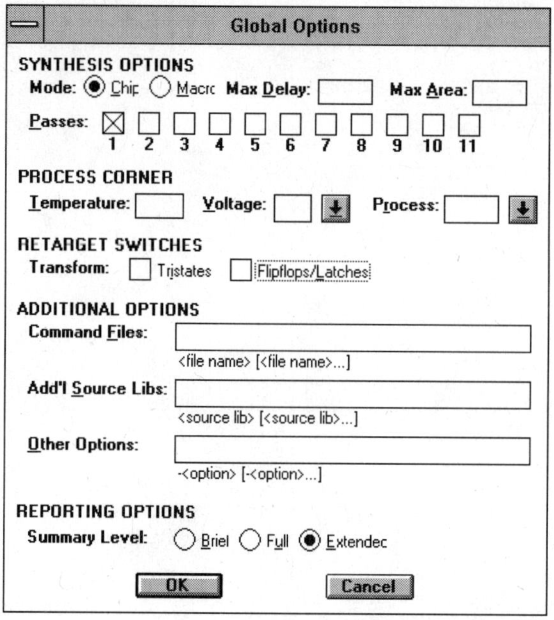

Figure 17-13
*The **Chip** option specifies that all input and output signals are to be attached to device pins via I/O buffers.*

Controlling Synthesis and Optimization

To give you some idea of how optimization options and synthesis strategies can affect the synthesis results, I'm going to present a slightly more complex design and synthesize it using different synthesis strategies. The design I'll be presenting is a state machine that is included in the PREP (Programmable Electronics Performance Corporation) benchmark suite. This benchmark circuit is good because it will allow us to examine not only how the features and options of synthesis tools can be tuned for a particular design, but how the design itself can be modified to enhance synthesis results.

PREP Benchmark Circuit 4

The state machine that we will be synthesizing, PREP benchmark circuit 4, is diagrammed in Figure 17-16. As you can see from the diagram, this state machine has 16 unique states and includes many transitions from state to state, triggered by values observed in the input bus **I** (which is composed of signals **I7** through **I0**).

In addition to the state diagram defining transitions between states, the specification for the state machine includes an encoding of the outputs for each state, shown in Figure 17-17. The specified encoding of the outputs includes some

```
CORE - V2.1.4
Copyright 1990-1994, Exemplar Logic, Inc.  All rights reserved.

- Reading file d:\exemplar\data\packages.syn\standard.vhd for
 primary unit STANDARD
- Reading root vhdl file D:\VHDL\ROTCOMP\ROTCOMP.VHD
- Reading file d:\exemplar\data\packages.syn\std_1164.vhd for
 primary unit STD_LOGIC_1164
- Compiling root entity ROTCOMP, architecture STRUCTURE
"ROTCOMP.VHD",line 25: Warning, component COMPARE has no
 definition.
"ROTCOMP.VHD",line 26: Warning, component ROTATE has no
 definition.
- VHDL source successfully analyzed
Reading library file 'd:\exemplar\lib\act120.syn'...
Library version = 1.14
Delays assume: Temp= 25.0 C  Voltage=5.00 V  Process=typical

Exemplar Logic's CORE  Sun Jun 12 20:31:42 1994

Pass    Area      Delay      Io              -CPU-
     (modules)     (ns)   (modules)          min:sec
1          0         0       20               00:02
   .
   .
   .
                    Resource Use Estimate

     Design:           ROTCOMP
     Technology:       act1
     File:             D:\VHDL\ROTCOMP\ROTCOMP.VHD
     Area:             0 modules
     Critical Path:    0 ns
     Io modules:       20 modules
```

Figure 17-14
Synthesizing the rotcomp top-level module.

don't-care information, and I'll show how we can use that information to advantage when writing a synthesizable design.

Synthesis Conventions for State Machines

As I indicated earlier, there are any number of ways to describe a complex circuit such as a state machine using VHDL. Since state machines have an inherently sequential operation, and languages such as VHDL have sequential programming language features, it makes sense to describe the machine using a higher-level representation that takes advantage of the sequential features of the language.

Another factor to consider when describing a state machine for synthesis is that synthesis tool vendors have determined that state machines are good candidates for special kinds of optimization. Because of this, it is important to write a state machine design using a well-established synthesis convention—one that synthesis

Figure 17-15
ADL netlist for the rotcomp top-level module.

```
; PROGRAM D:\EXEMPLAR\BIN\PC\FPGA.EXE
D:\VHDL\ROTCOMP\ROTCOMP.VHD D:\EXEMPLAR\DEMO\ROTCOMP.ADL
-COMMAND_FILE=D:\EXEMPLAR\DEMO\TMP5.$$$
; VERSION V2.1.4
DEF ROTCOMP; CLK, RST, LOAD, INIT_0_, INIT_1_, INIT_2_,
 INIT_3_, INIT_4_, INIT_5_, INIT_6_, INIT_7_, TEST_0_,
 TEST_1_, TEST_2_, TEST_3_, TEST_4_, TEST_5_, TEST_6_,
 TEST_7_, MATCH.
USE ADLIB:COMPARE; $1I97.
USE ADLIB:ROTATE; $1I98.
USE ADLIB:OUTBUF; $1I99.
USE ADLIB:INBUF; $1I100.
USE ADLIB:INBUF; $1I101.
USE ADLIB:INBUF; $1I102.
USE ADLIB:INBUF; $1I103.
USE ADLIB:INBUF; $1I104.
USE ADLIB:INBUF; $1I105.
USE ADLIB:INBUF; $1I106.
USE ADLIB:INBUF; $1I107.
USE ADLIB:INBUF; $1I108.
USE ADLIB:INBUF; $1I109.
USE ADLIB:INBUF; $1I110.
USE ADLIB:INBUF; $1I111.
USE ADLIB:INBUF; $1I112.
USE ADLIB:INBUF; $1I113.
USE ADLIB:INBUF; $1I114.
USE ADLIB:INBUF; $1I115.
USE ADLIB:INBUF; $1I116.
USE ADLIB:INBUF; $1I117.
USE ADLIB:INBUF; $1I118.
NET CLK; CLK, $1I118:PAD.
NET RST; RST, $1I117:PAD.
NET LOAD; LOAD, $1I116:PAD.
NET INIT_0_; INIT_0_, $1I115:PAD.
NET INIT_1_; INIT_1_, $1I114:PAD.
NET INIT_2_; INIT_2_, $1I113:PAD.
NET INIT_3_; INIT_3_, $1I112:PAD.
NET INIT_4_; INIT_4_, $1I111:PAD.
NET INIT_5_; INIT_5_, $1I110:PAD.
NET INIT_6_; INIT_6_, $1I109:PAD.
NET INIT_7_; INIT_7_, $1I108:PAD.
NET TEST_0_; TEST_0_, $1I107:PAD.
NET TEST_1_; TEST_1_, $1I106:PAD.
NET TEST_2_; TEST_2_, $1I105:PAD.
NET TEST_3_; TEST_3_, $1I104:PAD.
NET TEST_4_; TEST_4_, $1I103:PAD.
NET TEST_5_; TEST_5_, $1I102:PAD.
NET TEST_6_; TEST_6_, $1I101:PAD.
NET TEST_7_; TEST_7_, $1I100:PAD.
NET MATCH_internal; $1I97:EQ, $1I99:D.
NET Q_0_; $1I98:Q(0), $1I97:A(0).
NET Q_1_; $1I98:Q(1), $1I97:A(1).
NET Q_2_; $1I98:Q(2), $1I97:A(2).
NET Q_3_; $1I98:Q(3), $1I97:A(3).
NET Q_4_; $1I98:Q(4), $1I97:A(4).
NET Q_5_; $1I98:Q(5), $1I97:A(5).
NET Q_6_; $1I98:Q(6), $1I97:A(6).NET Q_7_; $1I98:Q(7),$1I97:A(7).
```

```
NET CLK_internal; $1I118:Y, $1I98:CLK.
NET RST_internal; $1I117:Y, $1I98:RST.
NET LOAD_internal; $1I116:Y, $1I98:LOAD.
NET INIT_0__internal; $1I115:Y, $1I98:DATA(0).
NET INIT_1__internal; $1I114:Y, $1I98:DATA(1).
NET INIT_2__internal; $1I113:Y, $1I98:DATA(2).
NET INIT_3__internal; $1I112:Y, $1I98:DATA(3).
NET INIT_4__internal; $1I111:Y, $1I98:DATA(4).
NET INIT_5__internal; $1I110:Y, $1I98:DATA(5).
NET INIT_6__internal; $1I109:Y, $1I98:DATA(6).
NET INIT_7__internal; $1I108:Y, $1I98:DATA(7).
NET TEST_0__internal; $1I107:Y, $1I97:B(0).
NET TEST_1__internal; $1I106:Y, $1I97:B(1).
NET TEST_2__internal; $1I105:Y, $1I97:B(2).
NET TEST_3__internal; $1I104:Y, $1I97:B(3).
NET TEST_4__internal; $1I103:Y, $1I97:B(4).
NET TEST_5__internal; $1I102:Y, $1I97:B(5).
NET TEST_6__internal; $1I101:Y, $1I97:B(6).
NET TEST_7__internal; $1I100:Y, $1I97:B(7).
NET MATCH; $1I99:PAD, MATCH.
END.
```

tools will recognize as a state machine. The convention that has evolved for defining state machines in VHDL involves describing the machine using one or more process statements, and describing the states and transitions of the machine using enumerated types and one or more **case** statements. Let's take a look at the VHDL description for the PREP benchmark 4 state machine to see how this design representation works. The complete VHDL source file for the circuit is shown in Figure 17-18.

Like the earlier shift/rotate design, this design makes use of the IEEE 1164 **std_logic** and **std_logic_vector** data types. **Std_logic** includes don't-care values ('-' and 'X') in addition to the logic values '0' and '1'. These special values can help when there are don't-cares that you want to capture in a design.

Let's take a close look at the design. Reading from the top of the VHDL file, we can see

- ☐ **Library** and **use** statements making the **std_logic_1164** package, and all its contents, visible to the subsequent entity and architecture.
- ☐ An **entity** declaration specifying the ports of the design (as shown in the earlier block diagram).
- ☐ An **architecture** declaration, containing:
  - A **type** declaration for an enumerated type, **states**, that will be used to represent all the possible states of the machine.
  - Signal declarations for two buses, **present_state** and **next_state**, of type **states**. These signals will be used to store the present state of the machine and to decode the next state, respectively.

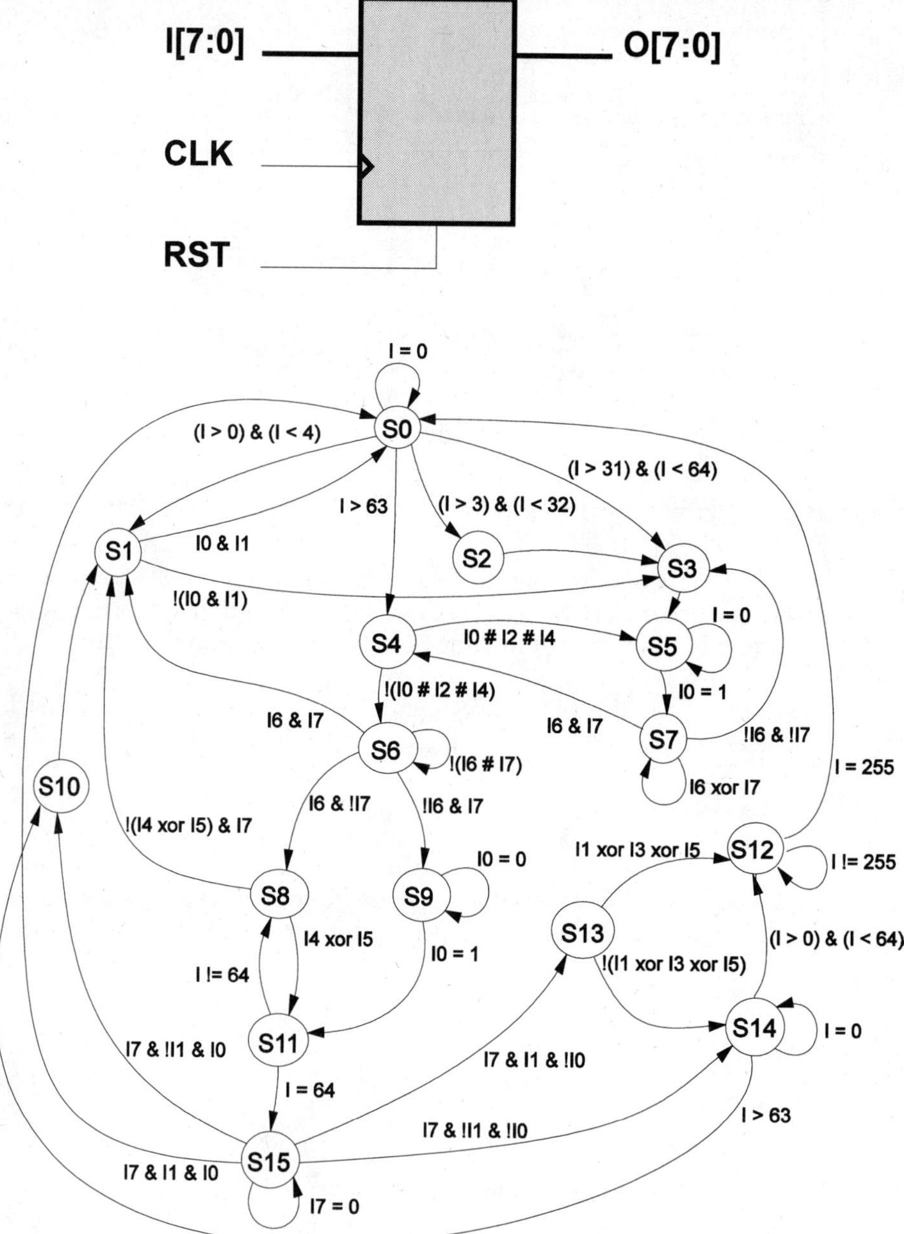

Figure 17-16
The PREP benchmark circuit 4 state machine.

State	Output Encoding (O[7:0])
S0	0, 0, 0, 0, 0, 0, 0, 0
S1	0, 0, 0, 0, 0, 1, 1, 0
S2	0, 0, 0, 1, 1, 0, 0, 0
S3	0, 1, 1, 0, 0, 0, 0, 0
S4	1, X, X, X, X, X, X, 0
S5	X, 1, X, X, X, X, 0, X
S6	0, 0, 0, 1, 1, 1, 1, 1
S7	0, 0, 1, 1, 1, 1, 1, 1
S8	0, 1, 1, 1, 1, 1, 1, 1
S9	1, 1, 1, 1, 1, 1, 1, 1
S10	X, 1, X, 1, X, 1, X, 1
S11	1, X, 1, X, 1, X, 1, X
S12	1, 1, 1, 1, 1, 1, 0, 1
S13	1, 1, 1, 1, 0, 1, 1, 1
S14	1, 1, 0, 1, 1, 1, 1, 1
S15	0, 1, 1, 1, 1, 1, 1, 1

Figure 17-17
The PREP benchmark circuit 4 output encodings include don't-care information.

- A **process** statement describing the behavior of the state registers: if the **RST** input is high, the machine will reset to state **ST0**. Otherwise, the next state value decoded onto **next_state** will be loaded into the state registers. (If there were any state machine outputs that were registered, then these outputs would be described in this first process as well.)
- A second, much longer, **process** statement describing the transition logic for each state of the machine. Each state of the machine is represented by a unique choice in a **case** statement, and includes conditional (**if-then**) logic

Figure 17-18
The PREP benchmark circuit 4 state machine, described in VHDL.

```
--------------------------
-- Prep Benchmark circuit #4
--
library ieee;
use ieee.std_logic_1164.all;

entity prep4a is
    port (CLK,RST : std_logic;
          I : std_logic_vector(7 downto 0);
          O : out std_logic_vector(7 downto 0));
end prep4a;

architecture behavior of prep4a is
    type states is (st0,st1,st2,st3,st4,st5,st6,st7,st8,st9,
                    st10,st11,st12,st13,st14,st15);
    signal present_state,next_state : states;
begin

    registers: process (CLK,RST)
    begin
        if RST = '1' then
            present_state <= st0;
        elsif CLK = '1' and CLK'event then
            present_state <= next_state;
        end if;
    end process;

    transitions: process (present_state,I)
    begin
        case present_state is
            when st0 =>
                O <= "00000000";
                if I = "00000000" then
                    next_state <= st0;
                elsif I > "00000000" and I < "00000100" then
                    next_state <= st1;
                elsif I > "00000011" and I < "00100000" then
                    next_state <= st2;
                elsif I > "00011111" and I < "01000000" then
                    next_state <= st3;
                else
                    next_state <= st4;
                end if;
            when st1 =>
                O <= "00000110";
                if I(1 downto 0) = "11" then
                    next_state <= st0;
                else
                    next_state <= st3;
                end if;
            when st2 =>
                O <= "00011000";
                next_state <= st3;
            when st3 =>
                O <= "01100000";
                next_state <= st5;
```

```
when st4 =>
    O <= "1——0";
    if (I(0) or I(2) or I(4)) = '1' then
        next_state <= st5;
    else
        next_state <= st6;
    end if;             when st5 =>
    O <= "-1——0-";
    if (I(0) = '0') then
        next_state <= st5;
    else
        next_state <= st7;
    end if;
when st6 =>
    O <= "00011111";
    if I(7 downto 6) = "00" then
        next_state <= st6;
    elsif I(7 downto 6) = "01" then
        next_state <= st8;
    elsif I(7 downto 6) = "10" then
        next_state <= st9;
    else
        next_state <= st1;
    end if;
when st7 =>
    O <= "00111111";
    if I(7 downto 6) = "00" then
        next_state <= st3;
    elsif I(7 downto 6) = "11" then
        next_state <= st4;
    else
        next_state <= st7;
    end if;
when st8 =>
    O <= "01111111";
    if (I(4) xor I(5)) = '1' then
        next_state <= st11;
    elsif I(7) = '1' then
        next_state <= st1;
    else
        next_state <= st8;
    end if;
when st9 =>
    O <= "11111111";
    if I(0) = '1' then
        next_state <= st11;
    else
        next_state <= st9;
    end if;
when st10 =>
    O <= "-1-1-1-1";
    next_state <= st1;
when st11 =>
    O <= "1-1-1-1-";
    if I = "01000000" then
        next_state <= st15;
    else
        next_state <= st8;
    end if;
```

```
            when st12 =>
                O <= "11111101";
                if I = "11111111" then
                    next_state <= st0;
                else
                    next_state <= st12;
                end if;          when st13 =>
                O <= "11110111";
                if (I(5) xor I(3) xor I(1)) = '1' then
                    next_state <= st12;
                else
                    next_state <= st14;
                end if;
            when st14 =>
                O <= "11011111";
                if I = "00000000" then
                    next_state <= st14;
                elsif I > "00000000" and I < "01000000" then
                    next_state <= st12;
                else
                    next_state <= st10;
                end if;
            when st15 =>
                O <= "01111111";
                if (I(7) = '1') then
                    if I(1 downto 0) = "00" then
                        next_state <= st14;
                    elsif I(1 downto 0) = "01" then
                        next_state <= st10;
                    elsif I(1 downto 0) = "10" then
                        next_state <= st13;
                    else
                        next_state <= st0;
                    end if;
                else
                    next_state <= st15;
                end if;
            when others => null;
        end case;
    end process;
end;
```

describing the transitions, along with an assignment statement defining the encoding of output **O** for each state. Although this process statement is written using sequential statements such as **if-then-else**, it describes combinational logic. When a **process** statement is used to describe combinational logic, all of the combinational inputs must be listed in the sensitivity list of the process. In this case, the sensitivity list contains the signals **present_state** and **I**.

This design file is representative of state machines of all kinds, and can act as a model for state machine designs that you create yourself. If you are creating designs with multiple, communicating state machines, this model can be easily extended using multiple registered and combinational processes.

Designing for Synthesis

Before running this design through synthesis, let's look at a few things that have been done to make it synthesize into an efficient circuit. First, consider the enumerated type definition for the state register. The type **states** consists of 16 unique state identifiers that are declared symbolically with the names **st0**, **st1**, and so on. The design has been entered symbolically because, as the specification indicated, we don't actually care how the states of the machine are encoded internally in the hardware realization of the circuit. In fact, we don't even need to care about how many registers are used to represent the current state value—all that matters is the value of **O**, as observed on the outputs of the machine for each state. Using enumerated types gives the synthesis tool the freedom to choose whatever representation it determines is best for the specified implementation technology.

Because this design description has effectively hidden the encoding of the state register values, and has even failed to specify the number of registers required, doesn't it violated the rule I stated in the previous chapter about knowing where your registers are? Not really; using two process statements, one for the state machine's registered operation and one for the combinational logic of the transitions and of the output, has made it quite clear what is registered and what is not. If the synthesis tool does its job correctly, any extraneous logic or signals (such as the signal **next_state**) will be collapsed away, leaving us with a compact implementation of the circuit, using however many registers, and whatever encoding, is best for the design and target technology.

Taking Care of Don't-Cares

This state machine design is a good example of where don't-cares can be used to help optimize a circuit. In a circuit such as this one, there are two primary places where don't-cares can have an impact: in the state encoding and in the output encoding.

To understand where don't-cares help in state encoding, consider the number of states in the machine. This state machine has 16 states, which is a simple power of two. This means that the states of the machine can be encoded using four registers with no undefined states, using one of a variety of possible encoding methods (e.g. sequential binary, reflected code, or a pseudorandom assignment). If, however, the state machine was encoded in some larger number of registers (to simplify the transition logic) or had a number of states that did not map directly into some number of registers, there would be one or more states that were undefined—states that could become don't-cares in the generated logic. Most synthesis tools will automatically extract don't-care logic in situations like this; your only responsibility is to make sure the design is provided with a global reset or other circuitry to make sure it is always capable of escaping from the illegal states that are possible in a state machine design that includes don't-care logic.

A second type of don't-care optimization is demonstrated in this design in the encoding of the **O** outputs. If you refer back to the output encoding (Figure 17-17) you will see that some of the states of the machine specify only a subset of the eight bits of the output—the remaining bits are don't-cares. The **std_logic** data type includes a special, *meta-logic* value that can be used to specify such a don't-care to the synthesis tool. This value, '-', is recognized by VHDL simulators and simulated as a value distinct from '0' or '1', which makes the simulation of circuits containing don't-cares much more accurate. In addition, some synthesis tools (although unfortunately, not the current version of Exemplar's CORE) recognize this special value and will process signal assignments and other uses of the '-' value as don't-cares in the generated logic.

As a general rule, the more don't-cares your design has (whether created as a side effect of a state encoding or specified directly in the design), the more opportunity the synthesis tool will have to reduce the size of the generated logic. You need to be careful, however, to make sure that a design that includes don't-cares is provided with appropriate hazard-free logic and/or global resets to allow recovery from undefined circuit conditions.

Specifying Custom Encodings

In some synthesis tools (such as the Synopsys VHDL Compiler or Data I/O's Synario VHDL Compiler), the use of the special value '-' during synthesis can be expanded to other uses of enumerated types. In these tools, a special attribute called **enum_encoding** can be used to specify the precise encoding of an enumerated type, including don't-cares. For example, the outputs of the PREP benchmark state machine could be specified as an enumerated type with a specific 8-bit encoding using the following type and attribute declarations:

```
type state_outputs is (O0,O1,O2,O3,O4,O5,O6,O7,O8,O9,
                       O10,O11,O11,O12,O13,O14,O15);
attribute enum_encoding of state_outputs: type is
    "00000000 00000110 00011000 01100000 1——0 " &
    "-1—0- 00011111 00111111 01111111 11111111 " &
    "-1-1-1-1 1-1-1-1- 11111101 11110111 11011111 " &
    "01111111";
```

Note: *The use of don't-cares in enumerated types is an area of VHDL that is hotly debated in some VHDL circles. Be sure to check with your synthesis tool vendor before attempting to use don't-cares for optimization, and be sure that the approach that you take for synthesis does not result in a design that cannot be simulated properly. (In the previous encoding example, the fifth and sixth values specified for the* **state_outputs** *type could appear to be the same value during simulation, possibly leading to problems during debugging.)*

Processing the Design

To demonstrate how synthesis strategies effect the results of synthesis, I'll process this state machine design twice using the CORE synthesis program, and will specify different synthesis strategies for each run. There are many synthesis options that I can specify in CORE; since this is a state machine design, we will be experimenting with the state machine encoding options. First, we'll run the synthesis using a pseudorandom approach to encoding, which usually results in compact minimal encoding for complex state machines. A minimal encoding is an encoding in which the fewest possible registers are used. In this case the number of registers will be four in a minimal encoding, since there are 16 unique states. The most optimal minimal encoding for this design would be an encoding onto those four registers that results in the smallest amount of combinational logic resources being required.

Targeting a Device

The optimal encoding of a state machine, and the most compact representation of the combinational logic that implements the state transitions and stimulates the outputs, depends to a large extent on the specific architecture of the target technology. The technology that we will specify as a target for synthesis is the Xilinx 4000 series LCA, which is a field programmable gate array (FPGA) rich in registers, but somewhat limited in its supply of wide (six input or greater) combinational logic functions.

Synthesis with Random Encoding

The first synthesis run we're going to invoke on this circuit, again using CORE, will be with a pseudorandom encoding for the state machine, with the default values specified for all other optimization options (Figure 17-19).

When we run the program, it reads in the design and begins the synthesis process. On a typical system, the program takes about 10 minutes to finish processing before generating an XNF netlist. XNF is the format required by the Xilinx place-and-route tools. Examining the summary report created by CORE, we can get a general idea of how many of the device's resources will be required to implement this circuit.

Measuring Gates

The summary report produced by CORE (Figure 17-20) includes a series of numbers to help you determine how much of the target device you have used. If you are comparing gate capacity for devices within the same family (4000 series FPGAs, for example) or want to compare different design, synthesis or optimization strategies for a circuit, you can use these numbers for comparison. Things get a little trickier, though, if you are trying to compare synthesis results across device families. This is because the measurement used for one device family

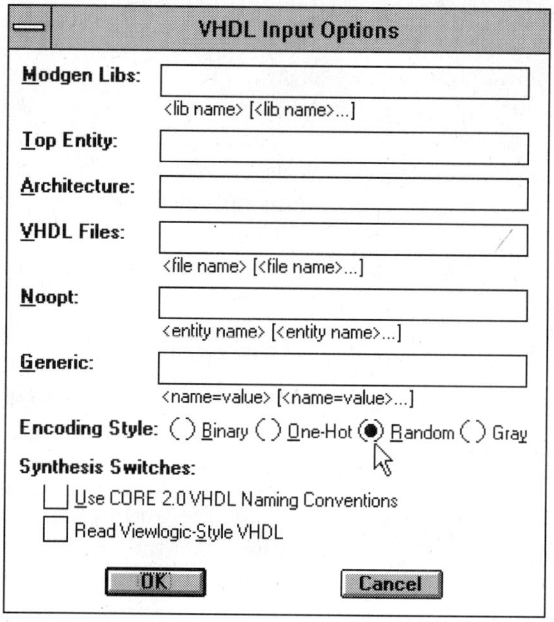

Figure 17-19
Selecting random encoding.

(CLBs, in the case of Xilinx parts) may not provide a useful comparison to numbers produced for other types of devices. This is not something to worry much about, though; it is unlikely that you will be making implementation decisions based on the absolute size of your circuit when synthesized to different device types, or based on the relative sizes of two devices from different manufactures. The most likely reasons to choose one device family over another are operational (speed, temperature and power) and cost factors, rather than capacity.

Looking at the Results

The summary report show that the best result CORE can come up with for this circuit, using random state encoding, is 46 CLBs. A CLB is the basic unit of logic in a Xilinx LCA device. Each CLB in a 4000 series LCA includes two flip-flops and a lookup table that can be configured to create combinational functions. The CORE program has estimated that the four state register flip-flops, combined with the combinational logic for the state machine transitions, will consume 46 of these logic blocks. The program has also estimated and reported the delay parameters for the outputs, based on its knowledge of the 4000-series LCA architecture. These delay numbers are rough at best, since the timing behavior of a Xilinx LCA is highly dependent on the actual routing of interconnects in the device. The numbers are useful for determining the effect of multilevel logic and other factors that can increase signal delays. Notice also that the summary report has indicated a critical path delay value of seven. This is an indication that the optimizer has had to break one or more large combinational logic functions into a multilevel logic circuit in order to fit the constraints of the CLB's lookup-table architecture.

Improving the Results

If we look at the summary results in terms of the percentage of resources used, we can quickly conclude that we are underutilizing the register resources of the 4000 series family of devices. Look, for example, at the line showing the resource usage for the smallest device in the family, the 4005 device. If implemented in this device, the state machine circuit would require an estimated 25% of the logic blocks in the device, but would only use 1% of the more than 600 available flip-flops.

Since we know that a complex state machine can be encoded using alternate encoding strategies that trade-off register resources for transition logic, we know that we can probably get better results for this design by using such an encoding. To test this assumption, we're going to run the CORE program again, but this time specify that we want a one-hot state encoding (Figure 17-21).

This time the program runs much faster, finishing in only a few minutes. As the new summary report shows (Figure 17-22), it also results in a much smaller implementation of the circuit. In this version the circuit requires four times the number of flip-flops (for a total of 16), but now only requires 15% of the 4005's CLB resources (a total of 35 CLBs). In addition, the critical path delay value has been reduced to only four.

Using Module Generation

In the previous chapter, I described how a module generation strategy can help to optimize a circuit for a specific device type. To show how module generation works, we're going to use another of the PREP benchmark circuits. This circuit, PREP benchmark 2, is a data path-intensive circuit that consists of two 8-bit registers, an 8-bit 2-to-1 mux, a counter and an 8-bit comparator. The circuit is diagrammed in Figure 17-23.

Entering the Design

This circuit has also been described in VHDL; the complete design file is listed in Figure 17-24. Starting from the top of the file, we see

- ☐ A **package** declaration creating an 8-bit integer data type called **byte.** This will simplify the design description that follows.

```
    Pass      Area     Delay      PACKED DFFs    PIs     POs  -CPU-
             (FGs)  (levels)     (CLBs)                       min:sec
    1          95       11          47      4     10       8   01:52
    2         105        7          51      4     10       8   01:19
    3          95        8          44      4     10       8   00:53
    4          98       16          45      4     10       8   01:34
    5          96       10          46      4     10       8   00:44
    6         101       13          47      4     10       8   01:13
    7          94        7          46      4     10       8   01:35
    8         102       14          49      4     10       8   01:24

                      Resource Use Estimate

     Design:            PREP4A
     Technology:        xi4
     File:              D:\EXEMPLAR\PREP4\PREP4A.VHD
     Area:              94 Function Generators
     Packed Area:       46 CLBs
     Critical Path:     7 levels
     DFFs:              4 (in CLBs or IOBs)
     IOFFs:             0 (in IOBs)
     HM CLBs:           0
     Modgen CLBs:       0
     Input Pins:        10
     Output Pins:       8

                      Device Utilization Report

Device             FGs      Registers       IOBs
            avail util    avail util    avail util
4005PC84      392  24%      616   1%       61  30%
4005PG156     392  24%      616   1%      112  16%
4005PQ160     392  24%      616   1%      112  16%
4005PQ208     392  24%      616   1%      112  16%
4006PG156     512  18%      768   1%      128  14%
4006PQ160     512  18%      768   1%      128  14%
4006PQ208     512  18%      768   1%      128  14%
4008PG191     648  15%      936   0%      144  13%
4008PQ208     648  15%      936   0%      144  13%
4008MQ208     648  15%      936   0%      144  13%
4010PG191     800  12%     1120   0%      160  11%
4010PQ208     800  12%     1120   0%      160  11%
4010MQ208     800  12%     1120   0%      160  11%
4013MQ208    1152   8%     1536   0%      192   9%
4013PG223    1152   8%     1536   0%      192   9%
4013MQ240    1152   8%     1536   0%      192   9%
4013PQ240    1152   8%     1536   0%      192   9%

                         Delay Summary

     Node:     Slack      Arrival          Required        Load
                         rise    fall     rise    fall
     O(2)  :    2.00     7.00    7.00     9.00    9.00     2.00
     O(4)  :    2.00     7.00    7.00     9.00    9.00     2.00
     O(3)  :    3.00     6.00    6.00     9.00    9.00     2.00
     O(0)  :    3.00     6.00    6.00     9.00    9.00     2.00
     O(1)  :    3.00     6.00    6.00     9.00    9.00     2.00
     O(6)  :    4.00     5.00    5.00     9.00    9.00     2.00
     O(5)  :    4.00     5.00    5.00     9.00    9.00     2.00
     O(7)  :    4.00     5.00    5.00     9.00    9.00     2.00
```

Figure 17-20
The synthesis results obtained with random encoding could be improved.

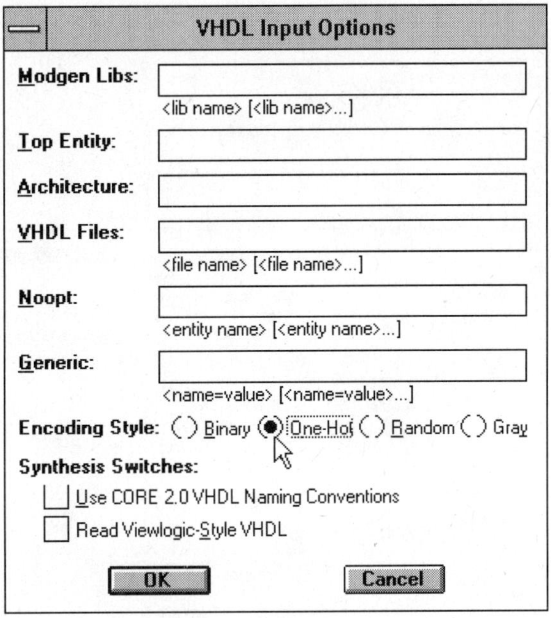

VHDL Input Options

Modgen Libs:
<lib name> [<lib name>...]
Top Entity:
Architecture:
VHDL Files:
<file name> [<file name>...]
Noopt:
<entity name> [<entity name>...]
Generic:
<name=value> [<name=value>...]
Encoding Style: ( ) Binary (●) One-Hot ( ) Random ( ) Gray
Synthesis Switches:
☐ Use CORE 2.0 VHDL Naming Conventions
☐ Read Viewlogic-Style VHDL
OK Cancel

Figure 17-21
Specifying a one-hot encoding.

- ☐ A **work** statement making the new type definition visible to the subsequent entity and architecture declarations.
- ☐ An **entity** declaration declaring the input and output ports of the design, as they were specified on the block diagram.
- ☐ An **architecture** declaration, containing:
  - Signal declarations for the internal signals that will carry data between different blocks in the circuit.
  - A **process** statement containing the logic for the three registered elements of the design (represented by the internal signals **q1**, **q2** and **count**).
  - Concurrent assignments for the multiplexer and comparator and for the connection between the counter and the **DATA0** output.

Processing the Design

When this design is processed with CORE, using the default synthesis and optimization options, the resulting circuit requires 15 4000 series CLBs. (The complete summary report is shown in Figure 17-25.)

Pass	Area (FGs)	Delay (levels)	PACKED (CLBs)	DFFs	PIs	POs	—CPU— min:sec
1	63	5	34	16	10	8	00:44
2	65	6	32	16	10	8	00:26
3	63	5	35	16	10	8	00:22
4	61	5	34	16	10	8	00:27
5	62	4	32	16	10	8	00:25
6	61	5	32	16	10	8	00:33
7	67	6	34	16	10	8	00:18
8	60	5	35	16	10	8	00:38

Resource Use Estimate

Design:	PREP4A
Technology:	xi4
File:	D:\EXEMPLAR\PREP4\PREP4A.VHD
Area:	60 Function Generators
Packed Area:	35 CLBs
Critical Path:	5 levels
DFFs:	16 (in CLBs or IOBs)
IOFFs:	0 (in IOBs)
HM CLBs:	0
Modgen CLBs:	0
Input Pins:	10
Output Pins:	8

Device Utilization Report

Device	FGs avail	FGs util	Registers avail	Registers util	IOBs avail	IOBs util
4005PC84	392	15%	616	3%	61	30%
4005PG156	392	15%	616	3%	112	16%
4005PQ160	392	15%	616	3%	112	16%
4005PQ208	392	15%	616	3%	112	16%
4006PG156	512	12%	768	2%	128	14%
4006PQ160	512	12%	768	2%	128	14%
4006PQ208	512	12%	768	2%	128	14%
4008PG191	648	9%	936	2%	144	13%
4008PQ208	648	9%	936	2%	144	13%
4008MQ208	648	9%	936	2%	144	13%
4010PG191	800	8%	1120	1%	160	11%
4010PQ208	800	8%	1120	1%	160	11%
4010MQ208	800	8%	1120	1%	160	11%
4013MQ208	1152	5%	1536	1%	192	9%
4013PG223	1152	5%	1536	1%	192	9%
4013MQ240	1152	5%	1536	1%	192	9%
4013PQ240	1152	5%	1536	1%	192	9%

Delay Summary

Node:		Slack	Arrival rise	Arrival fall	Required rise	Required fall	Load
O(2)	:	1.00	6.00	6.00	7.00	7.00	2.00
O(4)	:	1.00	6.00	6.00	7.00	7.00	2.00
O(3)	:	2.00	5.00	5.00	7.00	7.00	2.00
O(0)	:	2.00	5.00	5.00	7.00	7.00	2.00
O(1)	:	2.00	5.00	5.00	7.00	7.00	2.00
O(6)	:	3.00	4.00	4.00	7.00	7.00	2.00
O(5)	:	3.00	4.00	4.00	7.00	7.00	2.00
O(7)	:	3.00	4.00	4.00	7.00	7.00	2.00

Figure 17-22
A one-hot encoding has dramatically improved the synthesis results.

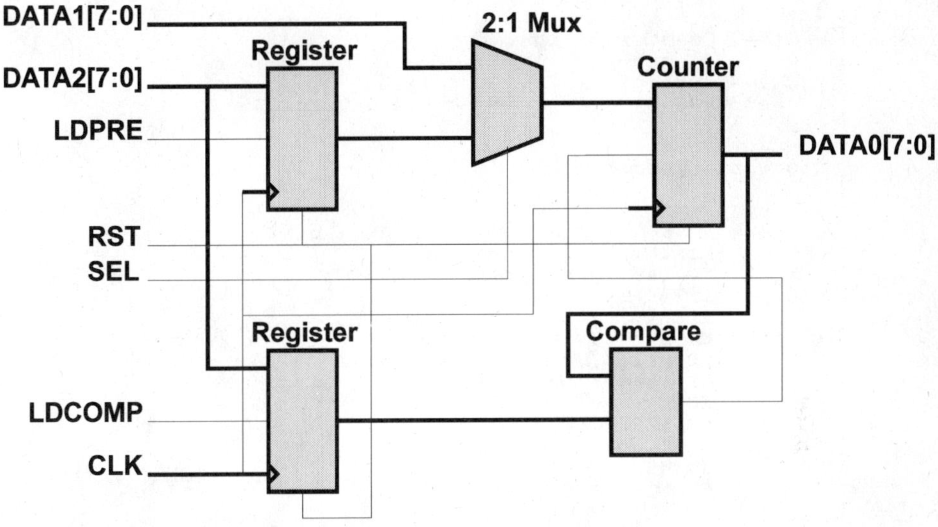

Figure 17-23
PREP benchmark circuit #2 timer/counter.

To improve the results, we can specify the Xilinx 4000 family module generation library (Figure 17-26) before invoking the synthesis program.

Module Generation: How It Works

When CORE is run with a module generation library specified, it attempts to make use of predefined, presynthesized modules that are specific to the type of device being targeted.

There are many types of logic functions that are difficult for a synthesis tool to efficiently synthesize. These functions, which are usually related to data path applications, may require large amounts of combinational logic arranged in a multilevel gate structure, or may make use of specialized register or I/O features that are specific to the target device, and outside of the scope of logic synthesis. This is especially true in FPGA architectures, which may have vastly different internal structures from what is normally expected by general-purpose logic synthesis algorithms.

In a synthesis program like CORE that supports module generation, a device-specific library is provided to the synthesis program. This library contains information about the preoptimized modules that are available, and instructs the synthesis tool on how to reference these modules from within the generated netlist (or other hierarchical output format). During operation, the synthesis tool attempts

```
------------------------------
- PREP Benchmark Circuit #2
-
- Timer/Counter (1 instance)
-
package typedef is
    subtype byte is integer range 0 to 255;   - 8 bit
end;

use work.typedef.all;

entity prep2 is
   port (CLK,RST,SEL,LDCOMP,LDPRE : bit;
         DATA1, DATA2 : byte;
         DATA0: out byte);
end prep2;

architecture dataflow of prep2 is
    signal q1,q2,mux,count : byte;
    signal load : boolean;
begin
    process(RST,CLK)
    begin
        if RST = '1' then
            q1 <= 0;
            q2 <= 0;
            count <= 0;
        elsif CLK = '1' and CLK'event then
            if LDPRE = '1' then
                q1 <= DATA2;
            end if;
            if LDCOMP = '1' then
                q2 <= DATA2;
            end if;
            if load then
                count <= mux;
            else
                count <= count + 1;
            end if;
        end if;
    end process;

    mux   <= q1 when SEL = '1' else DATA1; - mux
    load  <= q2 = count;                   - compare
    DATA0 <= count;                        - output

end dataflow;
```

Figure 17-24
The timer/counter VHDL source file includes a type ***byte*** *that simplifies the design.*

to match high-level operators (such as '=', '+', and other operators) to corresponding predefined modules in the library. While doing this, the synthesis tool has to consider the width of the operation being performed, and whether there are additional signals (such as carry out) that must be taken into consideration. The synthesis tool may perform local optimization to break a large function into smaller functions appropriately sized for the predefined module, or may rely on the

```
Pass     Area    Delay     PACKED DFFs     PIs     POs -CPU-
        (FGs) (levels)     (CLBs)                     min:sec
  1       37        6         18     24     21       8   00:19
  2       37        6         18     24     21       8   00:21
  3       27        4         15     24     21       8   00:18
  4       27        4         14     24     21       8   00:15
  5       29        5         14     24     21       8   00:12
  6       34        7         21     24     21       8   00:21
  7       27        5         13     24     21       8   00:12
  8       27        4         14     24     21       8   00:14

                 Resource Use Estimate

    Design:            PREP2A
    Technology:        xi4
    File:              D:\EXEMPLAR\DEMO\PREP2A.VHD
    Area:              27 Function Generators
    Packed Area:       15 CLBs
    Critical Path:     4 levels
    DFFs:              24 (in CLBs or IOBs)
    IOFFs:             0 (in IOBs)
    HM CLBs:           0
    Modgen CLBs:       0
    Input Pins:        21
    Output Pins:       8

                 Device Utilization Report

Device               FGs     Registers         IOBs
               avail util   avail util   avail util
4005PC84         392   7%     616   4%      61  48%
4005PG156        392   7%     616   4%     112  26%
4005PQ160        392   7%     616   4%     112  26%
4005PQ208        392   7%     616   4%     112  26%
4006PG156        512   5%     768   3%     128  23%
4006PQ160        512   5%     768   3%     128  23%
4006PQ208        512   5%     768   3%     128  23%
4008PG191        648   4%     936   3%     144  20%
4008PQ208        648   4%     936   3%     144  20%
4008MQ208        648   4%     936   3%     144  20%
4010PG191        800   3%    1120   2%     160  18%
4010PQ208        800   3%    1120   2%     160  18%
4010MQ208        800   3%    1120   2%     160  18%
4013MQ208       1152   2%    1536   2%     192  15%
4013PG223       1152   2%    1536   2%     192  15%
4013MQ240       1152   2%    1536   2%     192  15%
4013PQ240       1152   2%    1536   2%     192  15%

                       Delay Summary

    Node:          Slack      Arrival         Required        Load
                           rise    fall     rise    fall
    DATA0(0)   :    5.00   2.00    2.00     7.00    7.00      2.00
    DATA0(1)   :    5.00   2.00    2.00     7.00    7.00      2.00
    DATA0(2)   :    5.00   2.00    2.00     7.00    7.00      2.00
    DATA0(3)   :    5.00   2.00    2.00     7.00    7.00      2.00
    DATA0(4)   :    5.00   2.00    2.00     7.00    7.00      2.00
    DATA0(5)   :    5.00   2.00    2.00     7.00    7.00      2.00
    DATA0(6)   :    5.00   2.00    2.00     7.00    7.00      2.00
    DATA0(7)   :    5.00   2.00    2.00     7.00    7.00      2.00
```

Figure 17-25

Timer/counter synthesis results using default synthesis options.

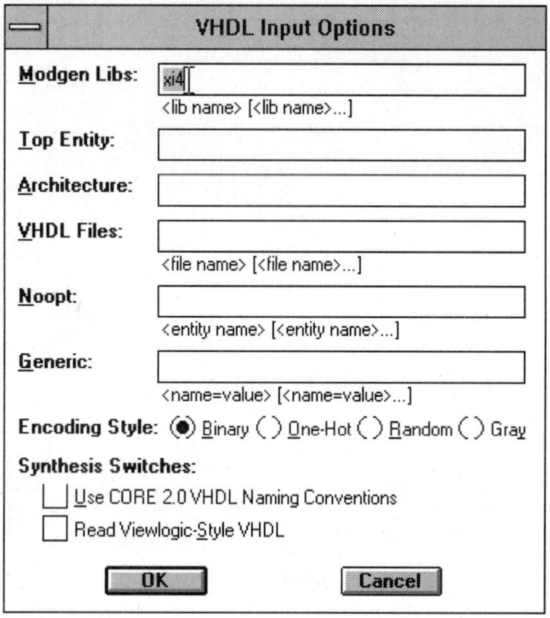

VHDL Input Options

Modgen Libs: xi4

<lib name> [<lib name>...]

Top Entity:

Architecture:

VHDL Files:

<file name> [<file name>...]

Noopt:

<entity name> [<entity name>...]

Generic:

<name=value> [<name=value>...]

Encoding Style: (●) Binary ( ) One-Hot ( ) Random ( ) Gray

Synthesis Switches:

[ ] Use CORE 2.0 VHDL Naming Conventions

[ ] Read Viewlogic-Style VHDL

OK Cancel

Figure 17-26
Specifying a module generation library.

modules' ability to accept size parameters (as is the case in LPM library implementations).

What kind of gains can be expected from module generation? That depends entirely on how well the design being processed matches the module library being used. For PREP benchmark circuit 2 the results are quite dramatic, since the design uses a variety of data path elements that have direct equivalents in the Xilinx 4000 module library.

Figure 17-27 lists the summary report for the design after processing with module generation. As you can see, the circuit size has been reduced dramatically, and now requires only eight CLBs to implement, with two levels of delay estimated. When you consider that the design requires 24 flip-flops for the counter and input registers, you begin to see why it makes sense to use preoptimized modules—there is simply no way for general-purpose synthesis algorithms to figure out how to cram that much functionality into that small a space.

Moving On

In this chapter we have taken a detailed look at how synthesis programs operate. In doing so, we have learned a little more about VHDL, and about how designs can

```
     Pass     Area    Delay     PACKED DFFs    PIs    POs —CPU—
             (FGs) (levels)    (CLBs)                     min:sec
     1        18       3          9     24      21      8   00:23
     2        18       3          9     24      21      8   00:15
     3        16       2          8     24      21      8   00:20
     4        16       2          8     24      21      8   00:15
     5        18       3          9     24      21      8   00:15
     6        18       3          9     24      21      8   00:15
     7        16       2          8     24      21      8   00:16
     8        16       2          8     24      21      8   00:16

                        Resource Use Estimate

       Design:          PREP2A
       Technology:      xi4
       File:            D:\EXEMPLAR\DEMO\PREP2A.VHD
       Area:            16 Function Generators
       Packed Area:     8 CLBs
       Critical Path:   2 levels
       DFFs:            24 (in CLBs or IOBs)
       IOFFs:           0 (in IOBs)
       HM CLBs:         2
       Modgen CLBs:     6
       Input Pins:      21
       Output Pins:     8

                        Device Utilization Report

Device               FGs   Registers        IOBs
              avail util  avail util  avail util
4005PC84        392   4%    616   4%     61  48%
4005PG156       392   4%    616   4%    112  26%
4005PQ160       392   4%    616   4%    112  26%
4005PQ208       392   4%    616   4%    112  26%
4006PG156       512   3%    768   3%    128  23%
4006PQ160       512   3%    768   3%    128  23%
4006PQ208       512   3%    768   3%    128  23%
4008PG191       648   2%    936   3%    144  20%
4008PQ208       648   2%    936   3%    144  20%
4008MQ208       648   2%    936   3%    144  20%
4010PG191       800   2%   1120   2%    160  18%
4010PQ208       800   2%   1120   2%    160  18%
4010MQ208       800   2%   1120   2%    160  18%
4013MQ208      1152   1%   1536   2%    192  15%
4013PG223      1152   1%   1536   2%    192  15%
4013MQ240      1152   1%   1536   2%    192  15%
4013PQ240      1152   1%   1536   2%    192  15%

                            Delay Summary

       Node:        Slack    Arrival        Required      Load
                            rise   fall    rise   fall
       DATA0(0)  :   6.00   2.00   2.00    8.00   8.00    2.00
       DATA0(1)  :   6.00   2.00   2.00    8.00   8.00    2.00
       DATA0(2)  :   6.00   2.00   2.00    8.00   8.00    2.00
       DATA0(3)  :   6.00   2.00   2.00    8.00   8.00    2.00
       DATA0(4)  :   6.00   2.00   2.00    8.00   8.00    2.00
       DATA0(5)  :   6.00   2.00   2.00    8.00   8.00    2.00
       DATA0(6)  :   6.00   2.00   2.00    8.00   8.00    2.00
       DATA0(7)  :   6.00   2.00   2.00    8.00   8.00    2.00
```

Figure 17-27
Synthesis results with module generation.

be written with synthesis in mind. We'll be continuing our discussions of synthesis (and even encounter more VHDL along the way) in the next three chapters as we explore the world of programmable logic.

CHAPTER 18

FOCUS ON TECHNOLOGY: PROGRAMMABLE LOGIC

Programmable logic devices (PLDs) first appeared in the mid-1970s and have grown steadily in popularity ever since. PLDs are the ideal solution for designs that must be quick to develop, easy to maintain, and reasonably compact. PLDs are small-scale ASICs that can be configured (using relatively cheap programming hardware) to implement a specific logic function. PLDs offer the advantages of fixed-function devices (short design cycles, low development cost, less reliance on specialized skill) and of ASICs (higher densities, lower production costs, design security).

In terms of density, a typical PLD can be used to replace anywhere from a few to a few dozen fixed-function (TTL or equivalent) devices. Larger, complex PLDs (CPLDs) and field programmable gate arrays (FPGAs) with 48 or more pins can be used to perform functions that rival mask-programmed gate arrays or standard cell devices.

What Is a PLD?

For the purposes of this chapter, I'm going to define a PLD to be any integrated circuit intended for logic applications that can be programmed by the customer using software and programming equipment costing less than $10,000. Why the need for such a definition? Because the lines between what have traditionally been thought of as PLDs (ranging from simple PAL devices such as the 22V10 to more complex FPGA class devices), and mask programmed gate arrays has been blurred considerably. Laser-programmed gate arrays, FPGA conversion services that offer one-day turnaround, and other emerging technologies have made it more difficult than ever to catagorize devices by technology. Instead, it is better to catagorize devices by the design techniques required, and by their costs.

Falling into my definition of PLDs are two basic types of devices that can be further described in terms of their typical design environment, application and cost. These two types of devices are traditional PLDs based on the programmable logic array (PLA) structure (and their more complex siblings, the CPLDs) and the finer-grained field programmable gate arrays (FPGAs).

PLA-Based Devices

In the mid-1970s, Monolithic Memories, Inc. (which was later acquired by Advanced Micro Devices) introduced a series of programmable devices they called PAL (for Programmable Array Logic) devices. These devices (which are still in widespread use today) were similar in technology to common programmable read-only memory (PROM) devices, but featured programmable AND gate connections allowing them to efficiently implement general-purpose logic functions.

The PAL devices (such as the 22V10 diagrammed in Figure 18-1) are one form of PLD based on the programmable logic array (PLA), a two-level structure of logic gates (AND and OR gates, arranged in a sum-of-products structure) that theoretically allows any combinational logic function to be implemented. The PLA architecture is the basis for virtually every programmable logic device produced for the past twenty years. (The exceptions to this are the FPGA devices, which I'll get to in a moment.)

Devices based on a PLA architecture range from the simple 16L8 and 16R8 devices (the "popcorn PALs") to large, complex PLDs such as the AMD MACH series, Altera's MAX EPLD series and many other high-density programmable logic devices.

The distinguishing characteristics of PLA-based PLDs are

- ☐ A sum-of-products (or similar) arrangement of combinational logic, allowing wide (many input) logic functions to be implemented.
- ☐ A limited number of registers, with registers usually being associated with specific output pins or with a limited number of buried nodes.
- ☐ Predictable timing characteristics, with the timing behavior being dependent to only a small degree on how a design is implemented in the device.
- ☐ High speeds, with pin-to-pin delays approaching those of the fastest discrete logic components.

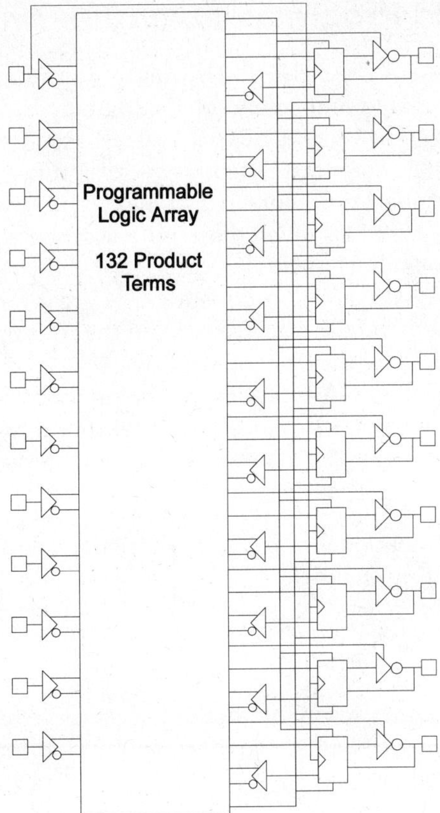

Figure 18-1
A typical PLD based on the PLA structure (22V10 PAL device).

Design Tools for PLA-Based Devices

The design tools used for PLA-based devices are almost exclusively language based. Users of these tools write their design descriptions in some form of hardware description language (PALASM, ABEL, CUPL, or perhaps more advanced languages such as VHDL) and compile the design into a form that can be transfered to the programmable device. This compiled form is usually a Joint Electron Device Engineering Council (JEDEC) standard data file, and is transfered to the programmable device by means of a device programmer—a specialized piece of hardware that the PLD is plugged into for programming. (Some newer PLDs dispense with the programming equipment entirely, and require only a modified parallel port cable and some special software to download the JEDEC programming data into the chip.)

FPGAs: Field Programmable Gate Arrays

Like the simpler PLA-based PLDs, field programmable gate arrays (FPGAs) are user programmable and intended for logic applications, but their similarity to simpler PLDs stops there. Unlike the PLA-based devices, FPGAs use a cell-based approach to their architecture, and require significant amounts of on-chip routing resources to connect different parts of the design being implemented (Figure 18-2). While PLA-based PLDs (even those with segmented architectures and inter-block routing channels) have relatively consistent and predictable timing behaviors, the timing behavior of an FPGA depends to a great extent on the application that is being implemented in the device, and on the routing method used to interconnect the different parts of the design.

Examples of FPGA-type devices being sold include the LCA devices from Xilinx, the ACT devices produced by Actel, and devices sold by Quicklogic, AT&T, Motorola and others. The distinguishing characteristics of FPGAs are

- ☐ Smaller logic blocks (or cells) that can be independently configured to implement combinational or registered functions and then connected via programmable routing channels.
- ☐ Ample register resources, with each logic block typically having one or two dedicated registers.
- ☐ Flexible routing resources, making it possible to connect any logic block with any other logic block, or connect any block directly to an input or output pad or macrocell.
- ☐ Computationally intensive design tools, with the routing of the logic blocks requiring minutes, hours, or even days to complete.
- ☐ Timing behavior that is difficult to predict until the design has been completely mapped to the device.

Design Tools for FPGAs

Because of these unique requirements, and because the architecture of an FPGA does not have the simple sum-of-products logic arrangement of a PLA-based device, design tools for FPGAs have historically been quite different from those used for simpler PLDs. While most PLD design tools are language-based, very few FPGA design tools (until quite recently) support or promote language-based design entry. Instead, FPGA users have traditionally entered their designs in schematic form using libraries of primitives (or larger macrofunctions) provided by the FPGA vendors. As FPGA applications (and the devices themselves) have grown in size and logic synthesis technology has improved, FPGA users have been moving to languages such as VHDL (or to PLD languages such as ABEL) to express their

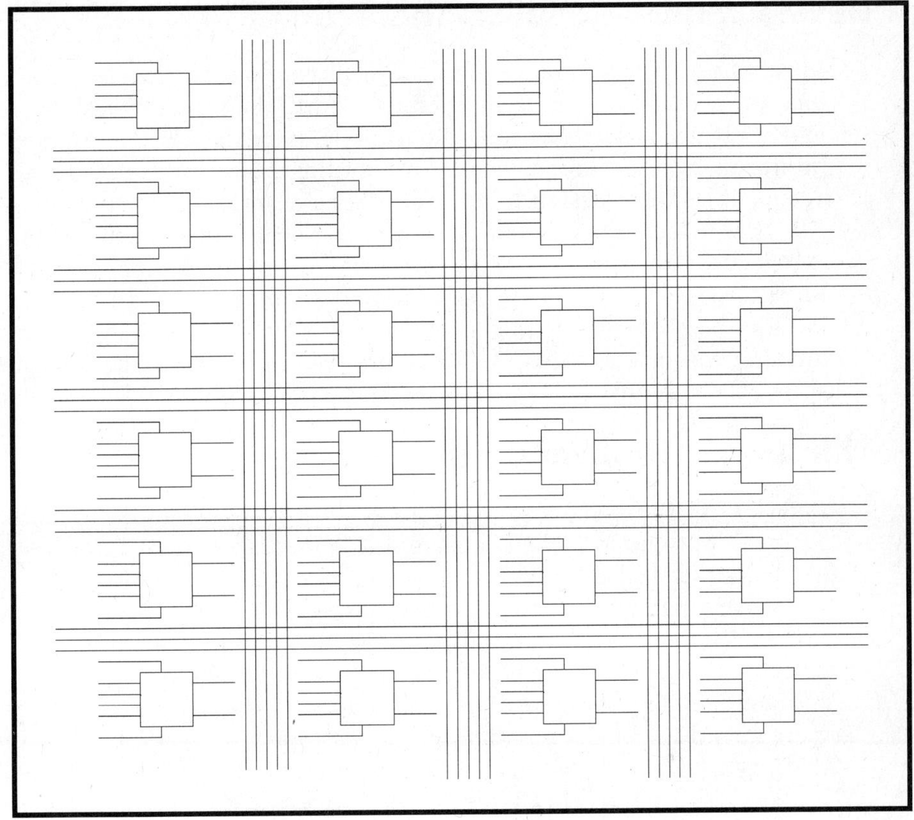

Figure 18-2
Programmable routing channels connect configurable logic modules in an FPGA.

designs, and FPGA design tool vendors have responded by adding language-based design entry features to their proprietary development tools.

Sources for PLD Tools

There are many development tools available for PLDs and FPGAs. PLD tools, in fact, were among the first true EDA tools to reach broad acceptance among mainstream engineers. In recent years, there have been a spate of new tools with more sophisticated features and better integration with other, more broadly focused tools.

Device Vendor-Supplied Tools

Many of the design tools available for PLDs are provided free of charge (or at a minimal cost) from device vendors such as AMD, Lattice, Atmel, and others. These tools are generally restricted to a small number of devices (naturally, those produced by the device vendor distributing the software) but are generally adequate for most design needs. The classic example of this type of software is PALASM, which was originally developed at Monolithic Memories, Incorporated (MMI) and later absorbed (along with the rest of the company) into Advanced Micro Devices (AMD). More full-featured products offered by device vendors include the MAX+PLUS tools provided by Altera Corporation, and customized, low-cost versions of Data I/O's ABEL product distributed by device vendors such as Atmel and Xilinx.

Third-Party Tool Vendors

Data I/O Corporation, Logical Devices, Inc., and MINC, Incorporated, are all examples of companies that were created to serve the needs of the programmable device market. Data I/O Corporation and Logical Devices are long-time producers of device programming hardware, and have developed or acquired software tools to enhance their product offerings. MINC, on the other hand, is a company that produces only software for programmable logic users. All three companies, in addition to selling software directly to end users, also supply technology to other, more broad-line EDA companies such as Viewlogic, Mentor Graphics, and Cadence.

The third-party PLD tool vendors have traditionally provided the most complete and full-featured software tools for PLDs. Languages such as ABEL, CUPL and MINC's DSL are optimized for PLD applications, and include features that give you precise control over PLD implementations, while at the same time allowing designs to be easily moved between alternative PLD architectures.

Broad-Line EDA Suppliers

The larger EDA tool suppliers are yet another source for programmable logic tools, and this is the area that is currently seeing the most action. For a variety of reasons, the major suppliers of broad-line EDA tools (including Cadence, Viewlogic and others) were somewhat slow in adding PLD design tools to their environments. This has changed in the last few years, however. PLD design support is now considered a critical item in a broad-line EDA tool's feature list, and there are new tools for PLDs (and relationships between tool vendors) being announced all the time. Even the lower-cost EDA suppliers such as Protel, OrCAD and MicroSim now offer PLD development software. This software is usually obtained from one of the three programmable logic tool companies previously mentioned. Protel, for example, has integrated Logical Device's CUPL product into its design system, while MicroSim and Viewlogic resell technology obtained from MINC and Data I/O, respectively.

Why the sudden interest in PLD software? Simply because PLDs are one of the fastest growing technologies in use by mainstream designers. PLDs are cheap, and low risk, and their use can result in a system that is cost effective, maintainable and fast to develop. PLDs are also ideal for prototyping activities. There are now companies that exist solely for the purpose of converting PLD- or FPGA-based designs into mask-programmed equivalents, making this application of PLD technology even more attractive.

Typical PLD Tool Features

What does a PLD design tool look like? In most cases, PLD design tools are oriented toward text-based design entry, rather than traditional schematic-based design. This is partly because of the influence of PALASM (which was first released many years before HDLs became popular in other design areas) and because the restrictive structure of most PLDs makes them naturally easier to work with using more abstract methods. (It is rarely the case that a schematic-oriented design will map directly into a PLD architecture, and many—perhaps most—designs being targeted to the more modern PLDs are large enough that a schematic representation would be unmanagable anyway.)

To allow designs to be entered textually, each of the PLD tools has some kind of hardware description language (HDL) that provides enough features to access the various features in the programmable devices being supported. AMD (and other PLD vendors) use PALASM (or its more-modern counterpart, PDS, which is shown in Figure 18-3) as its primary input language. MINC, Incorporated (Colorado Springs, Colorado) uses a language it calls DSL, and Logical Devices, Inc. (LDI) has its CUPL (Figure 18-4). Perhaps the most popular of these languages is Data I/O's ABEL, which has been in use for over a decade.

ABEL: Advanced Boolean Expression Language

ABEL (Advanced Boolean Expression Language) is a design language and set of supporting software programs that allow complex logic designs to be entered, compiled, optimized, simulated, and then implemented in programmable logic. ABEL is a device-independent language, meaning that a design written in ABEL does not have to explicitly state what device or technology will be used for implementation. The language does, however, include many features and constructs that give you control over a variety of device-specific circuit elements.

```
;****************************************************************
    TITLE Latch Design File
  PATTERN Latch.PDS
REVISION 1.1
   AUTHOR Nick Schmitz
  COMPANY ADVANCED MICRO DEVICES, INC.
     DATE 9/16/93        -

  CHIP  Ltch_Tst  MACH435

;****************************************************************
PIN 20 LE
PIN 5 RST
PIN 4 SET

PIN 9 Q1
PIN 8 Q2
PIN 3 D

;; PIN 10 Q3 ; Unused
;; PIN 6 Q4

;****************************************************************

EQUATIONS
;****************************************************************
; With explicit S/R equations "Native" Latch in Macrocell

     Q1 *= D
     Q1.CLKF  =  LE
     Q1.RSTF  =  RST
     Q1.SETF  =  SET

Minimize_off ; must be off to retain redundant logic

     Q2 = D   *  LE              ; Loading Term - LE dominates
        + D   *  Q2   * /RST     ; Transient race - redundant logic
        + Q2  * /LE   * /RST     ; Data Holding term
        + SET * /LE   * /RST     ; Set term - LE & RST dominate

Minimize_on
```

Figure 18-3
AMD's PDS language.

Design Entry Using ABEL

ABEL (like its two chief competitors, Logical Devices' CUPL and MINCs DSL) provides three different design representations that you can combine as needed to completely specify a design. These representations are equations, truth tables, and state diagrams. ABEL also includes a test vector language that can be used to describe circuit stimulus and expected outputs for simulation.

Equations are most useful when the design to be described has some underlying pattern or regularity. Multiplexers, shift registers, and counters are all examples of circuits that have these attributes. ABEL raises the level of design abstraction for circuits such as these by incorporating high-level equation features

```
Name      Adder;
Partno    CA0016;
Date      10/08/85;
Rev       01;
Designer  Woolhiser;
Company   Assisted Technology;
Assembly  None;
Location  None;
Device    p1618;

/************************************************************/
/*                                                          */
/* Four bit adder using the CUPL function statement.        */
/*                                                          */
/* 4-bit asynchronous adder implemented as a ripple-carry   */
/* through four adder-slice circuits.  Each adder-slice     */
/* takes a pair of 1-bit numbers (Xi, Yi) and the carry from*/
/* a previous slice (Cin) and produces their 1-bit sum (Zi) */
/* and carry (Cout).  Each adder-slice circuit is defined   */
/* using the CUPL function adder_slice(), which returns     */
/* the product directly and the carry as Cout.              */
/************************************************************/
/* Allowable Target Device Types :  PAL16L8                 */
/************************************************************/

/** Inputs **/

Pin [1..4] = [X1..4];              /* First 4-bit number    */
Pin [5..8] = [Y1..4];              /* Second 4-bit number   */

/** Outputs **/

Pin [12..15] = [Z1..4];            /* 4-bit sum             */
Pin [16..18] = [C1..3];            /* Intermed carry vaules */
Pin 19 = Carry;                    /* Carry for 4-bit sum   */

/* Adder-slice circuit - add 2, 1-bit, numbers with carry */

function adder_slice(X, Y, Cin, Cout) {
        Cout    = Cin & X                 /* Compute carry */
                # Cin & Y
                # X & Y;
     adder_slice = Cin $ (X $ Y);      /* Compute sum   */
}

/* Perform 4, 1-bit, additions and keep the final carry */

Z1 = adder_slice(X1, Y1, 'h'0, C1);  /* Initial carry = 'h'0 */
Z2 = adder_slice(X2, Y2,   C1, C2);
Z3 = adder_slice(X3, Y3,   C2, C3);
Z4 = adder_slice(X4, Y4,   C3, Carry);  /* Final carry value */
```

Figure 18-4
Logical Devices' CUPL.

such as sets, arithmetic operators, and relational operators. These features, which are found in all modern hardware description languages, allow more abstract forms of expression than are possible using simple sum-of-products Boolean equations.

```
Module counter
Title '8-bit Loadable Counter'

    Clear,Clock,Load    pin;
    D7..D0              pin;  "Data inputs
    Q7..Q0              pin istype 'reg,buffer';  "Counter bits

    Data  = [D7..D0];
    Count = [Q7..Q0];

Equations

    Count.clk = Clock;   "Clock
    Count.clr = Clear;   "Synchronous clear

    when Load then
        Count := Data;
    else
        Count := Count.fb + 1;

Test_Vectors([Clock,Clear,Load,Data]->[Count])
             [ .C. ,  1  ,  0,    0]->[   0 ];
             [ .C. ,  0  ,  0,    0]->[   1 ];
             [ .C. ,  0  ,  0,    0]->[   2 ];
             [ .C. ,  0  ,  0,    0]->[   3 ];
             [ .C. ,  0  ,  1,  128]->[ 128 ];
             [ .C. ,  0  ,  0,    0]->[ 129 ];
             [ .C. ,  0  ,  0,    0]->[ 130 ];
             [ .C. ,  0  ,  0,    0]->[ 131 ];
             [ .C. ,  0  ,  0,    0]->[ 132 ];
             [ .C. ,  0  ,  0,    0]->[ 133 ];
             [ .C. ,  0  ,  0,    0]->[ 134 ];
             [ .C. ,  0  ,  0,    0]->[ 135 ];

End
```

Figure 18-5
ABEL's high-level equation language.

Figure 18-5 lists a complete ABEL design description that describes an 8-bit loadable counter. (This design file also includes test vectors, which I'll describe a bit later.)

Truth tables are most useful for designs that have no underlying pattern or order. A typical example of such a circuit is a code converter. Figure 18-6 lists an ABEL truth table description of a seven-segment decoder. This small example demonstrates another useful feature of truth tables—the ability to specify (or imply) don't-care conditions in a circuit. In this example, only 10 of the 16 possible values are listed in the truth table. The 6 remaining conditions are therefore not significant to the operation of the final circuit and can be treated as don't-cares during optimization.

The third form of entry supported by ABEL, the state diagram, is useful for state machines—circuits that are sequential and depend on feedback to control their next state. ABEL's state diagram language can be used to describe finite state machines at a high level, by specifying each state of the machine, the transitions between

```
module BCD7
title 'BCD to 7-segment display driver'
////////////////////////////////////////////////////
// Seven-segment display driver with active-low   //
// outputs. Segments:       -a-                   //
//                         f| |b                  //
//                          -g-                   //
//                         e| |c                  //
//                          -d-                   //
////////////////////////////////////////////////////

    D3..D0          pin;                      "BCD input
    a,b,c,d,e,f,g   pin istype 'dc,com';      "Segment outputs
    OE              pin;                      "Output enable

    BCD     = [D3..D0];
    LED     = [a,b,c,d,e,f,g];
    ON,OFF  = 0,1;                            "Inverted sense

equations

    LED.oe = !OE;       "Define output enable

truth_table(BCD->[  a ,  b ,  c ,  d ,  e ,  f ,  g ])
              0 ->[ OFF, OFF, OFF, OFF, OFF, OFF,  ON];
              1 ->[  ON, OFF, OFF,  ON,  ON,  ON,  ON];
              2 ->[ OFF, OFF,  ON, OFF, OFF,  ON, OFF];
              3 ->[ OFF, OFF, OFF, OFF,  ON,  ON, OFF];
              4 ->[  ON, OFF, OFF,  ON,  ON, OFF, OFF];
              5 ->[ OFF,  ON, OFF, OFF,  ON, OFF, OFF];
              6 ->[ OFF,  ON, OFF, OFF, OFF, OFF, OFF];
              7 ->[ OFF, OFF, OFF,  ON,  ON,  ON,  ON];
              8 ->[ OFF, OFF, OFF, OFF, OFF, OFF, OFF];
              9 ->[ OFF, OFF, OFF, OFF,  ON, OFF, OFF];

test_vectors ([OE,BCD]->[  a ,  b ,  c ,  d ,  e ,  f ,  g ])
              [ 0, 0 ]->[ OFF, OFF, OFF, OFF, OFF, OFF,  ON];
              [ 0, 1 ]->[  ON, OFF, OFF,  ON,  ON,  ON,  ON];
              [ 0, 2 ]->[ OFF, OFF,  ON, OFF, OFF,  ON, OFF];
              [ 0, 3 ]->[ OFF, OFF, OFF, OFF,  ON,  ON, OFF];
              [ 0, 4 ]->[  ON, OFF, OFF,  ON,  ON, OFF, OFF];
              [ 0, 5 ]->[ OFF,  ON, OFF, OFF,  ON, OFF, OFF];
              [ 0, 6 ]->[ OFF,  ON, OFF, OFF, OFF, OFF, OFF];
              [ 0, 7 ]->[ OFF, OFF, OFF,  ON,  ON,  ON,  ON];
              [ 0, 8 ]->[ OFF, OFF, OFF, OFF, OFF, OFF, OFF];
              [ 0, 9 ]->[ OFF, OFF, OFF, OFF,  ON, OFF, OFF];
              [ 1, 5 ]->[ .z., .z., .z., .z., .z., .z., .z.];

end
```

Figure 18-6
ABEL's truth table language.

states, and the output logic. Figure 18-7 shows a complete ABEL design file that uses a state diagram to define the behavior of a four-state state machine with combinational and registered outputs.

```
module SM4
title 'State machine output example'
/////////////////////////////////////////////////////////////////
// 4-state state machine with state transition outputs.       //
/////////////////////////////////////////////////////////////////
     Clk,Hold,OE pin;                      "Inputs
     Q1,Q0 pin istype 'reg';               "State bits
     REG1 pin istype 'reg';                "Reg output
     COM1 pin istype 'com';                "Com output

     A = ^b00; B = ^b01; C = ^b11; D = ^b10;    "State values

Equations

     [REG1,Q0,Q1].clk = Clk;
     [REG1,Q0,Q1].oe = !OE;

State_Diagram [Q1,Q0]

     State A: REG1 := 0;
              COM1  = 0;
              If !Hold Then A Else B ;

     State B: REG1 := 1;
              COM1  = 1;
              Goto C;

     State C: COM1 = 0;
              If Hold Then C With REG1 := 0;
              Else D With REG1 := 1;

     State D: REG1 := 1;
              COM1 = 1;
              If Hold Then D Else A;

Test_Vectors ([Clk,OE,Hold] -> [[Q1,Q0],REG1,COM1])
               [.C., 0,  0 ] -> [  .X. , .X. , .X.];
               [.C., 0,  0 ] -> [  .X. , .X. , .X.];
               [.C., 0,  0 ] -> [  .X. , .X. , .X.];
               [.C., 0,  0 ] -> [   A  ,  0  ,  0 ];
               [.C., 0,  0 ] -> [   A  ,  0  ,  0 ];
               [.C., 0,  1 ] -> [   B  ,  0  ,  1 ];
               [.C., 0,  1 ] -> [   C  ,  1  ,  0 ];
               [.C., 0,  1 ] -> [   C  ,  0  ,  0 ];
               [.C., 0,  0 ] -> [   D  ,  1  ,  1 ];
               [.C., 0,  1 ] -> [   D  ,  1  ,  1 ];
               [.C., 0,  1 ] -> [   D  ,  1  ,  1 ];
               [.C., 0,  0 ] -> [   A  ,  1  ,  0 ];
               [.C., 0,  0 ] -> [   A  ,  0  ,  0 ];
End
```

Figure 18-7
State diagram languages allow state machines to be described in terms of their possible states..

Test Vectors and Simulation

The three preceding ABEL source files (the counter, display driver, and state machine) all included test vectors as a part of the design specification. Test vectors are lists of values representing inputs to, and corresponding outputs of, a design under test. In ABEL, test vectors are entered into source files as an integral part of the design process, using language features that look very much like a truth table representation. The ABEL software includes two simulators (an equation-level simulator and a JEDEC file simulator) that can be used to test the functionality of the design, and the test vectors can also be used to test the programmed device using the test features built into most device programmers.

Using VHDL for PLD Designs

A recent trend that should be noted here is the sudden, rapid acceptance among PLD tools vendors of VHDL as a standard design entry language. At this writing it is too early to tell if VHDL will replace the widely used ABEL, CUPL, and PALASM/PDS languages, but indications are positive that VHDL will be a significant force in the PLD design tool industry. VHDL does offer some significant advantages over existing PLD languages, but also has its disadvantages.

Advantages of Using VHDL for PLD Design

The most obvious benefit to using VHDL is that it is a standard language. Because it's a standard, designs entered using VHDL can easily be migrated to alternative technologies such as gate arrays. Being a standard also means that there are many choices of design tools available, and these design tools include advanced simulation tools (including source-level debuggers) that simply aren't available for designs written in a PLD language.

VHDL also has some built-in advantages not directly related to PLDs and FPGAs:

- The same design language can be used for system design, ASIC and PLD design, simulation modeling, and for test development. Since VHDL is both a design description language and a test language, you only have to learn one language for many different applications.

- VHDL supports hierachy and design management features that make it much easier to reuse existing design, and to work on large designs in a top-down manner. This is particularly useful for PLDs, since designs spanning more than one PLD are often reworked and combined into a larger programmable device or gate array.

- VHDL is also a commonly used netlist language, making it easy to integrate VHDL designs with other parts of the design that were entered in schematic (or other) form. Since many of the more popular schematic editors will output a VHDL netlist, it is quite possible to use schematics in concert with hand-written

VHDL code, without having to buy an expensive design tool that directly supports this feature.

Disadvantages of Using VHDL for PLD Design

So what are the down-sides to using VHDL for PLD applications? Here are a few things to consider.

- ☐ Did I say VHDL is a standard? Guess what: it's not. While the language as it is defined in IEEE standards 1076-1987, 1076-1993, 1164, and 1076.3 (which should be released by the time you read this) is implemented fairly consistently in simulation tools, for synthesis (the primary focus of PLD design tools) there is no clear standard for many important aspects of PLD design (such as how to express pin assignments, or describe a three-state output). Instead, there are only conventions. In addition to those things that are missing in the language, there are many language elements included in the VHDL standards that are not synthesizable. (These include such things as file I/O.) Because of this, you must write your VHDL designs using a subset of the language, and this subset may not exactly match the subset used in other tools.
- ☐ VHDL does not provide the language features needed to specify all the information about a PLD-based design. Although all PLD languages provide statements for defining basic physical information such as pin assignments, these features are lacking in VHDL. To get around this, PLD tool vendors must establish a convention (special comment fields, or custom attributes) to embed this kind of information in the design.

The bottom line is: if you are happy with the PLD design environment you have (or are on a tight budget), you may want to stick with a PLD design language and design environment for the time being.

PREP: A Standard VHDL For PLDs?

In an attempt to resolve the preceding issues for VHDL and PLD users, the Programmable Electronics Performance Corporation (the PREP committee, headed by Stan Baker) has established a working group to agree on a set of standard methods by which PLD- and FPGA-specific physical data can be represented in VHDL, and to foster communication between design tool vendors so that new conventions and subsets are reasonably compatible. It remains to be seen whether this effort can keep up with the rapid changes occurring in PLD and FPGA device architecture, and with the rapid evolution of VHDL-oriented design tools. The best advice I can give at this point is: if you are going to choose VHDL as your primary design entry method then you would be well advised to acquire at least two different VHDL compilers. If you only use one compiler in your work, you may well lose track of what are well-established synthesis conventions and what are requirements peculiar to the synthesis tool you have chosen.

Simulation of PLDs and FPGAs

Simulation is increasing in importance for PLD and FPGA applications. Designs being implemented in these devices are growing in size, and the devices themselves are getting larger and more complex. Another important factor increasing the need for simulation is the speed at which modern circuits are expected to operate. These high speeds, coupled with changes in packaging technologies, make it difficult or even impossible to effectively debug large PLD- or FPGA-based circuits using traditional prototyping methods.

Simulation has long been a part of the programmable logic design process. When the first widely-available PLDs appeared in the late 1970s, they were accompanied by design software (most notably MMI's PALASM and, somewhat later, Data I/O's ABEL and Assisted Technologies' CUPL) that included rudimentary simulation technology. These PLD simulators were intended to emulate the behavior of a device programmer by accepting data in the form of test vectors and applying that data to verify the correct function of the programmed device.

The early simulators were quite effective at identifying the most common functional errors in PLD-based designs, but were not nearly as useful for verifying the timing behavior of these devices. The lack of true timing-based simulation was not seen as a serious problem, however, because PLD devices had consistent and predictable timing characteristics, and the speed requirements of most PLD-based designs did not pose a serious challenge to the relatively high speeds of the devices themselves.

The introduction of FPGAs, however, changed the requirements for simulation of programmable logic devices. The widely varying internal delay paths of these new devices, coupled with their much higher complexities, resulted in new simulation requirements, and approaches to simulation that were more akin to the simulation methods used for large ASIC-based designs. To accurately simulate FPGA devices, users of these devices needed to acquire and learn comprehensive simulation tools, and FPGA vendors needed to work closely with simulation tool vendors to provide accurate timing models for their customers. This trend—the close relationship between FPGA and complex PLD vendors and simulation tool vendors—continues today, as device vendors work to make sure their devices are fully supported in the tools being used by their customers.

Functional And Timing Simulation For PLDs

Although timing simulation is important for verification of FPGA and PLD-based circuits, it is not necessary to perform a complete timing simulation as the first step in the verification process for a design. In fact, a more efficient approach is to use a combination of functional and timing simulation during the design process. This is particularly important for FPGAs, since the process of creating an accurate timing model for the entire design can be a time-consuming process, with each iteration of the design requiring many minutes—perhaps even hours—of painstaking and computation-intensive work before a timing-annotated netlist (or other format) is ready for simulation.

The purpose of a functional simulation is to test the logical operation of a circuit. This kind of test can be performed at any point in the design process, on the entire design or on a smaller segment of the design. Functional testing can catch the most common design errors, and is relatively quick and easy to perform.

For PLD and FPGA applications, functional simulation is most effective when applied incrementally, with each segment of the design being entered and debugged completely before moving on to the next segment.

Of course, functional simulation cannot provide complete assurance that the design will actually work when implemented in the target device. Since this type of simulation ignores actual path and gate delays, the real-world attributes of the device may invalidate the results obtained before these factors were taken into consideration. If you know that the design is functionally correct, however, you can more easily determine whether a problem found later on is due to a timing problem, rather than a functional design error.

Timing simulation differs from functional simulation in that the simulator is provided with information about the actual timing delays (path delays and gate delays) that will exist in the design as implemented in the target device. Additional information is provided to the simulator to allow it to check for timing violations such as setup and hold, and to identify and flag other common timing-related errors.

Because this information can only be determined after the design has been mapped into the actual part, timing simulation must be deferred until the latter stages of the design process, and usually involves the entire design, rather than smaller portions of a design. In many design environments, system-level testing is also important, so the timing simulation of the programmable device may be performed in concert with other devices in the simulated system.

Timing simulation can be used to verify the correct operation of a device, at the speed it is intended to operate in circuit, with nearly the same level of confidence as would be obtained if the physical device had been plugged into a hardware prototype and tested. Simulation can do more than a hardware prototype, however. With simulation, you can experiment with differing system speeds, apply stimulus that is difficult or impossible to generate in hardware, and observe the inner workings of the device while it is operating.

For those engineers who have had to opportunity to develop a large-scale ASIC (such as a gate array or standard-cell device), nothing about FPGA and complex PLD simulation will seem new. There are some important differences between simulation for ASICs and simulation for programmable devices, however.

The most important difference is related to risk. When designing a chip that will be produced by an ASIC foundry, it is imperative that the design be completely debugged prior to the production of the first silicon. This is because the cost of failure (both in terms of money and in time) can be enormous. Accurate and comprehensive simulation is therefore a prerequisite to ASIC production, and the process of developing adequate test vectors and other test data can actually consume far more time than the process of developing the circuit itself.

In contrast, FPGA and complex PLD devices are relatively low-risk. Because the devices can be reprogrammed or replaced at a relatively low cost, comprehensive simulation for these devices is less critical. Programmable devices therefore lend themselves well to an iterative approach that combines functional simulation, limited timing simulation, and actual hardware prototyping.

Another important distinction between designs intended for ASICs and those intended for FPGA or complex PLDs is the sheer size of the designs. A typical gate array design may have 10 times the density of a typical FPGA or complex-PLD design. For this reason the simulation tools—and the computing platforms on which those tools run—for ASIC simulation are quite different and usually far more expensive than the equivalent tools for FPGAs and complex PLDs.

Moving On

In this chapter, we have taken a high-level look at the two fundamental types of programmable logic devices, and have gained some insight into the kinds of design tools used to develop PLD-based circuits. In the next two chapters we'll see examples of PLD design tools in action.

Other Resources

Alford, Roger, *Programmable Logic Designer's Guide*, Howard W. Sams, Indianapolis, IN, 1989.

Chan, Pak K., *Digital Design Using Field Programmable Gate Arrays*, Prentice Hall, Englewood Cliffs, NJ, 1994.

Jenkins, Jesse, *Designing with FPGAs and CPLDs*, Prentice Hall, Englewood Cliffs, NJ, 1994.

Lala, Parag K., *Digital System Design Using Programmable Logic Devices*, Prentice Hall, Englewood Cliffs, NJ, 1990.

Pellerin, David, and Michael Holley, *Digital Design Using ABEL*, Prentice Hall, Englewood Cliffs, NJ, 1994.

Pellerin, David, and Michael Holley, *Practical Design Using Programmable Logic*, Prentice Hall, Englewood Cliffs, NJ, 1994.

Treseler, Michael, *Designing State Machine Controllers Using Programmable Logic*, Prentice Hall, Englewood Cliffs, NJ, 1992.

CHAPTER 19

HANDS-ON EDA: USING FPGA DESIGN TOOLS

In this Hands-On chapter, I'll be presenting an example circuit that has been described using a combination of ABEL and schematic representations and implementated using a Xilinx FPGA. Designing for FPGAs is quite a bit more complicated than designing for simpler PLDs, and often involves using a combination of design tools obtained from different sources. In this example, I'll be using a design tool specifically created to combine the strengths of a device-independent design entry environment with device-specific software provided by device vendors.

Note: *The information in this chapter is based on a sample project and descriptions supplied by Data I/O with their Synario 2.0 product. An evaluation version of the Synario 1.0 software has been porovided on the companion CD-ROM, and you are encouraged to install this software and try it for yourself.*

Data I/O's Synario

Data I/O Corporation released its Synario FPGA design tool in October 1993. This Windows-based design environment combines and integrates a full-featured schematic editor with Data I/O's ABEL design language, and includes a Verilog-based simulator, Silos III, licensed from Simucad Corporation. An optional version of Synario includes support for VHDL entry and simulation. This combination of software provides a powerful set of design entry features for PLD and FPGA devices.

Synario also includes FPGA optimization and fitting software obtained from the major FPGA device vendors and has a user interface called the Project Navigator that helps FPGA users make their way through the sometimes complex process of converting designs into actual working FPGA devices.

The key features of Synario are

- ☐ Support for all common PLDs, complex PLDs and FPGAs.
- ☐ A Project Navigator that tracks design sources (schematics, ABEL or VHDL source files, Verilog HDL test fixtures and document files) and ensures that they are processed with the right set of tools to produce an appropriate format of output for the selected device type.
- ☐ Dependency features that track which portions of the design are out of date and reprocess only those portions that require processing after a change.
- ☐ An enhanced version of the ABEL language that supports hierarchical designs, and allows lower-level ABEL modules (or schematics) to be included into larger designs.
- ☐ Simulation back-annotation features that allow simulation results to be viewed directly on the schematic.
- ☐ Integration with PLD vendor-supplied fitting or place-and-route software. (For PLDs and complex PLDs, Data I/O's own fitting software is bundled in with the product. For FPGA devices, the FPGA vendors supply Data I/O with the appropriate back-end software.)
- ☐ Optional support for VHDL design entry and simulation.
- ☐ Cross-probing features that allow schematic wires (nets) to be selected dynamically for display during simulation.

Entering a Design in Synario

Designs can be entered in Synario as schematics, ABEL or VHDL language files, or a combination of these entry methods. A design being entered in Synario is called a Project, and the various schematics, language files, and other files associated with that project are called Sources. Figure 19-1 shows a Synario project that includes both ABEL and schematic sources, as well as including a Verilog test fixture and a document file (in Microsoft Write format). This design (which will be described in detail later in this section) is intended for a Xilinx FPGA device. Synario's Project

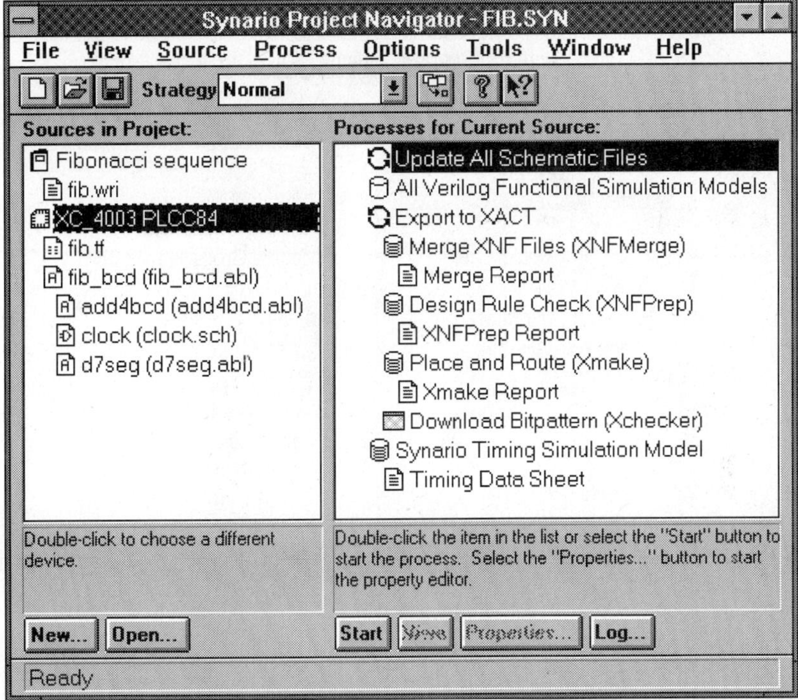

Figure 19-1
Synario's Project Navigator displays the design's sources (as a hierarchy of files) in the Sources window, and displays the processes available for each source in the Process window.

Navigator understands the unique requirements for each type of device and for this design displays the processes required to create a Xilinx FPGA.

Figure 19-2 shows a second project loaded into the Project Navigator, this one intended for a complex PLD (a MACH 435 device) . This example shows how the Project Navigator adjusts itself to meet the requirements of a particular device. In this case, a JEDEC format file is required to create the working (programmed) device.

After a project has been created, project sources are either created within the project navigator or imported into the project. To modify any source in a Synario project, you double-click on the source name in the Project Navigator's Sources Window (the area on the left side of the Project Navigator Window). Synario keeps track of the source types, so if you double-click on a schematic source, the schematic editor will be invoked, while double-clicking on an ABEL file or Verilog test fixture will cause the Synario text editor to be invoked. The source window actually operates in much the same way as does Windows File Manager; if you set up an association between a file extension (such as .DOC for a document file) and a

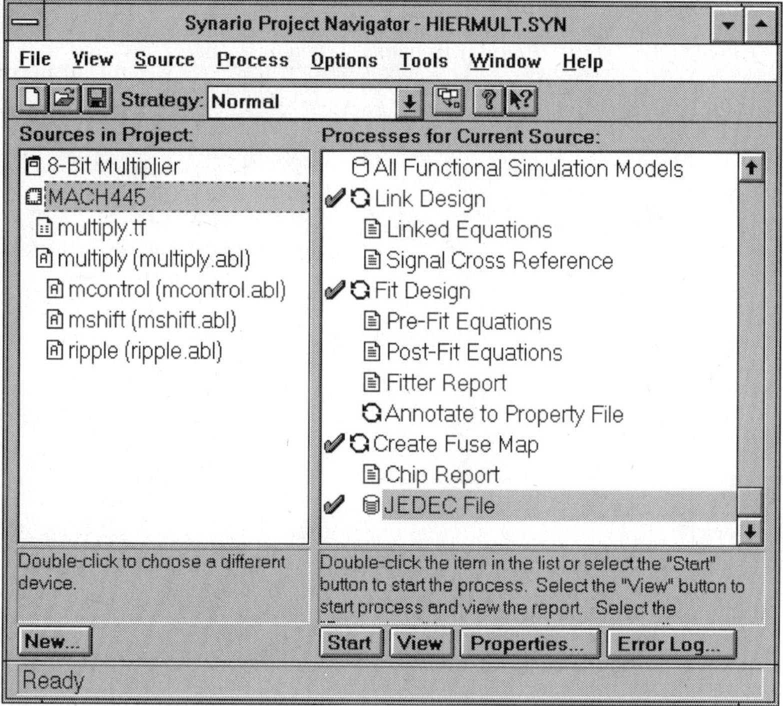

Figure 19-2
The processes that will be needed to complete a design depend on the type of device selected. In this case, a complex PLD has been selected, so a JEDEC file is the desired result of processing.

corresponding application (such as Microsoft Word for Windows,) you can drag and drop virtually any type of file into the Synario source window, and double-clicking on the name of that file will cause Synario to invoke the proper application to edit or process the file. Document types that are not immediately understood by Synario as being project sources (such word processing documents) display under an icon in the Source display called the Project Notebook.

Synario Design Example

The Synario project that we will be looking at in this tutorial is a standard example included with the Synario product. The design, a Fibonacci sequence generator, is composed of three ABEL source files and one schematic.

Xilinx Demonstration Board

The Fibonacci sequence generator is a standard example that is intended for use with the 4000 series LCA demonstration board supplied by Xilinx. The demonstration board is available directly from Xilinx, and consists of

- One XC4003 LCA device in an 84-pin PLCC socket
- Two seven-segment displays
- One eight-segment bar display
- Eight DIP switches to control the device inputs
- Momentary contact switches for Program, Reset, and Spare inputs (for device programming)
- A download (programming) cable kit that plugs into the parallel port on a personal computer

The demonstration board allows a wide variety of circuits to be implemented, so you can quickly learn about the FPGA design process.

Fibonacci Sequence Generator

The Fibonacci sequence generator that we will implement in the demonstration board is a decimal number generator, with each clock cycle resulting in a new number in the Fibonacci series being displayed on the demonstration board's seven-segment displays. (A Fibonacci sequence is a series of numbers, each of which is the sum of the previous two numbers. For example, the series 0, 1, 1, 2, 3, 5, 8, 13, 21, 34 is a Fibonacci sequence.)

This design has been entered primarily in the ABEL language, with only the clock generator circuit having been entered in schematic form. Hierarchy features in ABEL are used to connect the four design modules into a complete circuit. Let's look at each of the four source files.

Top-Level ABEL File (FIB_BCD.ABL)

The **fib_bcd.abl** file uses a mixture of hierarchy references and logic descriptions to implement a state machine and tie together the three lower-level modules. The complete ABEL source file for this module is listed in Figure 19-3.

Starting at the top of the file, we see

- A module statement and title defining the name of the module and briefly describe its purpose.
- Node declarations for intermediate signals that will be used in the adder portions of the design. The registered signals **A7—A0** and **B7—B0** represent the

previous two numbers in the sequence, while **S7—S0** represent the sum of the two numbers. The **Cout** and **C1** signals provide a carry out function and a carry between the two stages of the 8-bit adder, respectively.

- ☐ Set declarations that define groupings of signals into sets named **SumA** and **SumB**. These two sets represent the previous two sums in the sequence, while the **Sum** set represents the calculated next sum. Set declarations such as these—like buses on a schematic—can dramatically simplify the description of complex circuits.

- ☐ After the signal and set declarations, interface declarations defining the three lower-level modules in the design (**add4bcd**, **clock**, and **d7seg**). Each declaration includes a list of input and output ports, and the **add4bcd** declaration also includes a default value (0) for its **Cin** (carry-in) input. These interface declarations don't actually create any logic; their only purpose is to define the module and port names, and the port direction, for subsequent uses (or *instances*) of the modules.

- ☐ After the interface declarations, functional block declarations creating unique instances of the three lower-level modules. The **add4bcd** module is a 4-bit adder, and is instantiated twice. These two adders will be chained to create an 8-bit adder. The **d7seg** module is also instantiated twice, once for each of the two LED displays. The **clock** module is instantiated once, and will provide a clock signal (**Clk**) for the other modules.

- ☐ Pin declarations describing the design inputs and outputs related to the clocking function. The purpose of the **clock** module is to slow down the system clock (**ExtClk**) so that the sequence is displayed on the LEDs at a rate allowing the numbers to be observed, and the **UseExt** and **Speed** inputs control the rate at which the **Clk** signal will be cycled.

- ☐ Simple equations tying the input signals (**ExtClk**, **UseExt** and **Speed**) to the appropriate ports of the clock module (which has been given an instance name of **ClkGen**). Another simple equation connects the **Clk** port of the clock module with the **Clk** signal.

- ☐ Another set of simple equations creating an 8-bit adder by connecting the two instances of the 4-bit adder module (via the **C1** carry signal) and routing the resulting eight bits to the **S7—S0** sum signals.

- ☐ A set of declarations defining the signals necessary for the state machine portion of the design. The **Reset** input provides an asynchronous reset function for the design. **Sbits** is a specially declared state register signal that represents a symbolic state register of unknown width. **Clear**, **First** and **Add** are symbolic state names whose actual encodings will be determined automatically during synthesis.

Figure 19-3
The top-level ABEL source file.

```
module fib_bcd
title 'Decimal Fibonacci sequence generator for XC4000 Demo Board
Michael Holley and Steve Kaufer   Data I/O Corp.   21 July 1994';

" Every Fibonacci number is the sum of its two predecessors:
" 0,1,1,2,3,5,8,13,21,34,55,89,144,...

    A7..A0    node istype 'reg';
    B7..B0    node istype 'reg';
    S7..S0    node istype 'com';
    Cout,C1   node istype 'com';

    SumA = [A7..A0];
    SumB = [B7..B0];
    Sum  = [S7..S0];

"Sub-module declarations
    add4bcd interface (A3..A0,B3..B0,Cin=0 -> D3..D0,Cout);
    clock   interface (ExtClk,UseExt,Speed -> Clk);
    d7seg   interface (A3..A0,RBI=0 -> A,B,C,D,E,F,G,RBO);

"Sub Module instances
    adder1,adder2 functional_block add4bcd;
    bcd1,bcd2     functional_block d7seg;
    clkgen        functional_block clock;

Declarations " Clock
    ExtClk         pin 13;
    UseExt,Speed   pin 26,27;
    Clk            pin 10;

Equations
    clkgen.ExtClk = ExtClk;
    clkgen.UseExt = UseExt;
    clkgen.Speed  = Speed;
    Clk = clkgen.Clk;

Equations " BCD Adder
    adder1.[A3..A0] = [A3..A0];
    adder1.[B3..B0] = [B3..B0];
    [S3..S0] = adder1.[D3..D0];
    C1 = adder1.Cout;

    adder2.[A3..A0] = [A7..A4];
    adder2.[B3..B0] = [B7..B4];
    adder2.Cin = C1;
    [S7..S4] = adder2.[D3..D0];
    Cout = adder2.Cout;

Declarations " Control State Machine
    Reset   pin 28;

    Sbits   state_register;
    Clear   state;
    First   state;
    Add     state;

    " Make a set the width of set SumA with a value of 1
    One = [0,0,0,0,0,0,0,1];
```

```
Equations
    [SumA,SumB,Sbits].clk = Clk;

State_diagram Sbits
    State Clear:
        SumA := 0;
        SumB := 0;
        goto First;

    State First:
        SumA := One;
        SumB := Sum;
        goto Add;

    State Add:
        SumA := SumB;
        SumB := Sum;
        If (Cout) Then Clear Else Add;

    Async_Reset Clear: Reset;

Declarations "Display
    O7..O0 pin 61,62,65,66,57,58,59,60;
    CR4A,CR4B,CR4C,CR4D,CR4E,CR4F,CR4G pin 49,48,47,46,45,50,51;
    CR3A,CR3B,CR3C,CR3D,CR3E,CR3F,CR3G pin 39,38,36,35,29,40,44;
    CR3_DP                             pin 37;

Equations
    ![O7..O0] = [S7..S0];

    bcd1.[A3..A0] = [S3..S0];
    bcd2.[A3..A0] = [S7..S4];

    ![CR4A,CR4B,CR4C,CR4D,CR4E,CR4F,CR4G] = bcd1.[A,B,C,D,E,F,G];
    ![CR3A,CR3B,CR3C,CR3D,CR3E,CR3F,CR3G] = bcd2.[A,B,C,D,E,F,G];
    !CR3_DP = Cout;

End
```

- ☐ Before the state diagram section, a simple equation defining the clocking for the state machine and the two previous sum registers. The internal clock (**Clk**) is used for both the state machine and the sum registers.

- ☐ After the clock equation, a state diagram describing the operation of the circuit at a high level. The first state of the machine, **Clear**, simply sets the two sum registers (**SumA** and **SumB**) to a cleared state, then advances to the **First** state. In state **First**, an initial value (binary 00000001) is loaded into the **SumA** register. **SumB** is loaded with the result of the combinational add function (the sum of **SumA** and **SumB**). In this state of the machine, the result of this operation is always a value of 1 being loaded into **SumB**. In the **Add** state, the value appearing in **SumB** is transferred to the **SumA** register, and **SumB** is loaded with the sum of the previous two values. If the value exceeds the maximum value (indicated by the **Cout** signal), the machine automatically resets to state **Clear**.

- A final set of declarations and equations describing the connections between the LED outputs and the display decoders **bcd1** and **bcd2**, each of which is an instance of the **d7seg** module. The LED outputs are inverted before going off-chip, allowing them to properly drive the LED segments.

Adder Module (add4bcd.abl)

The **add4bcd** module is an ABEL source file (Figure 19-4) that implements a 4-bit adder with a BCD (binary coded decimal) decoder at the output. The Fibonacci design calls for an 8-bit adder with a decoder, but the best implementation of an adder for this FPGA implementation is two chained 4-bit adders.

The ABEL source file for the adder consists of

- Pin declarations: These pin declarations do not actually represent pins on the device; since this is a lower-level module, the pins that are declared at this level are actually module ports that will become intermediate signals at the next higher module in the hierarchy, as we saw in the top-level ABEL file **fib_bcd.abl**.
- Set declarations: In this example, the set groupings make it possible to describe the function of the adder in just two lines of equations.
- An ABEL truth table: Describing the BCD decoder portion of the module, the truth table simply associates the sum and carry values (appearing on set **S** and signal **C4**) with the appropriate binary coded decimal values. Values that exceed the maximum decimal value (9) trigger the carry-out bit **Cout**.

Seven-Segment Display Decoder (d7seg.abl)

The final ABEL source file in this design is a seven-segment display decoder. This source file, which is shown in Figure 19-5, consists of

- Pin declarations representing the 4-bit BCD input (**A3—A0**), a blanking input (**RBI**) and the seven outputs corresponding to the display segments.
- A truth table specifying the decoding of the seven segments for each input combination.

This module actually corresponds directly to a hard macro provided by Xilinx for the 4000 series devices. This design could therefore have eliminated the **d7seg** module and specified a hard macro (**d7segh**) directly, either by instantiating two **d7segh** symbols in a lower-level schematic or by referencing the hard macro directly from within the top-level ABEL source file. To make this design easier to

Figure 19-4
The add4bcd.abl source file describes a 4-bit adder with a BCD decoder at the output.

```
module add4bcd
title 'BCD Adder for FPGA   Michael Holley  1 Oct 1993'

    A3..A0      pin;
    B3..B0      pin;
    D3..D0      pin istype 'com';

    Cin         pin;
    Cout        pin istype 'com';
    S3..S0      node;
    C4..C1      node istype 'com';

    A = [A3..A0];
    B = [B3..B0];
    C = [C3..C1,Cin];
    D = [D3..D0];
    S = [S3..S0];

equations " Adder
    S = A $ B $ C;
    [C4..C1] = A & B # (A # B) & C;

@dcset
truth_table([  S , C4] -> [Cout, D ]);
            [  0 , 0 ] -> [  0 , 0 ];
            [  1 , 0 ] -> [  0 , 1 ];
            [  2 , 0 ] -> [  0 , 2 ];
            [  3 , 0 ] -> [  0 , 3 ];
            [  4 , 0 ] -> [  0 , 4 ];
            [  5 , 0 ] -> [  0 , 5 ];
            [  6 , 0 ] -> [  0 , 6 ];
            [  7 , 0 ] -> [  0 , 7 ];
            [  8 , 0 ] -> [  0 , 8 ];
            [  9 , 0 ] -> [  0 , 9 ];
            [ 10 , 0 ] -> [  1 , 0 ];
            [ 11 , 0 ] -> [  1 , 1 ];
            [ 12 , 0 ] -> [  1 , 2 ];
            [ 13 , 0 ] -> [  1 , 3 ];
            [ 14 , 0 ] -> [  1 , 4 ];
            [ 15 , 0 ] -> [  1 , 5 ];
            [ 16 , 1 ] -> [  1 , 6 ];
            [ 17 , 1 ] -> [  1 , 7 ];
            [ 18 , 1 ] -> [  1 , 8 ];
            [ 19 , 1 ] -> [  1 , 9 ];

end
```

transfer to different device families, however, it was decided to use the more portable ABEL description for this part of the design.

Figure 19-5
The d7seg.abl source file describes a BCD to 7-segment display decoder.

```
module d7seg

title 'BCD-to-7-Segment Decoder'

    A3..A0          pin

    RBI             pin;
    A,B,C,D,E,F,G   pin istype 'com';
    RBO             pin istype 'com';

@dcset
truth_table
        ([RBI,A3,A2,A1,A0] -> [A,B,C,D,E,F,G,RBO])
         [ 1 , 0, 0, 0, 0] -> [0,0,0,0,0,0,0, 1 ];    "Blank
         [ 0 , 0, 0, 0, 0] -> [1,1,1,1,1,1,0, 0 ];    "0
         [.X., 0, 0, 0, 1] -> [0,1,1,0,0,0,0, 0 ];    "1
         [.X., 0, 0, 1, 0] -> [1,1,0,1,1,0,1, 0 ];    "2
         [.X., 0, 0, 1, 1] -> [1,1,1,1,0,0,1, 0 ];    "3
         [.X., 0, 1, 0, 0] -> [0,1,1,0,0,1,1, 0 ];    "4
         [.X., 0, 1, 0, 1] -> [1,0,1,1,0,1,1, 0 ];    "5
         [.X., 0, 1, 1, 0] -> [1,0,1,1,1,1,1, 0 ];    "6
         [.X., 0, 1, 1, 1] -> [1,1,1,0,0,0,0, 0 ];    "7
         [.X., 1, 0, 0, 0] -> [1,1,1,1,1,1,1, 0 ];    "8
         [.X., 1, 0, 0, 1] -> [1,1,1,1,0,1,1, 0 ];    "9
         [.X., 1, 0, 1, 0] -> [1,1,1,0,1,1,1, 0 ];    "A
         [.X., 1, 0, 1, 1] -> [0,0,1,1,1,1,1, 0 ];    "B
         [.X., 1, 1, 0, 0] -> [1,0,0,1,1,1,0, 0 ];    "C
         [.X., 1, 1, 0, 1] -> [0,1,1,1,1,0,1, 0 ];    "D
         [.X., 1, 1, 1, 0] -> [1,0,0,1,1,1,1, 0 ];    "E
         [.X., 1, 1, 1, 1] -> [1,0,0,0,0,1,1, 0 ];    "F

end
```

Clock Module (Schematic)

The final module of this design, and the only module that relies on features specific to LCA type devices, is the clock divider module. This module has been entered in schematic form (Figure 19-6) and consists of two multiplexers, three flip-flips, and a clock generator. This circuit provides three possible speeds for the internal clock. If the **ExtClk** signal is active, the external clock is passed directly to the output (**Clk**). When **ExtClk** is not active, the clock generator (a Xilinx macro) is either passed directly to the output at 8 MHz or is divided to provide a very slow (2 Hz) clock. Control over the internal clock speed is provided by the **Speed** input to the circuit.

Simulating the Design

To simulate a design with Synario, you must first create a type of source file called a test fixture. A test fixture is a file written in the Verilog language (or VHDL, if you

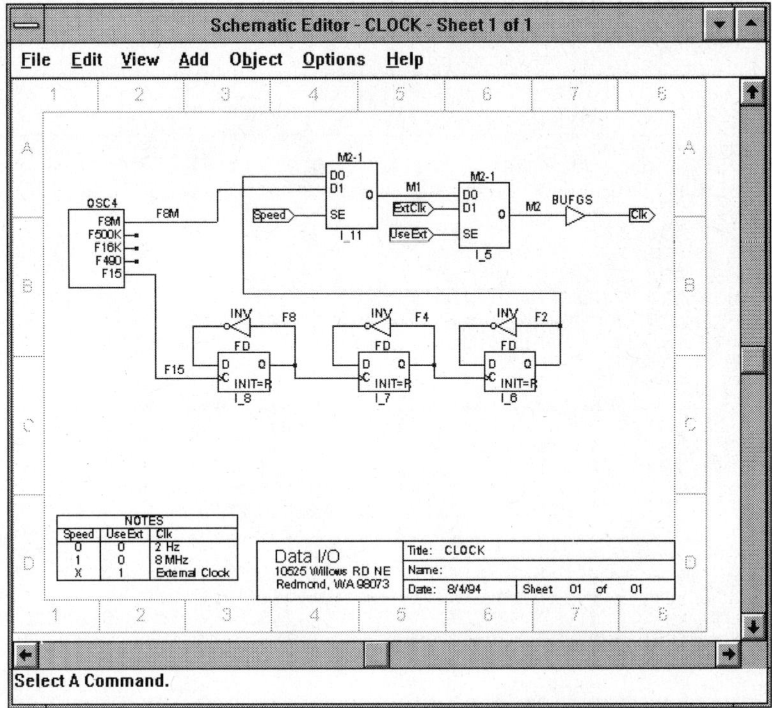

Figure 19-6
The clock schematic utilizes an oscillator macro provided by Xilinx for the 4000 series devices.

are using the Synario VHDL option) that defines stimulus and, optionally, checks for correct behavior of the design outputs when processed with the simulator. (If you want, you can create a test fixture that does nothing more than refer to a lower-level design file, and use the simulator's command language to type in simulation commands, set input values, and advance the simulation time. This is a tedious way to run simulation, however, and it is well worth your time to learn the minimal amount of Verilog required to create a real test fixture.) Figure 19-7 shows a simple Verilog test fixture for this design. This test fixture has been simplified through the use of a Verilog **'include** statement that references an automatically generated file (**fib_bcd.tfi**). The **.tfi** file, which was generated by the Synario Project Navigator, contains all the signal declarations, component instantiations, and name aliases needed to write stimulus for the design, for either functional or timing (post-route) simulation.

A design can have many different test fixture, depending on the compexity of the project. For example, a large design with many hierarchical submodules might include smaller test fixtures that exercise parts of the design, a test fixture written

```
`timescale 10 ns / 100ps
module t;

`define auto_init
`include "fib_bcd.tfi"

// Clock Selection
// Speed UseExt  Clock
//   0      0    2 Hz
//   1      0    8 MHz
//   X      1    ExtClk

always
    begin
    #10
          ExtClk = ~ExtClk;
    end

initial
    begin
    #10   Speed = ;
          UseExt = 1;
          Reset = 1;
    #100  Reset = 0;
    #400  $stop;

    end

endmodule
```

Figure 19-7
The test fixture provides a free-running system clock with a 20 ns cycle time, and a sequence of test inputs.

to perform a functional test of the entire design, and yet another test fixture specifically written to perform a timing simulation of the completed PLD or FPGA.

In Synario, there are two basic ways to attach test fixtures to a design. If you want to perform a functional simulation (prior to mapping the design to an actual device), you associate the test fixture with one of the modules in the design. If you will be performing a functional simulation of the entire design, you must associate the test fixture with the top-level module in the design, or with the device, as is done in this example.

If you want to perform an accurate timing simulation of your design, you must associate the test fixture with the device rather than with a module. You can perform either functional or timing simulation by associating a test fixture with a device. The difference between functional simulation of the top-level module and functional simulation of the device is simply in how the simulation models are created—from the design data or from the programmed device data.

Before the simulator can process the design, each module (source file) in the design must be converted into a format appropriate for the simulator. The simulation model format used for the Synario simulator is Verilog, so each of the source files (the three ABEL-HDL files and the schematic) must be converted into

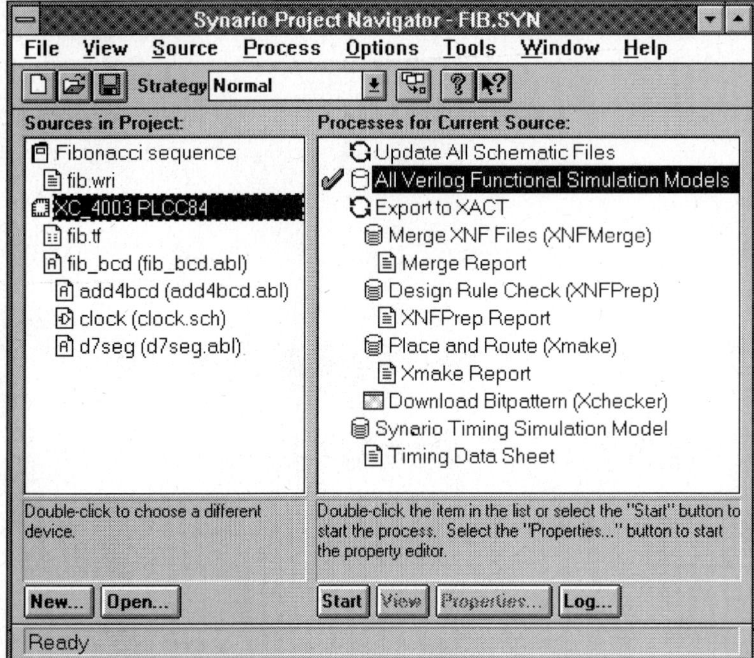

Figure 19-8
The Project Navigator builds Verilog functional simulation models for all modules in the design.

Verilog netlists. Using the Project Navigator, you can either create these models by double-clicking on the **All Functional Simulation Models** process (Figure 19-8), or you can simply invoke the simulator and let the Project Navigator determine which simulation models need to be created or updated for you.

To simulate the design, you highlight the test fixture (in the Sources window) and double-click on the appropriate simulation process (Functional Simulation, in this case) to invoke the Synario simulator. Before invoking the simulator, the Project Navigator automatically updates the necessary files and invokes whatever processes are required to create simulation models. For ABEL source files, the ABEL compiler is invoked, followed by a Verilog HDL model generator. For schematic files, simulation models are created that are composed of a netlist of simulation primitives representing the function of each symbol on the schematic. The exact format of these models depends on the type of device you have selected, and the kinds of symbols you have referenced.

When all the necessary simulation models have been created or updated, the Project Navigator invokes the simulator control panel (Figure 19-9) and the simulation is ready to begin. To start the simulation, you set an end time and other simulation parameters (or simply accept the default values) and click on the **Run**

Synario Simulator - fib

File Reports Window Help

Run From: .0 ns

To: 6,000.0 ns

Step Interval: 1,000.0 ns

Run

Step

Mode: Unit Delay

Stop

Debug >>

Figure 19-9
Synario's simulator control panel.

button. When the simulation has finished, you can bring up the Waveform Display window to view the results (Figure 19-10).

The Synario waveform display includes features common to most waveform tools, including selectable cursors, multiple zoom levels, buses and multiple display formats (such as binary, decimal, and hexadecimal) and also supports more advanced features such as schematic cross-probing. Cross-probing is particularly useful for designs that are composed primarily of schematics and allows simulation values to be displayed dynamically both on the waveform display and on the schematic. Cross-probing also allows signals to be selected from the schematic (by highlighting a net) for immediate display in the waveform window.

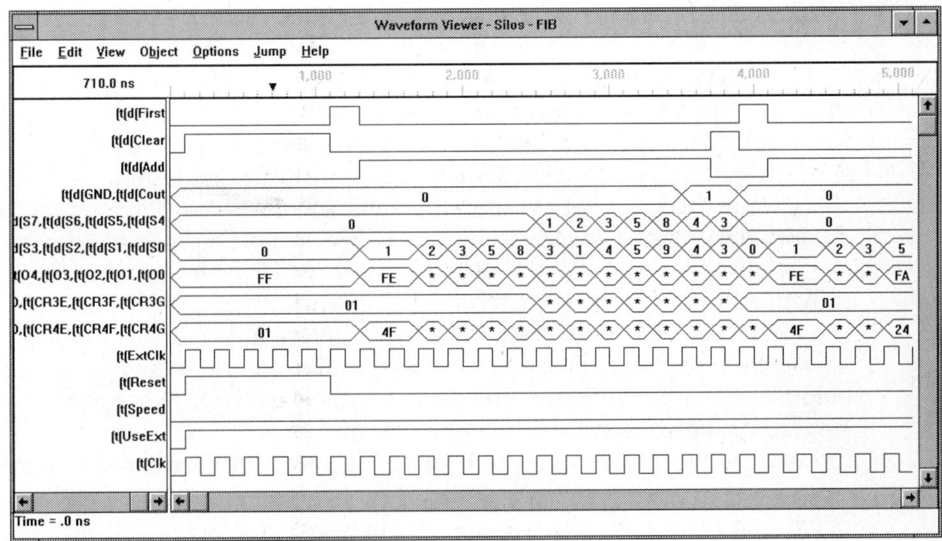

Figure 19-10
Synario's waveform viewer.

Mapping the Design to an FPGA

After functional simulation, the next step is to actually map the design into an FPGA device. For the Xilinx LCA devices, the process consists of

- ☐ Generating XNF netlists for all modules of the design
- ☐ Optimizing the XNF netlists for the 4000 series FPGA architecture
- ☐ Merging the XNF netlists into a single design file
- ☐ Mapping the design onto the 4000 series CLBs (configurable logic blocks)
- ☐ Placing the CLBs and routing the chip
- ☐ Generating a bitmap file, ready for downloading to the device

With the exception of the first step (generating the XNF netlists), all these steps will be performed using software obtained from Xilinx. (Other third-party sources do exist for the remaining steps, most notably from NeoCAD, Inc., of Boulder, Colorado, and these third-party tools can, for many examples, do a better job of mapping the device than the Xilinx software. For most designs, however, the Xilinx-supplied software is quite adequate.)

Generating XNF Netlists

The first step in mapping the design into an FPGA is creation of the XNF netlists representing the six design modules (the top-level file, two instances of the 4-bit adder, two instances of the seven-segment display decoder and the clock generator module). One of the most convenient features of Synario's Project Manager is its knowledge of device-specific processing requirements such as this. When you select a device in Synario the project navigator modifies all the process flows shown in the Process window to reflect the requirements of the selected device. For LCA devices, the project navigator knows that all source file types (ABEL, schematic, or VHDL) must be compiled or translated into the XNF netlist form before the device is mapped.

In Figures 19-11 and 19-12 you can see the steps required to translate ABEL source files and schematics to XNF netlist format. These steps are performed automatically by the Project Navigator, so you don't have to keep track of which steps have already been performed.

After the vendor-specific (XNF format) netlists have been generated, the design is ready to be processed by the Xilinx-supplied device fitting tools. For the Xilinx devices, there are many steps required to get a design into the actual device. Figure 19-13 diagrams the flow of a hierarchical design such as this one through the device fitting and mapping process. All these steps are accessed through the Synario

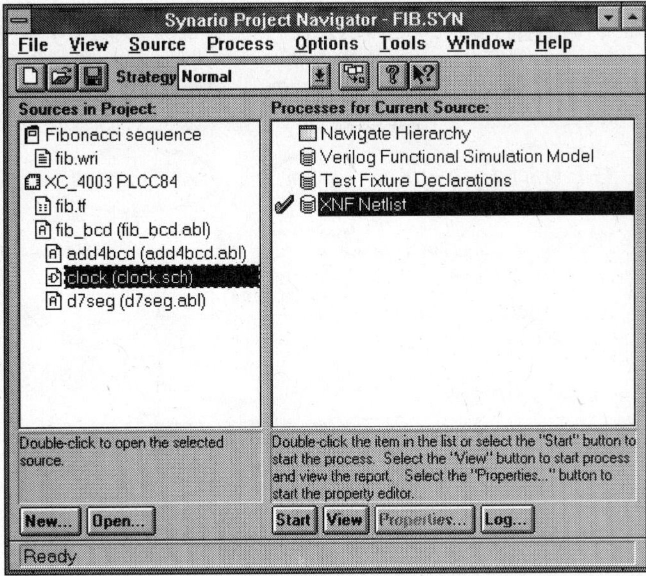

Figure 19-11
Schematic sources are translated into vendor-specific netlist formats.

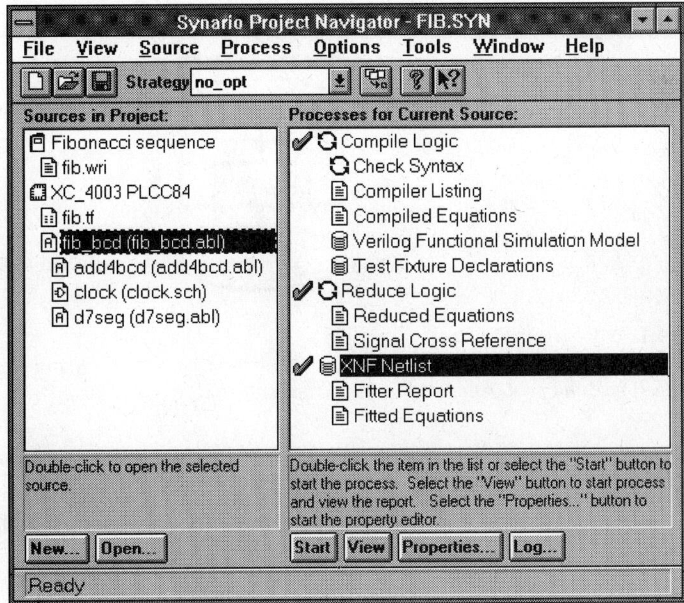

Figure 19-12
ABEL (or VHDL) sources must be compiled (synthesized) prior to translation into a netlist format.

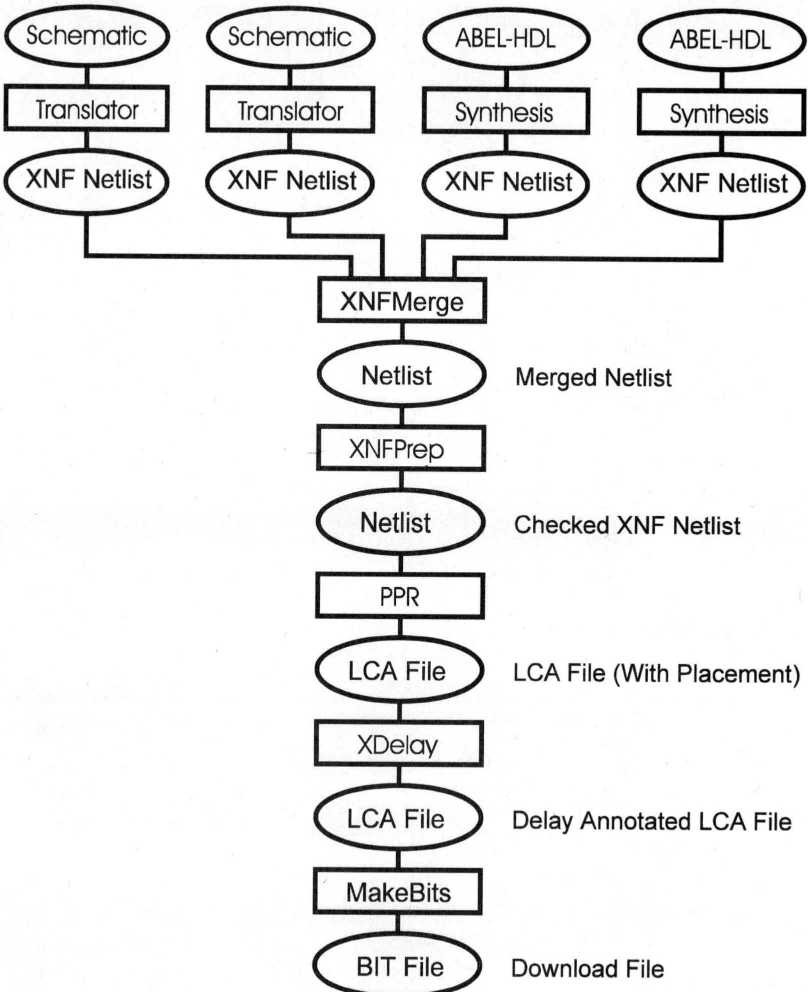

Figure 19-13
Processing a design into a downloadable LCA bit stream file requires many steps. For large designs, the PPR (place and route) step can be quite time consuming.

Project Navigator, although the programs that arc running are actually provided by Xilinx.

The merging step (Figure 19-14) reads in all modules of the design and creates a single XNF netlist representing the entire design. (It is also possible to perform the merge operation later in the process, during the actual device mapping process. This is is useful for designs that are simply too large to be processed as one XNF file.)

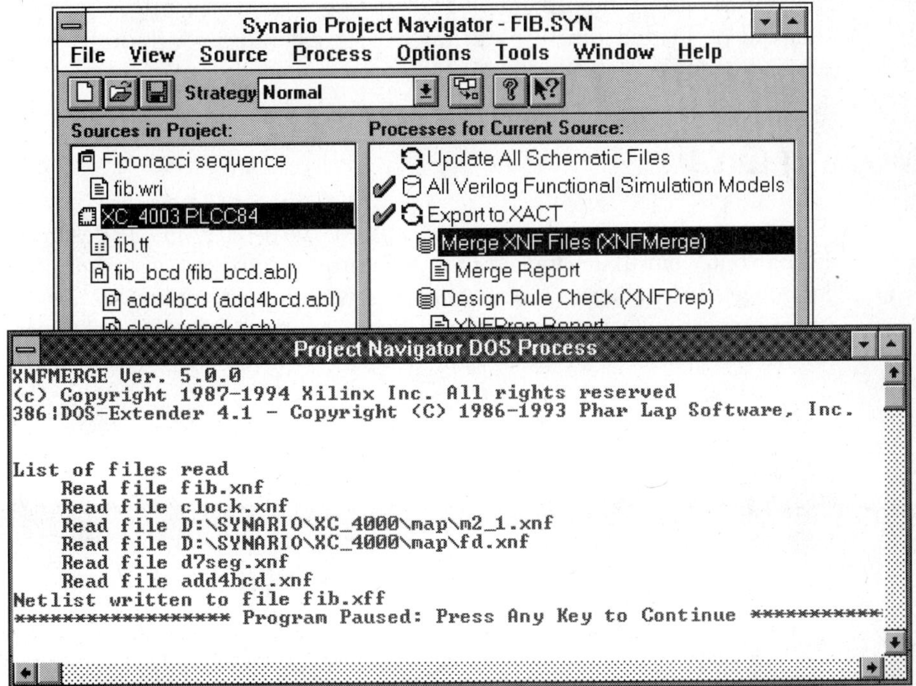

Figure 19-14
The Project Navigator invokes vendor-supplied device fitting programs (such as the Xilinx merge program shown here) as needed to create the final device download file.

After merging, the design is processed by a design rule checker. This design rule checker reports on potential problems with the design, as well as performing optimizations such as deletion of unused or disabled logic. After design rule checking, the design (in XNF netlist format) is ready for placement and routing.

Placement and Routing

Placement and routing for FPGAs can be a long and involved process. Depending on the complexity of your design, the placement of logic blocks within the device and the routing of interconnects between those logic blocks can take minutes, hours, or even days to complete. This is because the internal architecture of an FPGA may be quite restrictive in its routing resources, and the routing software required to find an efficient routing for many different types of applications is quite complex. (This problem is most evident in the Xilinx LCA devices and is not as common in other FPGA devices.)

During place-and-route, the software partitions the design and places the resulting blocks of logic into specific logic modules within the device. It then routes the design and, if the placement and routing was successful, creates a bitmap file that can be loaded directly into the device, or into a configuration PROM from which the device will later be loaded.

Moving On

This chapter has shown how a full-featured, third-party FPGA design tool can be used to enter, simulate, and synthesize a design composed of schematics and ABEL language source files. In the next chapter, we are going to be looking at one of the more powerful design tools offered by a leading vendor of PLDs and see how VHDL can be used for PLD design.

CHAPTER 20

HANDS-ON EDA: USING VHDL FOR PLDS

In this chapter, we're going to be looking at a full-featured PLD development tool that includes VHDL as one of its input options. We'll use a combination of schematic and VHDL source files to enter a relatively complex design, compile that design for a complex PLD, and simulate it. The design tool that we are going to be using is the MAX+Plus II package offered by Altera, and the design example is a driving game inspired by Altera's ChipTrip example.

Altera's MAX+Plus II

Note: *Although Altera has provided MAX+Plus II evaluation software on the companion CD-ROM (and you are encouraged to load the software and try it out for yourself), the evaluation version of software does not have the necessary capabilities to perform this tutorial. If you want to follow along with this tutorial, you will need to acquire the full-featured MAX+Plus II software directly from Altera. Refer to the vendor information listings in Appendix A for information about how to contact Altera Corporation.*

The Altera software, which first appeared (as A+Plus) in 1984, is a complete system for programmable logic development. Altera has always placed a strong emphasis on software tools, and the results have shown: MAX+Plus II is a powerful design system. With the addition of VHDL to their product (both for design entry and for simulation model generation) Altera has taken the lead in proprietary PLD development tools and has shown that design tools offered by device manufacturers can be every bit as feature laden as tools offered by so-called "universal" PLD tool suppliers.

In this tutorial, we're going to be exploring the MAX+Plus II software as we enter, synthesize, and simulate a design consting of a top-level schematic and lower-level VHDL design files. This design includes two state machines and a counter that is instantiated twice in the circuit through the use of hierarchy.

The Sample Design

The circuit we're going to be entering is a simple driving simulator—a game, really—that simulates a journey across town after work. The goal of the simulation—and the object of the game—is to create a set of input stimuli that will get the simulated vehicle from the office to the beach, stopping to pick up a pizza on the way, as quickly as possible (in a minimum number of clock cycles) and without getting any speeding tickets.

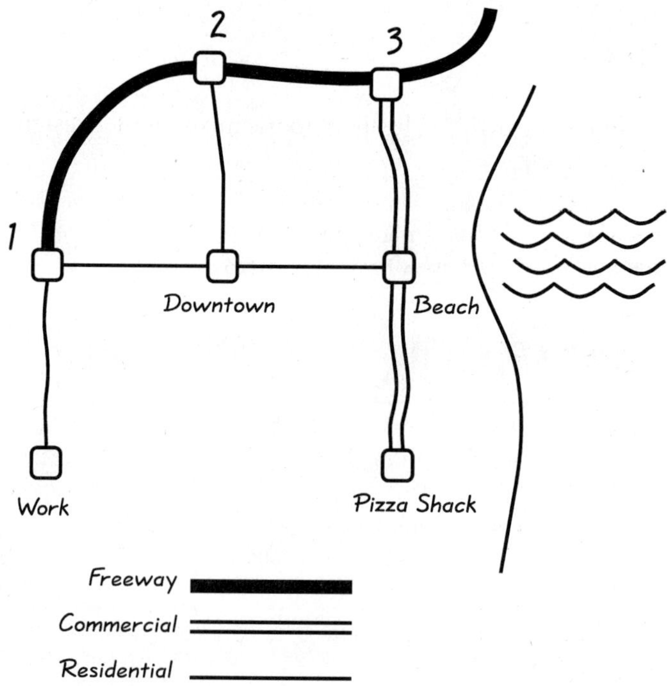

Figure 20-1
The simulated town. The object? Get from work to the beach (and pick up a pizza on the way) as fast as you can without getting a ticket.

A map of the simulated town is shown in Figure 20-1. On this map, there are seven intersections, or locations, to which the vehicle can drive. At each intersection, the vehicle can be given a new direction of either north, south, east or west. The vehicle can also be given a speed for the next leg of the trip: either fast or slow. When the vehicle is traveling slow, it progresses only one intersection per clock cycle; when is is traveling fast, it travels two intersections in a clock cycle.

There are many ways that the driver of the vehicle could navigate across town to the pizza place and to the beach. Complicating the trip, though, is the fact that the police are everywhere, and they have their radar traps set up and ready to catch any speeders. Although there is no speed limit on the freeway (the thick solid line), there is a strictly enforced speed limit on the residential sections—they'll nab you every time. On the commercial streets, you will be able to get away with a warning—but only once.

Entering the Design

Figure 20-2 is a block diagram showing the input and outputs of the driving simulator game. The design is composed of the four modules shown in Figure 20-3. Two of these modules, **navigate** and **trap**, are state machines, while the remaining two modules are simple counters.

To show how MAX+Plus II supports mixed-mode design entry, I have entered the top-level module using a schematic, while the remaining modules are entered using VHDL (Figure 20-4). MAX+Plus II allows the use of schematics, VHDL or AHDL—Altera's own design entry language—in an arbitrary hierarchical arrangement. I'll describe this design from the bottom up, starting with the two state machines that control the whole show.

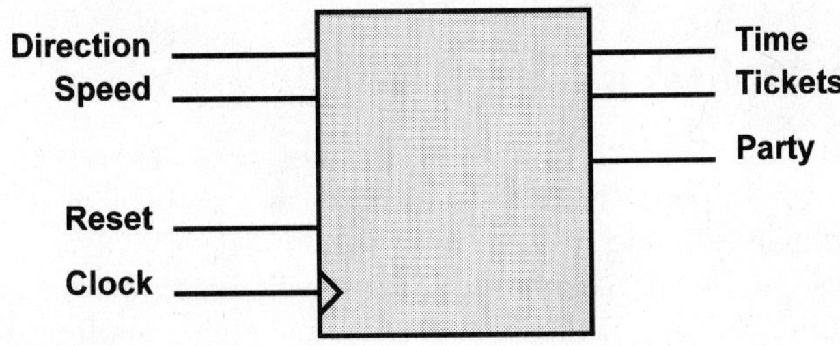

Figure 20-2
At the top level, the design accepts a speed (fast or slow) and direction for each clock cycle.

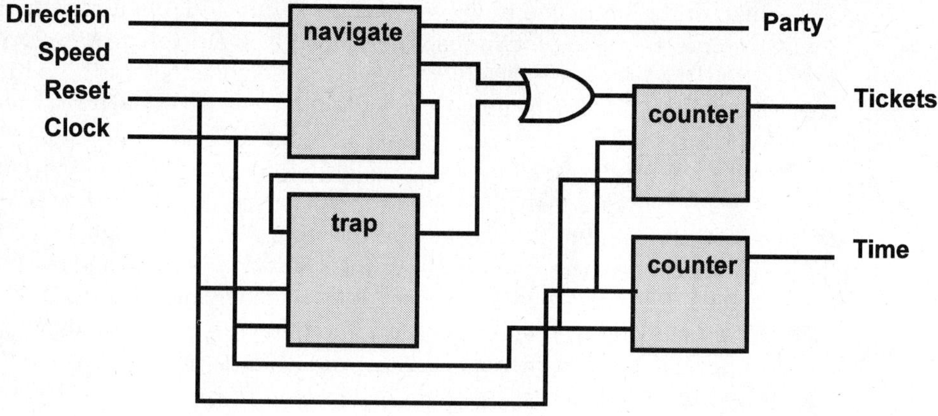

Figure 20-3
The design is decomposed into functional modules.

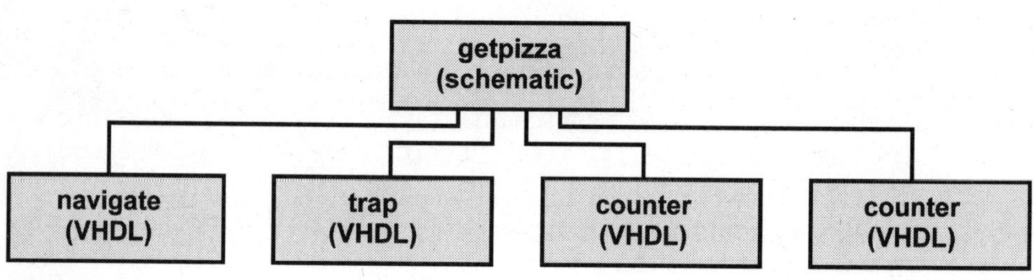

Figure 20-4
The design consists of four modules arranged in a hierarchy.

The Navigation Module: navigate.vhd

The first module of the design, and the most complex, is a state machine that defines each intersection in the simulated town, and defines what directions are valid for each intersection. Figure 20-5 lists the complete VHDL source file for this module. The design is written using the same synthesizable state machine style I presented in Chapter 17. Let's look at this file is some detail; reading from the top, we find

- **Library** and **use** statements allowing the IEEE 1164 data types to be used.
- A package (**getpizza_types**) defining a special type and constants for the **Direction** input (a 2-bit vector indicating the direction the vehicle is supposed to travel at the next clock cycle).

- **Library** and **use** statements making the IEEE 1164 library, and the **get-pizza_types** package, visible to the subsequent entity and architecture.
- **Entity** and **architecture** declarations for the **Navigate** module. The architecture declaration includes
    - Declarations for an enumerated data type (**state_machine**) and **present_state/next_state** signals for the state register.
    - A signal declaration for an intermediate signal, **have_pizza**, that will remain low until the simulated vehicle arrives at the pizza place, and will then remain high, indicating that a pizza has been acquired.
    - A process defining the registered behavior of the state machine, including the registered signal **have_pizza**, which is given a value of '1' when the machine is in the **Pizza** state.
    - A second process that defines all of the possible transitions from one intersection (state) to another. The transition logic is simplified through the use of a local procedure, **drive**, that takes care of determining whether the vehicle is going too fast for the type of road it is on, and whether a ticket should be immediately issued, in the case of a residential road. (Commercial roads result in a warning before a ticket is issued, and this function will be taken care of in the second state machine, **trap**.)

The state machine is designed so that any unknown transition (a turn that takes the vehicle off the road) will result in the machine landing in a state called **Lost**. This state has no escape, short of resetting the entire circuit with the asynchronous reset input. (Be careful not to make any wrong turns!)

The Speed Trap Module: trap.vhd

The second module of this design, **trap**, is also a state machine. This state machine has only three states, however, that keep track of the current "legal" state of the journey. The machine initializes (with a reset) to state **Legal**, and advances to state **Warning** any time the vehicle is caught speeding (as reported by the **Navigate** module). If the state is already **Warning** (meaning the vehicle has exceeded the speed limit in a commercial zone) the machine advances to the **Ticket** state, and a ticket is issued.

The complete VHDL source file for the **trap** module is listed in Figure 20-6. The source file includes

- **Library** and **use** statements for the IEEE data types.
- **Entity** and **architecture** declarations for the module. The architecture includes

Figure 20-5
The ***navigate*** *state machine.*

```
-------------------------------
-- Pizza game. Inspired by the Altera ChipTrip example
-- described in the Altera Max+Plus II Getting Started
-- manual.
--

library ieee;
use ieee.std_logic_1164.all;

package getpizza_types is
    subtype direction is std_logic_vector(1 downto 0);
    constant NORTH: direction := "00";        -- directions
    constant EAST:  direction := "01";
    constant WEST:  direction := "10";
    constant SOUTH: direction := "11";
end getpizza_types;

library ieee;
use ieee.std_logic_1164.all;
use work.getpizza_types.all;

entity navigate is
    port (clk,reset: std_logic;
          dir: direction;
          speed: std_logic;
          speeding, party, get_ticket: out std_logic);
end navigate;

architecture behavior of navigate is
    type state_machine is (Work,Ramp1,Ramp2,Ramp3,Downtown,
                           Beach,Pizza,Lost);
    signal present_state,next_state: state_machine;
    signal have_pizza: std_logic;
begin

    registers: process(clk,reset)
    begin
        if reset = '1' then
            present_state <= Work;
            have_pizza <= '0';
        elsif clk = '1' and clk'event then
            present_state <= next_state;
            if present_state = Pizza then
                have_pizza <= '1';
            end if;
        end if;
    end process;

    transitions: process(present_state,dir,speed,have_pizza)
        type road is (Residential,Commercial,Expressway,OffRoad);
        procedure drive(dest1,dest2: state_machine;
                        road_type: road) is
        begin
            if speed = '0' then
                next_state <= dest1;
                speeding <= '0';
                get_ticket <= '0';
```

```
            else
                next_state <= Dest2;
                if road_type = Residential then
                    speeding <= '1';
                    get_ticket <= '1';
                elsif road_type = Commercial then
                    speeding <= '1';
                    get_ticket <= '0';
                else            -- Expressway (or lost)
                    speeding <= '0';
                    get_ticket <= '0';
                end if;
            end if;
        end drive;

    begin
        case present_state is
        when Work =>
            party <= '0';
            if dir = NORTH then
                drive(Ramp1,Ramp2,Expressway);
            else
                drive(Lost,Lost,OffRoad);
            end if;
        when Ramp1 =>
            party <= '0';
            if dir = NORTH then
                drive(Ramp2,Ramp3,Expressway);
            elsif dir = EAST then
                drive(Downtown,Beach,Residential);
            else
                drive(Lost,Lost,OffRoad);
            end if;
        when Ramp2 =>
            party <= '0';
            if dir = WEST then
                drive(Ramp1,Ramp1,Expressway);
            elsif dir = EAST then
                drive(Ramp3,Ramp3,Expressway);
            elsif dir = SOUTH then
                drive(Downtown,Downtown,Residential);
            else
                drive(Lost,Lost,OffRoad);
            end if;
        when Ramp3 =>
            party <= '0';
            if dir = WEST then
                drive(Ramp2,Ramp1,Expressway);
            elsif dir = SOUTH then
                drive(Beach,Pizza,Commercial);
            else
                drive(Lost,Lost,OffRoad);
            end if;
        when Downtown =>
            party <= '0';
            if dir = NORTH then
                drive(Ramp2,Ramp2,Residential);
            elsif dir = EAST then
                drive(Beach,Beach,Residential);
            elsif dir = WEST then
                drive(Ramp1,Ramp1,Residential);
            else
                drive(Lost,Lost,OffRoad);
            end if;
```

```
        when Beach =>
            party <= have_pizza;
            if dir = NORTH then
                drive(Ramp3,Ramp3,Commercial);
            elsif dir = WEST then
                drive(Downtown,Ramp1,Residential);
            elsif dir = SOUTH then
                drive(Pizza,Pizza,Commercial);
            else
                drive(Lost,Lost,OffRoad);
            end if;
        when Pizza =>
            party <= '0';
            if dir = NORTH then
                drive(Beach,Ramp3,Commercial);
            else
                drive(Lost,Lost,OffRoad);
            end if;
        when Lost =>
            party <= '0';
            drive(Lost,Lost,OffRoad);
        end case;
    end process;
end behavior;
```

- An enumerated type declaration for the three states of the machine, and signal declarations for the **present_state** and **next_state** signals.
- A declaration for an intermediate signal, **gt**, that represent the combinational function determining whether a ticket has been issued.
- Two processes representing the state machine, using the same synthesizable style as was used previously. Note that the intermediate signal **gt** is used to maintain the convention of having only combinational outputs in the transition process, and registered outputs in the register process. This is not actually necessary, but makes the design easier to read. (The **gt** signal will be collapsed out of the logic by the synthesis program, so there is no additional overhead in using a style like this.)

The Counter Modules: counter.vhd

The final two lower-level modules are actually multiple instances of the same VHDL source file, named **counter**. This simple counter circuit has a count enable input, a clock and a reset. The complete VHDL source file is listed in Figure 20-7. The file contains

- ☐ **Library** and **use** statements, just as in the other VHDL source files.
- ☐ **Entity** and **architecture** declarations for the module. The architecture includes

Figure 20-6
The speed trap state machine.

```
library ieee;
use ieee.std_logic_1164.all;

entity trap is
    port (clk,reset,speeding: std_logic;
          get_ticket: out std_logic);
end trap;

architecture behavior of trap is
    type state_machine is (legal,warning,ticket);
    signal present_state, next_state: state_machine;
    signal gt: std_logic;
begin

    registers: process(clk,reset)
    begin
        if reset = '1' then
            present_state <= legal;
            get_ticket <= '0';
        elsif clk = '1' and clk'event then
            present_state <= next_state;
            get_ticket <= gt;
        end if;
    end process;

    transitions: process(present_state,speeding)
    begin
        case present_state is
        when legal =>
            if speeding = '1' then
                next_state <= warning;
                gt <= '0';
            else
                next_state <= legal;
                gt <= '0';
            end if;
        when warning =>
            if speeding = '1' then
                next_state <= ticket;
                gt <= '1';
            else
                next_state <= warning;
                gt <= '0';
            end if;
        when ticket =>
            next_state <= legal;
            gt <= '0';
        end case;
    end process;
end behavior;
```

Figure 20-7
The counter module.

```
library ieee;
use ieee.std_logic_1164.all;

entity counter is
    port(clk,reset,increment: in std_logic;
         count: out integer range 0 to 15);
end counter;

architecture behavior of counter is
    signal q: integer range 0 to 15;
begin
    process(reset,clk)
    begin
        if reset = '1' then
            q <= 0;
        elsif (clk = '1' and clk'event) then
            if increment = '1' then
                if q = 15 then
                    q <= 0;
                else
                    q <= q + 1;
                end if;
            end if;
        end if;
    end process;

    count <= q;

end behavior;
```

- A **process** statement defining the operation of the counter, using integer data types. (**Std_logic_vector** data types could have been used, but would have required a special overloaded function to perform the "+" operation, which is not defined in the IEEE 1164 standard.)
- A concurrent signal assignment statement assigning the value of the counter to the output of the module.

Putting It All Together: The Top-Level Schematic

The top-level module that puts the design together could be entered using either VHDL, or a schematic. To show how the Altera software allows mixed-mode design entry, I have chosen to use a schematic. The top-level schematic for this design was entered using the MAX+Plus II schematic editor, and is shown in Figure 20-8. In the schematic, the four functional blocks (**navigate**, **trap**, and the two counters)

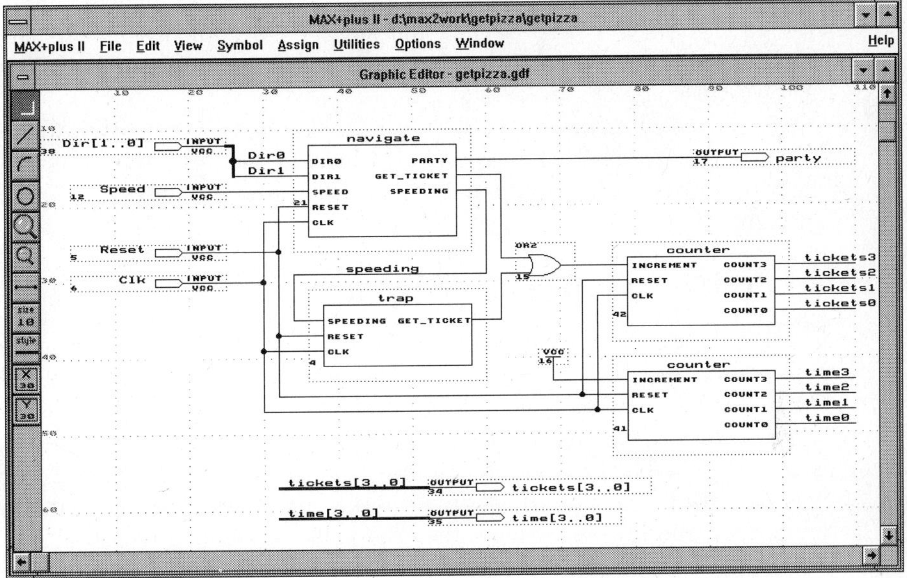

Figure 20-8
The driving game's top-level schematic.

have been defined as symbols in the schematic, and contain pointers to the lower-level VHDL modules.

In addition to the four block symbols reference the lower-level VHDL files, the schematic includes one gate primitive (the OR gate) and input and output symbols. The input and output symbols are important, as they inform the MAX+Plus II system that the indicated signals are to be mapped onto device pins during processing.

The connections between symbols on a schematic can be made by drawing wires or by using common signal names. Both methods are used in this schematic. For the outputs of the two counters, bus names are used to associate the four outputs of each counter block to a 4-bit bus that is connected to the output. (This method of connecting buses can become a little confusing, as I'll describe in a moment.)

Hierarchy Navigation

MAX+Plus II keeps track of the hierarchy of a design, so you can "push" into a lower-level module simply by double-clicking on one of the functional blocks. The

MAX+Plus interface can display multiple documents (of multiple types, such as VHDL or AHDL files, or schematics) and has a hierarchy display window (Figure 20-9) that helps you keep track of the modules in your design. The Auto Device Selection window (Figure 20-10) lets you choose the family of devices into which the design is to be implemented.

For designs that include HDL files in the hierarchy (particularly those that have VHDL or AHDL at higher levels in the hierarchy), the MAX+Plus II interface builds the hierarchy from information obtained at the time the VHDL or AHDL modules are compiled.

Bus Limitations In MAX+Plus II

One feature that is a little awkward in MAX+Plus II (and in most other design systems that attempt to mix traditional schematics with language-based entry) is the treatment of buses and vectors. Although the MAX+Plus II schematic editor supports the uses of buses to collect two ore more signals into a single data path (as is done for the **Dir**, **tickets**, and **time** signals in this design), there is currently no way to carry those buses through a symbol and into a lower-level module, if that lower-level module is a VHDL file. The reason (and this reason applies to most schematic/HDL hybrids) is that the schematic capture package does not have a built-in knowledge of VHDL's many data types, and does not know, for example, which direction a given data type should be, or its width.

In this design, I'm actually taking some liberties with integer data types in the connections between the top-level bus signals **Tickets** and **Time**. Although I have split these buses into their component signals before connecting them to the outputs of the two counters, I have not attempted to do the same thing within the VHDL source files. This means that there is an implied connection between the **Count** object (which is a 4-bit integer data type) within the **count.vhd** file and the corresponding pin stubs on the two counter symbols. This is only possible because the rules for conversion of lower-level multibit object names (e.g., vectors and integers) are simple: the VHDL compiler simply appends numbers to the object names to create names for each bit in the object. The result? The design works as entered, but might not work if entered identically in another design system that used a different scheme for name expansion.

As VHDL becomes more prevalent in schematic-oriented design tools, I expect the integration between schematic symbols and underyling VHDL files to be improved. For now, however, it is safest to avoid implied connections such as those used in this design and to pass signals between different design representations in the hierarchy one bit at a time.

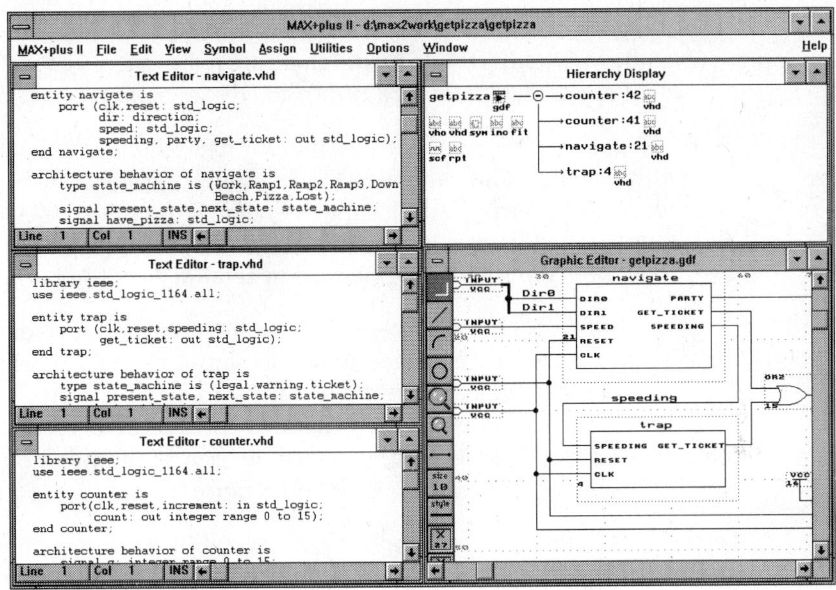

Figure 20-9
The MAX+Plus II interface.

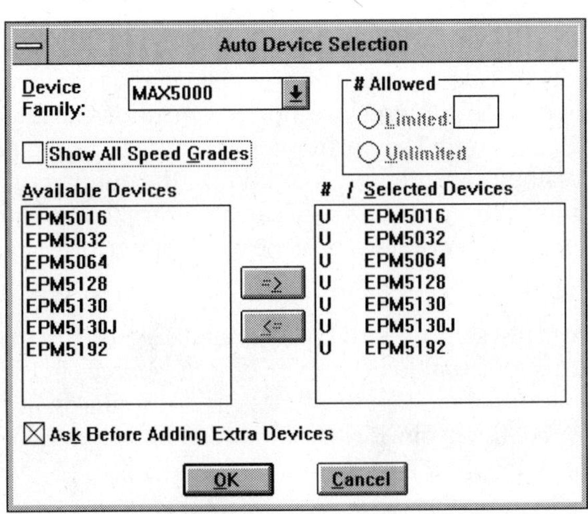

Figure 20-10
The device selection dialogue box.

Processing the Design

Once the design has been entered, it can be processed by selecting the **Compile** option from the MAX_Plus II **File** menu There are many steps that the system must go to create a mapped device (Figure 20-11), and these steps are summarized below:

- ☐ Netlist Extractor: This step reads each input file (schematic, VHDL, AHDL, or other form of entry) and generates a binary netlist format. It also creates one or more hierarchy interconnect files the define how the source files in the project are interconnected. Syntax or electrical connection errors are reported during this phase, and compiler listing files are generated as needed.

- ☐ Database Builder: This step converts the hierarchical representation of the design into a flattened representation. Each input module is inserted into the resulting circuit as indicated in the hierarchy map, with multiple instances of modules being created as needed. Hierarchical names are created and substituted to maintain the electrical connectivity across module boundaries, and hierarchy-related errors are detected and reported.

- ☐ Logic Synthesizer: This step applies logic reduction and other general-purpose optimization algorithms to generate an efficient representation of the design—one that uses as few logic gates as possible. The logic synthesizer also searches for and deletes unused nodes in the design. If the Design Doctor is enabled, the optimization step also checks for certain logic conditions that may affect the reliability or testability of the circuit. Situations such as asynchronous feedback, static hazards, and lack of a global reset are checked, along with other useful design rules that can be selected as needed.

- ☐ Partitioner: This step checks to ensure the design will fit (using general information such as the number of registers and combinational logic used) and, in the event the design does not fit, partitions it into multiple devices of the specified family. The partitioner attempts to fit the design into as few devices as possible, and attempts to minimize the number of pins used for inter-device communication. This process can be controlled, so that you can specify the type and/or number of devices to be used, or perform your own manual allocation of logic into the devices.

- ☐ Fitter: This step uses detailed knowledge of the selected device to map the circuit into actual logic cells or other resources in the target device. Input and output pins are automatically assigned to pins on the device (while preserving any predefined pin locations), and reports are generated to help you make changes should the program fail to find a fit.

- ☐ Timing SNF Extractor: This step calculates and generates detailed timing parameters for the design for the purposes of timing simulation. This data is used by the MAX+PLUS simulator to report simulation results with accurate timing

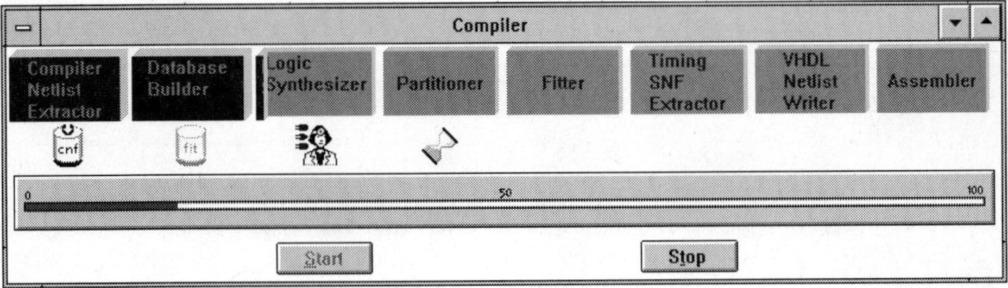

Figure 20-11
The Compiler reports its status using a combination of indicators.

delay values, and is used when EDIF, VHDL, or Verilog HDL netlists are generated.

- VHDL Netlist Generation: This step uses the information generated as a result of fitting the design in combination with the extracted timing data to create an accurate netlist for timing simulation.
- Assembler: This step converts the information generated in the Fitter step (the pin assignments, resource assignments, etc.) into a form ready for downloading to a device programmer. The format that is generated depends on the family of device used, and the type of programming system being employed. Altera's POF (Programmer Object File) is the default format generated, although the JEDEC (Joint Electron Device Engineering Council) standard format is also supported.

After the Compiler has finished, all error, information, and warning messages are available for viewing in a message window (Figure 20-12). A **Help on Message** button makes it easy to get detailed information (including suggested design resolutions) for most messages that are generated.

Simulating the Design

The MAX-PLUS II system includes a built-in simulator that can perform either functional or timing simulation. Since the design has been mapped into a device (an EPM 5032 device), we'll be performing timing simulation.

Since the object of the "game" this design represents is to navigate through or around the city, get to the pizza joint, and then to the beach, the game is actually "played" during simulation. To play the game, we'll be supplying inputs (direction and speed) to the simulator, which will then model the behavior of the circuit over time and report if we have received a ticket and when we have successfully made our way to the beach.

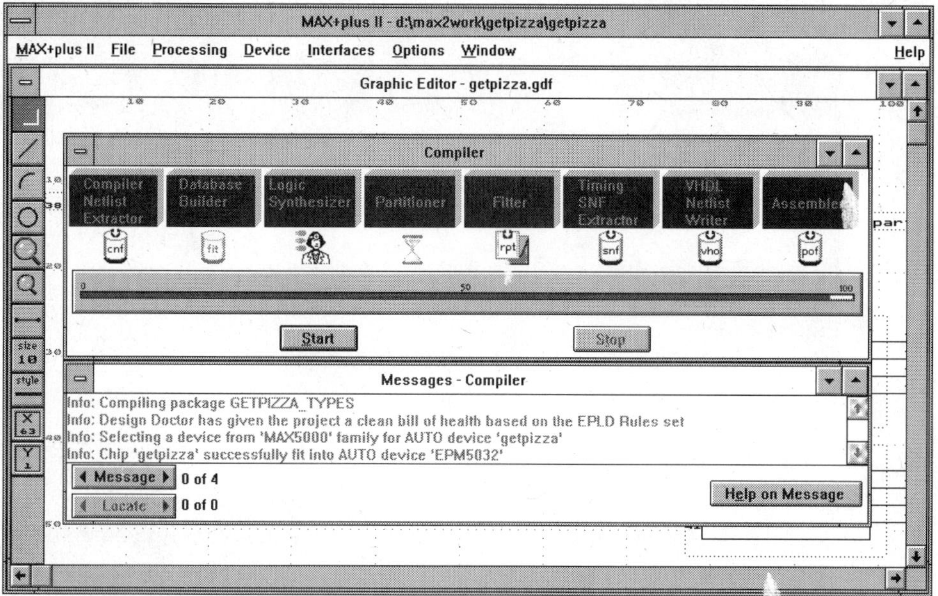

Figure 20-12
Status messages are written to a message window during compilation.

Choosing the Route

The best route for the simulated vehicle to take is

1. From the start (work), drive north at a slow speed to freeway on-ramp number one.

2. From freeway on-ramp number one, go north at high speed, using one clock cycle to get to freeway ramp number three.

3. From freeway ramp number three, speed south past the beach (in one clock cycle) to get to the pizza place.

4. From the pizza place, drive north at normal speed to the beach.

Following this route, the vehicle will make it to the beach, with a pizza and no tickets, in four clock cycles. Let's try it!

Setting Up the Stimulus

Stimulus to be used during simulation can be entered in either of two ways. The first way is to write test vectors in an ASCII file. This is the traditional way in which

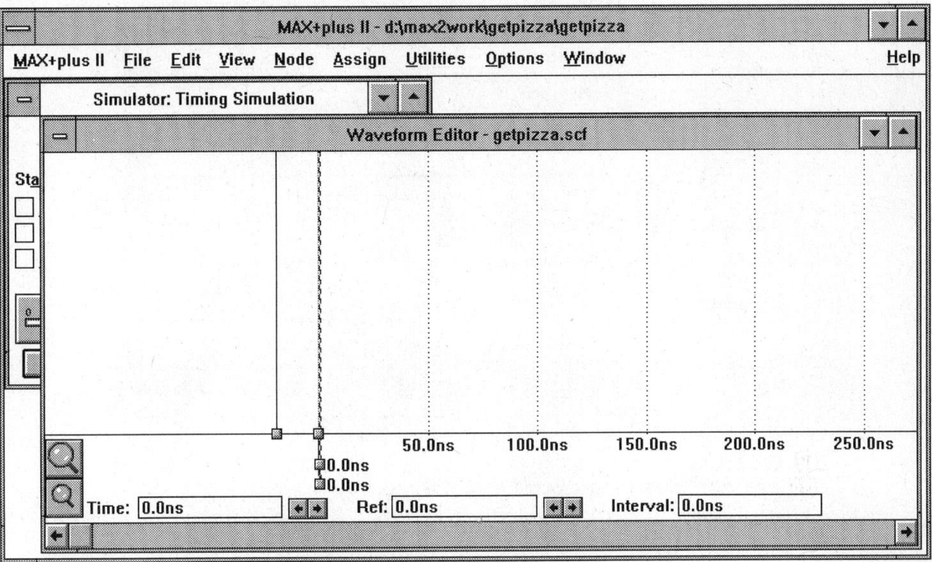

Figure 20-13
The MAX+Plus II waveform editor.

PLD devices are tested. The second way to enter stimulus into MAX+PLUS II is to use the waveform editor, and this is what we'll be doing for this simulation.

The Waveform Editor

The first step in creating a simulation waveform file is to invoke the MAX+PLUS II waveform editor. This editor (shown in Figure 20-13) shows signal names on the left side of the waveform, while waveforms are displayed to the right of each signal. The waveform display includes selectable cursors that can be used to measure the time between events and has zoom features so you can get a close look at part of a waveform, or see the entire waveform if needed.

To add signals to the waveform display, you simply double-click in an empty area in the signal list area, and a dialogue box (Figure 20-14) appears. Signals can be specified by their individual names (as shown) or can be specified as buses.

Once all the desired signals have been added to the waveform display, you can modify the waveform values of the circuit inputs to describe the input stimulus over time for the circuit. Figure 20-15 shows a set of input values already entered into the waveform. The stimulus will first simulate the vehicle traveling the route that I described earlier, which should result in a safe arrival at the beach with the pizza in hand and no tickets. Following the succesful journey, additional stimulus has been provided to check the operation of the ticket counter. The result of this is

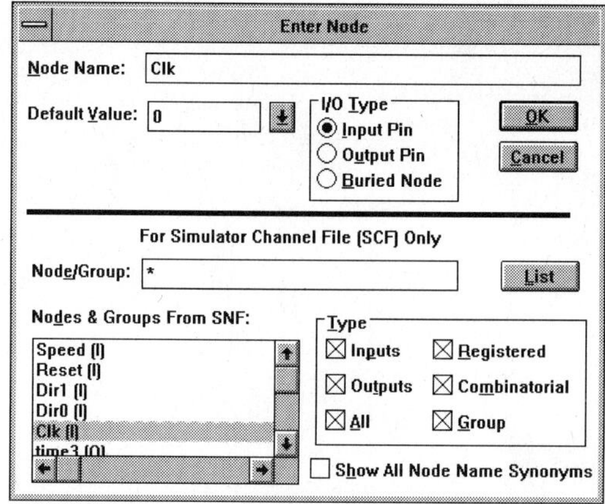

Figure 20-14
Selecting from a list of nodes to add to the display.

another successful trip to the beach, but a couple of tickets should be issued along the way.

To see the results of the simulation, we'll have to add the outputs (**party**, **time** and **tickets**) to the waveform display. This is done using the same double-clicking method used to add input waveforms.

Running the Simulation

To run the simulation, we'll go to the Simulator control window (Figure 20-16) and select the **Start** button. The simulator begins its operation, processing the input vectors and simulating the design based on a simulation model generated during the compilation process. As the simulation progresses, the status bar in the Simulator control windows moves from left to right, and the values in the waveform display window are dynamically updated to show the simulated output values. (If we have selected simulation options such as setup and hold checking, the simulator will report violations during simulation.)

When the simulation completes, the results are displayed in the waveform editor as shown in Figure 20-17. If you look carefully at the waveforms, you will see there is a delay (of about 20 ns) between the rising edge of each clock cycle (input **Clk**) and the subsequent changes in output values such as **time**. This delay has been determined by the MAX+PLUS II software and is based on the actual type of device that was selected for implementation.

Running a Timing Analysis

The timing analyzer included with MAX+PLUS II offers three analysis modes:

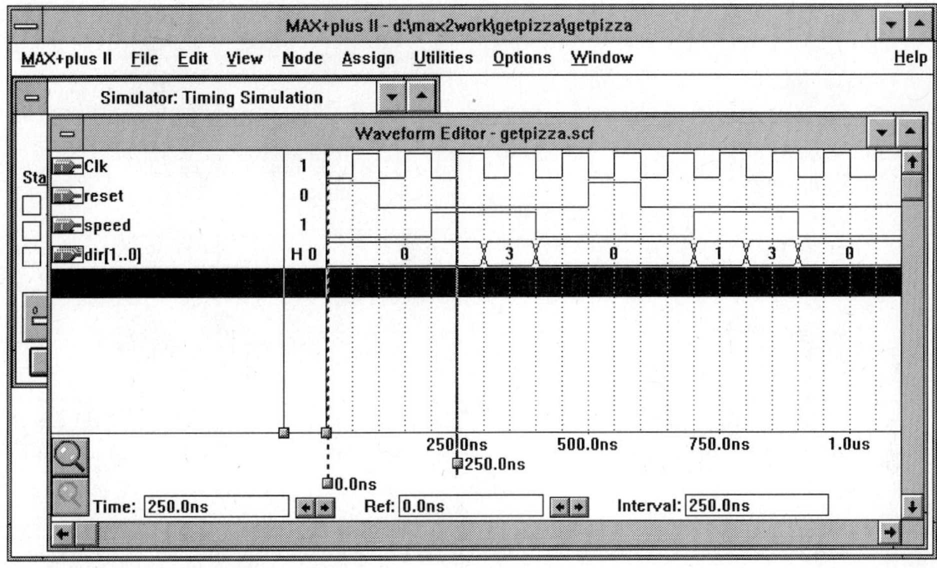

Figure 20-15
The waveform display can be zoomed out so the entire waveform can be viewed.

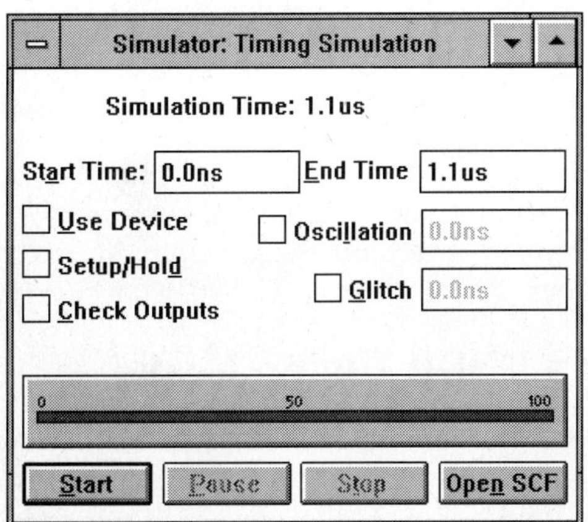

Figure 20-16
The simulator control panel.

- Delay Matrix: This mode analyzes the propagation delay paths between multiple source and destination nodes.

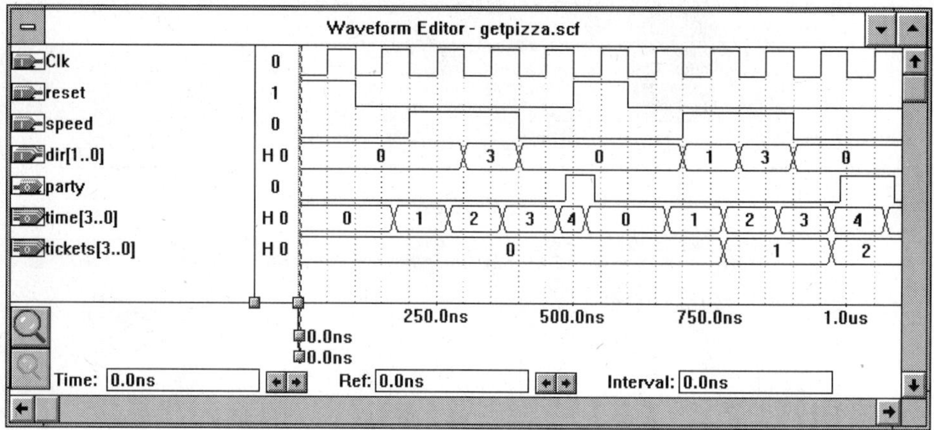

Figure 20-17
The simulation results are displayed as generated waveforms for the specified outputs.

- Registered Performance: This mode analyzes registered logic for performance-limiting delay and the resulting minimum clock period (maximum operating frequency).
- Setup and Hold Matrix: This mode calculates the minimum setup and hold time requirements from the input pins to the inputs of flip-flops and latches.

The first analysis, the delay matrix, is generated by invoking the timing analyzer, selecting the Delay Matrix mode, and running the analysis. The Delay Matrix, Registered Performance, and Setup/Hold Matrix displays for this design are shown in Figures 20-18, 20-19, and 20-20, respectively.

Generating a VHDL Timing Model

One very useful feature of MAX+PLUS II, for those who use VHDL or Verilog for system-level simulation, is its ability to generate a complete timing model for the programmed device. This file (a portion of which is shown—in VHDL form—in Figure 20-21) is completely self-contained (it does not rely on external files or special libraries of timing data) and can be used to perform simulation of the device within a larger circuit, using a variety of VHDL simulation environments.

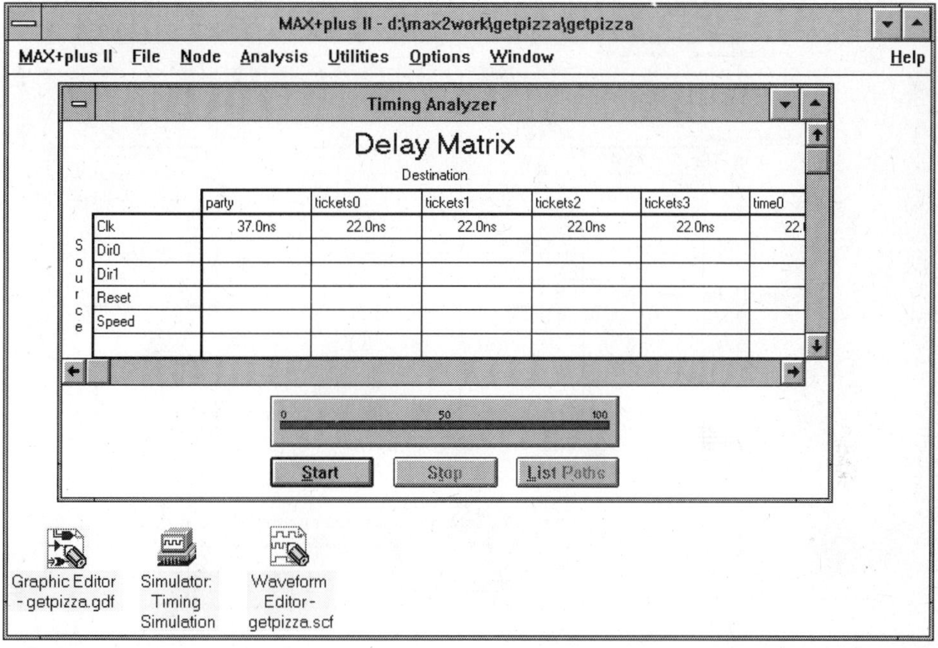

Figure 20-18
The Delay Matrix display.

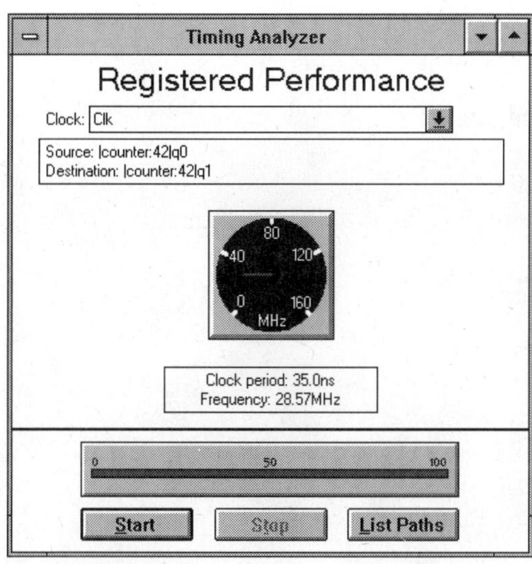

Figure 20-19
The Registered Performance display.

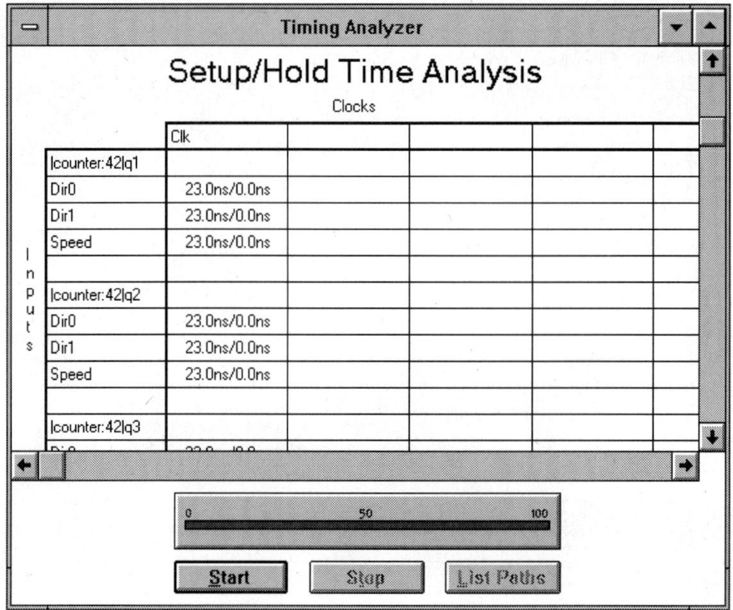

Figure 20-20
The Setup/Hold Matrix shows the minimum required setup and hold times from input pins to the D, Clock, and Latch Enable inputs of flip-flops and latches.

Moving On

This completes out look at PLDs, FPGAs and the design tools for these devices. In the next chapter, we are going to move ahead and find out about larger-scale devices: ASICs.

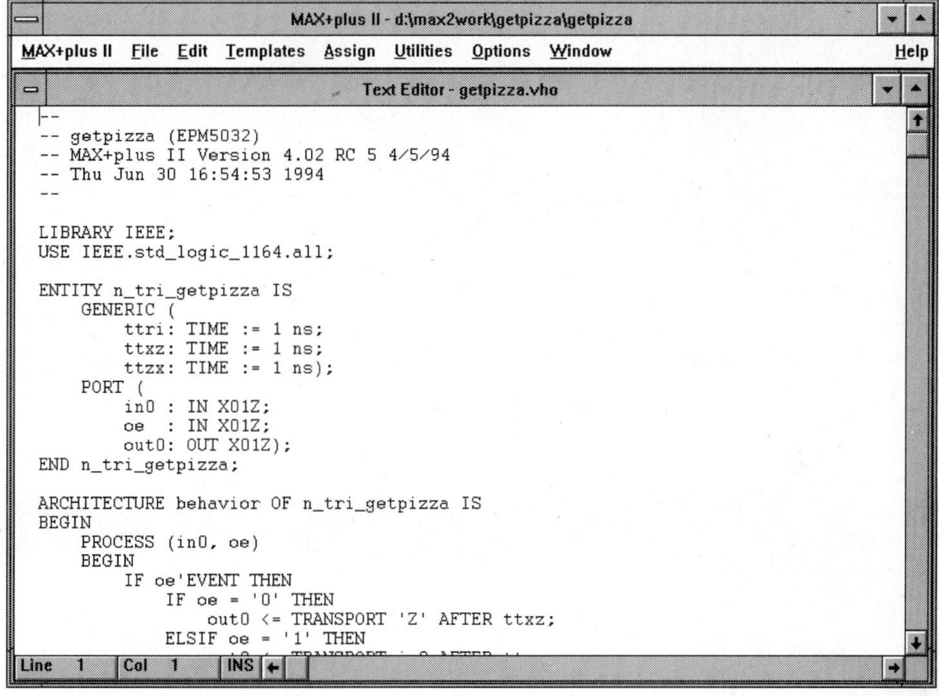
MAX+plus II - d:\max2work\getpizza\getpizza
MAX+plus II File Edit Templates Assign Utilities Options Window Help
Text Editor - getpizza.vho
--
-- getpizza (EPM5032)
-- MAX+plus II Version 4.02 RC 5 4/5/94
-- Thu Jun 30 16:54:53 1994
--
LIBRARY IEEE;
USE IEEE.std_logic_1164.all;
ENTITY n_tri_getpizza IS
GENERIC (
ttri: TIME := 1 ns;
ttxz: TIME := 1 ns;
ttzx: TIME := 1 ns);
PORT (
in0 : IN X01Z;
oe : IN X01Z;
out0: OUT X01Z);
END n_tri_getpizza;
ARCHITECTURE behavior OF n_tri_getpizza IS
BEGIN
PROCESS (in0, oe)
BEGIN
IF oe'EVENT THEN
IF oe = '0' THEN
out0 <= TRANSPORT 'Z' AFTER ttxz;
ELSIF oe = '1' THEN
Line 1 Col 1 INS

Figure 20-21
VHDL timing model for the programmed device.

CHAPTER 21

FOCUS ON TECHNOLOGY: INTEGRATED CIRCUITS

Your design is getting large. Very large. The prototype consumes 17 FPGAs plus a handful of TTL components and smaller PLDs and uses so much power that the lights dim whenever the system is powered up. It runs at only 2 MHz. It's time to start thinking about an ASIC—an application-specific integrated circuit.

As we have seen in previous chapters, programmable logic devices—and FPGAs in particular—are a popular way to get reasonably high device densities without going through a risky, costly, and prolonged ASIC design process. But when a design—or segment of a design—becomes to big for programmable logic (currently topping out at around 20,000 equivalent gates for a practical implementation) or you need to lower the build cost for a high-volume product, you need an ASIC.

ASICs find their way into end products in many ways. They may be introduced into a design right at the start, when both the design complexity and production volumes are going to be high, or they may be introduced later, after an initial production run is made using programmable logic or some other lower-risk technology.

Just how challenging is it to move into ASICs? Are there low-cost ASIC design options available? I'll try to answer these questions in this chapter, and in the tutorial chapter that follows. While examining the ASIC design process, we'll be looking at ways to minimize the cost and risk of ASIC prototyping and fabrication. I won't be spending much time discussing large-scale ASIC projects; if you are engaged in a project that requires a very large ASIC, then you will need much more expertise and information than I could possibly collect in one chapter. If you need more information about large ASIC projects, then you should explore some of the resources listed at the end of this chapter. You should also consider soliciting the help of an experienced ASIC designer, either by hiring one or by making use of an ASIC consultant.

What Is an ASIC?

Like most electronics-oriented acronyms, the term *application-specific Integrated circuit* has come to represent a narrower area than its component words might indicate. Loosely defined, an ASIC is any integrated circuit that is designed, customized, or programmed to perform a function that has been defined by the IC customer, rather than by the IC manufacturer. In common use, however, the term ASIC normally excludes programmable logic of any kind and includes only those ICs that must be fabricated by an IC foundry or other specialized manufacturing service. These chips include mask- and laser-programmed gate arrays, standard cell, semicustom, and full-custom ICs.

Using this definition, an ASIC might be a full-custom design that performs complex, high-speed video signal processing, or it might be a relatively low density, mask-programmed version of an FPGA design that is already in production. Because ASICs are used in so many different applications, it is difficult to characterize them by function. Instead, they are normally grouped by their underlying technology. Let's examine some of the broad classes.

Gate Arrays

Gate array devices are the most common type of ASIC in use today. They are the natural next step after programmable logic, and normally have lower up-front costs and shorter turnaround times than other types of ASICs. With the advent of laser-programmed gate arrays, it is possible to have a 30,000 gate ASIC prototype turned around in less than a day. More typically, though, you can expect a mask-programmed ASIC to require at least a few weeks between the time you submit your design (in the form of both netlists and test vectors) to the manufacturer until the time you recieve your completed prototype. Although each iteration of the design has a time penalty (and a cost penalty for the fabrication process), the overall risk is much less in gate arrays than it is for other, more custom ASIC technologies.

A gate array device is characterized by a basic array of transistors arranged on a wafer. The transistors are laid out in fixed, predetermined locations, and cannot be modified in any way. The customization of a gate array for a particular application involves specifying a custom set of conductive mask layers that create an application-specific pattern of transistor interconnections in the finished chip. The primary differences in different gate array architectures are the sizes and arrangements of the transistor arrays and the type of interconnection strategy employed.

Types of Gate Arrays

The most common gate arrays are those based on a channeled architecture, in which pairs of transistors are arranged in rows separated by empty channels. To create the desired function in the device, the final interconnections are made in custom layers (usually one or two metal mask layers).

For higher-density gate array devices, the routing channels are left out, and the entire die is composed of what is called a *sea of gates*. To customize this type of gate array, the metal layers are deposited not in routing channels, but directly over the transistors, so that many (perhaps most) of the transistors in the chip become routing channels, rather than logic gates.

As in FPGA devices, routing of the interconnect signals is a major limiting factor in gate arrays of any size. Although gate array devices can contain 100,000 or more equivalent gates, it is unusual for a design implemented in a gate array to exceed 50% of that amount. (These numbers should be viewed as being relative; new gate array architectures are being introduced constantly, and gate counts are rising quickly.)

Counting Gates

Just as in complex PLD and FPGA architectures, relative gate counts are rarely a complete indication of whether a given design will fit into a chosen gate array architecture. Routing problems in the chosen architecture may result in a significant waste of die resources, and additional complexities can be introduced by designs that are routing intensive (such as those with large amounts of combinational logic or those that implement RAM blocks).

Cell-Based ASICs

Unlike gate arrays (and FPGAs), cell-based ASICs (usually called *standard cell* devices) require that a complete set of masks be specified that is unique to the application being created.

In a cell-based ASIC, the ASIC vendor (or a vendor of design tools who supports that vendor) provides a library of cells that represent gate-level functions such as AND gates and flip-flops and higher-level functions such as multiplexers, counters and comparators, and even such things as RAM blocks, EPROMs, and controllers. These cells are called "standard cells" because they are designed according to a single set of guidelines (height, positioning of power and ground, arrangement of I/O, etc.), allowing the cells to be placed virtually anywhere on the completed chip.

These cells are predesigned by the ASIC vendor for implemention in its process technology, and may be either fixed or configurable for various input and output requirements. Once specified (usually in schematic form), the cells can be implemented as needed using predefined arrangements of transistors and interconnected as specified by the end user. This task of placing cells onto the chip and determining an efficient interconnect strategy is called *place and route* and can be performed automatically by specialized routing software.

The actual architecture of an ASIC constructed using standard cell technology is, in most respects, kept hidden from the end user. This allows you to concentrate on the design itself, rather than on the underlying process required to implement that design. To design a standard cell ASIC, you will normally use a schematic approach and will instantiate and connect the ASIC vendor's higher-level symbols as needed to create the circuit. You can then use digital and/or analog simulators to verify that the design does what it is expected to do before submitting it for fabrication.

Cell-based architectures become more attractive as you begin to create designs that exceed the practical gate count limitations of gate arrays, and as you begin to incorporate circuit elements (such as RAM, or complex datapath elements) that do not map efficiently into a gate array architecture.

Full-Custom ASICs

To create a full-custom ASIC, you must create every element (transistor, capacitor, resistor, and interconnect channel) in the device and determine the layout for the entire chip. This "hand-crafted" approach to IC design requires significant expertise on the part of the designer, and is usually reserved for very large projects that can afford to hire IC design specialists. Gate array and semicustom ICs have advanced in capabilities to the point where it makes sense to consider a full-custom IC only if you intend to market the device directly or if your requirements are so unusual that there are no semicustom libraries that will fulfill your needs.

Do You Need an ASIC?

The decision on when and whether to use ASIC technology requires an analysis of the quantities of product to be produced, the likelihood of the design being changed, the market window, and many other factors. Before deciding that an ASIC is the right choice, you should be very sure that there is no possibility of using an FPGA for your design. There are many FPGA vendors and architectures available, and just because one FPGA family operates too slowly, or is too expensive or hard to find sources for, does not mean that other device families will have the same limitations. Every type of FPGA has its own strengths and weaknesses; some are faster than others, some are known for their lower cost per gate, some are power misers, and others are easier to design for or program.

If you have decided to use an ASIC only because of production cost considerations, you should consider using an FPGA in the prototyping stage, and use an FPGA translation service to create an equivalent mask or laser-programmed version of your design. Taking this route can save you a tremendous amount of time, since you will have to spend far less time analyzing the detailed timing behavior of the circuit—you can just try it out in-circuit.

What Are the Trade-offs?

Every potential circuit implementation has its strengths and weaknesses. When you are evaluating using an ASIC for a design, you should consider the following factors:

- Up-front development engineering (*nonrecurring engineering*, or *NRE*) costs: What will it cost to obtain the needed design tools, and what specialized training or outside consulting will be needed? What involvement will be required from the ASIC vendor during the initial phases of the project, and how much will that involvement cost?
- Schedule risks: How long will it take to obtain the tools, learn the new design process, and produce the first prototype silicon?
- Production costs: What will it cost to produce the devices in quantity (and what is the quantity that you intend to produce)?
- Flexibility: What will the impact be when a redesign is required? Does the technology support the need for minor changes, or will the entire design need to be scrapped?
- Board space requirements: How costly will it be to use lower-density devices and correspondingly greater amounts of board space.

Although these, and other factors, are different for each project and implementation technology, there are generalizations that can be made. The chart of Figure 21-1 compares these and other factors for full-custom, cell-based, gate array and FPGA devices.

What Does It Cost?

The engineering costs for creating an ASIC are, of course, dependent on the size and complexity of the circuit. For gate array and standard cell devices, the use of a vendor's library can help to speed the development time dramatically. In fact, since the risk of making a mistake is high, and the cost of going through a second iteration of a chip is potentially very high, the majority of the engineering time for gate array and standard cell devices may be spent in verifying (through the use of a vendor-qualified simulator and thousands of test vectors) the circuit prior to submitting it to the ASIC foundry. It's important not to underestimate this phase of the ASIC design process: you may spend only a few weeks entering the circuit and verifying its basic function, but spend months creating the necessary test vectors,

Trade-off	Full Custom	Cell-Based	Gate Array	FPGA
Multisourcing Difficulty	Highest	Low-Medium	Low-Medium	Lowest
Development Cost (NRE)	Highest	High	Medium	Lowest
Mask Costs	High	High	Low-Medium	None
Design Time	Highest	Medium	Medium-High	Lowest
Redesign Flexibility	Lowest	Low	Low-Medium	Highest
Cost of Iteration	Highest	High	Medium	Lowest
Production Unit Cost	Lowest	Low	Medium	Highest
PCB Costs	Lowest	Low	Low	High
Layout Efficiency and Flexibility	Highest	Medium-High	Low-Medium	Lowest
I/O Flexibility	Highest	Medium-High	Low-Medium	Lowest
Level of Integration	Highest	High	Medium	Lowest

Figure 21-1
Device trade-offs. (Adapted from ***Surviving the ASIC Experience****, Prentice Hall, 1992.)*

running simulations, and correcting minor problems in the design. If the vendor insists on using a "golden" simulator that you do not have access to, you can expect the costs to mount as you send one or more members of your design team off-site to make use of the vendor's own in-house simulation tools.

For full-custom designs (and some standard cell designs), you can count on many months of painstaking work on the part of an experienced IC designer but, in many cases, the full-custom chip can actually be done more cheaply than the equivalent gate array or standard cell version of the design. This is because every aspect of the chip design is in your control. Rather than submitting a netlist (and thousands of test vectors) to the ASIC vendor, you will be submitting a complete mask-level description of the design.

To do this, you need to have access to tools that allow you to specify the design and generate a netlist that can be fed to a silicon compiler, or have access to and control over the actual arrangement of transistors on the wafer. Both these methods require that the design tool have knowledge of the target device architecture and its capabilities (its *permissible geometries*) .

Full-custom designs are normally carried out with the help of a special type of graphical editor called a *layout editor*. This editor allows you to create a mask-level description of your design and provides tools for design rule checking specific to the type of device (the process) being used. Layout editors also include netlist extractors that can generate a SPICE (or other format) description of the circuit that can be compared with an original schematic-based circuit for verification. After this verification step, the extracted circuit is simulated using vendor-supplied timing parameters.

Historically, the software required to do netlist-level or mask-level design has been very expensive, and available only on Unix workstation-class platforms. In recent years, however, tools have appeared on personal computers that allow semicustom and full-custom ASIC designs to be developed. This, coupled with dramatic reductions in the cost of certain fabrication services, has made it possible for ASICs to be used in designs that would not have made economic sense earlier.

Fabrication Costs

Estimating the cost of an ASIC requires knowledge of many factors. These factors include the number of devices per wafer (a function of the die size), the number of pins on the device, the packaging technology being used, the expected yield (failure rate, in terms of a percentage of device per wafer), and the cost of the process technology being employed.

For a given run of chips, you will also need to consider the tooling costs associated with getting your netlist or mask-level design into production. These costs can be quite large, and can easily bring the total cost of your first wafers (and corresponding first batch of chips) to many tens of thousands of dollars.

Wafer-Sharing Services

Until recently, high start-up costs in production have precluded the use of ASICs for low-volume applications—which are the majority of designs produced today. With the advent of wafer sharing programs, it is now possible to create an ASIC for little more than the cost of creating a comparable FPGA prototype. A wafer-sharing service places numerous IC designs on a single wafer, so that entry-level fabrication costs are shared among all those who use the wafer. With a wafer-sharing service such as the DARPA-funded MOSIS service or the Foresight program offered by Orbit Semiconductor, prototype chips can be produced for as little as $600 per chip. When combined with the low-cost ASIC design tools now appearing, it is actually possible to create a prototype ASIC for less than $10,000, including the cost of the tools.

The MOSIS Service

In addition to low-cost gate array prototyping services (some of which appear in the vendor listings in Appendix A), there is an alternative service provided by the Information Sciences Institute at the University of Southern California in Marina Del Ray, California. For projects on a strict budget, MOSIS (which stands for MOS Implementation System) can be useful option.

The MOSIS service was started in 1980, and was originally intended to provide low-volume fabrication services for academic users and government contractors and government agencies. The program is funded by the Defense Advanced Research Projects Agency (DARPA) with assistance from the National Science Foundation (NSF).

In recent years, the MOSIS service has been expanded to address the needs of commercial users, with MOSIS foundries now providing services to a number of commercial ASIC users. The service is particularly well suited for prototyping activities that do not have critical schedules to meet. The services operates by combining multiple projects on a single wafer, thereby spreading the costs of prototype production among multiple customers.

When a design is submitted to MOSIS (as mask layout geometry data in magnetic tape or email format), the service checks the design for correct syntax, but does not perform any additional verification or validation prior to production. When all of the projects for a particular run have been collected, the service writes tapes and submits them to a mask maker for phototooling. After this is complete, the resulting wafer masks are inspected and forwarded to the fabrication line. The entire process, from design submission to prototype chips (bonded and packaged) can take as little as two or three weeks to complete.

Moving On

In this chapter, we have surveyed the basic types of ASICs in common use today, and have examined some of the trade-offs involved in using them. In the next chapter, we're going to be looking at a set of design tools that make it possible to create ASIC designs (including standard cell and full-custom chips) on a shoestring budget.

Other Resources

DiGiacomo, Joseph, *Designing with High-Performance ASICs*, Prentice Hall, Englewood Cliffs, NJ, 1992.

Pucknell, Douglas, and Kamran Eshraghian, *Basic VLSI Design Systems and Circuits, 3rd ed.*, Prentice Hall, Englewood Cliffs, NJ, 1994.

Schroeter, John, *Surviving the ASIC Experience*, Prentice Hall, Englewood Cliffs, NJ, 1992.

Wolf, Wayne, *Modern VLSI Design*, Prentice Hall, Englewood Cliffs, NJ, 1994.

CHAPTER 22

HANDS-ON EDA: CREATING AN INTEGRATED CIRCUIT

In this chapter, we're going to be examining two sample ASIC designs, each of which illustrates a different method of producing an ASIC. The first example uses a standard cell-based design and fabrication method (using the MOSIS service to provide low-cost fabrication), while the second example will be of a full custom CMOS chip design entered at the transistor level.

While both designs are relatively simple, they nevertheless illustrate issues related to standard cell and full-custom design methods and to ASIC design in general. In the standard cell example, we will be implementing a traffic light controller, and in the second example, we will be creating an operational amplifier.

Note: *The information in this chapter is based in large part on design examples and information provided by Tanner Research. The example screens shown in this chapter have been captured using Tanner's DOS-based products; evaluation versions of these products can be found on the companion CD-ROM.*

Tools for Standard Cell Design

Designing for a standard cell device requires the same basic design tools as other types of automated circuit design (a design entry program, functional simulator and libraries, etc.) as well as other tools specific to ASIC design. The software tools generally needed for standard cell designs include

- ☐ Schematic capture (or HDL synthesis software)
- ☐ Schematic symbol (or module generation) libraries
- ☐ Timing libraries for simulation
- ☐ Layout libraries
- ☐ Timing simulator
- ☐ Standard cell place and route tools
- ☐ Mask or layout editor
- ☐ Verification tools, including
  - Design rule checkers
  - Netlist extractors
  - Layout verification tools

To demonstrate that low-cost ASIC design is possible, these examples have been developed using tools available from Tanner Research, of Pasadena, California. Tanner specializes in low-cost tools for gate array, standard cell and full-custom design and emphasizes ASIC vendor independence in their tools.

Tanner Research Tools

Tanner Research is a company specializing in low-cost, vendor-independent tools for ASIC design. The Tanner Tools Pro software supports ASIC technologies including field programmable gate arrays (FPGAs), mask-programmed gate arrays, and semicustom and full-custom chips. A flowchart representation of the Tanner Tools software is shown in Figure 22-1.

Standard Cell Design Process

A design concept intended for standard cell implementation is typically entered using a schematic capture program. (An alternative is to use a hardware description language such as VHDL or Verilog HDL, but we will only consider the schematic capture approach in these examples).

When entering the design, the libraries used are critical, and the issues of schematic capture, netlist formats, and libraries must be addressed together. First, a library of schematic symbols appropriate for the target technology is needed to

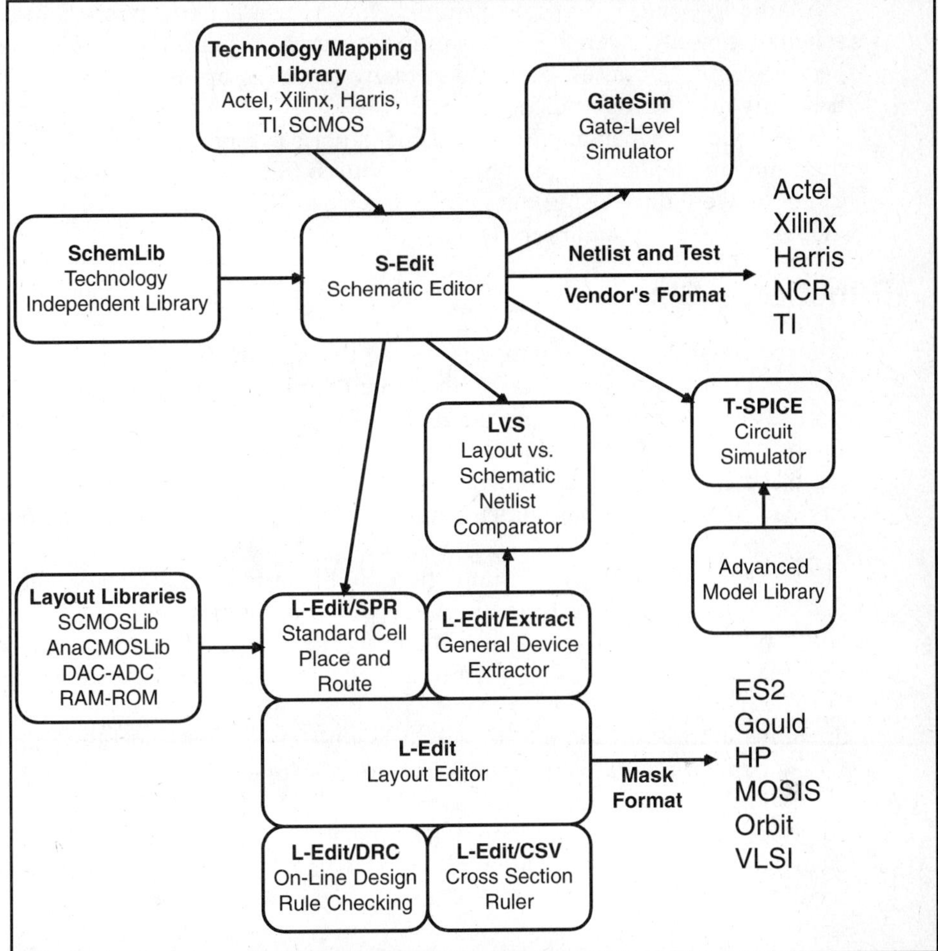

Figure 22-1
Tanner Tools Pro design flow.

describe the design in schematic form. Once the design has been entered, it must be simulated using detailed timing information specific to the schematic symbols and ASIC process used. This timing information is specific to a particular ASIC vendor or process, but you can decide at the outset to take either a vendor-specific approach or a vendor-independent approach.

In the typical vendor-specific approach, the schematic symbols and timing models are supplied by the silicon vendor for use with a vendor approved schematic capture package. Using such an approach, a design that has been entered for one vendor's ASIC technology cannot easily be moved into an alternate ASIC supplier's technology.

With a vendor-independent approach, you use generic symbols to enter the schematic, which can be subsequently mapped (automatically) to a set of vendor-specific libraries. This one-to-many mapping approach gives you greater flexibility in selecting a silicon vendor.

Although a schematic entered using generic symbols is vendor independent, the timing models and layout libraries produced from the design are not. In this first example, we will be using the MOSIS service as the silicon vendor, so the timing models and cell layout library will be specific to that technology.

Functional Simulation

After schematic entry, simulation is needed to verify the functionality of the design. Most standard cell-based designs implement digital circuits, and therefore a digital simulator is used for functional simulation. There are three important methods that can be used to simulate a standard cell-based design. First, a functional simulation can be performed with a unit delay assigned to each of the logic gates. This type of simulation will catch most functional errors and is highly recommended as a first step.

Next, a prelayout timing simulation can be performed, based on gate-specific delays. This gate delay information is provided in the timing model for each gate, and is based on the process that will be used to fabricate the chip (in this case the MOSIS process). In prelayout simulation, load-based delays resulting from the wires are assumed to be zero. Depending on the technology chosen for implementation and the speed at which your circuit will operate, this level of timing simulation may or may not provide a useful level of verification.

Once the design is placed and routed into the chip, a post-layout simulation can be performed. Before simulation, load capacitance information is back-annotated from the chip router to the timing models. Postlayout simulation provides the most accurate simulation possible, but can be done only after the chip is successfully routed.

Placing and Routing the Design

A standard cell-based design is composed automatically at the mask level. The tool used for this purpose is called a *standard cell place and router*. A netlist description generated from the schematic, combined with a mask-level layout library is provided as input to the tool, which then generates the entire chip layout. The layout of the chip consists of a *pad frame*, a *core*, and the *core-to-pad frame routing*. The pad frame provides the interface to the outside world, while the core represents the internal logic of the chip.

A standard cell core typically consists of rows of logic connected together through routing channels. Most routers use optimization algorithms to yield a compact arrangement of cells in the final chip.

Verifying the Layout

Once the chip's mask-level description is generated, a mask-level layout editor is typically used to view and edit the result. A layout editor is a graphical tool somewhat akin to a printed circuit board layout program used to edit a design at the mask level. A design that requires no manual mask-level editing can be forwarded directly to a semicustom chip service (*foundry*) for fabrication. However, most designers prefer to run some error checks before doing so. Error checks are recommended for all designs, no matter how simple or complex, before submitting them for fabrication. Handcrafted designs (those composed at the mask level) should never be fabricated without substantial error checking and verification.

Verification tools, in the form of a *design rule checker* (DRC) and a *layout vs. schematic comparator* (LVS) are used to check for errors in a design. The DRC checks for any geometrical rule errors that might have occurred in the mask-level description of the design. These rules are determined by the process to be used for fabrication. For example, a given process might dictate that two metal lines be separated by some number of microns.

The LVS tool compares the topology of the mask level to the schematic level. For a design to work, there must not be any differences between the two. An LVS accomplishes this by comparing two netlists. One of the netlists is generated from the schematic, and the other is extracted from the mask layout. A *netlist extractor* tool is used to extract the netlist from the layout. In our case, the format of the netlist will be SPICE.

At this point the design is ready to be submitted to a fabrication service. The MOSIS services (described in the previous chapter) will accept the mask-level description of a design and return the first set of prototype chips in a matter of weeks. Commercial services can typically turn around a design somewhat faster, depending on the complexity of the design and the production volumes requested.

Example Design: A Traffic Light Controller

We'll begin by entering the schematic representing the traffic light controller. This circuit is commonly found in logic design textbooks and represents a controller used to regulate the traffic lights in an intersection.

The schematic will be entered using S-Edit, Tanner's schematic capture tool. The schematic uses a technology-independent set of schematic symbols to represent the logical function of the circuit. This library is shown in Figure 22-2.

Unlike schematics entered for circuit board layout, most ASIC schematics use hierarchical structures. For example, at the very top level a chip may be represented as a packaged part with various pins. One level down in the hierarchy, a lower-level schematic may represent the top level of the design, and consist of the design core and the I/O pads. Moving down farther in the hierarchy, the design core may in turn be composed of various logic blocks representing high-level logic functions such as counters or multiplexors. Pushing down into the logic blocks themselves,

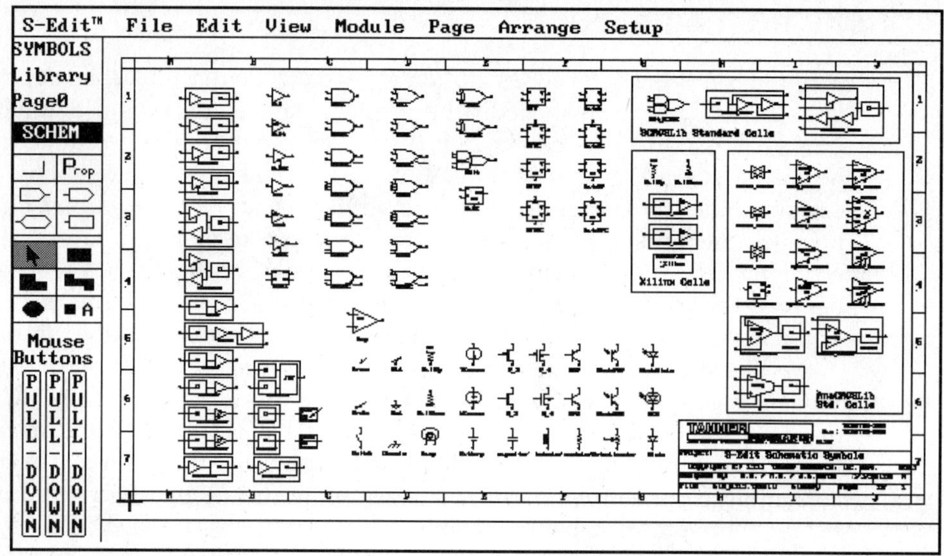

Figure 22-2
S-Edit symbol library.

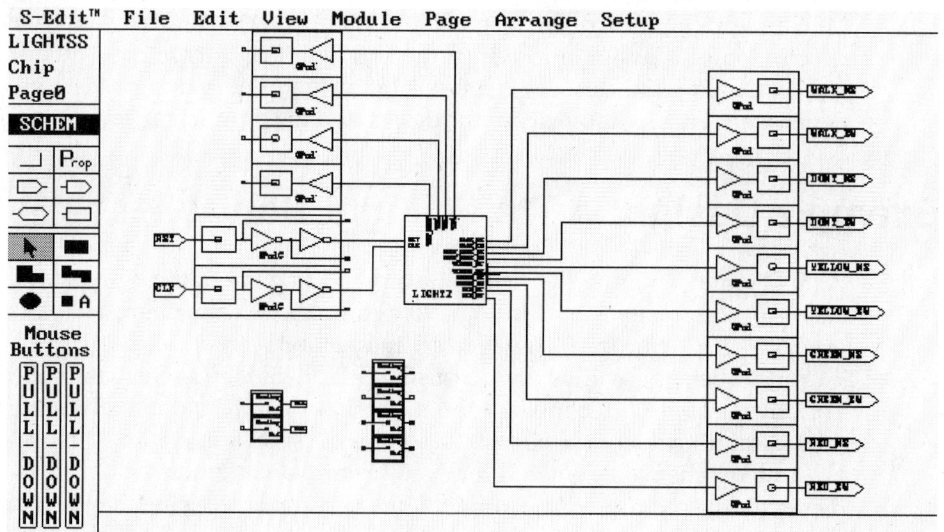

Figure 22-3
Traffic signal controller top-level schematic.

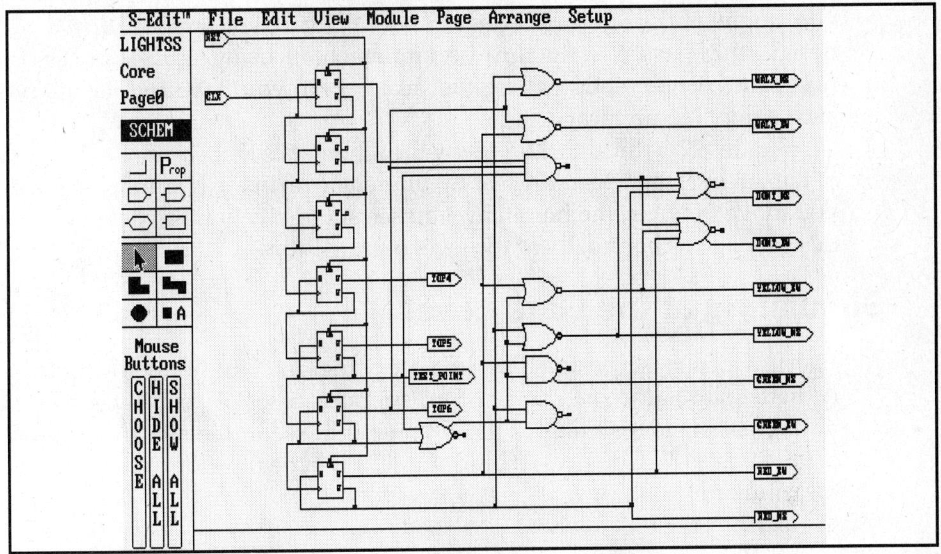

Figure 22-4
Schematic view of module core.

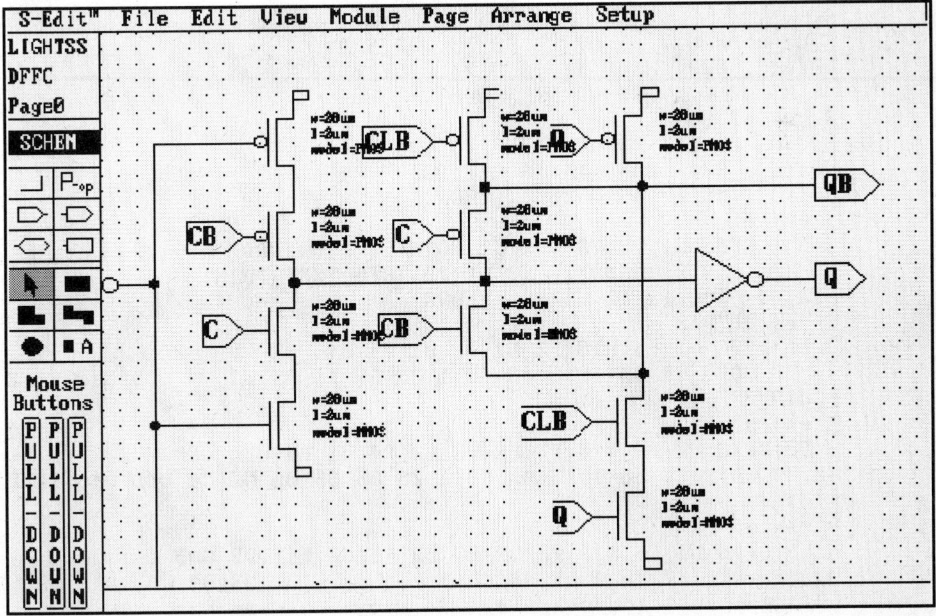

Figure 22-5
Schematic of DFFC.

you might find basic logic gates. And finally, if you are creating a full-custom design, the gates may in turn be implemented using actual transistors. With a full-featured schematic editing tool like S-Edit, you have the flexibility to create such a fully hierarchical design.

Figures 22-3 through 22-5 show the schematics that comprise this design. Each of the three schematics represents a different level in the hierarchy in the design. As you move down in the hierarchy, you see successively more detailed views of the design, concluding finally at the level of transistors.

Simulating at the Gate Level

The next step in the design is to simulate using GateSim, Tanner's digital simulator. A digital simulator such as GateSim supports a set of primitives modeled using timing parameters similar to those you might see in the specifications of discrete chips (such as TTL devices). For example, a D-type flip-flop may be represented by the simulator as follows:

```
Q       .DFF    [tRiseQ] [tFallQ] [tsetQ]
                [tRiseQB] [TfallQB] [tsetQB] [tclrQB]
                [tsetup] [thold] [tMinPulseWidth]
                QBAR SETBAR CLRBAR D CLFK
```

```
 File  Edit  Window  Search  Process  Utility  Help
$ U8=AND2 U17_P3 U7_P3 U8_P3 VDD GND
U8<0<___000 .NAND 14 16 U17_P3 U7_P3
U8_P3 .INV 17 15 U8<0<___000
$ end of U8
$ U9=AND2 U17_P3 U7_P4 U9_P3 VDD GND
U9<0<___000 .NAND 14 16 U17_P3 U7_P4
U9_P3 .INV 17 15 U9<0<___000
$ end of U9
$ U12=AND3 U1_P3 TOP6 TEST_POINT U12_P4 VDD GND
U12<0<___000 .NAND 20 19 U1_P3 TOP6 TEST_POINT
U12_P4 .INV 13 12 U12<0<___000
$ end of U12
$ U1=DFFC U1_P4 U18_P2 U1_P3 U1_P4 U19_P2 VDD GND
U1_P3 .DFF 38 38 1 16 48 48 1 25 65 55 35 U1_P4 VDD U18_P2 U1_P4
+ U19_P2
$ end of U1
$ U2=DFFC U2_P4 U18_P2 U2_P3 U2_P4 U1_P4 VDD GND
U2_P3 .DFF 37 36 1 15 48 48 1 25 65 55 35 U2_P4 VDD U18_P2 U2_P4
+ U1_P4
$ end of U2
$ U3=DFFC U3_P4 U18_P2 U3_P3 U3_P4 U2_P4 VDD GND
U3_P3 .DFF 37 36 1 15 48 48 1 25 65 55 35 U3_P4 VDD U18_P2 U3_P4
-- lights.net [Fundamental] 0% --
```

Figure 22-6
Design netlist, ready for gate-level simulation or layout.

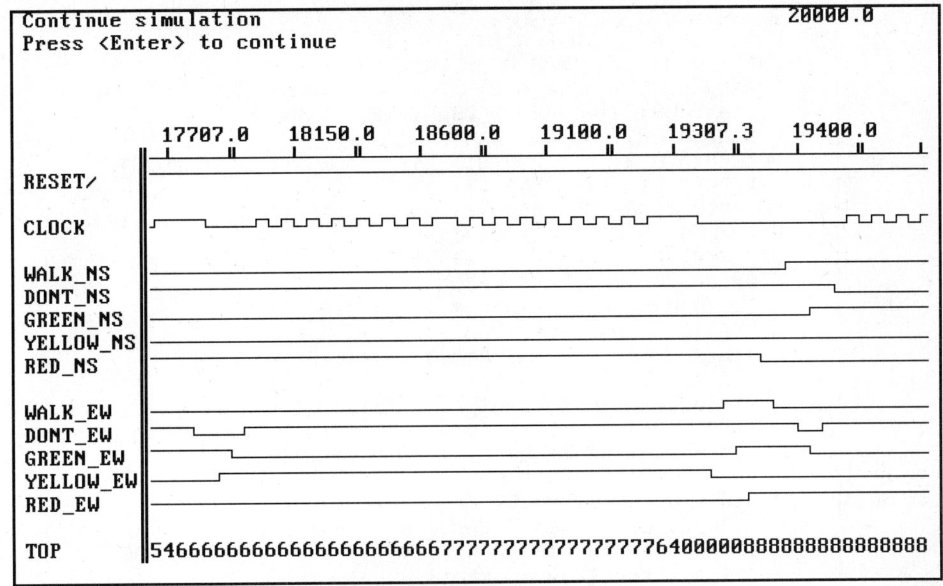

Figure 22-7
Sample simulation result.

As you can see, the simulator expects various timing parameters for each instance of a simulation primitive. For this design, the timing models are supplied in a file consisting of gate-level timing data based on the MOSIS technology.

To simulate the operation of a circuit, a simulator needs several inputs. It needs a command file with the simulation input, a netlist of the design to simulate, and an input vector file that provides the input stimuli for the design. The netlist format, ready for gate-level simulation, is illustrated in Figure 22-6. Figure 22-7 shows the results of simulating the traffic signal controller example.

The next step in creating the traffic signal controller is to use the place and router to generate the layout. L-Edit/SPR accepts the gate-level netlist description of the design, fetches core cells from a library and organizes them into rows of logic. It routes the logic, generates the pad frame, and routes the core to the pad frame.

The resulting standard cell netlist is shown in Figure 22-8. After this netlist has been generated, the final results are displayed in the L-Edit layout editor as shown in Figure 22-9. In Tanner Tools Pro, the standard cell place-and-route (SPR) tool is integrated into the L-Edit layout editor. Because of this tight integration, the results can be viewed immediately after the SPR has completed.

At this point the standard cell design is almost complete. All that remains is to run the DRC and LVS for error checking. We'll defer a discussion of this aspect of the design process, however, to the second part of this chapter, since the DRC and LVS processes are the same whether you are creating a standard cell or full-custom design.

```
 File  Edit  Window  Search  Process  Utility  Help
C NAND2C OUT1 OUT2 A B;
UU8<0<0 U8<0<___000 U8_P3 U17_P3 U7_P3;
C NAND2C OUT1 OUT2 A B;
UU9<0<0 U9<0<___000 U9_P3 U17_P3 U7_P4;
C NAND3C OUT1 OUT2 A B C;
UU12<0<0 U12<0<___000 U12_P4 U1_P3 TOP6 TEST_POINT;
C DFFC Q QB DATA CLK CLB;
UU1<0<0 U1_P3 U1_P4 U1_P4 U19_P2 U18_P2;
C DFFC Q QB DATA CLK CLB;
UU2<0<0 U2_P3 U2_P4 U2_P4 U1_P4 U18_P2;
C DFFC Q QB DATA CLK CLB;
UU3<0<0 U3_P3 U3_P4 U3_P4 U2_P4 U18_P2;
C DFFC Q QB DATA CLK CLB;
UU4<0<0 TOP4 U4_P4 U4_P4 U3_P4 U18_P2;
C DFFC Q QB DATA CLK CLB;
UU5<0<0 TOP5 TEST_POINT TEST_POINT U4_P4 U18_P2;
C DFFC Q QB DATA CLK CLB;
UU6<0<0 TOP6 U6_P4 U6_P4 TEST_POINT U18_P2;
C DFFC Q QB DATA CLK CLB;
UU7<0<0 U7_P3 U7_P4 U7_P4 U6_P4 U18_P2;
CP IPADC PAD DATAIN DATAINB DATAINUNBUF;
UU18<0<0 RESET/ U18_P2 U18<0<___000 U18<0<0<___000;
— lights.tpr [Fundamental] 0% ——————————————
```

Figure 22-8
Standard cell netlist generated from place and route.

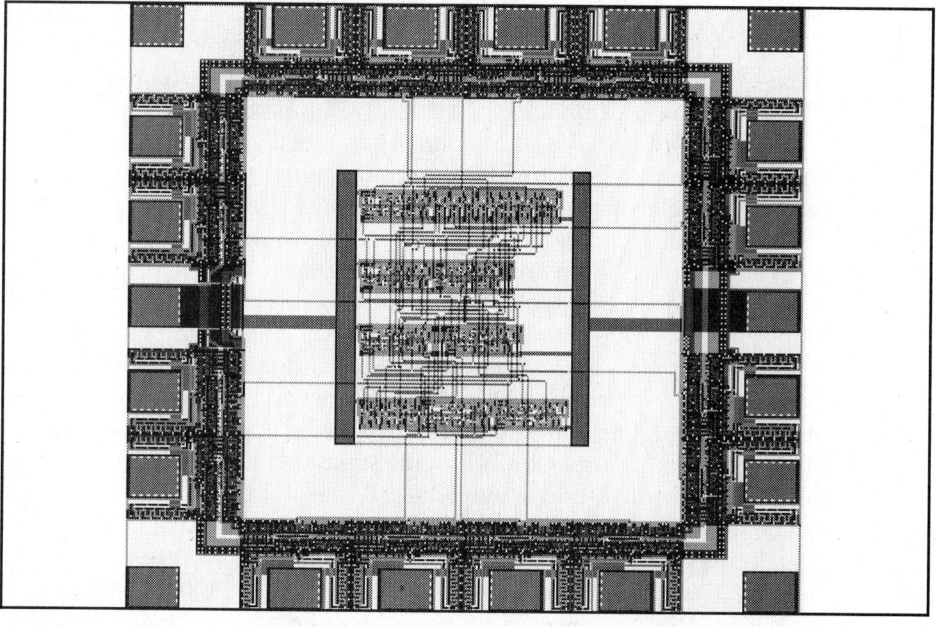

Figure 22-9
Standard cell layout for the traffic light controller.

The Full-Custom Design Process

The process of creating a full-custom chip is similar to that of designing a standard cell chip, but rather than developing the design using a high-level set of primitives (or high-level language, in the case of HDL-based designs), we will create the design at the level of the actual transistor level.

Creating a design at the level of a mask requires a certain level of specialized expertise, since you will be creating every transistor and interconnect path in the chip by hand. If you have the necessary knowledge of IC design, the full custom approach can be the lowest-cost method of IC design. In addition, there are certain classes of circuits (most notably analog designs) that do not lend themselves to automated layout generation.

Creating a Full-Custom CMOS Amplifier

Now we'll consider the full-custom design of a simple CMOS operational amplifier. Unlike the previous traffic light controller design, we're going to begin this design at the transistor level and create the mask layout manually.

Entering the Design

As with the traffic lights example, we begin with the schematic editor. The schematic primitives used in this example are NMOS and PMOS transistors. After the schematic is completed, we will perform a functional simulation.

Figure 22-10 illustrates the two types of transistors, NMOS and PMOS, used for this design. These transistors are provided in the schematic editor's component library, and correspond directly to transistors that will be generated in the custom chip.

Figure 22-11 shows the complete transistor-level description of the operational amplifier circuit.

Simulating the Design

Unlike the previous example, in which a gate-level simulation was performed, this design will require simulation at the transistor level. We'll perform this simulation of the design using T-Spice, Tanner's SPICE-based analog simulator. The results of this simulation can be displayed as SPICE simulation plots (Figure 22-12).

Laying Out the Mask

After the transistor-level simulation, the next step is to lay out the design at the mask level. In the layout, a transistor consists of a collection of *mask layer geometries* dictated by the process in question. For example, Figure 22-13 illustrates the

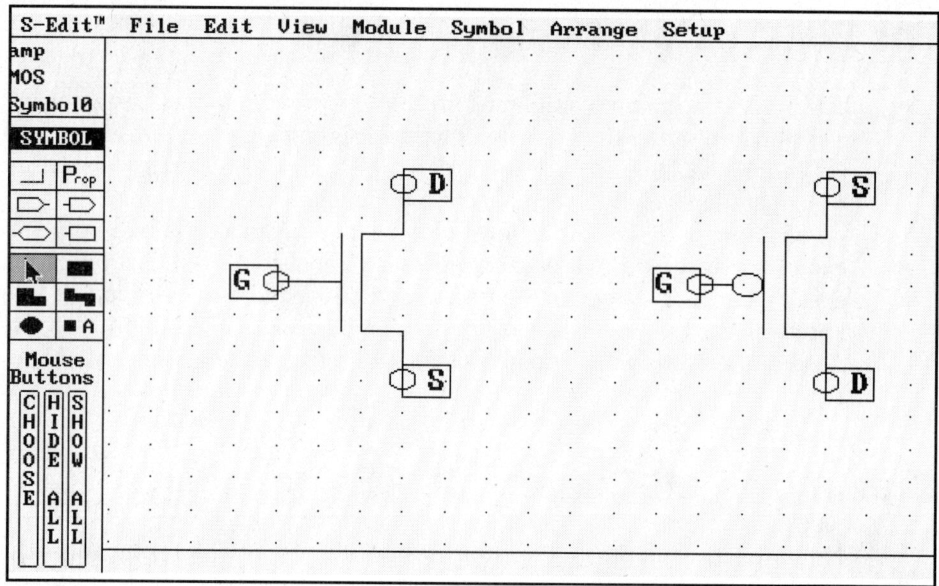

Figure 22-10
Creating PMOS and NMOS transistors .

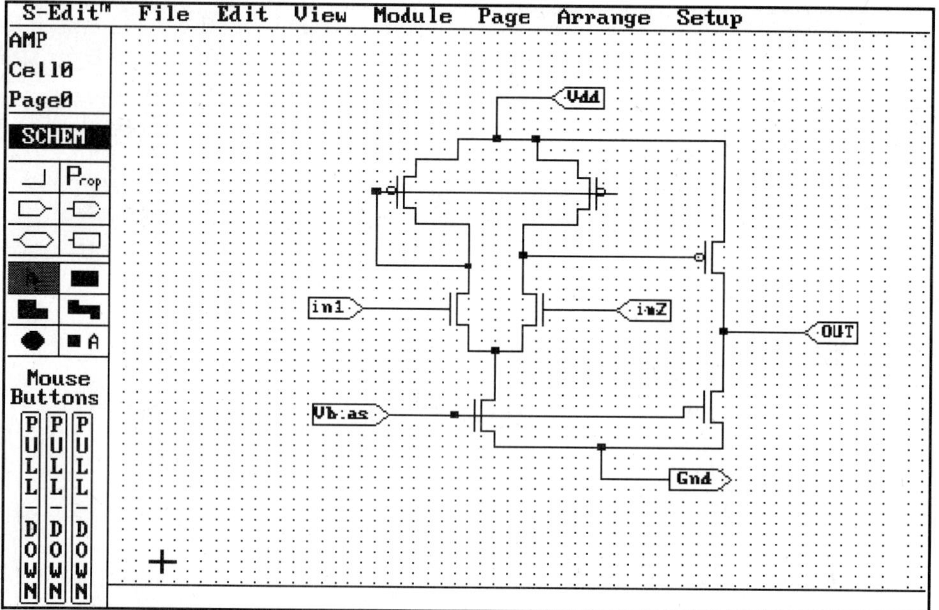

Figure 22-11
The operational amplifier circuit.

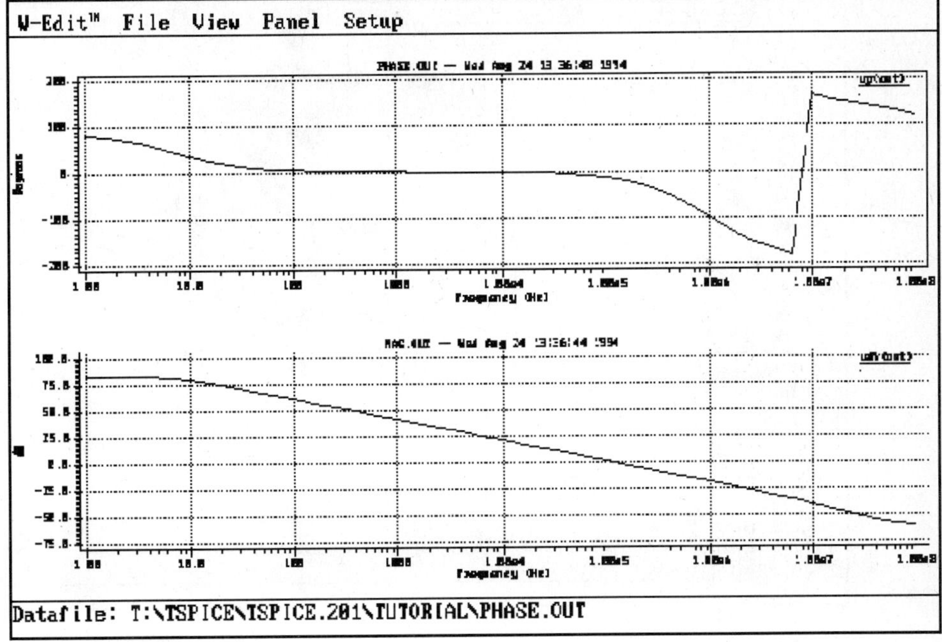

Figure 22-12
Generating magnitude and phase plots in T-Spice.

creation of a simple transistor. Figure 22-14 shows the same transistor viewed in cross section.

In this fashion we proceed to lay out the entire operational amplifier. The completed layout of the circuit is shown in Figure 22-15.

Verifying the Design

The next step in this full-custom design process is to verify the design. We use the DRC, Extract, and LVS tools to accomplish this. As mentioned in the previous example, DRC checks for geometry rule violations. In Tanner Tools Pro, the DRC is integrated within L-Edit and can be set up and run on-line.

To set up a DRC, we must define the set of rules corresponding to the fabrication process being used. The DRC is set up within L-Edit/DRC. First, each rule is given a meaningful name. Next, the type of rule is chosen and the corresponding layers and distances are defined. After running the DRC, violations are reported, both graphically and textually. Figure 22-16 illustrates the results of running the checker on the design after setting up DRC checks for field overlaps and distance checks. DRC such as the one shown can be view directly on the mask display, or can be written to a text file for later analysis.

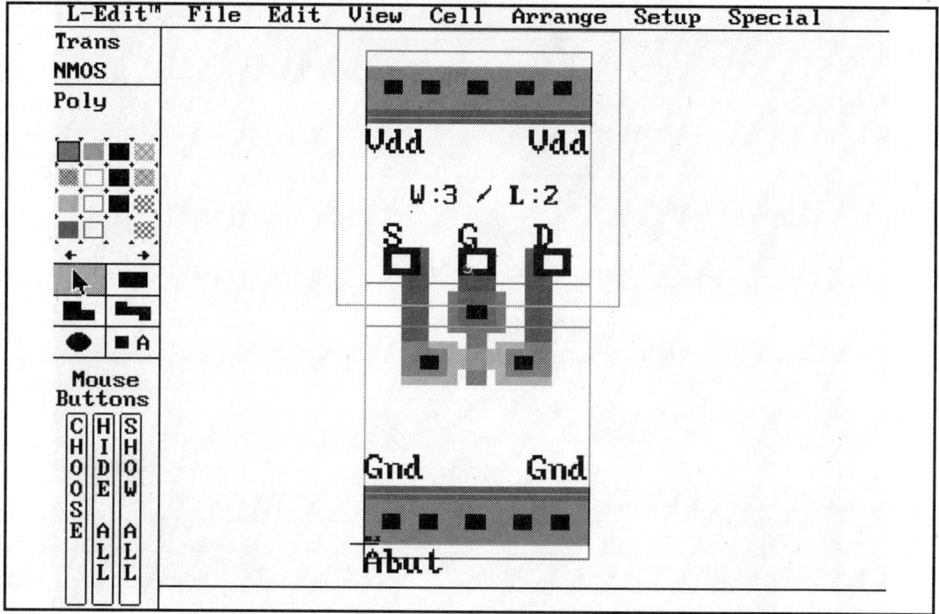

Figure 22-13
Mask design of a transistor.

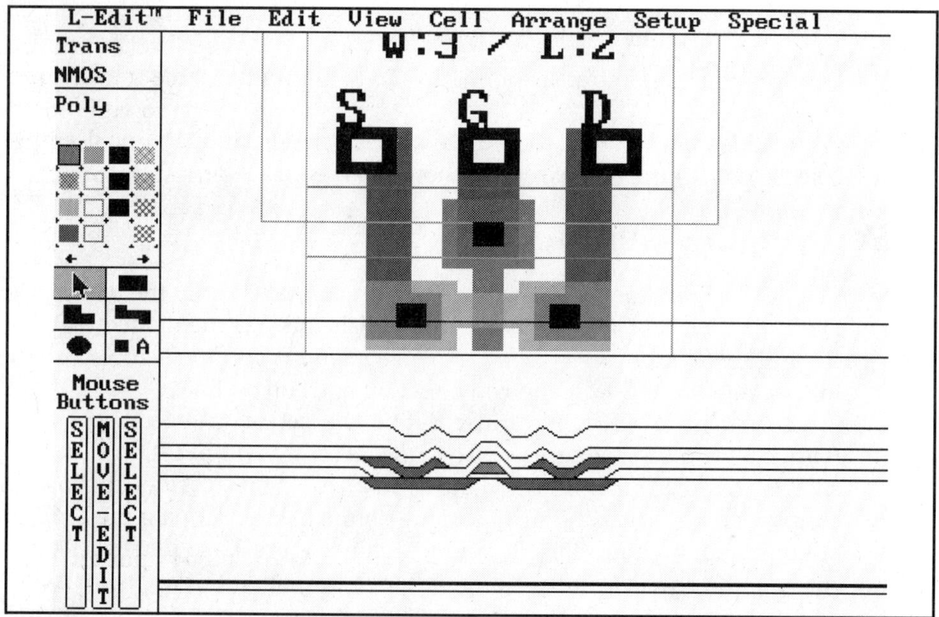

Figure 22-14
Cross section view of transistor.

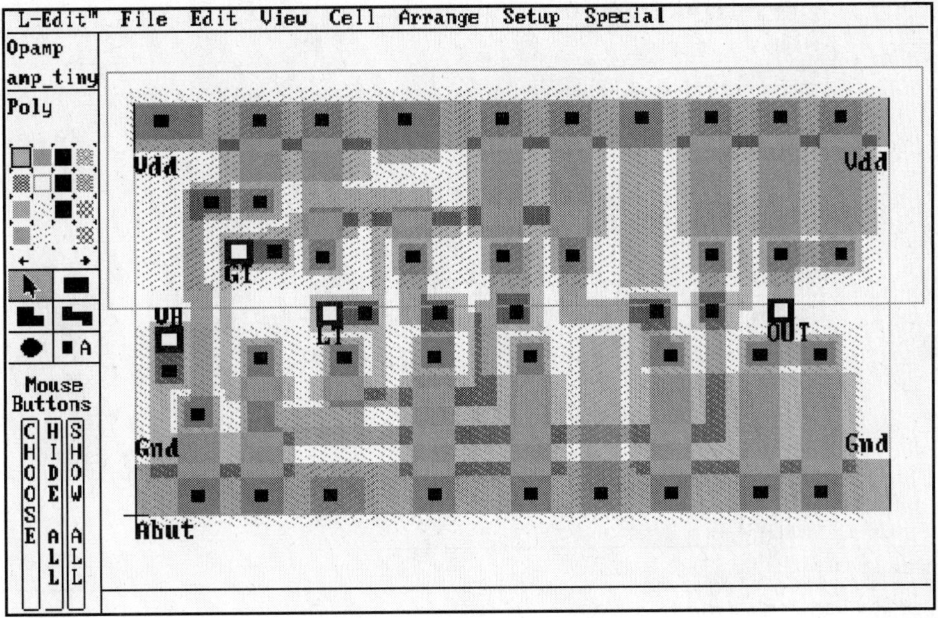

Figure 22-15
Operational amplifier layout.

Once the DRC errors are corrected, L-Edit/Extract is used to extract a SPICE netlist based on the layout. This SPICE netlist is subsequently used to simulate the layout and to compare it against a schematic-based netlist to verify the topology and the parameters. The L-Edit/Extract tool uses a definition file to derive the electrical devices and the connectivity from the geometrical description found in the layout. A portion of the extracted netlist is shown in Figure 22-17.

The extracted netlist can be simulated in T-Spice as before, and the LVS tool can be used to verify that it matches the original schematic.

Moving On

In this chapter, we have seen examples of the design methods and tools used in the creation of both standard cell and full-custom designs. We have also seen examples of both digital and analog circuits being implemented in ICs. Mixed-signal designs, those that include both digital and analog portions, can be created using the methods just described. In a mixed-signal design, the digital portion may be done using a standard cell approach while the analog portion is handcrafted.

The ASIC design process is somewhat different from the process of design using discrete components. There are new tricks to learn and a different set of tools and technology issues to be aware of. While explaining the complexity of a full-size

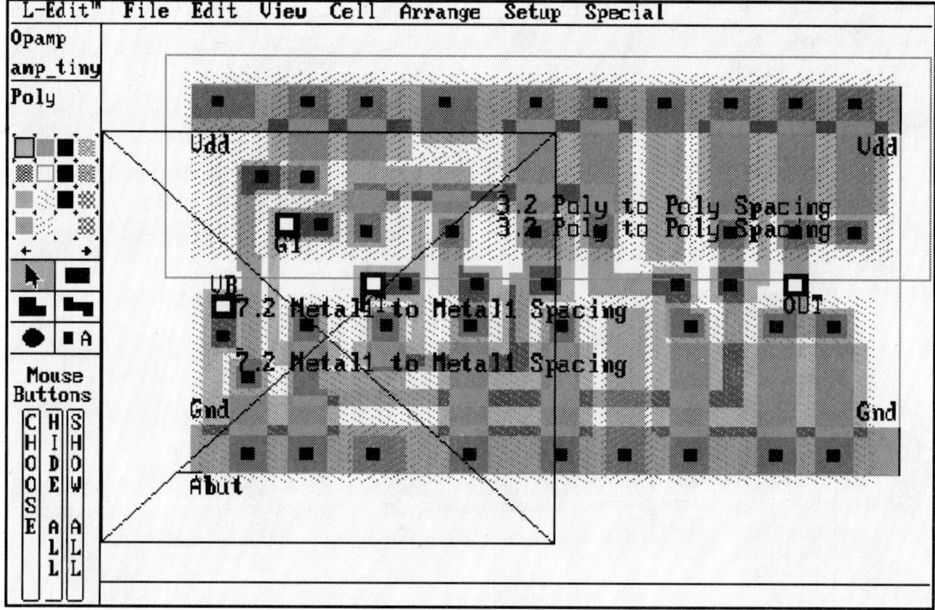

Figure 22-16
Viewing DRC errors.

```
* Circuit Extracted by Tanner Research's L-Edit V5.14 / Extract V2.06 ;
* TDB File trans, Cell NMOS, Extract Definition File morbn20.ext ;

.MODEL NMOS
.MODEL PMOS
.MODEL poly2NMOS
.MODEL poly2PMOS
.MODEL NPN
M1 15 14 16 8 NMOS L=2U W=3U
* M1 Drain Gate Source Bulk (11 24 13 27) A = 6, W = 3
* Total Nodes: 5 ;
* Total Elements: 1 ;
* Extract Elapsed Time: 0 seconds ;
.END
```

Figure 22-17
A portion of the extracted netlist.

ASIC design is beyond the scope of this book, you should now have a better understanding of the basic methods and design tools involved.

CHAPTER 23

FOCUS ON TECHNOLOGY: PCB LAYOUT

In electronic product marketing, there are two factors that never change: the product must be infinitely small, and it must be infinitely cheap to produce. In no area of electronics technology does this have a greater impact than in the area of interconnect design. Modern electronic systems, with their ever-increasing speeds and seemingly impossible physical contraints demand careful attention to factors such as manufacturability, testability, and reliability. All these factors come into play when taking a circuit concept—or a prototype circuit—and making it work full speed on a manufactured printed circuit board (PCB).

PCB layout is the most physical aspect of the circuit design process. At its simplest, layout involves finding space on the board for all the needed components and figuring out how to most efficiently make the connections between those components—how to *route* the board—to complete the circuit. At is most complex, the layout process can be a nightmare project, involving advanced theories of transmission line effects, capacitance, and thermal behavior.

There are many parallels between the art of ASIC design and the art of printed circuit board design. With boards operating at very high signal frequencies, the problems of signal interference and signal delay are very much the same sorts of problems faced by ASIC designers, and similar tools are often employed to solve these problems. In this chapter, we'll be examining some of the basic layout and routing tools available. (For information about signal integrity analysis tools, refer back to Chapter 9.)

The Language of PCB Layout

A printed circuit board seems, on the surface, to be a rather simple concept to understand. For the most part, every part of it appears visible to you (never mind the fact that there may be multiple layers), and there seems to be little magic required to create one. But the fact is, modern printed circuit boards, with their hundreds—or even thousands—of components, offer topological challenges that turn what appears to be a simple technician's job into a form of high art. Like every form of art (and high technology), PCB layout offers its own unique vocabulary. To help understand this language, let's take a quick look at what a "typical" printed circuit board is composed of.

Printed Circuit Board Materials

Most rigid printed circuit boards in use today are constructed out of thin sheets of epoxy-impregnated fiberglass alternated with layers of copper *traces* or *planes*. These copper conductive layers are created directly on the layers of nonconducting fiberglass through a photographic process similar to silkscreening or lithographic printing. As techniques for creating the copper traces have become more precise, it has been possible to create boards with traces that a separated by only small fractions of a millimeter (as little as .08 mm, at this writing). This density of signals, combined with increasingly small component *footprints* and *pin pitches* (the terms used to describe the amount of space—or *real estate*—required by a component, and how close together that component's leads are), has made it possible to create extremely dense circuits. This increased density, and the need to keep signal paths as short as possible for reasons of delay and capacitance, creates a need for creative ways of resolving problems in interconnect strategies—workarounds to use when a signal "just can't get there from here."

Multiple-Layer Boards

The most important method used to resolve routing conflicts on a board is to use multiple layers of copper traces. When *multiple-layer* boards are used, the board designer may alternate the predominant direction in which traces are created on each *signal layer*. On one layer, the traces may run primarily "north-south," while on the next layer they run "east-west." This strategy helps to reduce conflicts that occur when a signal needs to be routed between layers (using special conductive holes known as *vias*) and can also help to reduce parasitic effects that can effect the circuit's operation. A common way to reduce a multiple-layer board's vulnerability to external noise is to dedicate two or more copper layers (usually the center layers) as power and ground planes.

Multiple-layer boards would seem to be the best way to accomodate a very dense circuit with many interconnects. The trade-off, of course, is cost; the expense of producing a printed circuit board goes up dramatically as layers are added. If there are *buried vias* required to carry signals between the internal layers (without going through the entire board), the manufacturing process becomes even more complex, and the price rises accordingly. For this reason, designing a board that uses as few layers as possible can be of paramount importance.

Component Technology

The kind of board required for a circuit and the complexity of the routing are determined in large part by the number and types of components being used. If the components are of the traditional *through-hole* type (in which device or socket pins are inserted into holes in the board and soldered into place on the reverse side), then the routing method may be quite different than that required for a board populated—perhaps on both sides—with *surface-mount* components. Surface-mount components can dramatically reduce the cost of a printed circuit board (since there are fewer holes to drill), with the trade-off being a more expensive manufacturing process. (Surface-mount technology requires expensive and specialized manufacturing equipment that only pays off at high production volumes.)

Thermal Relief

Unless a board is going to be assembled (populated with components and soldered) by hand, it will need to be designed in such a way that the thermal stresses of wave soldering (or other form of automated assembly) do not cause the board to overheat, reducing the quality of the solder joints or, in the extreme case, causing the board to delaminate. The most common technique to control the heat distribution in a board during assembly is to incorporate specially designed copper areas called *thermal relief pads* into the design of the board. Thermal relief pads are most often added at the power and ground connections to help dissipate heat from the otherwise-insulated—and heat-absorbing—power and ground planes.

PCB Layout Tools

There are three basic types of computer-aided tools for PCB design: PCB layout editors (which are special-purpose schematic editors; see Figure 23-1), auto-routers (which help to determine an efficient routing path for all or part of a board), and signal integrity analysis tools (which were described in an earlier chapter).

Component Libraries

Just as in schematic editors, the value of a good PCB package is not reflected entirely in its drawing and graphics display features. The real value is found in the library of components the package supports. It doesn't matter how pretty the output of the package is, or how quickly you can create a complex routing or move a

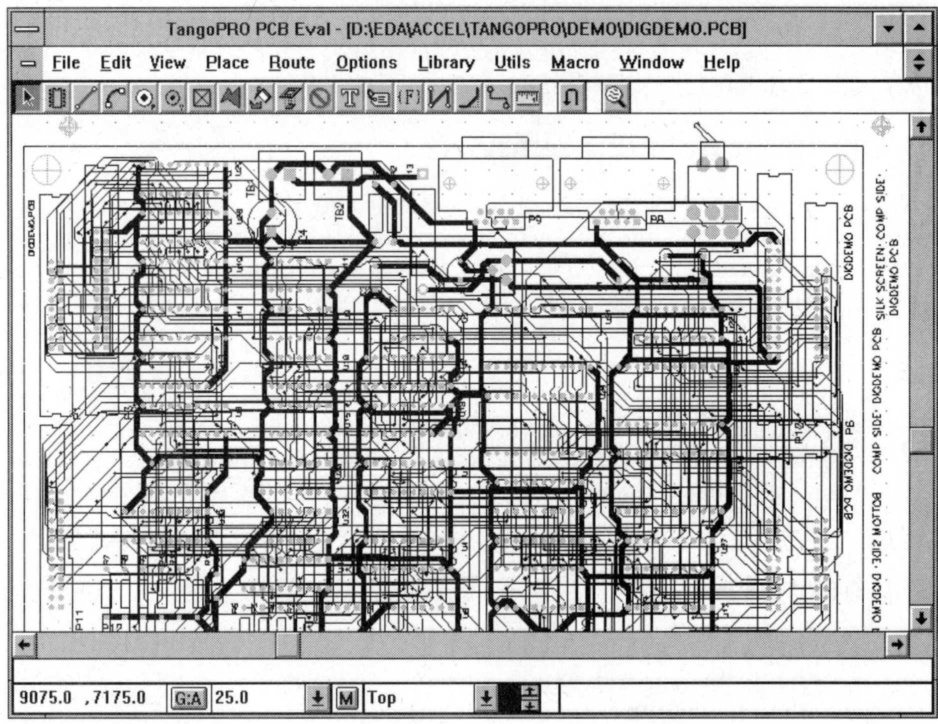

Figure 23-1
A PCB layout editor. (Accel's TangoPRO.)

component's location. If you don't have access to a comprehensive component library—one that includes all the component patterns you are likely to use—then you aren't going to get very far.

Output Format

For most board designs, the goal is to create a special type of file that can be given to a printed circuit board service bureau. The Gerber format is the most common format in use today, and is a photoplot representation of the masks used to screen each layer of the board.

Laying Out a Board

The first step in creating a board design is setting up the various parameters and options to be used during the place and route process. These parameters and options include such things as the unit of measure (eg. mils or millimeters), the number and types of layers, the line width, and various editing and display options that are specific to the board layout program being used.

The next step is to either create a design by placing components from the library, or by loading a netlist. Virtually all designs that you will be laying out will have been entered using a separate schematic capture package, so it is unlikely that you will ever need to use the manual method to select components. Instead, you will use your schematic capture package to produce a netlist that can be read by your PCB layout software. There are a variety of netlist formats in use today. Some of more common ones are the OrCAD netlist format, Tango-Schematic, Schema, ViewLogic and FutureNet. Most PCB layout tools can handle any of these netlist formats, so you can easily mix schematic and PCB design tools from different tool vendors.

When you first load a new netlist into a board layout program, the components are connected by straight lines in what is known as a *rat's nest*. The rat's nest represents the electrical connections between the components, and will be modified (either manually or automatically) during routing to create the final routed circuit. Figure 23-2 is an example of such a rat's net displayed in ACCEL's TangoPRO layout editor.

After the netlist has been loaded, you will begin moving the components into position on the board. Efficient placement of components is something of an art and involves factors such as manufacturability, noise and EMI considerations, and other considerations that are outside the scope of this brief description. Experienced board designers find visual cues such as those provided by a rat's nest useful in determing an initial placement, and in estimating where there may be later routing density problems.

Routing the Board

When you have determined an initial placement, you can move on to the next step: routing. To set up for routing, you will need to specify an initial number of layers, a placement grid to work within, the clearances between traces, the size of traces, and other impornant constraints. The options that you specify to the routing program (or that you specify to help with manual routing) will depend on many factors, such as the types of components being used (the pin pitches and other physical constraints), the speed at which the circuit will operate, and the manufacturing process being used for the actual board.

Most PCB layout software packages include a number of design rule checking (DRC) features, and you can use the design rule checking features to help ensure that the board is going to be manufacturable and that you don't miss connections while you create the routing.

To help with complex manual routes, most PCB layout programs include features such as

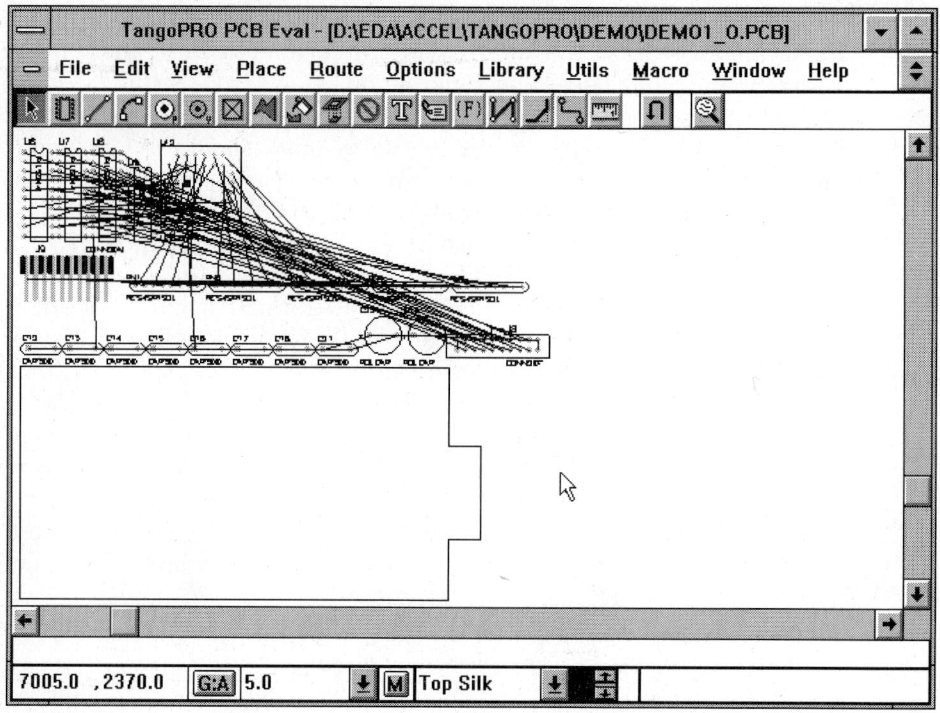

Figure 23-2
A rat's nest (prior to placement and routing).

- Automatic vias: When crossing an existing routing trace (a *blockage*), you will need to change layers. A board layout program with automatic vias will automatically create a via on the board to maintain connectivity across the layers.

- Backup and retry features: To back up and try another route, most layout programs provide a way to *unwind* multiple segments of a route, such as by repeatedly pressing the backspace key.

- Partial routes: Before reaching a destination pad, you may want to pause the current route, remove a blockage (by rerouting) and then continue the original routing. Partial routes allow you to leave a route only partially complete, so you can go back and complete it later.

- Arcs and mitres: For signal integrity, routing convenience, or unusual board geometries, it is often desirable to create arcs or mitred corners on routing traces. Most PCB layout tools provide a variety of features to simplify this task.

Connectivity and Design Rule Checking

Before going on to produce any board, it is important to use the connection and design rule checking features built into all modern board layout tools. Netlist comparison features, for example, are important because they verify that the connectivity of the original netlist matches that of the routed board. This comparison is an excellent way to quickly identify missing components, or connections, or uncover other basic placement and routing errors.

Design rule checking goes farther than simple netlist comparison, however, by actually applying a set of rules to the routed board to ensure that it meets specifications for routing clearance and has acceptable (and manufacturable) screened copper areas.

Creating the Artwork

When it comes time to actually produce a board, you need to output the board design as a series of artwork files. These files include photoplots, N/C drill files, and ink screens. While PCB layout tools differ in how these files are generated and managed, the resulting set of files is nearly identical, no matter which PCB design tool you have used.

Generating Gerber Format Files

Gerber format plotter files are a common way to produce high quality-output for board production. Some layout programs allow generated Gerber photoplots to be displayed superimposed over a board (Figure 23-3). Using this feature, it is easy to spot discrepencies in the output. These features allow you, if you wish, to import all of the Gerber files for a design to view a composite image of the entire board.

Automatic Board Routing

Automated board routing requires highly complex, computationally intensive software that is usually sold as an extra-cost option to printed circuit layout tools. The purpose of an automated routing system is to generate a complete (or nearly complete) routing implementation that meets specified constraints (trace clearances, "keep out" areas, and copper pour areas such as ground planes and thermal relief pads).

For very complex boards, it is unlikely that an automated routing program will be able to completely route the board. For this reason, the processes of component placement, hand routing and automatic routing are often performed in an iterative fashion, and having an integrated layout system that supports such iteration is important.

Automated routing software typical includes features such as

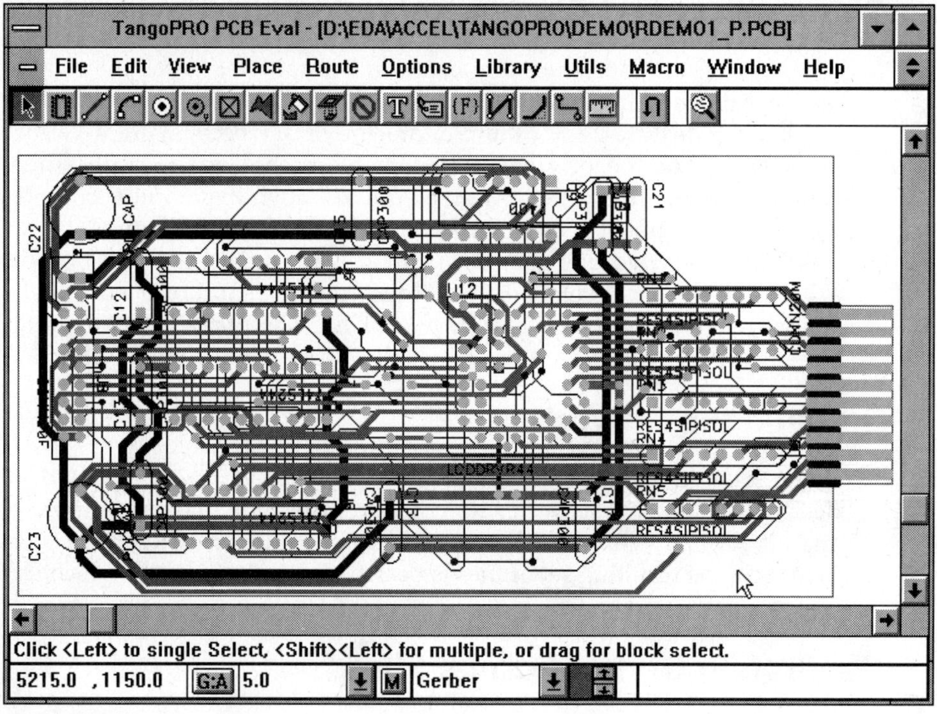

Figure 23-3
Viewing a Gerber file .(TangoPRO PCB.)

- User-definable keep-out areas and pre-routes
- Diagonal routing
- User-enabled blind and buried vias
- User-specified routing grids and spacings
- Special contraints for critical signals (nets)
- Special routing features for surface mount components
- Manufacturability features (e.g., reduced number of vias, trace spreading)
- Integration with manual placement and routing tools (for design iteration)
- Ability to suspend the routing process at any point to make manual edits
- Generation of backup files for restarting the autorouter

Moving On

PCB design and layout truly is an art, and its practitioners possess specialized skills, knowledge, and experience. In this chapter we have only skimmed the surface of the layout process and the tools that are available to help in this process.

Other Resources

Byers, T. J., *Printed Circuit Board Design with Microcomputers,* McGraw-Hill, New York, NY, 1991.

Capillo, Carmen, *Surface Mount Technology,* McGraw-Hill, New York, 1990.

Ginsberg, Gerald, *Printed Circuits Design,* McGraw-Hill, New York, 1991.

Ginsberg, Gerald, *Multichip Modules and Related Technologies,* McGraw-Hill, New York, 1994.

CHAPTER 24

SOME FINAL WORDS

If there is one idea that I have tried to get across in this book, it is this: EDA tools on personal computer platforms are becoming increasingly powerful, and are now competitive with similar tools offered on higher-priced engineering workstations. In surveying the kinds of tools now available, I hope I've made it easier for you to choose a set of tools to do your job, have helped you to ask the right questions of EDA vendors, and have helped you to make effective use of the tools you already have.

Before leaving, however, I would like to spend a moment examining the current trends in design tools.

Where Are EDA Tools Going?

If we look at the direction that EDA tools have been taking in the past decade, we see a continuous movement away from specific implementation issues and toward a higher level of design abstraction. Design tool developers are constantly working to remove the drudgery from the electronic design process and give the design engineer the power to work at the system level, rather than at the level of specific components or subcircuits. (A noble goal, but I did hear one design engineer moan that the newer tools were taking the "fun" out of design.)

There are some in the industry who feel that abstract design entry methods like VHDL and Verilog HDL will become the predominant method of design. While it does seem that these design languages are increasing in popularity, my feeling is that their use as a primary design representation will be rather short-lived. If we look at what has happed in the software development tools industry of late, we see development tools that are going a step beyond mere languages and are taking a more high-level, "component-based" view of the software design problem. If this can happen in software (a discipline with a long history of language-based design). then it is bound to happen in hardware as well. As such, I predict that electronic design automation tools will come full circle, and schematics (albeit much higher-level ones) will once again be the prefered form of design entry.

Have EDA Tools Shortened the Design Cycle?

Because the goal of EDA is to remove the "hard stuff" from the design process, it has often been claimed that EDA tools will dramatically reduce the time in which products are completed, will improve quality, and will make future design iterations even quicker. All this may be true when EDA tools are applied to an existing project, but such statements obscure an important fact: project development times are not actually getting any shorter. Why? Because the products and systems being developed are growing in complexity just as fast as (perhaps even faster then) the tools being created to support them. While it may be true, for example, that logic synthesis tools make it possible to create a 20,000 gate ASIC in a fraction of the time it would have taken a few years ago, it may also be true that that same product would now be obsolete, having been replaced by a product requiring the equivalent of a 100,000 gate ASIC.

The point I'm trying to make is that both the tools and the design requirements are moving ahead at a high speed, and it is foolhardy to think that all your design problems will be solved if you can just get the capital budget for new tools or can just get your hands on that next release of software.

If there is one truth in all this, it is that you need information about the tools that are out there to keep up with the fast pace of change. I hope this book and the companion CD-ROM have helped to provide some of that information.

APPENDIX A

EDA VENDOR DIRECTORY

This directory includes the names, addresses and phone numbers of a large number of EDA vendors. Information on each vendor has been obtained either by direct contact (in the form of a questionnaire) or from industry press accounts. Brief summaries of each vendor's company or product focus are also included. (Summaries written in quotes have been supplied by the vendors themselves.) The listings include vendors of Windows-based software products, as well as vendors that provide products only on workstation or other platforms.

Vendors that have supplied demonstration software or product information for inclusion on the companion CD-ROM are indicated with the following symbol:

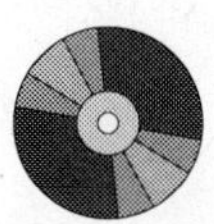

For information about specific products or services provided by these companies, and for the most up-to-date product information, you are encouraged to contact the vendors directly at the phone numbers or addresses shown.

Note *Many of the vendors listed in this directory maintain on-line services on CompuServe or the Internet and World Wide Web. Be sure to ask about such services, or check the resources listed in Appendix C for a starting point.*

Accel Technologies, Inc.

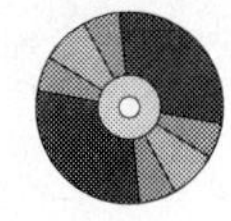

6825 Flanders Drive
San Diego, CA 92121-2986
(800) 488-0680
(619) 554-1000
(619) 554-1019 fax
sales@acceltech.com

- ☐ **TangoPRO Schematic**
- ☐ **TangoPRO PCB**
- ☐ **TangoPRO Route**

"ACCEL develops and sells a complete line of high-end, Windows-based software for schematic entry and PCB design. The TangoPRO line was introduced in 1993, and includes TangoPRO Schematic, TangoPRO PCB, TangoPRO Route, and interfaces to other popular CAE and CAD tools.

"ACCEL has been a leader in electronic design software since 1986. We built our Tango design tools for engineering professionals emphasizing innovation, excellence, and exceptional value. Our customer service and technical support groups are staffed with knowledgable professionals. ACCEL is also committed to research and development. Each release is well documented, rigorously tested, and backed by an unconditional money-back guarantee."

ACEO Technology

Fremont, CA
(510) 656-2189

- ☐ **Asyn**

ACEO develops and markets EDA tools that include the Asyn Verilog HDL synthesis product. ACEO tools operate on Sun workstations.

Actel Corporation

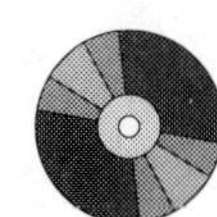

955 East Arques Avenue
Sunnyvale, CA 94086
(408) 739-1010
(408) 739-1540 fax

- ☐ **ACT Series FPGAs**

☐ Designer Series FPGA Software

"Actel Corporation is a leading supplier of high-performance field programmable gate arrays (FPGAs) and currently provides the dominant antifuse-based architecture in the FPGA market. As a Sunnyvale-based startup in 1988, Actel was the first company to successfully develop and manufacture and antifuse based FPGA, enabling its products to surpass the performance, density and cost-per-gate of existing memory-based FPGAs. Actel's product line consists of the ACT 1, ACT 2 and ACT 3 FPGA families with devices spanning the density between 1,200 and 10,000 gates.

"Actel offers the Designer and Designer Advantage Development Systems for the design and implementation of its FPGAs. The Development Systems offer links to today's popular EDA environments. Development systems are available that interface to Cadence Design Systems, Mentor Graphics, OrCAD, and Viewlogic EDA tools. Additionally, synthesis support is available for Cadence Design Systems, Exemplar Logic, Mentor Graphics, Synopsys and Viewlogic synthesis products."

Acugen Software, Inc.

427-3 Amherst St.
Suite 391
Nashua, NH 03603
(603) 881-8821
(603) 881-8906 fax

☐ ATGEN

☐ SHARPEYE

"Designing with or testing devices such as Actel's ACT, AMD's MACH, Altera's MAX and FLEX, Xilinx LCAs, Lattice pLSI and ispLSI or most popular PLDs? Consider ACUGEN Software's ATGEN test generation and/or SHARPEYE testability analysis software products. These products automatically generate test vectors or testability reports for an extensive library of devices. Translators to most automated test equipment (ATE) are also available."

Advanced Microcomputer Systems

1460 SW 3rd Street
Pompano Beach, FL 33069
(800) 972-3733
(305) 784-0904 fax

- ☐ **EZ-Route**

Advanced Microcomputer Systems is a personal computer peripheral supplier that also offers a software package, EZ-Route, for printed circuit board layout.

Advanced Micro Devices, Inc

One AMD Place
P.O. Box 3453
Sunnyvale, CA 94088-3453
(408) 732-2400
(800) 222-9323

- ☐ **PAL® Programmable Logic Devices**
- ☐ **MACH Series PLDs**
- ☐ **PALASM 4 Software**
- ☐ **MACHXL Software**

Advanced Micro Devices, Inc. (AMD), produces a wide range of bipolar and CMOS programmable logic devices, including the widely used PAL devices, and the MACH family of complex PLDs (CPLDs).

Agape Design Automation

528 Weddell Drive, Suite #3
Sunnyvale, CA 94089
(408) 745-6785
(408) 745-6783
mycad@netcom.com

- ☐ **MyCAD**
- ☐ **MyLogic**
- ☐ **MySPICE**
- ☐ **MyChip**

Agape Design Automation produces low-cost solutions for design entry and IC layout.

Alta Group

919 East Hillsdale Blvd.
Foster City, CA 94404
(415) 574-5800
(415) 358-3601 fax

- ☐ **BONeS™**
- ☐ **SPW™**
- ☐ **HDS™**
- ☐ **Race™**
- ☐ **Reveal™**

"The Alta Group is the leading supplier of ESDA solutions, focusing on wireless communications, networking, and multimedia applications. Alta's products include system-level simulators and graphical entry tools, and are customized to specific applications with specialized libraries and interactive analysis."

Altera Corporation

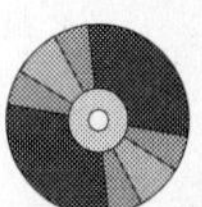

2610 Orchard Parkway
San Jose, CA 95134-2020
(800) 767-3753
(408) 428-9220 fax

- ☐ **MAX, FLEX Programmable Devices**
- ☐ **MAX+PLUS II Software**

"Altera Corporation, founded in 1983, is a world-wide leader in high-performance, high-density programmable logic devices and associated computer-aided engineering logic development tools. Programmable logic devices are semiconductor chips that offer on-site programmability to customers. User benefits include ease-of-use, lower-risk, and fast time-to-market. The Company offers the broadest line of CMOS programmable logic devices that address high-speed, high-density, and lower power application. Altera products serve a broad range of market areas, including telecommunications, data communications, computers, and industrial applications."

Altium

One Almaden Blvd.
Suite 1200
San Jose, CA 95113
(800) 255-5710
(408) 266-4189
(408) 534-4189 fax

- ☐ **LogicBench™**
- ☐ **TestBench™**
- ☐ **ChipBench™**
- ☐ **Wizard™ Design Entry**
- ☐ **BooleDozer™ Synthesis**
- ☐ **AUSSIM™ Simulation**

Altium (IBM EDA) brings to market IBM's extensive suite of EDA tools. These tools are intended for the design of highly complex, leading-edge integrated circuits, and include top-down design, test pattern generation, ASIC layout editors, and static timing analyzers.

American Microsystems, Incorporated (AMI)

1651 Alvin Ricken Drive
Pocatello, ID 83201

- ☐ **PEEL™ Programmable Logic Devices**
- ☐ **PEEL Development Software**
- ☐ **PLACE Software**

AMI produces the popular PEEL electrically reconfigurable PLDs and offers development software for PLD users.

ANACAD

Milpitas, CA
(408) 954-0600

- ☐ **HDL-A™ Analog Simulation**

☐ VHDeLDO™ Mixed-Signal Simulator

☐ VEReLDO™ Mixed-Signal Simulator

ANACAD develops and markets systems for HDL-based analog simulation.

Annapolis Micro Systems, Inc.

190 Admiral Cochrane Drive
Suite 130
Annapolis, MD 21401-7386
410-841-2514
410-841-2518 fax

Analogy, Inc.

Beaverton, OR
(503) 626-9700

☐ Saber Simulator

Analogy offers high-performance mixed-signal simulation tools that operate on engineering workstations (DEC, HP, Sun, IBM).

AnalySYS, Inc.

25 Loiselle St.
Suite 201
Embrun, ON
CANADA KOA 1W1
(603) 443-0428

☐ VMK

AnalySYS produces VMK, a productivity-enhancing tool for VHDL model developers. VMK integrates with Model Technology's V-System Simulator and Mentor's QuickVHDL and System 1076 VHDL simulators and adds "makefile" capabilities for design processing.

Ansoft Corporation

4 Station Square
Suite 660
Pittsburgh, PA 15219
(412) 261-3200
(412) 471-9427 fax
info@ansoft.com

☐ Maxwell® SI Field Simulator

"Ansoft's Maxwell® Field Simulators let design engineers building motors, transformers, relays, and other electrical equipment simulate product performance quickly and accurately—saving time, money, and market share.

"Maxwell 3D Field Simulator is a dedicated simulation tool for electromechanical, high-voltage, and magnetic applications. Based on Ansoft's Maxwell finite-element technology for electromagnetics, this product offers 2D, axisymmetric, and full 3D modeling for electrical and magnetic field applications. Aimed at electrical engineering applications, the simulator includes a specialized mesh-building system that renders the FEA process completely transparent to the user. The Maxwell 3D Field Simulator can link to solid model files generated in SDRC I-DEAS, Parametric Technology's ProEngineer, EDS' Unigraphics, and others."

APSI

Tuscon, AX
(602) 577-8886
(800) 975-2774

☐ Aztec

☐ APLGRL

APSI produces tools for signal integrity analysis. The Aztec series of products operate only on Sun workstations, while the APLGRL product is also available on 386/486/Pentium platforms.

Atmel

2125 O'Nel Drive
San Jose, CA 95131
(408) 441-0311
(408) 436-4200 fax

- ☐ **Programmable Logic Devices**
- ☐ **Atmel-ABEL**
- ☐ **Atmel-CUPL**
- ☐ **Atmel-ViewPLD**

Atmel is a producer of complex and in-circuit reprogrammable PLDs, and offers PLD development software tightly integrated with products offerered by major vendors of universal PLD tools.

AT&T Microelectronics

555 Union Blvd.
Allentown, PA 18103
(800) 372-2447
(620) 712-4085 fax

- ☐ **ORCA™ FPGA Devices**
- ☐ **ORCA Development System (ODS)**

"High-performance cell libraries to innovative ORCA FPGAs, AT&T Microelectronics offers an unparalleled mix of products, technology, and support to provide powerful, cost-effective ASIC solutions."

AT&T Design Automation

600 Mountain Ave.
Rm. 3B-414
Murray Hill, NJ 07974
(800) 875-6590
(908) 582-5145

- ☐ **ATTSIM**
- ☐ **ATTDFT**
- ☐ **Synovation**

"AT&T Design Automation is a leading producer of electronic design automation software for high performance integrated circuits and systems. Products offered today are primarily in simulation, synthesis and design for testability."

Attest Software

4677 Old Ironsides Drive
Suite 100
Santa Clara, CA 95054
(800) 982-0244
(408) 982-0248 fax
info@attest.com

☐ Tdx Testability Analysis Tools

"TDX is a high-performance, interactive fault simulation and automatic test generation software system for VHDL. Testability analysis and Iddq test software are also available.

"The software is built around a high performance concurrent fault simulator accurate on a wide range of state and timing sensitive circuits. It supports synchronous and asynchronous designs containing logic gates, MOS transistors, tri-state buffers, flip-flops, single/multi-port RAMs, and complex bus resolution functions. The software also supports the detailed pin timing and strobing features found on "tester-per-pin" automatic test equipment.

"Demo software is available via anonymous ftp. General-use licenses can be provided free to accredited universities for educational purposes. The demo software is functional on small circuits, and is also fully functional on the GL85 microprocessor circuit (an 8085 clone) included with the suite of tools. The software is available by ftp at the location **ftp.netcom.com** in the **/pub/at/attest** directory."

Automata Publishing

San Jose, CA
(408) 255-0705

☐ Viper Verilog HDL Simulator

☐ Book and Simulator Package

Automata Publishing destributes low-cost, PC-based Verilog HDL simulation products and training materials.

Automated Logic Design Company, Inc. (ALDEC)

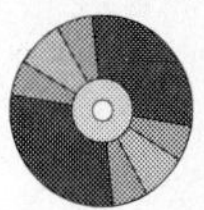

3525 Old Conejo Road, Suite 111
Newbury Park, CA 91320
(805) 499-6867
(800) 48-SUSIE
(805) 498-7945 fax
(805) 498-4086 bbs

- ☐ **ACTIVE-CAD™**
- ☐ **SUSIE-CAD™**

"Low-cost SUSIE-CAD CAE tools provide a complete design environment for PLD, CPLD and FPGA devices. SUSIE-CAD includes the Schematic Editor with an on-line Logic Simulator, Design Manager, Symbol Editor, Waveform Editor and Library Manager. The Design Manager integrates the SUSIE-CAD software with the IC vendor layout tools and provides seamless design file transfer. Patented incremental compilation allows the user to make changes on the schematic and simulate without recompiling the schematic netlist. Back annotated simulation results are displayed directoy on the schematic. VHDL and Equation design entry are optional. SUSIE-CAD can be upgraded to a system-level design environment that includes MPUs, memories, TTL, CMOS and other libraries."

Beige Bag Software

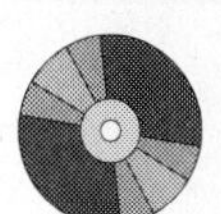

2000 Hogback Road, Suite 2
Ann Arbor, MI 48105
(313) 971-4227
(313) 971-3632 fax

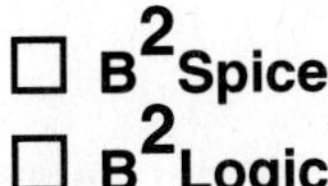

- ☐ **B^{2}Spice**
- ☐ **B^{2}Logic**

"In 1990 Beige Bag Software was founded to create software that would be both affordable and essential to engineering students, engineering faculty, and professional engineers. Since then, Beige Bag Software has developed low-cost and easy-to-use digital and analog circuit simulation programs that fulfill this purpose. Currently, over 100 major universities, over 30 Fortune 500 companies, as well as other engineering firms and hobbyists use Beige Bag products.

"B^{2}Logic and B^{2}Spice are affordable, user friendly circuit design and simulation tools for the Macintosh and Windows platforms. B^{2}Logic provides over 100 components for digital circuit designs. The user views simulation results by probing signals in the schematic and in a timing diagram. B^{2}Spice provides most

Spice components and supports Transient, AC and DC analyses. Simulation results may be graphed or tabulated. B^2 Logic is a digital simulator that boasts EDIF format output, enhanced PLD simulation capabilities, and much more."

CAD Artisans

Escondido, CA
(619) 739-1845

- ☐ **AuSIM-VX VHDL Simulator**

CAD Artisans produces VHDL design entry and simulation tools that operate on a wide variety of engineering workstations.

Cadence Design Systems

555 River Oaks Parkway
San Jose, CA 95134
(408) 943-1234
(800) 746-6223
(408) 943-0513

- ☐ **Verilog-XL Simulation**
- ☐ **Leapfrog™ VHDL Simulation**
- ☐ **Veritime™ Timing Analysis**
- ☐ **Synergy™ Synthesis**
- ☐ **Composer™ Design Entry**
- ☐ **Concept™ Design Entry**

"Cadence Design Systems, Inc. is the worldwide leader in the development and marketing of design automation software and services that accelerate and advance the process of designing electronic systems. Cadence combines leading-edge technology with a complementary set of services that enable customers to improve the quality and time-to-market performance of innovative electronic products."

Cad-Migos Software Tools, Inc.

1975 Fernside Street
Redwood City, CA 94061
(415) 369-5853 voice/fax

☐ SPICE-IT!™ For Windows™

"CAD-Migos Software Tools, Inc. is a California corporation dedicated to developing, marketing, and distributing affordable advanced engineering software tools (EDA/CAE/CAD) for the product design and development fields. The current 'populations' of workstation platforms in these fields have guided the company to develop tools for the high-end PC-compatible workstation utilizing the extremely popular Microsoft Windows™ user interface as their desktop environment."

SPICE-IT!TM for Windows™ v1.0 is a powerful, integrated electronic circuit design and simulation system. This CAE tool package includes full-featured design entry tools, interactive circuit debugging, extensive device model libraries and enhanced plotting features. Our electronic design and engineering system, THE WHOLE ENCHILADA™ for Windows v1.0 (which includes SPICE-IT! for Windows) provides a graphical logic simulator, interactive and fully automatic PCB layout tools, post-processing utilities and thermal analysis tools."

CAESIUM, Inc.

Santa Clara, CA
(408) 248-4603

☐ Model Libraries

Capilano Computing

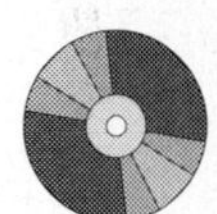

960 Quayside Drive, Suite 406
New Westminster, B.C.
Canada V3M 6G2
(604) 522-6200
(800) 444-9064
(604) 522-3972 fax

☐ DesignWorks™ for Windows

"DesignWorks™ for Windows is the most powerful and easy to use Windows-based schematic entry package on the market, featuring:

- ☐ Advanced schematic editing with bussing, hierarchy, integrated symbol editing, error checking, text attributes, etc.
- ☐ Optional digital logic simulation with completely interactive operation; presents a 'live' circuit on the screen that responds immediately to connection, input and parameter changes.

- ☐ Libraries of thousands of standard logic and analog devices.
- ☐ Netlist and back-annotation interfaces to most popular PCB systems.
- ☐ Powerful custom report generation for netlists, bills of materials, etc.
- ☐ Imports schematics from OrCAD™, FutureNet™ and EDIF."

Cascade Design Automation

Bellevue, WA
(800) 258-8574

☐ Epoch™ High Level Physical Design™ System

Cascade Design Automation offers physical design tools that accept VHDL, Verilog or schematic input and generate VHDL gate-level output with accurate timing. Epoch includes a library of models for standard-cell and parameterized components such as memories and datapath elements. An interface to the Synopsys Design Compiler is available. Epoch software is available for engineering workstation platforms.

Chip Express

2903 Bunker Hill Lane
Suite 105
Santa Clara, CA 95054
(408) 988-2445
(408) 988-2449 fax

☐ Laser Programmed Gate Arrays

Chip Express offers laser-programmed gate arrays (LPGAs) with 24-hour turnaround. LPGAs provide up to 45,000 gates, 300 I/Os, and 460 MHz speeds and are a practical alternative to large (and more expensive) FPGAs or low-end mask-programmed gate arrays.

Chronologic Simulation

(800) 837-4564
(415) 965-2705
info@chronologic.com

☐ VCS Simulator

Chronologic Simulation produces the high-performance VCS Verilog HDL simulator. Chronologic Simulation is a Viewlogic company.

Chronology Corporation

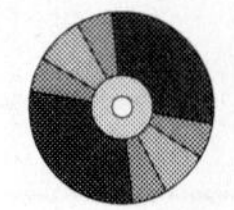

17411 NE Union Hill Road
Suite 100
Redmond, WA 98052
(206) 869-4227
(800) 800-6494
(206) 869-4229 fax
sales@chronology.com

☐ Timing Designer™

"Interactive Timing Analysis
Over 10,000 engineers now use TimingDesigner® — the state-of-the-art software that accurately models, analyzes, and documents digital circuit timing. TimingDesigner is the best way to create and analyze timing diagrams, compute worst-case timing margins, instantly see the effects of design tradeoffs, andlyze the interface between complex chips, visualize timing relationships in complex clock trees, and communicate timing specifications. Netlists and test vectors aren't needed. Used with all types of designs, at all stages of designs. Several editions and platforms are available. Call for a free demo — (800) 800-6494."

Chrysalis Symbolic Design

100 Burtt Road
Andover, MA 01810
(508) 475-7700
(508) 475-7745 fax
info@chrysalis.com

☐ Design Verifyer™

Chrysalis provides tools that perform formal verification of RTL and gate-level design descriptions to their previously verified functional equivalents. The Chrysalis tools read both VHDL and Verilog hardware description languages.

CINA, Inc.

P.O. Box 4872
Mountain View, CA 94040
(415) 940-1723

☐ **SmartCAT**

CINA's SmartCAT is a design tool that looks for logic and testability errors in combinational logic circuits.

Compass Design Automation

San Jose, CA
(408) 433-4880

☐ **ASIC Navigator**

☐ **ASIC Synthesizer**

☐ **VHDL Scout**

Compass Design Automation produces design tools intended for ASIC development. The synthesis and simulation tools include support for both VHDL and Verilog HDL. Compass tools are available on engineering workstations including DEC, HP, Sun, and IBM.

CONTEC Microelectronics USA

San Jose, CA
(408) 434-6767

☐ **ContecSI**

☐ **ContecRADIA**

☐ **ContecPLANE**

☐ **ContecSPICE**

CONTEC Microelectronics supplies SPICE-based simulation and signal integrity analysis tools that operate on workstation and PC platforms.

Cooper & Chyan Technology, Inc.

1601 Saratoga-Sunnyvale Road
Suite 255
Cupertino, CA 95014
(408) 366-6966

- ☐ **EditRoute**
- ☐ **AutoPlace**
- ☐ **AutoRoute**

Cooper & Chyan Technology specializes in high-performance tools for printed circuit board layout and automatic placement and routing.

Cypress Semiconductor

3901 North First Street
San Jose, CA 95134
(408) 943-2600
(800) 858-1810
(408) 943-4897 fax

- ☐ **Cypress Programmable Logic Devices**
- ☐ **Warp 2™ VHDL Design Software**
- ☐ **Warp 3™ VHDL Design Software**

Cypress Semiconductor produces a wide range of programmable logic devices and offers VHDL-based software for synthesis and simulation of those devices. The software is available on Sun workstations and PCs.

Data I/O Corporation

10525 Willows Road NE
P.O. Box 97046
Redmond, WA 98073-9746
(206) 881-6444
(800) 426-1045
(206) 882-1043 fax
corpsales@data-io.com

- ☐ **ABEL-6 PLD Design Software**

- ☐ **Synario™ Design System**
- ☐ **ECS Schematic Capture For Windows**
- ☐ **V-System VHDL Simulator**
- ☐ **FPGA Vendor Place and Route Tools**
- ☐ **Open-ABEL™ CPLD FItters**

"Data I/O is a 21 year old publicly traded company (DAIO - NASDAQ) that specializes in solutions for users of programmable integrated circuits. Data I/O is focused on three main areas:

1. Manufacturing programming solutions for customers who need to program high volumes of devices at the lowest possible cost per device.

2. Engineering programming solutions intended for design teams needing to program the latest devices during the development of leading-edge electronic products.

3. Windows™-based EDA tools supporting the broad range of design activities required to complete a complex electronic product.

Data I/O's unique approach of using experienced FPGA and CPLD designers to architect the products results in design tools that operate intuitively and truly increase the productivity of hardware design engineers."

Design Acceleration

San Jose, CA
(408) 559-8500

- ☐ **Signalscan**

Design Acceleration supplies an analog/digital waveform display system compatible with Verilog, EPIC, and HSPICE simulators. The software is available for workstation and Windows PC platforms.

Deutsch Technology Research

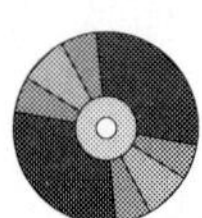

5150 El Camino Real
Suite D-15
Los Altos, CA 94022
(415) 390-8510
(415) 390-8513 fax

☐ SPICEWindows

Deutsch Technology Research offers high-performance SPICE0-based analog simulation products, including the SPICEWindows professional simulator.

dQdt

5962 La Place Court
Suite 201
Carlsbad, CA 92008
(619) 929-9250
(619) 929-0280
info@dqdt.com

☐ DSP ASIC Libraries

"DQDT has developed an advanced, top-down VHDL-based DSP ASIC design methodology which cuts industry standard design times in half. This methodology is being made available both as a design service and as libraries of DSP VHDL models and cores."

Dynamic Soft Analysis, Inc.

Pittsburgh, PA
(412) 683-0161

☐ BETAsoft-Master

Dynamic Soft Analysis develops and sells software for the thermal analysis of systems, boards, and components.

Engineerium

San Diego, CA
(619) 292-1900

☐ dV/dt Timing Diagram Accelerator

Engineering produces the dV/dt timing diagram analysis product.

Escalade

1210 E. Arques Ave.
Sunnyvale, CA 94086
(408) 481-1308
(408) 481-1313 fax

Esperan

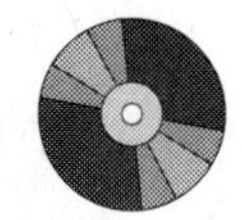

Unit 1, Hilldrop Lane
Ramsbury, Wilts SN8 2RB
England
+44 672 20101
+44 672 21039 fax

- ☐ **VHDL Language Training**
- ☐ **MasterClass Multimedia VHDL Tutorial**

"Esperan is an independent company specializing in training and education for engineers who use high-level design techniques. We offer many different courses and seminars on VHDL related topics, covering both the language and its application in a wide range of areas such as system-level modeling, ASIC and FPGA synthesis."

Our MasterClass multimedia tutorial series is designed for a new VHDL user, and covers the VHDL constructs most commonly used in RTL code, as well as discussing how coding styles influence synthesis results."

Evaluations Per Second, Inc.

Waltham, MA
(617) 487-9959

- ☐ **SIMETRI-FX**
- ☐ **SIMETRI-LX**

Evaluations Per Second offers high-performance Verilog-compatible simulators for workstation (Sun, HP) platforms.

Exemplar Logic

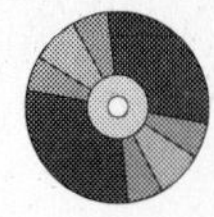

2550 Ninth Street, Suite 102
Berkeley, CA 94710
(510) 849-0937
(510) 849-9935 fax
info@exemplar.com

☐ CORE Synthesis

Exemplar Logic provides synthesis tools for complex PLD, FPGA and gate array design. The tools support a variety of input formats, including VHDL and Verilog HDL.

Fintronic USA, Inc.

1360 Willow Road
Suite 205
Menlo Park, CA 94025
(415) 325-4474
(415) 578-0260 fax

☐ FinSim™ Verilog Simulator

☐ FinVA™/FinUA™ Verilog Analyzers

Fintronic USA offers a variety of Verilog-related tools, including the FinSim family of workstation and PC-based simulators.

Frontline Design Automation

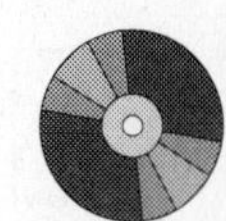

2860 Zanker Road
Suite 203
San Jose, CA 95134
(408) 456-0222
(408) 456-0265 fax

☐ BaseLine Simulator

☐ SimLine ASIC Simulator

"FrontLine is focused on delivering leading edge digital simulation products on both the PC and Unix platforms. BaseLine, the FrontLine offering on the PC, targets the fast-growing FPGA marketplace. BaseLine provides a full-featured, high-compatibility, Verilog simulation environment to handle the largest of FPGAs being designed today. SimLine, FrontLine's high end offering, runs on Unix platforms and targets designers of advanced ASICs."

Harris EDA

7796 Victor-Mendon Road
Fishers, NY 14453
(716) 924-9303
(716) 924-4729

- ☐ **EDAnavigator**
- ☐ **EDAvalidator**
- ☐ **EDAassimilator**
- ☐ **FINESS MCM**

"Harris EDA offers fully integrated software for the design-through-manufacture of PCBs, MCMs and hybrid ICs. Client-server architecture and object-oriented technologies provide integation with existing environments."

High Level Design Systems

3945 Freedom Circle, 4th Floor
Santa Clara, CA 95054
(408) 748-3456
(408) 748-3499
info@hlds.com

- ☐ **Logic DP™**
- ☐ **Physical DP™**

"High Level Design Systems is the leading supplier of design planning tools for submicron IC design."

HP-EEsof, Inc.

5601 Lindero Canyon Road
Westlake Village, CA 91362-4020
(818) 879-6200
(800) 343-3763
(818) 879-6467 fax

☐ HP Momentum

☐ HP Impulse

☐ HP Microwave Design System

Hyperception

9550 Skillman LB125
Dallas, TX 75243-8250
(214) 343-8525
(214) 343-2457 fax
(214) 343-4108 bbs
info@hyperception.com

☐ Hypersignal® for Windows

"The Hypersignal® for Windows RT-4 software package provides an integrated digital signal processing (DSP) design environment for the simulation and implementation of DSP-based products. Block Diagram, a key component of RT-4, is a real-time visual programming application in which designs can be created by connecting functional block icons and selecting operational parameters. A block diagram can be simulated on the host PC or executed real-time on one of several supported DSP boards. The C Code Generator application provides the source code for complete DSP designs that can be cross-compiled for a specific DSP. RT-4 provides an excellent rapid-prototyping and product design tool that dramatically reduces the cost and technical risk that is typically associated with DSP development projects."

HyperLynx

Redmond, WA
(206) 869-2320
(206) 881-1008 fax

☐ LineSim Pro

☐ BoardSim

HyperLynx offers signal integrity analysis software for single-wire, full-board, multiboard, and MCM applications. HyperLynx products are available on DOS and Windows PC platforms.

IKOS Systems

19050 Pruneridge Avenue
Cupertino, CA 95014
(800) 223-3987
(408) 366-8689 fax
events@ikos.com

- ☐ **Voyager-VS**
- ☐ **Voyager-CS**
- ☐ **Voyager-CSX**

"IKOS Systems is a technology leader in high-performance, mixed-level hardware and software simulation for VHDL-based high-level design. The company's Voyager® Series products help designers dramatically reduce the design cycle for very complex, high-performance systems containing multiple ASICs and full-custom ICs."

i-Logix, Inc.

Three Riverside Drive
Andover Park, MA 01810
(508) 682-2100
(508) 682-5995 fax

- ☐ **ExpressV-HDL**

i-Logix develops and markets software tools for high-level VHDL and mixed-signal design. ExpressV-HDL is a front-end to traditional electronic design automation tools and provides engineers with a graphical design environment for behavioral simulation.

Innovative Software Design, Inc.

Two English Elm Court
Baltimore, MD 21228
(410) 788-9000
(410) 788-9001 fax

- ☐ **Relex Reliability Software**

"Innovative Software Designs produces the highly-acclaimed Relex Reliability Software. Available for Windows, Macintosh, and DOS, Relex aids the user in evaluating and improving the reliability of electronic and mechanical products. Features of Relex include CAD interfaces, system modeling, parts libraries and scientific graphics."

Innovative Synthesis Technologies (IST)

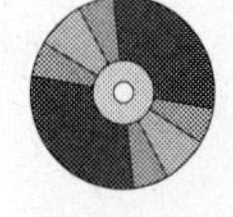

4, Place Robert Schuman
Grenoble, Isere 38000
France
(33) 76 70 5100
(33) 76 84 1261 fax

P.O. Box 1897
Danville, CA 94526
(510) 736-2302
(510) 736-6199 fax

☐ ASYL+ VHDL Synthesis

The ASYL+ VHDL synthesis system is intended primarily for control-dominated designs. The system supports graphical state chart and VHDL language input formats and synthesizes logic for gate array, FPGA, or standard cell ASICs.

Integrity Engineering

Minneapolis, MN
(612) 636-6913

☐ CALIF

☐ SImnet

☐ SImnet X

☐ AUTOSPICE

Integrity Engineering develops and markets software tools for signal integrity analysis. The software operates on workstation platforms as well as DOS and Windows PCs.

Interactive CAD Systems

P.O. Box 4182
Santa Clara, CA 95056-4182
(408) 970-0852
(408) 986-0524 fax

Intergraph Electronics

VeriBest Direct
6101 Lookout Road, Suite A
Boulder, CO 30801
(800) VERIBEST
(205) 730-8543
(303) 581-9973 fax

- ☐ **ACEPlus Design Entry**
- ☐ **VeriBest Designer**
- ☐ **VeriBest Simulator**
- ☐ **PLDSyn**
- ☐ **LogSyn**
- ☐ **VeriBest States**
- ☐ **Analog Designer**
- ☐ **VeriBest PCB Designer**

Intergraph is a broad-line supplier of EDA tools, including the VeriBest series of cross-platform products. Intergraph offers software for workstation platforms, as well as for Windows and Windows NT PC platforms.

InterHDL, Inc.

1270 Oakmead Pkwy
Suite 207
Sunnyvale, CA 94086
(800) 8-VIPER1
(415) 428-4200
(415) 428-4201 fax

- ☐ **Viper™**

☐ **Verilint™**

☐ **VLTool™**

"InterHDL designs, develops, and markets EDA tools for high level design in Verilog and VHDL. InterHDL sells Verilint, a Verilog design checker for language semantics, and Viper, a Verilog simulator."

International CMOS Technologies, Inc

2123 Ringwood Avenue
San Jose, CA 95131
(408) 434-0678

☐ **PEEL™ Programmable Logic Devices**

☐ **PLACE Design Software**

ICT develops and markets electrically erasable CMOS programmable logic devices and related software.

Intusoft

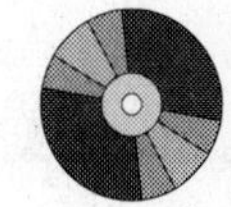

222 West 6th St.
Suite 1070
San Pedro, CA 90731
(310) 833-0710
(310) 833-9658 fax
74774,2023 CompuServe
74774.2023@compuserve.com
CompuServe CADD/CAM/CAE Vendor Forum, Library 21

☐ **ICAP/4 Software**

"Intusoft's ICAP/4 is an integrated system that allows you to simulate all types of designs including power, RF, ASIC, mixed mode, control system, and mixed technology (mechanical, physical, and electrical). ICAP/4 includes an integrated schematic entry front-end, extensive model libraries, and interactive 32-bit SPICE 3F.4 based simulator and a powerful data post processor. Intusoft is the leader in low-cost, full featured design tools with support for Windows, Windows NT (PC, Alpha and Mips), DOS, Macintosh and Power Macintosh platforms."

ISDATA

Oakland, CA
(510) 531-8553
(800) 777-1202

☐ LOG/iC PLD and FPGA Software

☐ Hint VHDL Synthesis

ISDATA produces design tools for PLDs and FPGAs. The LOG/iC products are available on a wide variety of platforms, including engineering workstations and DOS/Windows PCs.

Ivex Design International

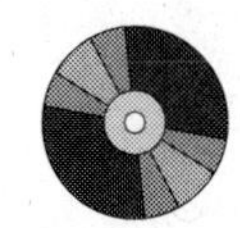

15232 NW Greenbrier Parkway
Beaverton, OR 97006-5746
(503) 531-3555
(503) 629-4907 fax

Ivex Europe GmbH
Arnulfstrasse 27
80335 Munich
Germany
89 5904 7121
89 5904 7200 fax

☐ WinBoard

"Ivex was formed in 1993 by former Orcad founders who wanted to provide a new generation of affordable Windows and Windows NT design tools. Products include a 90 day satisfaction guarantee and life-time technical support. WinBoard for Windows offers the industry's most acclaimed manual router for PCB layout, including unsurpassed editing capabilities, powerful copper pour, and advanced on-line Design Rule Checking (DRC). Designed specifically for manual routing, this offers true support for analog and high-speed designs. Call for pricing and availability of other Ivex products."

Lattice Semiconductor

5555 NE Moore Ct.
Hillsboro, OR 97124-6421
(503) 681-0118
(503) 681-3037 fax

- ☐ **pLSI and ispLSI Programmable Logic Devices**
- ☐ **pDS Development Software**

"Lattice Semiconductor develops and manufactures high performance programmable logic devices and associated logic design CAE tools. Lattice offers both low-density GALTM and pLSITM, and ispLSI complex PLD architectures for logic design. Lattice's tools include its low-cost pDS PC-based software, as well as pDS+ logic fitters compatible with major third-party CAE tool environments."

Logical Devices, Inc.

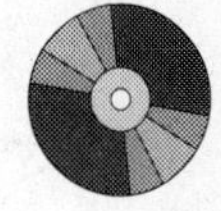

692 South Military Trail
Deerfield Beach, FL 33442
(800) 331-7766
(305) 428-1811 fax

- ☐ **CUPL**
- ☐ **Total Designer**

Logical Devices, Inc., is a manufacturer of device programming equipment and programmable logic design software. Logical Devices products include the popular CUPL programmable logic compiler, as well as the Windows-based Total Designer PLD development system.

Logic Modeling Corporation

P.O. Box 310
Beaverton, OR 97075-9962
(800) 346-6335
(503) 690-6900
(503) 690-6906 fax

- ☐ **SmartModel Simulation Libraries**

Logic Modeling Corporation offers simulation models for over 12,000 standard components. The model libraries are simulator independent and support a wide variety of simulation environments.

Massteck, Ltd.

95 Russell Street
Littleton, MA 01460
(508) 486-0197
(508) 486-1084 fax

Massteck is a provider of printed circuit board (PBC) layout software. Massteck software is available on engineering workstations and Windows-based PCs.

MATRA MHS, Inc.

2201 Laurelwood Road
Santa Clara, CA 95056
(408) 970-5858
(800) 554-5565
(408) 748-0439 fax

Mental Automation, Inc.

5415 136th Place SE
Bellevue, WA 98006
(206) 641-2141
(206) 649-0767 fax

- ☐ **SuperCAD**
- ☐ **SuperPCB**
- ☐ **SuperSIM**

Mental Automation offers low-cost, Windows-based software for electronic design automation.

Mentor Graphics

805 SW Boekman Road
Wilsonville, OR 97070
(800) 592-2210

- ☐ **System Architect**
- ☐ **Design Architect**
- ☐ **DSP Architect**
- ☐ **AutoLogic Synthesis**
- ☐ **VHDLsim**
- ☐ **QuickVHDL**
- ☐ **PLDSynthesis II**
- ☐ **Board Station 500**
- ☐ **MCM Station**

Mentor Graphics is a broad-line supplier of EDA tools. Mentor tools include system-level design tools, ASIC development systems, and VHDL simulation and synthesis packages.

Meta-Software

1300 White Oaks Road
Campbell, CA 95008
(408) 369-5400
(408) 371-5638 fax

- ☐ **HSPICE**

Meta-Software specializes in high-performance SPICE-based simulation for signal integrity analysis and performance modeling of analog circuits. They offer software products on engineering workstation platforms (Sun, HP, DEC, IBM) as well as on 386/486/Pentium PCs.

Micro Analog

P.O. Box 1208
Alpharetta, GA 30239-1208
(404) 410-0653
(404) 410-0556 fax

- ☐ **EE-Z-X Transformer Design Tool**

The EE-Z-X Transformer Design Tool is a DOS-based program intended to aid in and simplify the task of designing magnetic core transformers.

MicroSim Corporation

20 Fairbanks
Irvine, CA 92692
(714) 770-3022
(800) 245-3022
(714) 455-0554 fax
sales@microsim.com

- ☐ **The Design Center**
- ☐ **PSpice**
- ☐ **PSpice A/D**
- ☐ **PLSyn**
- ☐ **Paragon**
- ☐ **Polaris**

"The Design Center products consist of schematic entry (Schematics), analog simulation (PSpice), digital simulation (PSpice A/D), programmable logic synthesis (PLSyn), analog performance analysis (Paragon), and signal integrity analysis (Polaris). Used in any combination, they form a powerful, tightly integrated development environment with which you can produce superior analog and/or digital circuits. As your needs grow, you can be assured that your personal Design Center system can grow with them, including not only the foundation products but also these options: Mentor Integration, Caadence Integration, Filter Synthesis, and Device Equations."

MINC, Inc.

6755 Earl Drive
Colorado Springs, CO 80918
(719) 590-1155
(800) 755-3742
(719) 590-7330 fax

- ☐ **PLDSynthesis II**

MINC offers its PLDSynthesis II programmable logic design system, which allows logic to be specified and partitioned automatically into multiple PLDs. The system includes support for virtually all programmable logic devices, ranging from simple PAL devices to complex PLDs and FPGAs. The MINC software is also available through broad-line EDA suppliers such as CADENCE and Mentor Graphics.

Model Technology

15455 NW Greenbrier Parkway
Suite 240
Beaverton, OR 97006
(503) 641-1340
(503) 526-5410 fax

☐ V-System™ Simulator

Model Technology's V-System simulator is a popular product for VHDL simulation. The simulator supports IEEE 1076-1987 and IEEE 1076-1993, and is available on workstation computers and on Windows-based PCs.

Motorola Semiconductor Products, Inc.

2200 W. Broadway Road
Mesa, AZ 85202
(800) 441-2447
(602) 655-2597
(602) 655-5755 fax

☐ MPA1000 FPGA Family

☐ Timing Wizard Development Software

Motorola produces a family of FPGA devices and companion development tools and provides interfaces to third-party tool vendors such as Viewlogic, Mentor, Synopsys, and Exemplar.

National Semiconductor

2900 Semiconductor Drive
P.O. Box 58090
Santa Clara, CA 95052-9898
(800) 628-7364
(800) 888-5113 fax

☐ MAPL Complex PLDs

☐ OPALjr Development Software

National Semiconductor produces a series of programmable logic devices, including the MAPL family of complex PLDs.

NeoCAD, Inc.

2585 Central Avenue
Boulder, CO 80301
(303) 442-9121
(800) 888-3742
(303) 442-9124 fax

- ☐ **FPGA Foundry**
- ☐ **Timing Wizard**
- ☐ **Prism**

"NeoCAD, Inc. is the only independent FPGA CAD tools supplier providing a single design environment, FPGA Foundry, that supports many different architectures offered by an increasing number of FPGA vendors. FPGA Foundry currently supports Xilinx XC4000/4000a, XC3100, XC3000/3000a, AT&T 3000, AT&T ORCA and Motorola MPA 1000 device families. FPGA Foundry enables technology-transparent design, the ability to design without regard to implementation technology, and is timing and frequency driven. FPGA Foundry also offers post-mapped, multi-chip partitioning capabilities and eliminates the need for a designer to become an expert in target architectures. FPGA Foundry provides faster clock speeds, shorter design cycles and higher chip utilization."

Nextwave Design Automation

Palo Alto, CA
(415) 855-9791

- ☐ **EPILOG Verilog HDL Simulator**
- ☐ **NextView Debugger**

Nextwave Design Automation develops and markets Verilog HDL simulation and debugging tools. Nextwave's products are available on engineering workstations including Sun and IBM.

Orbit Semiconductor

1215 Bordeaux Drive
Sunnyvale, CA 94089
(408) 744-1800
(800) 331-4617
(408) 747-1263 fax

☐ Encore! Gate Array and FPGA Conversion

Orbit Semiconductor specializes in quick turn-around for prototype ASICs and mask-programmed conversions of FPGA-based designs.

OrCAD

9300 SW Nimbus Avenue
Beaverton, OR 97005
(503) 671-9500
(503) 671-9501

☐ OrCAD Schematic

☐ OrCAD PCB

OrCAD produces Windows-based software for design entry and printed circuit board (PCB) layout. OrCAD pioneered low-cost EDA tools for the PC platform and today offers 32-bit DOS and Windows products.

PADS Software, Inc.

165 Forest Street
Marlboro, MA 01752
(508) 485-4300
(508) 485-7171 fax

☐ PADS-PCB

"PADS is a leading supplier of printed circuit board layout and design software. Our goal is to provide exceptional value, and to provide our customers with a competitive edge. We are a TechWin sponsor and a full supporter of integration and standards. As and example of our committment, our newly announced Vendor Integration Alliance (VIA) program is open to all vendors committed to interfaces to PADS products."

Paradigm Logic

2328G Walsh Avenue
Santa Clara, CA 95051
(408) 988-5016
(408) 988-5017 fax

☐ ASIC Consulting Services

"Paradigm Logic is an engineering consulting firm specializing in ASIC and systems engineering solutions. We apply state of the art design methodologies including top-down design, Hardware Description Language and logic synthesis to provide solutions for a full range of ASIC and systems engineering issues. Let our experienced team of top-down design engineers be your Engineering Partner."

Performance Signal Integrity

Pittsburgh, PA
(412) 682-7101

Performance Signal Integrity offers software products for signal integrity analysis. The products are available only on Sun workstations.

Phase Three Logic

Beaverton, OR
(503) 531-2410

- ☐ **CapFast Schematic Capture**

Protel Technology

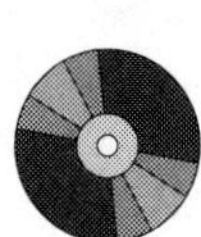

4675 Stevens Creek Blvd.
Suite 200
Santa Clara, CA 95051
(408) 243-8143
(800) 544-4186
(408) 243-8544 fax

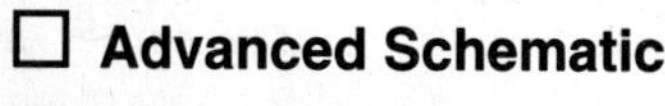

- ☐ **Advanced Schematic**
- ☐ **Advanced PCB**
- ☐ **Advanced SB Route**

Protel Technology offers Windows EDA tools for schematic capture and printed circuit board layout.

Quad Design

1385 Del Norte Road
Camarillo, CA 93010
(805) 988-8250
(805) 988-8259 fax

- ☐ **MOTIVE™ Timing Analyzer**
- ☐ **TLC™**
- ☐ **XTK Crosstalk Toolkit**

Quad Design offers tools for timing analysis of complex, high-speed circuits. Quad Design is a Viewlogic company.

Quicklogic Corp.

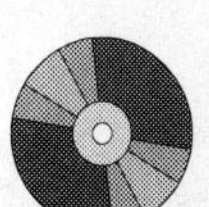

2933 Bunker Hill Lane
Santa Clara, CA 95054
(408) 987-2000
(408) 987-2012 fax

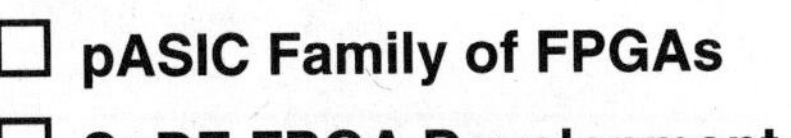

- ☐ **pASIC Family of FPGAs**
- ☐ **SpDE FPGA Development Tools**

"The SpDE design entry system for QuickLogic pASIC FPGAs supports place and route, physical view, timing analysis, schematic entry, Boolean entry and waveform simulation."

QuickTurn Design Systems

440 Clyde Avenue
Mountain View, CA 94043
(415) 967-3300

- ☐ **Enterprise/MARS IC Emulation Systems**

Quickturn Design Systems offers rapid prototyping and system verification systems for IC and ASIC design.

R-Active Concepts

20654 Gardenside Circle
Cupertino, CA 95014
(408) 252-2808
(408) 438-7684 fax

☐ BetterState Pro

"BetterState Pro V2.0 form R-Active Concepts, Inc. is an advanced state machine design tool that provides Extended State Diagrams (with hierarchy and concurrency) and Petri Net design entry methods, Automatic Code Generation for C, C++, Verilog HDL and VHDL, Visual Priorities, Visual Synchronization, State Visitation Statistics, Animated Playback, Interactive Visual State Traveler and a General Purpose Drawing Tool for design documentation. BetterState PRO with a choice of code generator is $495.00. Other configurations are available. BetterState Pro is a Microsoft Windows 3.X application and supports OLE and WorkGroups for Windows."

RAVIcad

1230 Oakmead Pkwy
Suite 216
Sunnyvale, CA 94086
(800) RAVICAD
(408) 720-6122 fax
sales@ravicad.com

☐ VHDL and Verilog Simulation Models

Simucad, Inc.

32970 Alvarado-Niles Road
Suite 744
Union City, CA 94587
(510) 487-9700
(510) 487-9721 fax

☐ SILOS III Verilog Simulator

"SILOS III is the latest advancement in high-performance digital simulation. SILOS III uses the Verilog Hardware Description Language to support top-down design methodology. Its highly efficient simulation algorithms accomodate large hierarchical designs while utilizing a limited amount of system memory. The SILOS

III Data Analyzer merges the waveform generator with the exclusive Graphical Trace Mode debugging tools to improve designer productivity by an order of magnitude. SILOS III is the most reliable, capable and affordable high performance simulation environment available today."

Simulation Technologies

New Brighton, MN
(612) 631-1858

☐ VirSim Verilog HDL Debugger

Simulation Technologies offers products for Verilog HDL simulation and debugging.

S-MOS Systems, Inc.

2460 North First Street
San Jose, CA 95131

☐ FPGA to Gate Array Conversions

☐ SDS Design System

S-MOS offers high-speed gate array conversion services from FPGA netlists. The services includes support for a wide variety of design formats, including Mentor, Valid, Viewlogic, Cadence, FutureNet, OrCAD, Dazix, Synopsys, and Exemplar.

Source III, Inc.

3958 Cambridge Road
Suite 247
Cameron Park, CA 95682
(916) 676-9329

☐ VGEN

☐ VTRAN

☐ VCAP

"SOURCE III provides a suite of CAE tools for dealing with the generation, translation, verification and analysis of logic simulation data files. The software is available on most workstation platforms and interfaces to over 25 popular logic simulators."

Spectrum Software

1021 S. Wolfe Road
Sunnyvale, CA 94086
(408) 738-4387
(408) 738-4702 fax

Summit Design, Inc.

9305 SW Gemini Drive
Beaverton, OR 97005-7158
(503) 643-9281
(503) 646-4954 fax

☐ Visual HDL

☐ Xpert HDL

Visual HDL allows the designer to enter a design using a mixture of textual and graphical representations, including block diagrams, flow charts, state diagrams, truth tables, and VHDL language. The system automatically generates VHDL code from graphical representations, and includes integrated high-level simulation tools. Xpert HDL is a VHDL design entry and design management system.

SUSIE-CAD, Inc.

1000 Nevada Hwy.
Suite 201
Boulder City, NV 89005
(702) 293-2271
(702) 293-1011 fax
support@aldec.com

☐ SUSIE-CAD™

☐ ACTIVE-CAD™

"SUSIE-CAD, Inc. offers Windows 3.1 based schematic capture and simulation tools (including functional, glitch and 10ps resolution timing simulation). SUSIE-CAD provides for a real-time, on the fly, design verification of the simplest TTL design to the most complex CPLD or FPGA design. Complete end-to-end design tool for all popular FPGA and CPLD vendors. SUSIE-CAD's product line includes SUSIE-CAD and ACTIVE-CAD."

SynaptiCAD, Inc.

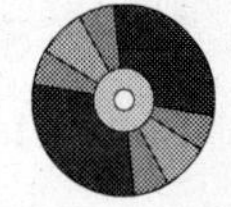

P.O. Box 10608
Blacksburg, VA 24062-0608
(703) 953-3390
(703) 953-3078 fax

☐ The Timing Diagrammer™

"The Timing Diagrammer by SynaptiCAD, Inc. is an EDA tool for drawing and analyzing timing diagrams. Signals, buses and clocks can be drawn faster and more accurately than pencil and paper versions. Timing parameters such as delays, setups and holds actively move and monitor signal transitions. Parameter values can be quickly edited using a custom spreadsheet, and timing diagrams automatically adjust to reflect parameter changes. The Timing Diagrammer also offers a copy-to-clipboard function making it easy to paste timing diagrams into your documents.

"The Timing Diagrammer is a Windows 3.1 program and is available for $249.99. Don't be fooled by crippled entry-level products; get professional quality for the same price. Quantity discounts and site licenses are available."

Synopsys, Inc.

700 East Middlefield
Mountain View, CA 94043-4033
(818) 792-3000

☐ Behavioral Compiler™
☐ Design Compiler™
☐ HDL Compiler
☐ VHDL Compiler
☐ FPGA Compiler™
☐ Test Compiler™
☐ VHDL System Simulator™

Synopsis offers high-level design automation (HLDA) tools that let engineers specify designs for synthesis using a higher level of abstraction. The synopsis synthesis tools support ASIC and FPGA design, and accept VHDL or Verilog input.

Synplicity, Inc.

465 Fairchild Drive, Suite 115
Mountain View, CA 94043
(415) 961-4962
(415) 961-4974
info@synplicity.com

☐ Verilog and VHDL Synthesis Tools

"Synplicity, Inc. develops and markets leading edge, easy to use logic synthesis products for designers using hardware description languages (Verilog HDL and VHDL) that run on PCs and Unix workstations. Synplicity's tools take industry standard VHDL and Verilog HDL designs as input and synthesizes, optimizes and maps them to popular FPGAs. ASIC support is planned for the future."

Tanner Research

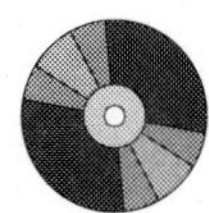

180 North Vinedo Avenue
Pasadena, CA 91107
(818) 792-3000
(818) 792-0300 fax

☐ S-Edit™ Schematic Editor

☐ L-Edit™ Layout Editor

☐ GateSim™ Simulator

☐ T-Spice™ Simulator"

"Affordable ASIC and MCM design software from Tanner Research, Inc. provides high performance and easy to use tools at superior value to users of PCs. Tanner Tools support FPGA, standard cell, and full custom designs with a tightly integrated design solution that includes the S-Edit™ schematic editor, L-Edit™ full custom layout editor, L-Edit/DRC™ design rule checker, LEdit/Extract™ netlist and parameter extractor, L-Edit/SPR™ standard cell place-and-route, and LVS layout vs. schematic module. GateSim™ provides gate-level simulation and T-Spice™ provides full chip circuit-level simulation. For MCM design L-Edit/Therm™ offers 3-Dimensional finite element thermal analysis. Tanner Tools support EDIF, GDS-II and CIF formats and offer an easy-to-use interface to low-cost prototyping or volume production services for ASIC and MCM fabrication."

Texas Instruments

Dallas, TX
(214) 644-5580
(800) 232-3200

☐ PLD Integrator Software

Texas Instruments offers a number of products in support of its ASIC and programmable logic products.

Topdown Design Solutions, Inc.

71 Spitbrook Road, Suite 210
Nashua, NH 03060
(603) 888-8811
(603) 888-7694 fax

☐ VHDL SelfStart Kit

☐ VBAK Timing Annotator

Topdown Design Solutions is a provider of VHDL-related products and services, including on-site training, VHDL simulation models, and VHDL-related software tools. Topdown Design Solutions is also a value-added reseller of Model Technology's V-System simulator.

UniCAD, Inc.

174 Littleton Road
Suite 103
Westford, MA 01886
(508) 692-8446
(508) 692-8197

☐ UniSolve

☐ UniCam

UniCAD, Inc. develops and markets tools for the analysis of physical effects in high-speed designs. These effects include emissions, signal integrity, RF/IF, thermal, and reliability. UniCAD's products are designed to be used in combination with leading EDA vendor's design environments.

Vantage

(510) 659-0901
(510) 659-0129 fax

- ☐ **SpeedWave™ VHDL Simulator**
- ☐ **Optium™ Simulation Environment**

Vantage supplies high-performance VHDL simulation tools, including the SpeedWave simulator. Vantage is a Viewlogic company.

VAutomation, Inc.

71 Spitbrook Road
Suite 306
Nashua, NH 03060
(603) 891-2424
(603) 891-2167 fax

- ☐ **HDL Models**

"VAutomation is a supplier of Synthesizable HDL models. We primarily focus on providing 8 and 16 bit microprocessors and their support peripherals. These models are ideal for creating 'Systems-in-Silicon' for embedded applications."

VEDA

Santa Clara, CA
(408) 970-1600

- ☐ **Vulcan Simulator**

VEDA provides VITAL-compliant VHDL simulation products. The software operates on engineering workstations including Sun, HP, and DEC.

Veritools

Los Altos, CA
(415) 941-5050

- ☐ **Verilog Simulation Tools**

Veritools produces software that can be used in conjunction with major Verilog simulators to enhance simulation analysis and design debugging.

Viewlogic Systems, Inc.

293 Boston Post Road West
Marlboro, MA 01752
(508) 480-0881
(800) 873-8439
(508) 480-0882 fax

- ☐ **ViewSim**
- ☐ **ViewVHDL**
- ☐ **VCS (Chronologic)**
- ☐ **ViewArchitect**
- ☐ **ViewSynthesis**
- ☐ **ViewFPGA**
- ☐ **ViewPLD**
- ☐ **PRO-Series Design Tools**

Viewlogic is a broad-line supplier of tools for system-level and ASIC design. Viewlogic tools are offered for a wide range of computing platforms, including DEC, Sun, HP, and Sun workstations, and DOS/Windows-based PCs.

Vista Technologies, Inc.

1100 Woodfield Road
Schaumburg, IL 60173-5124
(708) 706-9300
(708) 706-9317 fax
info@VistaTech.com

- ☐ **DesignVision™**
- ☐ **StateVision™**
- ☐ **Vista Model Creator™**
- ☐ **VHDL Developer Plus™**

"Vista provides Electronic System Design Automation (ESDA) tools for HDL design of ASICs, FPGAs, boards and systems. Vista's ESDA tools allow engineers to create HDL models for simulation or synthesis from graphical diagrams of behavior."

Vista provides five products for HDL design: DesignVision™, StateVision™, Vista Model Creator™, VHDL Language Assistant™, and The VHDL Developer Plus™. The entry methods for these tools are graphical behavior threads (DesignVision), state machine bubble diagrams (StateVision), spreadsheet tables (Vista Model Creator), syntax-directed editing (VHDL Language Assistant), or a combination (The VHDL Developer Plus). DesignVision, StateVision, and Vista Model Creator are available for both VHDL and Verilog."

Visual Software Solutions

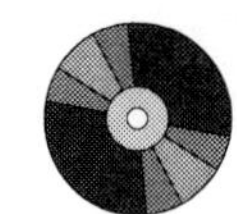

3057 Coral Springs Drive
Suite 203
Coral Springs, FL 33065
(305) 346-8890
(305) 346-9394 fax
(305) 423-8448 technical support

☐ StateCAD

"Visual Software Solutions develops and manufactures digital design software which it distributes stand-alone via regional VARs as well as bundled with other OEM tools such as Data I/O Corporation's Synario and ABEL products. Its premier product, StateCAD, delivers graphical state machine entry, analysis, HDL generation, and documentation capabilities to CPLD and FPGA designers. StateCAD not only locates bugs and provides solutions for them, but also generates ABEL-HDL and VHDL for synthesis, and ANSI C for simulation. Its automatic design analysis insures generation of streamlined HDL which is syntactically correct, logically consistent and, if desired, ready-to-burn."

Wellspring Solutions, Inc.

Wellspring Solutions
P.O. Box 150
Sutton, MA 01590
(508) 865-7271
(508) 865-1113 fax
info@wellspring.com

☐ VeriWell Simulator

☐ WellSpring Waves

"Wellspring Solutions, Inc. is the leading supplier of shrinkwrap priced Verilog Clones. Based in Sutton, MA with distributors in the U.S., Japan and the United

Kingdom, the company was founded in 1991 and is commited to full access to simulation for all engineers.

"The company provides VeriWell, a fully functional, XL-compatible, OVI compliant simulator for DOS, Unix, and Macintosh which is designed to fit into customers' existing design environments, and to provide an alternative ten times less expensive than higher-priced Verilog products.

"In keeping with its 'full access to all' philosophy, Wellspring Solutions announced in 1994 the release of VeriWell/Free, a 1000-line version of its unlimited registered VeriWell simulator. VeriWell/Free is available to anyone by FTP at iii.net:/pub/pub-site/wellspring, or via BBS by dialing the fax number 1-508-865-1113. VeriWell/Free can also be ordered on floppy. Contact the Wellspring Solutions main office for details."

WINTEK Corporation

1801 South Street
Lafayette, IN 47904
(800) 742-6809
(317) 448-1903

Xilinx, Inc

2100 Logic Drive
San Jose, CA 95124
(408) 559-7778
(800) 231-3386

☐ Xilinx FPGAs

☐ XACT Development System

"Founded in 1984, Xilinx is the world's leading supplier of CMOS programmable logic and related development system software. Xilinx products are standard integrated circuits that are programmed by Xilinx customers to perform desired logic operations. These products provide high integration and significant time and cost savings for electronic equipment manufacturers in the computer peripherals, telecommunications, industrial control and instrumentation, and military markets."

Zuken-Redac

1200 MacArthur Blvd.
Mahwaj, NJ 07430
(800) 356-8352
(508) 692-4725 fax

- ☐ **CAD Expert**
- ☐ **Route Editor**

Zycad

Fremont, CA
(510) 623-4400

- ☐ **Paradigm XP**
- ☐ **Paradigm ViP**
- ☐ **Paradigm RP**

Zycad provides hardware-accelerated simulation solutions for complex ASIC and large-scale system design. Zycad systems are available for major engineering workstations including those from IBM, HP, and Sun.

APPENDIX B

EDA PUBLICATIONS

The following periodicals contain useful information for users of electronic design automation tools and methods:

Computer Design

Circulation Department
P.O. Box 3466
Tulsa, OK 74101-3466

Electronic Design (ED)

Penton Publishing
1100 Superior Avenue
Cleveland, OH 44114

Electronic Design News (EDN)

Subscription Information
8773 South Ridgeline Blvd.
Highlands Ranch, CO 80126-2329

Electronic Engineering Times (EE Times)

Circulation Department
600 Community Drive
Manhassett, NY 11030

Electronic Products

Hearst Publications
Circulation Department
645 Stewart Avenue
Garden City, NY 11530-4709

Integrated System Design (ASI C & EDA)

Circulation Department
5150 El Camino Real
Suite D-31
Los Altos, CA 94022

Personal Engineering & Instrumentation

Circulation Department
Box 430
Rye, NH 03870

Printed Circuit Design

Circulation Department
P.O. Box 420235
Palm Coast, FL 32142-0235

APPENDIX C

ON-LINE RESOURCES FOR EDA USERS

The following on-line resources contain a wealth of information for electronic design automation users:

Usenet News Groups

Usenet news groups are a valuable forum for exchange of information, and there are many groups dedicated to electronic design issues. Most of these news groups post (or make available via FTP) a frequently asked questions (FAQ) document. Be sure to peruse each news group and check the appropriate FAQs before posting a question or request.

alt.cad

Alt.cad features general discussions relating to CAD applications.

alt.cad.autocad

Alt.cad.autocad focuses on the Autodesk AutoCAD tools.

alt.sys.intergraph

The **alt.sys.intergraph** news group is intended for discussions of Intergraph hardware and design tools.

comp.arch.fpga

The **comp.arch.fpga** news group is intended for discussions of field programmable gate arrays (FPGAs) used for reconfigurable computing. Discussions often broaden out into more general FPGA issues.

comp.cad.cadence

Comp.cad.cadence focuses on issues related to Cadence design tools.

comp.cad.compass

Comp.cad.compass focuses on issues related to Compass Design Automation tools.

comp.cad.synthesis

Comp.cad.synthesis is intended for users of logic synthesis tools. Issues discussed include VHDL and Verilog synthesis subsets, coding conventions, design methods, and comparisons of synthesis tools.

comp.lang.vhdl
comp.lang.verilog

The comp.lang.vhdl and comp.lang.verilog groups focus on the VHDL and Verilog hardware description languages (HDLs). Discussions often involve detailed language syntax questions, as well as debates about the relative merits of VHDL and Verilog and comparisons of HDL tools.

comp.lsi

Comp.lsi contains discussions on the subject of integrated circuit design. Topics include gate array, standard cell, full-custom, and FPGA technologies.

comp.lsi.cad

The **comp.lsi.cad** news group focuses on issues related to IC design tools.

comp.lsi.testing

Comp.lsi.testing is intended for discussions of integrated circuit testing issues.

comp.org.acm
comp.org.ieee

The **comp.org.acm** and **comp.org.ieee** news groups include discussions and announcements related to the ACM and IEEE organizations.

comp.sys.mentor

The **comp.sys.mentor** news group contains discussions by users of Mentor Graphics workstations and design tools.

comp.sys.dec

Comp.sys.dec is intended for users of Digital Equipment Corporation hardware.

comp.sys.sgi.announce

Comp.sys.sgi.announce contains product release information and other announcements related to Silicon Graphics workstations and software.

comp.sys.sun.announce

Comp.sys.sgi.announce contains product release information and other announcements related to Sun Microsystems workstations and software.

sci.electronics

The **sci.electronics** news group is intended for general electronics topics. Participants range from electronic engineering students and hobbyists to experienced project engineers and engineering managers.

sci.electronics.cad

Sci.electronics.cad contains discussions about electronic design automation tools. Low-cost design tools are often a topic of conversion on this group.

Mail Servers and Lists

Mail servers allow a group of users to exchange information using Internet mail addresses and a centralized list of participants. There are many lists in operation for EDA users, and new lists are being created constantly; here is a sampling:

Synopsys Network User's Group: jcooley@world.std.com

John Cooley moderates a regular electronic newsletter (ESNUG) for users of Synopsys tools. To subscribe, send email direct to John Cooley at the above address.

Signal Integrity Mail List: si-admin@silab.eng.sun.com

The signal integrity mail server allows those interested in signal integrity analysis to exchange messages. You can subscribe to this list by sending mail to the above address, and including the command SUBSCRIBE in the subject line of the message.

Xilinx Users Mail List: xilinx-users-request@somnet.sandia.gov

The Xilinx users mail server allows those interested in FPGA design issues to exchange messages. You can subscribe to this list by sending mail to the above address, and including the command SUBSCRIBE in the body of the message.

Web Sites

The following World Wide Web sites offer information and information links related to electronic design automation, electronic components, engineering computer systems and other useful topics. New Web pages are appearing constantly, so this list can only be considered partial. For a more up-to-date list, visit the author's home page at **http://www.seanet.com/Users/pellerin/**.

To access a World Wide Web page, you need a World Wide Web browser (such as Mosaic) and the appropriate Internet connection (SLIP/PPP or other service).

http:/www.amd.com/

Advanced Micro Devices, Inc. home page

http://www.info.apple.com/

Apple Computer home page.

http://www.cadence.com/

Cadence Design Systems home page.

http://www.data-io.com/

Data I/O Corporation home page.

http://www.digital.com/

Digital Equipment Corporation home page.

http://www.research.digital.com/

Digital Equipment Corporation Research home page.

http://www.dell.com/

Dell Computer home page.

http://techweb.cmp.com/eet/

EE Times Interactive home page.

http://www.hp.com/

Hewlett-Packard home page.

http://www.ibm.com/

International Business Machines home page.

gopher://gopher.ieee.org/

IEEE membership gopher server.

http://www.intel.com/

Intel Corporation home page.

http://www.marshall.com/

Marshall Industries home page.

http://www.mathworks.com/

Mathworks home page.

http://www.mathsoft.com/

Mathsoft home page.

http://www.microsoft.com/

Microsoft Corporation home page.

gopher://gopher.prenhall.com/

Prentice Hall Technical Reference gopher server.

http://www.sgi.com/

Silicon Graphics, Inc. home page.

http://www.sun.com/

Sun Microsystems home page.

http://www.synopsys.com/

Synopsys home page.

http://epimsl.nasa.gov/engineering/ee.html

NASA engineering resources home page.

ftp://vhdl.org/

VHDL international gopher server and home page.

http: / / www.xilinx.com /

Xilinx Corporation home page.

CompuServe Forums

CompuServe offers a number of forums of interest to electrical engineers. The EE Times-sponsored EETNet, for example, includes well-run forums with sections relating to many areas of electronic design.

To access the EETNet and other CompuServe forums, you will need to join CompuServe. Sign-up kits are available free of charge from many sources (such as modem and terminal emulator software suppliers) or can be purchased at a very low cost from any software retailer.

GO EET:ENGINEERING
GO EET:PROFESSIONAL
GO EET:STANDARDS

EETNet offers many forums and sections of interest to electrical engineers. The Engineering forum covers areas such as power, analog and digital design, PCB, packaging, and EDA tools. The Professional/International forum includes topics related to professional organizations, consulting and careers, and international topics. The Standards forum includes discussions related to domestic and international electronic product standards.

GO CADDVEN

The CADD/CAM/CAE Vendor forum is used for customer support and product information. A few low-cost EDA vendors (including Protel, Chronology and Intusoft) maintain sections on this forum.

GO AUTODESK

Autodesk's forum is used for customer support and product literature for AutoCAD and related products.

GO LEAP

The Engineering Automation forum includes discussions related to manufacturing, process control, CADD/CAM/CAE, and engineering technology.

APPENDIX D

The TechWin™ User Group

The following information has been provided by Stan Baker, founder and President of TechWin, Inc.

Join TechWin, the first and only independent forum for users and developers of EDA applications for Windows.

The EDA industry is evolving rapidly in response to the growing need for a new breed of EDA tools. Designers and companies are demanding tools that are easier to use, that can be used on an enterprise- wide computing basis, and that deliver higher performance and increased productivity at lower costs. The enabling technology to meet these demands is the new class of personal-computer operating systems, including Microsoft Windows, Windows NT, OS/2, and other future, low-cost Windows-like environments.

As EDA tools, technologies, and applications for these environments proliferate, you'll need a central source of information, education, and support for all aspects of windows-based EDA. TechWin, the EDA Users Group for Windows, gives you that support. TechWin puts you in touch with other users, developers, and vendors of EDA applications, and is developing a range of services targeted specifically to windows-based EDA:

Education

TechWin provides the following services:

- ☐ TechWin seminars, focusing on integration and interoperatility of applications, increasing general productivity and comparing the latest windows environments. TechWin members get substantial discounts for these seminars.

- ☐ TechWin on-line seminars and panel discussions, some exclusively for TechWin members.
- ☐ User-to-user education: participate on-line with an international membership. Support information sharing via a worldwide network of EDA users. TechWin members have an exclusive member forum for sharing information with each other and with EDA vendors.
- ☐ On-line references to industry activities, vendors, and products.
- ☐ On-line libraries of applications examples, conference papers, tutorials, utilities, etc.
- ☐ Semi-annual CD-ROM containing many current utilities and demos.

Learn More, Share More, Do More With TechWin

- ☐ Communicate with your peers about design and development issues, exchange application ideas, and compare vendor and product information.
- ☐ Learn how to increase productivity with other Windows-based tools (such as electronic mail and project management software) that work in concert with your EDA applications.

TechWin Works To Benefit You

TechWin operates independent of proprietary interests. Founded as a non-profit users-group organization, TechWin's charter is to benefit users, rather than support the interests of a particular company or organization.

TechWin focuses on the EDA needs of its members. As a result, you get a wide range of information and support for all aspects of EDA windows technology, from technical and business disciplines to company-wide enterprise computing.

Become a member today for just $50 per year. For more information contact Stan Baker at TechWin, phone (408) 356-5119, or Email *sbaker@techwin.org*.

TechWin™

EDA Users Group for Windows

504 Nino Ave.
Los Gatos, CA 95032
(408) 356-5119
(408) 356-9018 fax
sbaker@techwin.org
http://www.best.com/~sbaker/techwin/techwin.html

APPENDIX E

GLOSSARY

The following is a compendium of common electronic CAD terms:

ABEL Advanced Boolean Expression Language. A hardware description language specifically designed for programmable logic applications. ABEL is a trademark of Data I/O Corporation.

ACT Application Configurable Technology (Actel trademark). A family of field programmable gate arrays (FPGAs) sold by Actel corporation.

Analog simulation A simulation in which electrical signals are modeled or otherwise represented as actual voltage values, rather than as digital states. Analog simulators are used to model transistor and fundamental network circuits.

ASIC Application-Specific Integrated Circuit. Integrated circuits designed to be (to a greater or lesser degree) generic, and customized by the IC vendor or end-user for specific applications. ASIC device technologies include standard cell, gate array, semicustom and programmable logic.

Asynchronous A circuit (or signal within a circuit) that lacks a regular, predictable timing behavior. Asynchronous signals are not controlled by (or synchronized with) with a system clock.

Back annotation The updating of design or simulation data based on implementation-dependent factors. For example, the functional model of a system can be more accurately simulated if actual timing delays are back-annotated from known delays in the physical device implementation.

Behavioral model A representation of a system that reflects that system's operation over time, and allows the system to be simulated at its external interface.

Behavioral A level of abstraction in which a system is conceived of and described from its specified behavior, rather than from its underlying structure or physical make-up.

BiCMOS An integrated circuit process technology in which bipolar elements for output interfaces are combined with a CMOS core to combine the switching capabilities of bipolar with the power savings of CMOS.

Bidirectional A signal that, at various times, may act as an input to or output from a circuit. Bidirectional signals are normally associated with system interfaces such as buses.

Bipolar An integrated circuit process that employs two-junction (NPN and PNP) transistors. Bipolar circuits are being replaced, in most applications, by lower-power CMOS technology.

Boolean algebra A system of mathematics used for the description of logic functions. See *Switching algebra*.

Breakpoint A defined point at which a simulator, logic analyzer or other system monitoring tool is instructed to capture and hold the state of the system being tested. In simulation, breakpoints are used to pause the simulation at a certain point, allowing detailed analysis and debugging of the circuit to be performed.

Buffer A low-impedence driver used to amplify the current capability of a signal. Buffers can be used to drive other signals (such as buses) that have high loads, or may be used to improve the AC characteristics (such as rise and fall times) of the signal.

Bus A collection of two or more signals that have a data carrying relationship. Buses may have multiple drivers, in which case interface circuitry is required to resolve bus contention.

Bus contention A situation in which two or more drivers attempt to drive the same signal at the same time. Bus conflicts may occur due to the lack of adequate bus interface circuitry, or may occur because of timing skews in the interface circuitry.

CAD Computer Aided Design. An acronym that usually refers to mechanical drafting, 2D and 3D modeling, and other related computer applications. This acronym is sometimes used as a broad term describing the entire spectrum of technical/engineering applications, including electronic system design.

CAE Computer Aided Engineering. An acronym that generally refers to the areas of computer-based electronic system design, including design capture, simulation, and synthesis. This term has been replaced in recent years with the term *electronic design automation* (see *EDA*).

CFI CAD Framework Initiative. A consortium of design tool vendors and other interested parties created to standardize and promote inter-tool communication for Unix-based design tools.

CLB Configurable Logic Block. A configurable logic module found in Xilinx FPGA devices. Each CLB is composed of a small lookup table and one or more registers.

Clock skew A difference in the timing of various circuit elements due to the propogation delays associated with clock distribution paths.

Clock tree A physical (place and route) method of minimizing clock skew by carefully controlling the path delays of clock lines.

CMOS Complementary Metal Oxide Semiconductor. An integrated circuit process technology distinquished by low quiescent power requirements.

Concurrency Two or more events or systems operating independently, and in parallel. Electronic systems are inherently concurrent. In software simulations of electronic systems, concurrency must be taken into consideration in the software model of the system, and the simulator must have the ability to detect and calculate results that are dependent on parallel circuit behavior.

Controllability

The ability to observe, modify and otherwise excercise the internal elements (registers, control signals, etc.) of a circuit, or a component of that circuit, during simulation, or while that circuit is installed in a larger system.

Coverage

A measurement (typicall a percentage) of the relative "goodness" of a test, or suite of tests. Coverage is often measured in terms of a percentage of *faults* that are made observable and verifiable by the tests.

CPLD

Complex Programmable Logic Device. An acronym that generally refers to a programmable logic device that has enough functional complexity (programmable output macrocells, segmented architecture, routing blocks, etc.) that sophisticated design tools are required to effectively utilize the device. Examples of the more popular CPLDs include the AMD Mach and Altera MAX devices.

CUPL

A hardware description language intended for programmable logic applications. CUPL is a trademark of Logical Devices, Inc.

Delta cycle

A VHDL term refering to a sequence of simulation events that occur, in a simulated time of zero, in a defined order and manner to process all pending signal and variable assignments.

DRC

Design Rule Check. A set of rules that is applied (manually or by design software) to validate a design against a set of rules. These rules include such things as connectivity rules for schematics and netlists, electrical rules for physical implementation, and clearance rules for printed circuit board layout.

Digital simulation

A computer simulation of a circuit in which signals are modeled using a limited number of logic states, such as 1 (high), 0 (low), unknown and high-impedence. Digital simulators may use as few as two states (1 and 0) to model a circuit, or may have use many more states to accurately model complex digital circuits at the logic gate level.

EDA Electronic Design Automation. The currently-fashionable term describing applications used during the development of electronic systems. EDA tools assist in design capture, digital and analog simulation, ASIC synthesis, board layout, and other related application areas.

EDIF Electronic Design Interchange Format. A standard, netlist-based, format used to transfer circuit data between design tools.

ESDA Electronic System Design Automation. Depending on who who talk to (and what they are trying to sell you) this term may mean a higher level design entry tool such as a graphical block diagraming application that generates lower-level HDL, or may be a top-down design methodology that encompasses design entry, simulation and synthesis, as well as allowing hardware/software co-design..

Fault A point in an electronic circuit where a manufacturing defect could result in a failure of the circuit to operate correctly.

Fault coverage The percentage of faults observable and detectable by the application of a series of tests.

FPGA Field Programmable Gate Array. A configurable logic architecture in which a collection of cells (typically consisting of a small number of registers and some combinational logic elements) is interconnected by programmable routing channels.

Gate array An ASIC technology consisting of prefabricated wafers completed with customized metal interconnect layers. The final metal layers are defined by the end customer to create the desired interconnections and corresponding circuit function. Gate arrays may be composed of arrays of transistors and gates, or may have more complex macrofunctions (such as flip-flops) available.

Hard macro A high-level function (such as an adder, comparator or multiplexer) that is provided for use during design entry. Hard macros correspond directly to fixed sections of circuitry available in the target device.

HDL

Hardware Description Language. A programming language intended for the description of electronic circuits. HDLs are distinguished from software programming languages in that they support the description of systems that are inherently parallel.

Hierarchy

A method of representing and managing a complex design in which seperate modules of the design are arranged in an inverted tree structure. Hierarchy allows a large design to be viewed at different levels of abstraction, ranging from a high-level block diagram down to a detailed implementation consisting of gates, transistors and other circuit building blocks. The hierarchy of a design may or may not correspond to the actual structure that will be used in the final hardware implementation.

Instance

In a hierachical design representation, it is possible to refer to the same lower-level module (or component) of a design multiple times. Each of these references to a lower-level module results in one unique instance of that lower-level module being generated.

Instantiation

The process of creating one unique copy (instance) of a lower-level module by referencing that lower-level module in a higher-level module.

JEDEC

Joint Electron Device Engineering Council. An industry standards organization (created under the umbrella of the Electronics Industry Association) that develops package standards. In the programmable logic community, the term JEDEC is also used to refer to the JEDEC standard 3A data format used to transfer programming data to and from device programming hardware.

LSI

Large Scale Integration. Generally accepted to be an integrated circuit containing 200 or more equivalent gates.

Macrocell

A predefined or configurable block of circuitry in a chip, or a predefined high-level function in a design tool that may or may not correspond directly to a section of circuitry in the final implementation. Macrocells may include such things as adders, comparators and registers. (See also, *Hard Macro* and *Soft Macro*.)

MCM Multi Chip Module. A hybrid integrated circuit technology in which multiple IC dies are contained and intercorrected in a single package.

Mixed mode Simulation in which both transistor-level and gate-level (analog and digital) simulation are performed at the same time.

Mixed signal A circuit (typically an integrated circuit) which processes both analog and digital signals.

Module A segment of a design that is entered, simulated and otherwise processed independent of the rest of the design. Modules may be combined through the use of hierarchy, or may remain distinct throughout the design process. In a physical device, a module usually refers to a distinct segment of circuitry. Large devices such as ASICs and FPGAs may be designed a segment at a time, using software tools known as *module generators*.

Net A signal (circuit pathway) within a circuit, including all its branches.

Netlist A data representation that lists all components in the design, and the interconnections (the *nets*) between those components.

Node A distinct, observable point in a circuit, normally associated with a signal or signal branch. A node may or may not be observable off-chip, but is usually observable during simulation.

OLE Object Linking and Embedding. A Microsoft Windows technology used for communication of data between applications.

OVI Open Verilog International. An independent organization promoting the Verilog language as an open (non-proprietary) hardwave description language.

PAL Programmable Array Logic. A type of logic device distinguished by its use of a configurable sum-of-products logic array with programmable AND gate connections. PAL is a trademark of Advanced Micro Devices, Inc.

PALASM PAL Assembler. A design entry language and supporting software that is used to describe logic functions (in the form of Boolean Equations) for implementation in programmable logic devices.

Partitioning The logical segmentation of a design into smaller component parts or into managable collections of component parts. Partitioning may be performed at the design level (to aid in configuration management and team project management or to minimize size impacts on design tools) or may be performed automatically by partitioning algorithms, in order to place the design into multiple device targets.

PCB Printed Circuit Board. A common method of interconnecting electronic components on a physical surface. A PCB is composed of layers of conducting and non-conducting layers, and provides a rigid or semi-rigid fixture for the components as well as component interconnections.

PGA Pin Grid Array. A package type that is used for complex integrated circuits requiring a large number of pins.

Platform The computer and/or operating system environment on which a set of application development tools is used.

PLCC Plastic Leaded Chip Carrier. A small-footprint, low-cost packaging technology commonly used for surface-mount applications.

PLD Programmable Logic Device. An integrated circuit intended for applications that can be configured by the end-user to perform the required function. PLDs range in complexity from a few dozen equivalent gates (the simplest PAL-type devices) to many thousands of gates (the FPGA-class devices).

Primitive A software representation of a small, fixed-function circuit element such as a logic gate or flip-flop.

Routing The path taken to connect two points within a circuit. Also, the process of determining the connection paths within a circuit.

Routing delay The amount of time required for a change in a signal to be recognized at the receiving end of a path. The difference in time is due to the length and impedence of the path..

RTL Register Transfer Logic. A representation of a digital system in which registers are used to synchronize data, and in which the primary task during design is the development of the combinational logic that controls the movement of data through the registers in the system. RTL is the most common level of abstraction used when creating designs that will be processed by synthesis tools.

Simulation The creation and operation of an artificial system with the intent to model and analyze a correspoding real system. For electronic design systems, simulation may be performed at the transistor level (analog simulation) or the gate level (digital simulation).

Simulation model A software representation of a system component. Simulation models may be fixed-function models for off-the-shelf components, or may be generated and modified dynamically during simulation. Simulation models can be written in a software programming like C or Pascal, written in a hardware description language such as VHDL or Verilog, or may be composed of a netlist of simulation primitives. A simulation model can include only functional information, or may include detailed information about the timing delays and other factors that affect the real-world behavior of a circuit.

Soft macro A high-level function (such as an adder, comparator or multiplexor) is provided for use during design entry, but which is decomposed into lower-level functions before being implemented in the target device.

SPICE Simulation Program with Integrated Circuit Emphasis. A popular analog simulation and analysis program developed at the University of California at Berkeley.

Standard cell An ASIC technology in which primitive elements such as gates, flip-flips, multiplexers or other commonly used circuits are predefined with fixed physical and electrical characteristics.

Structural description
A design description that represents a circuit as a collection of connected components. The components may be data flow elements or control paths, or may be components described at a lower level in the design hierarchy.

Switching algebra
A form of mathematics used in the description, calculation and optimization of digital logic circuits.

Synchronous
A circuit or system in which the signals within the circuit or system are sampled or updated with respect to a global synchronizing signals (clocks).

Synthesis
The process of translating a design representation to a less abstract, more technology-specific form. Synthesis tools apply known constraints (both operational and implementation-dependent) to the design specification and produce a form of that design that is more appropriate for (and implementable in) the chosen technology.

Test vector
A set of circuit inputs and expected outputs that will be applied to a circuit, either during simulation or in the actual hardware testing process. Test vectors are often used for device or board-level testing during the manufacturing process.

Verilog
Verilog is a hardware description language (HDL) developed by Gateway Automation, a company which was later acquired by Cadence Corporation. The independent Open Verilog International (OVI) organization is currently promoting Verilog as an open (non-proprietary) language, and the IEEE may accept the OVI Verilog specification as an IEEE standard.

VHDL
VHSIC (Very High Speed Integrated Circuit) Hardware Description Language. VHDL is a hardware description language (*HDL*) developed under contract by the United States Department of Defense, and has been adopted as a standard by the IEEE.

Workstation
A computer system specifically designed for technical applications such as CAD, EDA or software development. Workstation computers are often based on the Unix operating system, and are most often found in larger, team engineering environments. Major workstation producers

include Sun, Digital Equipment Corporation, Hewlett Packard and IBM.

INDEX

D

E

F

G

H

I

J

L

R

S

T

U

V

W

X

Register Yourself!

EDA technology is changing fast, new EDA tools and vendors are appearing, and EDA software products are being updated constantly. To keep current on the latest Windows EDA technology, fill out and return this card. As a registered Windows EDA CD-ROM subscriber, you will be informed of updates to the CD-ROM, and will have the opportunity to receive updated CDs (for a nominal shipping and handling charge) as they are released.

Work is already under way on the next CD release, so don't delay...

Send in your card!

cut here ✂

Yes! Please keep me informed of future releases of the Windows EDA CD-ROM!

Name: ______________________

Title: ______________________

Address: ______________________

____

____

Email: ______________________

Phone: ______________________

Areas of Interest (check all that apply):

- ☐ Design entry tools
- ☐ Analog design tools
- ☐ Digital design tools
- ☐ Simulation
- ☐ ASIC design tools
- ☐ FPGA/PLD design tools
- ☐ DSP tools
- ☐ VHDL/Verilog
- ☐ Signal analysis tools
- ☐ Timing analysis tools
- ☐ Other: ______________

Did Somebody Swipe The Card?

Just send your name, address, phone number, email address (if you have one) and areas of interest (e.g., board-level design, ASICs, simulation, hardware description languages) to:

CD-ROM Project
Ptarmigan Design Group
26331 NE Valley Street
Suite 5-120
Duvall, WA 98019

cut here ✂

place stamp here

CD-ROM Project
Ptarmigan Design Group
26331 NE Valley Street
Suite 5-120
Duvall, WA 98019